CONIECTANEA BIBLICA • OLD TESTAMENT SERIES 29

CB
CONIECTANEA BIBLICA

OLD TESTAMENT SERIES 29

Present editors:
Tryggve N. D. Mettinger (Lund) and Magnus Y. Ottosson (Uppsala)

Lennart Boström

The God of the Sages

The Portrayal of God in the
Book of Proverbs

Almqvist & Wiksell International, Stockholm
1990

Language editor: Michael S. Cheney

Abstract:
The wisdom literature is unique within the Old Testament being characterized by a lack of references to key points of salvation history, the Exodus, Sinai, the law and the covenant. Instead we find an emphasis on creation, justice and individual ethics coupled with a belief in God as the sovereign Lord who stands in close relationship to man.
This study attempts to delineate the identifiable lines of theological thinking in the book of Proverbs by examining it from several different points of view. The focus of interest is on tracing the way the sages viewed their God and his relationship with the world. Following the discussion of a number of introductory issues, the first part discusses the occurrence of a number of themes in the book of Proverbs and interacts with previous scholarly discussions concerning the concept of God within the wisdom literature. The aim of this part is to describe the way in which the book of Proverbs regards the Lord's relationship to creation, world order and retribution. The second part demonstrates how two distinct yet complementary aspects of the deity's relationship to the world—namely, remoteness and nearness—have left their traces in the texts and both were essential ingredients in the Israelite sages' perception of the deity.
Comparisons between the book of Proverbs, other traditions of the Old Testament and non-Israelite wisdom exhibit a number of similarities—both in terms of content and form—between the book of Proverbs and the non-biblical texts. Most of the time, however, the closest correspondences are, first, to the other wisdom books and then to the other traditions of the Old Testament. This indicates that, though Israelite wisdom can be characterized as having an international flavour and outlook, it was integrated within the Israelite faith and its theological thought was regarded as complementary to the salvation historical approach that characterizes so much of the Old Testament's thought about God.

Keywords:
Bible, Old Testament, Wisdom literature, The book of Proverbs, Creation, Retribution, God, Yhwh, Supreme being, Personal god, Solomon, Israelite sages, Theodicy, Egyptian wisdom, Mesopotamian wisdom.

Almqvist & Wiksell International, Stockholm, Sweden
ISBN 91-22-01340-7

Table of Contents

Part two:
God's relationship to the world

Preface

My interest in the wisdom literature of the Old Testament can be traced back more than two decades. As teenagers, some friends of mine and I asked the newly installed pastor of our local Baptist church to hold Bible studies for us. When he generously offered to let us choose the subject, we decided, much to his surprise, that we would like to study the book of Ecclesiastes! These studies formed the beginning of a fascination with the wisdom books of the Old Testament that has followed me through the years and eventually led to this doctoral dissertation.

This study attempts to delineate the identifiable lines of theological thinking in the book of Proverbs by examining it from several different points of view. The focus of my interest is on tracing the way the sages viewed their God and his relationship with the world. Following the discussion of a number of introductory issues in the first chapter, the first part, which consists of two chapters, discusses the occurrence of a number of themes in the book of Proverbs and interacts with previous scholarly discussions concerning the concept of God within the wisdom literature. The aim of these two chapters is to describe the way in which the book of Proverbs regards the Lord's relationship to creation, world order, and retribution. The final two chapters demonstrate how two distinct yet complementary aspects of the deity's relationship to the world—namely, remoteness and nearness—have left their traces in the texts and both were essential ingredients in the Israelite sages' perception of the deity. The main scope of this study is the text of the Old Testament, but pertinent text material from the world of the Ancient Near East is also examined.

I am deeply grateful for all the assistance I have received from my friends, teachers, and colleagues in the Old Testament Senior Seminar at Lund. My advisers have been Professor Tryggve Mettinger and Dr. Fredrik Lindström to whom I express my deepest gratitude and appreciation. Without their advice and encouragement this project would probably never have been completed. To each participant in the Old Testament Senior Seminar at Lund I express my heartfelt thanks as well. Their critique of a number of chapters from the present work has at times been poignant and I have not been able to include all their suggestions in the continuing revision of this work, but their support and interest in my project has been much appreciated.

The first year of my dissertation work was spent in Israel where I had the privilege of spending each morning at the excellent scholarly library École Biblique. I would especially like to thank the librarians for their hospitality and helpfulness and also Professor Shemaryahu Talmon at the Hebrew University, Jerusalem, who was my adviser during that year and took the time to read through my second chapter, giving valuable criticism as well as advice on how to continue the project. My good friend and colleague in the Old Testament Senior Seminar at Lund, Michael S. Cheney, ThM, has been of invaluable help in taking upon himself, in the midst of his own dissertation project, the revision of my English manuscript. His wide knowledge of the Old Testament wisdom literature as well as other subjects, naturally led to a number of hints related to content as well. In addition, I would like to thank my colleague Åke Viberg, fil. kand., for his careful proof-reading of the final manuscript. Of course, I bear the responsibility for any deficiencies and errors which remain.

Lund in March 1990
Lennart Boström

Chapter one

Introduction to the wisdom literature and the book of Proverbs

A. The book of Proverbs: its relation to the wisdom literature of the Ancient Near East

1. Basic issues in the study of the book of Proverbs

The goal of the present work is to describe the concept of God reflected in the book of Proverbs. Therefore our discussion of introductory matters pertaining to the book of Proverbs will direct its focus upon issues that are of direct relevance to the question at hand. A fuller treatment of introductory matters is available elsewhere.[1]

a. The structure of the book
A preliminary reading of the book of Proverbs reveals several obvious divisions. The headings in 1:1; 10:1; 22:17; 24:23; 25:1; 30:1 and 31:1 indicate the disparity of the material. The sections set off by these headings are attributed to different authors and there is good reason to assume that the material in each section is of disparate origin. It may therefore be said that the book constitutes a "collection of collections."

The first section, Proverbs 1–9, consists of several large subsections, written mainly in an admonitory style. Attempts have been made to reconstruct from these chapters an original school book made up of ten discourses more or less patterned according to Egyptian prototypes.[2] The main problem with this approach is defining the criteria for determining what was included in these original discourses. Such criteria, of course, completely determine the outcome. Even though the methodology employed in such attempts at reconstruction may be somewhat problematic, the general outline of their conclusions is not to be doubted. Thus it should be noted that Proverbs 1–9 is, to a large extent, built up of pericopae characterized by admonitory style with the

---

[1] See esp. the monographs on wisdom literature by Fichtner (1933), von Rad (1981), Crenshaw (1982), Preuss (1987), and introductions to the commentaries of Toy (1977:V–XXXVI), Gemser (1963:1–16), Scott (1982:3–30), McKane (1985:1–47), Plöger (1984:XIII–XLIII).
[2] Whybray (1965 A:33–71), Scott (1982:14–17), Lang (1972:29–36).

specific form of address "my son."[3] Both of these features exhibit close formal and thematic parallels to Egyptian wisdom instructions.

The second section, Proverbs 10:1–22:16, consists of 375 short sayings,[4] almost exclusively sentences composed of two lines. Though it is clear at times that sentences dealing with a similar theme have been grouped together,[5] it is by and large difficult to discern a coherent structure in the placement of the individual sentences within the work as a whole.[6] This section may be divided into two more or less coherent units based on the observation that Proverbs 10–15 is characterized by antithetical parallelism while the following chapters are significantly less uniform.

The third section, Proverbs 22:17–24:22, became the focus of intense scholarly interest during the first part of this century because of its striking parallels with an Egyptian text—*The Instruction of Amenemope*. Again we have the admonitory style and longer units. Today, it is the consensus view that only 22:17–23:11 can be said to be closely related to *Amenemope*.[7] Of course parallels can be found elsewhere in this section, but not to any greater degree than is the case in the rest of the book of Proverbs.[8] The MT שלשום in the introduction, 22:20, has been the subject of dispute. This word is uncommon and seems to have been viewed as problematic from early times. The Ketib suggests שִׁלְשׁוֹם, probably meaning "previously" rather than literally "yesterday," but the Qere has שָׁלִישִׁים, a term for "officers" which is here usually interpreted to mean "excellent, noble [things, sayings]." Erman, who directed scholarly attention to the close relationship between this section and

---

[3] The formula, as it is used in Proverbs, refers to the listener, the disciple. Note the divergences in the use of the expression "my son" between Egyptian instructions and Proverbs, noted by Kitchen (1977:80–82). In Egypt the expression is very common in the titles of the books, but it never occurs in the text, while in Proverbs the opposite is the case.

[4] Whybray (1979:153). Preuss (1987:32): "Dass deren Gesamtzahl innerhalb der Sammlung genau 375 ist, was dem Zahlenwert der Summe der Buchstaben des Namens Salomo entspricht (das alte Hebräisch kannte keine Ziffern), dürfte kaum Zufall sein."

[5] E.g., 15:33–16:9 which all, except v 8, refer to Yahweh, and 16:10–15 , except v 11, refer to the king. See Murphy (1981 A:63–64) for a review of the attempts of Hermisson and Plöger to establish the existence of larger contextual unities.

[6] Hildebrandt's (1988:207–224) demonstration of proverbial pairs in Proverbs 10–29 is noteworthy and indicates one aspect of the editorial effort of the collectors of the proverbs. Though Hildebrandt succeeds in finding a large number of such pairs which amount to more than 20% of the total number in Prov 10–29, this is not sufficient evidence for a comprehensive, coherent structure of these chapters. Whybray (1979:154) reasons that the difficulty in discovering the principles behind arrangement is more likely due to the inability of the interpreter to find the key, rather than to the failure of the author or redactor to impose a logical structure on the ideas. Whybray (1979:155) reviews attempts to find a deliberate arrangement within these chapters and tries to demonstrate (1979:157–165) that the 55 Yahweh-sayings in the section are reinterpretations of sentences in their present context. He points out interesting connections between a number of Yahweh-sayings and their context, but at times the connections are judged to be farfetched (e.g., 14:1–2), and he himself admits eight doubtful cases and three without any relation to the context. The great value of Whybray's study is the demonstration of a close relationship between the Yahweh-sayings and the rest of the material in the book. An alternate view is put forward by McCreesh (1985:45) who believes that the lack of structure "is based on a refusal to see life as a neat system."

[7] See, e.g., Richter (1966 A:26), McKane (1985:371), Grumach (1972:4–6), Preuss (1987:33).

[8] See Ruffle's (1977:29–68) discussion of the relationship between the two texts.

Amenemope, proposed the reading שְׁלֹשִׁים, "thirty," indicating that the section, at least originally, consisted of thirty chapters as does *The Instruction of Amenemope*. A similar understanding of the word is found in the Septuagint which translates τρισσως, "three times, triply." The first problem with Erman's solution to this crux is that the material does not easily fall into thirty discrete units, a fact which has been amply demonstrated when scholars have sought to harmonize the text with Erman's thesis.[9] The second problem is that even though it can be argued that a close relationship exists between Proverbs 22:17–23:11 and *Amenemope*, this does not hold true for the rest of the material. This indicates that the third section is not a case of direct borrowing from an Egyptian text. The whole matter becomes even more complicated when one asks how the term "thirty," a word which does not occur in the Egyptian text, found its way into the Hebrew material.[10]

The fourth section, 24:23–34, is a short pericope whose form[11] and heading[12] indicate that it constitutes an addition to the preceding section. The last five verses are an interesting example of parallels within the book. The final two verses are identical to 6:10–11 while the imagery used in the first three is different from chapter 6, though the theme is the same. This parallel may serve as an example of the way in which the same material might be used in different ways within the wisdom tradition.

Like the second section, the fifth section, chapters 25–29, consists of short sentences. Here, however, or at least in chapters 25–27, there is considerable variation of form.[13]

The size of the sixth section, chapter 30, is debatable due to the difficulty of determining both the meaning and extent of Agur's words.[14] It seems clear that verse 4 in some respects responds to the verses which precede it. Verses 5–9 may also serve as a corrective to the preceding material while the rest of

---

[9] See, e.g., Scott's (1982:135–147), McKane's (1985:374–406), Römheld's (1989:59) reconstructions.

[10] See Richter (1966 A:25–37) concerning the relationship between the two texts where he makes a distinction between the translator of the Egyptian text and the collector of the Hebrew texts. Cf. the views of Grumach (1972:4–6), Ruffle (1977:55–66) and Römheld (1989:113–114).

[11] McKane (1985:572) does not regard these verses as instruction, except vv 27–29. But they cannot be regarded as sentences either, except vv 23 and 26 though without parallelism. Because of the parallel between vv 30–34 and 6:6–11 which at least occur in the context of instruction, there is reason to see the section as similar in form to the preceding section.

[12] גַּם־אֵלֶּה points back to the preceding and לַחֲכָמִים presupposes דִּבְרֵי חֲכָמִים in 22:17.

[13] See McKane's observations (1985:577–642) that simile is a prominent feature of chs. 25–27 while chs. 28–29 are dominated by antithetical parallelism. The difference in form, and to some extent, in content, indicates that the section is a collection from different sources.

[14] See McKane's (1985:643–647) discussion of the various alternatives. Crenshaw (1980:12) follows Scott (1982:175) and regards the words of Agur as an example of radical scepticism in Israel. See also Blenkinsopp (1983:47–48). The understanding of the MT לְאִיתִיאֵל as "there is no God" by way of Aramaic לָא אִיתַי אֵל is uncertain and can hardly serve as the sole argument for such a view, which, even if it is not to be understood as argument for "militant dogmatic atheism" (McKane 1985:647), is very radical and rare within the Old Testament context. Against the view of Agur as a sceptic, see Franklyn (1983:238–252) who convincingly argues for a single speaker in vv 1–9 who makes use of two rhetorical quotations and ends with a prayer.

the chapter, which mainly consists of numerical sayings, has no immediate
connection to the introduction.

The seventh section, chapter 31, as well as the preceding, are associated
with unknown figures[15] and it seems probable that both chapters have been
placed at the end of the book as a conclusion. Chapter 31 is divided into of
two parts,[16] verses 1–9 which contain a royal instruction to an unknown king
from his mother, and verses 10–31 which constitute an acrostic hymn about
the ideal wife highlighting the qualities of industry, creativity and independence.[17]

This brief survey of the different parts of the book of Proverbs indicates
the composite nature both of the structure of the work as a whole and of its
individual sections. Before we leave the question of structure, the works of
Kitchen and Skehan need to be mentioned. Kitchen approaches the question of
the literary structure of the book of Proverbs by comparing it to extant
wisdom books of the Ancient Near East and arrives at some remarkable
conclusions.[18] One is that the book consists of four parts with the following
divisions: chapters 1–24; 25–29; 30 and 31. Under this schema, chapters 1–9
form the prologue to the first section and 10:1; 22:17 and 24:23 serve as
subtitles.[19] Skehan admits the composite background of the material but
argues for a single editor of the whole book and finds evidence for this in the
arrangement of the material according to deliberate numerical patterns, e.g.,
that the number of sayings in the book correspond to the numerical value of
the proper names in the introductory verse of the book: שלמה, דוד, ישראל.[20]
Skehan even argues that the "author-compiler-designer" wrote the Hebrew text
"in such a way that its layout in the columns of his scroll visibly showed forth
the design of a house, which he himself identified (Prov 9:1) as Wisdom's

---

[15] The view forwarded by Albright and others that משא in 30:1 and 31:1 is a region in North-west
Arabia seems plausible, and explains our lack of knowledge of the persons mentioned, as well as the
presence of Aramaisms in 31:2–3, see Kitchen (1977:100–101, 107). It may also serve as the reason
for the MT's placement of the sections.

[16] Note Kitchen's observation (1977:101) that the subject-matter—the "good" wife—of the second
part, vv 10–31, is consistent with the reputed origin of the work—Lemuel's mother—both being
feminine. McCreesh (1985:40) sees a connection between the two parts in the various uses of the word
חיל. In v 3 Lemuel is admonished not to waste his חיל on, presumably, loose women. In vv 10–31 the
אשת־חיל is depicted—a woman who has חיל in herself and in whom the husband can put his trust.

[17] Wolters (1988:446–457) argues that the praise of the wife is in hymnic form, that the hymn genre is
not confined to theological purposes but that it springs from a tradition of heroic poetry. McCreesh
(1985:25–46) stresses the connection between Prov 31:10–31 as the book's conclusion and the
depiction of the Lady Wisdom in chs. 1–9. He regards 31:10–31 as a kind of riddle depicting wisdom
in an established setting no longer rivalled by Dame Folly. Lyons (1987:237–245) believes the
characterization of the woman represents the ideal of premonarchical Israelite society which is actualized
again in the similar situation of post-exilic times.

[18] Kitchen (1977:69–114; 1979:236–282).

[19] Kitchen (1977:70–86). To be exact, Kitchen (1977:80) terms 10:1 and 24:23 "sub-titles" and 22:17
a "titular interjection" (see 1979:246 for a definition of the latter term).

[20] Skehan (1971 A:25). The numerical value of the names is 930 and Skehan ends up with 932 lines
after having excluded the titles as well as 1:16, 8:11, 22:28 for different reasons.

house."[21] Skehan argues his points with great insight, although it must be said that his theories, though ingenious, seem rather fantastic. One of the problems with his views is that the text must be rearranged in several places to support the theory. The most noteworthy of Skehan's observations is that the number of sentences in the "Solomonic" collection, Proverbs 10–22:16, is equal to the numerical value of the name Solomon in Hebrew.[22]

b. Genres in the book

An understanding of form is essential to the study of the book of Proverbs.[23] The variety of forms represented in each section of the book as well as the different features which characterize each of the larger units are easily perceptible. Scholars' use of diverse form-critical terminology has created confusion in this area and Nel's attempt to establish a standard for this terminology is welcomed.[24] In his introductory chapter to *Old Testament Form Criticism,* Martin Buss notes that "OT form critics have often not seen, as others have, that genres are abstractions...."[25] This is a needed warning on the follies of narrow definitions of genres and rigid form criticism.

The forms found in the book of Proverbs can be divided into two main categories: longer units in admonitory style, chapters 1–9; 22:17–24:34, and short sayings in the indicative mood, chapters 10–22:16; 25–29.[26] The distinction between these two categories of material is based on both the length of the units as well as the mode of speech.[27] McKane regards these two categories—which he calls instruction genre and sentence genre—as the only two genres in the book.[28] Nel, who advocates genre definitions which allow the greatest possible number of structural variations, nevertheless finds McKane's genre classifications too broad and, therefore, untenable.[29] This may well be the case and such broad categories may necessitate a whole array of sub-genres to do justice to the texts. On the other hand, McKane's

---

[21] Skehan (1971 B:27).

[22] Skehan (1971 A:17; 1971 B:44) also finds that the number of lines in chs. 25–29 corresponds to the numerical value of the name Hezekiah which is mentioned in the first verse of the collection. In order to derive this value, however, he is compelled to modify the MT name from חזקיה to יחזקיה

[23] For wisdom and form, see esp. Crenshaw (1974 B), Murphy (1981 A), Nel (1981).

[24] Nel (1981; 1982:7–17).

[25] Buss (1974:53).

[26] Cf. Zimmerli (1933:181–184). Murphy (1981 A:9) notes that Sumerian wisdom contains far more genres than those found in Israel. Gordon (1960:122–152) classifies the Sumerian and Akkadian wisdom literature into the following 11 genres: proverbs, fables and parables, folk-tales, miniature "essays," riddles, "Edubba compositions" (school compositions), wisdom disputations or "tensons," satirical dialogues, practical instructions, precepts and "Righteous sufferer" poems.

[27] The terms "Mahnspruch" and "Aussagespruch" are often used to describe the different character of the categories, see, e.g., Zimmerli (1933:184), Westermann (1971:79–82).

[28] McKane (1985:1–22).

[29] Nel (1981:129). If McKane's classification is too broad in its general application, it seems too narrow when he insists that all material which is instruction must be imperative in form, a rule that would also exclude parts of the material in Egyptian instructions which to a large degree constitute the basis for the establishment of the genre.

categorisation serves the function of dividing the material into two natural groups that have much in common even though the structure of the book in fact is quite intricate. This discussion illustrates the previously mentioned problem of broad versus narrow form-critical categorisation and highlights the general difficulty of defining genres. Despite the protracted nature of this problem, we find McKane's broader classification useful and will refer to it in the following.

Murphy maintains that 22:17–24:22 is written in the typical form of Egyptian instruction with the customary prohibition followed by a motive clause. He argues that Proverbs 1–9, with its extended units, represents a developed form of the instruction genre.[30] Kayatz, on the other hand, maintains that it is especially the larger units and their structure which are a common element in both Egyptian instructions and Proverbs 1–9.[31]

Nel does not use the term instruction but uses "wisdom teaching" for "the systematic and logical combination of Sentences... about a specific topic" and notes that this genre can include other genres such as the hymn.[32] He finds the greater portion of Proverbs 1–9 to consist of wisdom teachings while Proverbs 22:17–24 are classified as admonitory sentences.[33] Though Nel, by means of this procedure, classifies these two sections as belonging to different genres, they have in common that they are dominated by admonitions.[34] The difference is, as was noted above, the relative length of units in Proverbs 1–9 in which elements of other genres are also included.

Nel defines the sentence as being in metric form, consisting mainly of a two-membered long verse (the basic form) with parallelism on both the "interpretive level" and on the structural and rhythmic levels.[35] He argues convincingly for the originality of the parallelistic character of these sentences and against an evolutionary view postulating a linear development from single sentence to two-membered sentence and to even longer units.[36]

---

[30] Murphy (1981 A:50). Lang (1972:27–28) prefers to relate Proverbs 1–9 to Egyptian school texts from the New Kingdom era. These texts are less organized and more anthology-like in structure.

[31] Kayatz (1966:74).

[32] Nel (1981:136). Gordon notes (1960:130) that the Sumerian proverb collections also include material of other genres like fables, parables, and miniature "essays." This indicates that genres are not completely distinct from each other, but should be viewed as secondary classifications which sometimes overlap and mix.

[33] Nel (1981:140) regards the wisdom saying and the admonition as the two basic forms of the sentence. This may be somewhat confusing and there seems to be good reason to regard the sentence and the admonition as different genres, one in the indicative mood and the other in the imperative. The small number of admonitions in Proverbs 10:1–22:16 and chs. 25–29 indicates that the two forms in Israel on the whole were separated.

[34] See Nel (1981:141) for a concise definition of admonition, an index and short characterization of all admonitions (1982:65–67) in Proverbs.

[35] Nel (1981:139).

[36] Nel (1981:139–140). Cf. Postel (1976:180), who in his investigation of the form and function of the motive clause, finds no support for a development from sentence to admonition. See also, e.g., von Rad (1981:27). An argument against the evolutionary view is the fact that a late instruction like *Onkhsheshonqy* consists mainly of short one-line sayings arranged without any recognizable pattern

The term "proverb" is today usually restricted to short, pithy sayings that can be documented as having currency among a people and which can apply to multiple situations.[37] The term is often qualified by being referred to as popular proverb or folk proverb.[38] If the currency criterion is maintained, the sentences in the book of Proverbs are excluded by definition since we cannot ascertain anything about their actual usage among people.[39] The lengths of folk proverbs found elsewhere in the Old Testament[40] differ from the two-stichoi, normally parallelistic, sentences of the book of Proverbs.[41] McKane proposes a more intricate definition of the proverb[42] and consequently ends up with a mere eleven proverbs for the entire book of Proverbs.[43] His narrower definition focuses upon a saying's concreteness and "hermeneutic openness" towards a variety of situations. It is certainly true that sentences may be more or less "open" and that some appear more apt to be extended when interpreted. The problem is defining criteria to aid in evaluating hermeneutic openness which will result in an accurate reconstruction of which sayings apply to situations other than the one actually depicted.[44] One cannot exclude the possibility that pure chance often played a role in the processes that made some proverbs more popular and widely used than others.[45]

Murphy makes a distinction between experiential and didactic sentences. The former are sentences that merely present some aspect of reality and leave the practical application to the reader, while the latter characterize a certain

---

(see Gemser [1960:127–128], cf. Lichtheim [1983:5]). It is also a fact that the longer units are found in Egypt from the earliest times (see R. J. Williams [1975:245]).

[37] E.g., Alster (1975:37).

[38] Scott (1961), Murphy (1981 A:4), Nel (1981:138). See Fontaine (1982:2–71) for an overview of the scholarly debate concerning the folk proverb, as well as a perceptive discussion of its form and function. For a short and instructive discussion of the proverb as an international phenomenon, see Alster (1975:1–13).

[39] Scott (1961:48) finds it possible that at times popular proverbs underlie the present sentences in Proverbs. There is a certain arbitrariness and generalization, though, in the criteria he establishes for identification of these cases. Sayings that are striking and picturesque he believes to have a popular background while the others he finds to be marked by academic moralizing as well as monotony are therefore the products of a school. J. G. Williams (1980:35–58) follows Scott in distinguishing between folk sayings and literary proverbs. Williams relates the biblical proverbs to aphoristic speech and demonstrates the role of artistic forms and methods in the construction of biblical proverbs. Hermisson (1968:36–64) asks for strict criteria concerning the popular background of sentences and finds those used earlier to be untenable. His conclusion is that the sentences of Prov 10–29 exclusively derive from the school setting.

[40] See Eissfeldt (1965:82–84) for a survey of popular proverbs in the Old Testament (see Fontaine [1982:4–5] for an overview of Eissfeldt's 1913 work,). Eissfeldt believes that the artistic saying, i.e. the sentence, to a large degree took over the function of these popular proverbs and that the sentences often included older proverbial material.

[41] Kovacs (1974:174).

[42] McKane (1985:23, 414, 594).

[43] McKane (1985:32): 10:5; 13:4, 7, 8; 16:26; 20:4; 24:27; 26:13, 15, 27; 27:7.

[44] McKane (1985:594, 605) calls, e.g., Prov 26:27 "proverbial," but not 26:6, 8; 27:18, also very concrete and possible to apply to different situations.

[45] Taylor (1931:3–5) illustrates the diversity in origin for proverbs and concludes that the distinction between "learned" proverbs with a long literary history versus "popular" proverbs is meaningless and "concerned merely with the accidents of history."

act or attitude in such a way as to influence another person's behaviour.[46] This distinction adequately describes one aspect of the variegation of the sentences, but it soon becomes evident that classifying all of the sentences in the book of Proverbs in one of these two categories is not adequate. It seems more correct to say that every sentence in the book must be regarded as didactic to some degree, but that the variations in this aspect cover the gamut from descriptive to admonitory sentences.

If we maintain that all the short sayings in Proverbs 10:1–22:16 and chapters 25–29 can be included in the sentence genre, we must allow for a number of divisions and subgenres under this broad classification. The Solomonic section is the most unified, being dominated in chapters 10–15 by sentences in antithetic parallelism.[47] In the subsequent chapters sentences containing synonymous, antithetical and synthetical parallelism are mixed together, with the added element of a number of "better" sayings.[48] In Proverbs 25–29 the variation in form is striking. The remarkable feature is the high frequency of similes in chapters 25–27[49] where we also find admonitions and "better" sayings, but relatively few sentences with parallelism. Chapters 28–29, on the other hand, are more conventionally patterned with parallelism as the dominating feature.

Proverbs 30 is especially noteworthy in terms of genre because of its numerical sayings. This form is also found in 6:16–19 and it is possible that behind the present form of, e.g., 25:3 is a numerical saying. Nel notes the possibility of a relationship between the riddle and the numerical saying.[50] A numerical saying has not yet been found among the extant texts of Mesopotamia and Egypt except in the Aramaic *Ahiqar*.[51] Interestingly enough, the form does occur in the Ugaritic texts, which has given rise to the suggestion that Biblical numerical sayings should be ascribed to Canaanite influence.[52]

Proverbs 31:1–9 contains typical instruction for royalty of the kind we find in Egypt in the instructions of *Amenemhet* and *Merikare,* and also in the

---

[46] Murphy (1981 A:4–5). The same distinction is maintained by Westermann (1971:84–85) who refers to early sayings, tied to a specific situation, and later, general-thematic, sayings. Von Rad (1981:31) has an interesting discussion concerning the difference between the exhortation and the plain statement where he asserts that the former suggests a definite mood of behaviour while the latter has "a characteristic openness, something that points beyond themselves, an element which leaves room for all kinds of associations and, in certain circumstances, even permits of a figurative interpretation."

[47] See Skehan (1971 A:18) for the exceptions which up to 14:26 total a maximum of nine.

[48] E.g., 16:8, 16, 19. Nel (1981:140) points out that the "better" saying is not to be regarded as a separate genre but a form of the sentence genre. Murphy (1981 A:66–67) distinguishes between the "good" saying, the simple "better" saying and its more sophisticated form which is formulated in a paradoxical way. See also Ogden (1977:489–492).

[49] See McKane (1985:578, 593–594) for a description of the different forms of the simile employed. See also Nel (1981:132).

[50] Nel (1981:134). Also Crenshaw (1974 B:236–238).

[51] Col. vi 92 (saying 12 acc. to Lindenberger [1983: 65–67; 1985:499]). See Murphy (1981 A:11–12).

[52] See Nel (1981:135, n. 30) for literature.

Babylonian *Advice to a Prince*.[53] The identities of both the king and his mother are unknown to us. The last unit of the book of Proverbs is an acrostic poem portraying the ideal wife.

The book of Proverbs itself defines its content as משלים, plural of משל.[54] The etymological and contextual meaning of משל has been discussed extensively.[55] Today when the etymology of words is considered less exegetically relevant than their actual usage and contextual understanding, there seems to be a consensus that the term is used in the Old Testament in such a broad way that it can not be regarded as a designation for a specific genre. Thus משל is best translated by a general term like "saying" which includes the whole spectrum of diverse genres within its scope.[56]

An issue of interest to us is the relationship between genre and content. Is it, e.g., possible that the absence of theological aspects in most sentences and in large sections of the instructions is due to form? This suggestion seems especially relevant to the sentence genre where the shortness of the units makes it difficult to take up the theological facets of each issue. These genres were used elsewhere in the Ancient Near East; short, sentence-like sayings, are already known especially from Mesopotamia and the instructions from Egypt, and are also characterized by a relative paucity of theological references. The sentence and instruction genres seem to have been employed predominantly in an educational context to give advice and directions on specific everyday life situations. The relative lack of theological references does not necessarily indicate a secular mindset, but only that theological arguments was not always necessary to establish a maxim's validity. Instead, a maxim was put forward for consideration on the basis of more direct grounds for motivation such as tradition, self-interest, concern for other people and common sense. Of course our knowledge of Israelite and other Ancient Near Eastern cultures indicates that none of these areas were separated from religion and theological thinking.[57] These considerations, together with the theological references that are found in the book of Proverbs, indicate that it may be very misleading to label wisdom a secular phenomenon.

Comparing Proverbs with the extant wisdom material from surrounding cultures reveals that the closest parallels to the sentence genre come from

---

[53] Murphy (1981 A:81).

[54] 1:1; 10:1; 25:1.

[55] For a review of the debate, see Nel (1981:130–131), and also Khanjian (1973:8). For a recent attempt to combine the two etymological roots of the verb, see Preuss (1987:40), and for an approach which finds the basic meaning of משל in a person who, in a representative fashion, stands out as a model or paradigm for something, see McKane (1985:26–33).

[56] See Nel (1981:130–131), Crenshaw (1982:67).

[57] Cf. Skehan's (1971 A:23) radical assessment of the argument that Prov 25–27 is the oldest portion in Proverbs because of its "secular" character.

Mesopotamia[58] while the examples of the instruction genre are mainly Egyptian.[59]

As in the book of Proverbs, a rational scheme for order of the short sayings in the Mesopotamian collections is often difficult to discern.[60] The subject matter of these sayings, like that of Proverbs, relates predominantly to everyday situations of common people. Different types of parallelism are extant already in Sumerian proverbs[61] as well as in Egyptian instructions.[62] Parallelism cannot be regarded as unique to Israelite poetry, but in no other wisdom book is this stylistic feature so consistently and regularly present in the material as in the sentence literature of the book of Proverbs, especially in chapters 10–15 and 28–29.

The comparison made by Scott between popular proverbs, taken mainly from the Old Testament and Mesopotamia, reveals significant similarities in form with the sentences in the book of Proverbs,[63] even though Scott maintains that there is a fundamental difference between the developed form of saying in the book of Proverbs and the popular proverb.

Much has already been said concerning the instruction genre. The Egyptians designated this genre *sb3yt,* and its form remained essentially the same throughout its long history of more than two thousand years.[64] Like Proverbs 1–9 it is composed of larger units whose structure normally consists of a casuistic introduction, followed by several imperatives, and a concluding motivation which can be arranged in different ways.

---

[58] See E. I. Gordon (1960:122–152) for a resumé of the wisdom material from Mesopotamia. Almost all Mesopotamian wisdom material is unilingual or bilingual Sumerian.

[59] R. J. Williams (1975:241), Waltke (1979:224). McKane (1985:151–182) includes only *Counsels of Wisdom* and *Ahiqar* in his treatment of Babylonian-Assyrian instructions. To these may be added *The Instructions of Suruppak* from Sumerian times and an Akkadian text from Ugarit (RS 22.439).

[60] The proverbs in Sumerian collections were at times gathered together into groups on the basis of their opening word, according to Gordon (1960:126). The "key sign" may also occur in the second place, or even further on in the proverb, and their arrangement together may also be based on subject matter (Gordon [1959:26, 154]).

[61] Alster (1975:55). Gordon (1959:16) notes that of the 300 proverbs translated by him 138 can be classified as parallelistic. Gordon refers to (1960:132) Kramer and Van Dijk in pointing out the use of both antithetic and synonymous parallelism in the Sumerian proverbs.

[62] Keel (1979:225–234) notes that antithetical thinking and formulations are also found in Egypt and cannot be regarded as something unique to Israel, as Schmid has argued(1966:155). The difference is that the antithetical character, esp. in Proverbs 10–15, appears more clearly.

[63] Scott (1961:47–56) points out seven common "idea patterns" upon which popular proverbs are patterned: 1) identity, equivalence; 2) contrast, non-identity, paradox; 3) similarity, analogy, typology; 4) contrary to order, futile, absurd; 5) characterization of persons, actions or situations; 6) value, lack of value, relative value, proportion or degree; 7) cause and consequence. These idea patterns apply to a large degree also to the sentences in Proverbs and certain forms like the simile, "better" saying, etc., found there.

[64] A difference in form can be observed in the latest instructions, *Papyrus Insinger* and *The Instruction of Onkhsheshonqy,* which both consist of short monostich sentences. In *Papyrus Insinger* the monostichs are imperative clauses grouped according to content, while in *Onkhsheshonqy* they are self-contained prose sentences usually without perceptible arrangement.

c. *Sitz im Leben*

The question of wisdom's Sitz im Leben is crucial to any reconstruction of their thinking. The problem is that the sages, who wrote or compiled the material in the book of Proverbs and the other wisdom books, on the whole are unknown to us. The Old Testament gives little information concerning their milieu and their position in society. We do not even know for certain if they constituted a professional class.[65] Their activity is shrouded in anonymity, except for the attribution of material to king Solomon and the "men of Hezekiah." The headings in the book of Proverbs indicate that the compilation of the material was an extended affair which took place in several stages over several centuries. These observations make it reasonable to surmise that circles of men who had an established position in society over an extended period of time did the work of compilation, rather than prominent individuals. Thus the book of Proverbs is to be understood as the end-product of a gradual process.

There are essentially four possible alternative settings for the sages and their teachings, though the combination and refinement of the various possibilities has produced a greater diversity of views among scholars. The first alternative, and today probably the most commonly advocated, is that the sages and the collections of the book are to be seen in relation to some sort of ancient Israelite school.[66] The second alternative is that the wise men who wrote and compiled the material were the advisers and scribes of the king.[67]

---

[65] The passage that might give the clearest indication that the wise men constituted a professional class is Jer 18:18 which refers to three groups: priest, wise man (חכם), and prophet, where it seems reasonable to assume that the term חכם along with the other two terms designates a distinct group of professionals. Against this, as noted by von Rad (1981:21), stands Ezek 7:26 which instead of חכם has elders, זקנים, which sounds less like a professional designation. There are also other passages within the prophetic books, e.g., Isa 44:25; Jer 50:35; 51:57, where non-Israelite חכמים are referred to in a way that indicates their professional status. See Crenshaw's discussion on the likelihood that the sages constituted a professional class (1982:28–29, also 1976 A:22) and Morgan's (1979:229–232) list of possible references to the wise men in the prophets. A related issue here is the relationship between the wise men, חכמים, and the scribes, ספרים. Brekelmans (1979:32, 36) argues that the two are not to be identified and that Jer 8:8 cannot be used as an argument for an identification of the scribes and wise men as a professional class. This applies also to McKane's (1965:40–47) views that the wise men were the statesmen, the royal counsellors of the court.

[66] Richter (1966 A:145), Hermisson (1968:97–136), Mettinger (1971:140–157), Khanjian (1973:268–269), Lang (1986:7–12), Shupak (1987:98–119).

[67] Von Rad (1981:15–17), Kovacs (1974:171–187), Morgan (1979:222). Von Rad notes, though, that the content of the sentences argues for a broader cultural setting and that wisdom was located not only at the court. This has also been demonstrated by Humphreys (1978:177–190) who examines the content of Proverbs 10–29 to see if it fits the picture of being directed to the young courtier. His conclusion is that only in Proverbs 16:1–22:16 and 25:2–27 does what he calls "the motif of the wise courtier" occupy a governing position. "Within Yahwism the motif of the wise courtier was limited in its potential for theological expression. Of the 538 sayings in Proverbs 10–29, only about 30 have the courtier as primary addressee.... Thus, while a court establishment for the training of courtiers may have played a role in the development of a limited segment of this material, the restricted use of the motif suggests that other areas of life be considered as well in the developmental history of Proverbs, and that the role of the royal court has been greatly exaggerated" (1978:187). Waltke (1979:230–232) believes that the original setting of the wisdom material in Israel as well as in surrounding cultures was the courtiers' homes and that the sayings later came to be used in schools. Concerning the present form of

The third alternative is that the teachings had their origin in the family and the clan. It was mainly the responsibility of the *paterfamilias* to transfer the teachings to the upcoming generation.[68] The fourth alternative is that the wise men never constituted a specific social group but were an intellectual class of relatively well-to-do citizens who had the interest and ability to occupy themselves with the traditional teachings—compiling, revising, and transmitting to future generations.[69]

The preceding discussion of genres suggested a possible popular origin especially for the sentences in the book of Proverbs. The question involves the original setting of at least part of the material in the book.[70] The main objections to a popular background for the sentences are 1) the developed and artistic form of the sentences, which imply a more uniform process of production, and 2) the difficulty of determining valid criteria for identifying sentences built upon earlier folk proverbs.[71] We agree that the present consistency in form tends to point away from a popular setting, but we question whether the possibility that parallelism was also a feature of sayings on a popular level can be completely ruled out,[72] even if the consistent use of the two-stichoi form in the Masoretic text may owe its origin to a secondary setting.[73] It seems reasonable to assume a popular background for at least a large part of the sentences and consequently some kind of relation to the popular proverb. This appears the more reasonable when we consider that the over-all content of the book contains few indications of class-orientation, but rather seems to be directed to Israelites in general.[74]

The assumption of a popular original setting for at least parts of the material in the book of Proverbs does not necessarily conflict with the view that the school was the setting for the compilation, redaction, and use of the present collections of the book. The problem with this view of the school as a setting

---

the material in Proverbs, he remarks (1979:232): "In Israel the sayings of its courtiers were democratized for the improvement of all Israel through such a work as the Book of Proverbs."

[68] Gerstenberger (1965), Morgan (1979:224–225), Blenkinsopp (1983). Similarly: Westermann (1971), Golka (1983).

[69] Whybray (1974:69–70). See also Whybray (1982:20–25) for a discussion of the possibilities of the existence of a highly sophisticated wisdom literature in premonarchical times.

[70] See Doll (1985:8–13) for an overview of the discussion of the two main alternatives: "Volksweisheit" or "Schulweisheit."

[71] See Hermisson (1968:36–64). Against Hermisson, see Gerstenberger (1969:40–44).

[72] See several of the African sayings referred to by Golka (1986), e.g., Mal. 1386, 1420.

[73] See Whybray (1982:20–23).

[74] See Zimmerli (1933:180), Crenshaw (1976 A:20–22). Cf. Kovacs (1974:171–189) who concludes that the book reflects the class-ethics of administrators and officials. Preuss (1987:40–44) makes a helpful survey of the content of the book with the intention of defining the addressee group. His conclusion is that the recipients must have been relatively well-to-do and with the potential of attaining to the higher positions in society. Pleins (1987:61–78) arrives at a similar conclusion by analyzing the way the theme of poverty is treated in Proverbs. He argues that "the values and interests of the wisdom writers are the same as those of the urban elite whom they serve" (1987:61). These observations correspond to some of Whybray's (1974) and indicate that a broad spectrum of middle-class people was the primary target of the teachings of the sages. At the same time, the generality of the content does not support any claim for class-orientation in a narrow sense.

for the book is the lack of evidence for the existence of schools in ancient Israel.[75] In later times, the book of Sirach refers to the school,[76] but concerning earlier days we can only surmise that some kind of school must have come into existence along with the state-like organization of the nation. The government organized by Solomon must have created an urgent need for the education of officials, scribes, etc. Furthermore, the fact that such schools existed in Egypt,[77] Mesopotamia,[78] and Ugarit[79] makes it probable that Israel also had similar institutions.

Westermann compares the sayings in the book of Proverbs to similar material from an African tribe and concludes that there is a fundamental difference between the primary Sitz im Leben of the "Imperativ-Sprüchen" and the "Indikativ-Sprüchen." The former belong to the area of education, the teaching and up-bringing of the young generation, while the latter, the "eigentliche Sprichwort," is built upon an equal relationship between the parties and is designed to simply relate an observation or a fact, leaving it to the listener to figure out the consequences.[80] We agree that there is good reason to distinguish between indicative and the imperative sayings, especially since the same distinction is relevant to the biblical texts. However, the radical differentiation between their original settings is more questionable because, among other things, it seems difficult to simply pass over the traces of admonition which are present in the sentences set in the indicative. It is an aspect of the geniality of the sentences that they do not explicitly prescribe, but in their description of the way things are and function there is certainly a strong element of warning and admonition which must be regarded as intentional as well as full of authority. The similarity in the aim and setting of the imperative and indicative forms provides an explanation for the dynamics of their combined use, especially in Proverbs 1–9, but also in the total structure of the book.

Regarding the identity of the sages, an observation made by Fox from the study of Egyptian wisdom literature is noteworthy. Fox does not find it necessary to postulate that different groups of people were responsible for distinct genres, and points out that in Egypt the scribes also wrote prayers, hymns, magic, etc.[81] Apparently the scribes in Ugarit and early Mesopotamia were

---

[75] For available material concerning schools in ancient Israel, see Hermisson (1968:113–136), Mettinger (1971:143–146), Lemaire (1981:7–45, 1984:270–281), Crenshaw (1985:601–615), Preuss (1987:45–46), Shupak (1987:98–119). For a different approach, see Golka (1983:257–270).

[76] Sir 51:23.

[77] See Hermisson (1968:103–107), Mettinger (1971:140–143), R. J. Williams (1975:239–240), Lemaire (1981:94, n. 73).

[78] See Hermisson (1968:107–113), Olivier (1975:49–54), Lemaire (1981:94, n. 74).

[79] See Rainey (1969:126–147), Khanjian (1973:125–139, 264–266), Lemaire (1981:94–95, n. 75).

[80] Westermann (1971:76). Cf. Zimmerli (1933:181–188).

[81] Fox (1980:128–129).

closely associated with the temple.[82] This observation may well be applicable to biblical studies[83] and indicates that different genres do not always originate from different settings. It also indicates that at times genre itself may hold as much sway over the content as the setting or the personality of the author. Similar observations have been made by Olsson in his study of the contemporary Masai tribe in Kenya. Olsson finds that genre to a large degree determines content and that the same people in different situations may refer to the deity in completely different, even seemingly contradictory, ways.[84]

Crenshaw differentiates between different categories of wisdom as family or clan wisdom, court wisdom, and scribal wisdom,[85] each with its own setting—clan, court, and school—and its own tradition.[86] We believe that each of these three settings can be traced within the corpus of the book of Proverbs and that such a multifaceted approach to setting is potentially fruitful for the understanding and interpretation of the material.[87] This approach is also supported by Nel, who, in his study of the wisdom admonitions, argues that the setting of wisdom needs to be determined not just by form but even more by reference to content. Nel's study of the content of wisdom sayings leads him to recognize different kinds of ethos in the sayings: family ethos, school ethos, official (court) ethos, priestly ethos, prophetic ethos and individual ethos.[88] Of these, the first three, which coincide with Crenshaw's categories, dominate.[89] Nel's attempt to grasp what kind of over-all life-setting might possibly be able to accommodate this differentiation of ethos leads him to the

---

[82] Rainey (1969:128). Khanjian (1973:66–67) notes that there were two circles of wisdom in Mesopotamia in the Akkadian period, but that the relationship of the wisdom circle to the temple is unclear. Khanjian (1973:268–269) more consistently relates Ugaritic wisdom to the scribal school milieu without any connections to the priestly circles.

[83] Cf. Perdue's conclusions (1977:225–226, 345–362) concerning the relationship between the sages and the cult in Israel. Perdue retains the classical division between the settings of wisdom and the cult, but points out connections in a way that nullifies the strict border-line between wisdom and cult maintained by many scholars.

[84] Olsson (1983:104–105, 1985 B:61).

[85] Crenshaw (1974 B:227; 1976 A:3).

[86] Crenshaw (1976 B:955). Crenshaw (1976 A:3) makes a short characterization of each tradition: the goal of clan wisdom is "the mastering of life, the stance hortatory and style proverbial." The goal of court wisdom is "education for a select group, the stance secular, and method didactic." The goal of scribal wisdom is "education for all, the stance dogmatico-religious, and the method dialogico-admonitory." Crenshaw's (1982:93–99) description of three types of wisdom: clan wisdom, court wisdom, and theological wisdom, is also instructive, though it can be debated whether they are to be regarded as "three fundamental stages."

[87] Cf. Morgan (1979:224–225).

[88] Nel (1982:79–81).

[89] Nel (1982:81) connects priestly ethos to the use of sacral law and cultic obligations. His only example of prophetic ethos is 1:20–33 and of individual ethos 30:1–9, which he regards as a unit of distinctive character.

conclusion that the most suitable milieu for the rise of the wisdom tradition encountered in the texts is the Israelite city:

> The Israelite city, the cultural, religious and educational centre, as life-setting enables the maintenance of the diversity of ethos which we encountered in Proverbs. The mutual influences of the various social groupings evident in the sayings presuppose geographical proximity.[90]

d. Date and authorship

At first glance, determining the authorship and date of the book of Proverbs may seem an easy matter since Proverbs 1:1 ascribes the book to Solomon. This appears credible in light of the depiction of Solomon in the historical books of the Old Testament where he is described as world-famous for his immense wisdom. A consideration of the other headings in the book hints that at least the compilation of some material is of later date[91] and explicitly ascribes some texts to other authors.[92] Another question is whether it is relevant to speak of one author when it comes to the type of material in the book of Proverbs. It seems more probable that the ascription of the book to Solomon would have been intended to convey the notion that he himself had both composed sayings as well as collected material. The heading in 25:1 indicates an awareness that the process of compilation was as yet unfinished when Solomon's days were over.

The Solomonic origin of the book has been called into question by modern scholars[93] who have often understood Solomon's role in the book's origin as minimal.[94] Instead it is common to regard Proverbs 25–27 or 25–29 as the oldest part,[95] because of certain "evolutionary" views concerning the develop-

---

[90] Nel (1982:82).

[91] See 25:1. Though the material is ascribed to Solomon, its compilation is located at a period around two centuries later.

[92] 22:17; 24:23; 30:1; 31:1. The general term חכמים in the two first passages may apply to Israelites or non-Israelites but it seems undeniable that at least the name in 31:1 was known to be non-Israelite. This indicates an openness to influences from the outside which does not characterize the Old Testament as a whole.

[93] For an overview of the book of Proverbs in modern scholarship see Lang (1972:11–26).

[94] Scott (1955:262–279) and Crenshaw (1982:42–54) interprets all the information in 1 Kings 5 and 10 concerning Solomon's wisdom as of a legendary nature and late additions without historic background. The reason Solomon came to be regarded as a king of great wisdom is supposed to be the remarkable and successful social, economic and political developments which took place during his reign, his great building enterprises, and the fact that the patron of wisdom, king Hezekiah, being first king since Solomon who could claim to be the sole Israelite monarch, modelled his national revival upon Solomon. Against Scott see Ruffle (1977:34–35). Another approach is represented by Alt (1976:102–112) who believes that the Deuteronomist must have relied on an authentic tradition and that Solomon did play a role in the international wisdom of his day. But the content of Proverbs does not correspond to the nature wisdom of 1 Kings 5:13, see Noth (1955:225–237). Solomon is regarded as a representative of wisdom, but his connection to the material in Proverbs is doubted.

[95] E.g., J. G. Williams (1987:268) and Kitchen (1977:71–73) refers to the following chronology as scholarly consensus.

ment of form and theology within wisdom.[96] The reference in the heading to
the men of Hezekiah is often regarded as authentic. This early material is
closely followed by Proverbs 10:1–22:16,[97] while Proverbs 1–9 is seen as
considerably later. The presumed Israelite adoption of Proverbs 22:17–24:34
from an Egyptian source is usually regarded as having occurred at about the
same time as the earliest parts of Proverbs were written, though the actual
incorporation of this material in the book might be ascribed to a later date
when Proverbs 1–9 and the earlier units were put together to form a book.
The date of chapters 30 and 31 is seldom included in the discussion probably
because the consensus view is that these parts should be regarded as late additions to the book, though their date of origin may be earlier.

R. J. Williams advocates the Egyptian influence upon Israel and points to a
number of factors that indicate that this was the case especially in Solomon's
and Hezekiah's days.[98] If Williams is right, it is less problematic to regard the
tradition that Solomon was the main patron of wisdom in Israel as authentic,
since it then seems highly probable that during his time Israel came in contact
with and was influenced by the ancient wisdom of Egypt.[99] Williams also
points out that the more recent attempts to date *The Instruction of Amenemope*
to the twelfth or even the thirteenth century provide "no reason to suppose that
the text was unknown in the days of Solomon."[100] This means that it is not
inconceivable that Proverbs 22:17–23:11, which undeniably stands in some
kind of relationship to *The Instruction of Amenemope,* can be traced back
even to Solomonic times.[101]

The view that Proverbs 1–9 is later than the sentences is still maintained[102]
but is more difficult to hold when neither form nor theological content can be
employed as arguments. Kayatz, who has demonstrated the close resemblance
between Proverbs 1–9 and Egyptian instructions especially in terms of form,

---

[96] R. J. Williams (1975:241, 244–245) notes that there is no longer any reason to regard Prov 1–9 and
22:17–24:34 on the basis of form as later than the compilations of aphorisms in the book, since these
units already had a long tradition in the Egyptian instructions. Cf. Gemser's (1960:127–128) warnings
against an evolutionary view based on his comparative study of *Onkhsheshonqy* and Proverbs.
Williams also argues against a gradual development from a secular to religious viewpoint in the wisdom
literature and notes that this view is no longer held by Egyptologists concerning Egyptian religion. See
also Kitchen's studies (1977, 1979) against an evolutionary view of form.

[97] Alternatively Proverbs 10:1–22:16 may be placed before Proverbs 25–29 and regarded as of pre-
Hezekian origin.

[98] Williams (1975:231–252), see also Shupak (1987:117–119). Waltke (1979:223), points out that
wisdom literature existed not only in Egypt but throughout the Fertile Crescent not only before Solomon
but even before the Hebrews appeared in history! The same is pointed out by Khanjian (1973:266–267)
in relation to Ugaritic wisdom which came from Mesopotamia long before Israel existed.

[99] Ruffle (1975:35–36) makes a case for the authenticity of the Solomonic "authorship." See Whybray
(1982:13–26 for a more sceptical evaluation).

[100] Williams (1975:242).

[101] See Ruffle (1977:65).

[102] McKane (1985:6–10) admits that Proverbs 1–9 cannot be assigned to a late date on form-critical
grounds. His late dating of the section is rather based on the view that its generalized and theologized
content represents a later stage in the history of the instruction genre in Israel, which at first, as in
Egypt, was used for the education of an *elite* that was trained for the service of the state.

points out that there is no reason to regard Proverbs 1–9 as later than the rest of the book.[103] Lang, who examines the arguments for a post-exilic dating finds them to be untenable, and, even if he is hesitant to fix a date for the section, opts for a pre-exilic alternative for most of the material.[104]

The conclusion we can make concerning authorship and dating is that evidence demanding an exilic or post-exilic date for any of the main sections in Proverbs 1–29 is lacking. It is even possible to argue in favour of the book's own claim—that Solomon is the originator of the process of composing and compiling the sayings that led to the formation of the different sections of the book and eventually the book in its present form.[105]

Essentially all Egyptian and Mesopotamian texts that can serve as comparative material to Israelite wisdom literature are of earlier date. Both Israelite culture and its wisdom literature are late-comers on the stage and it seems probable that Israelite wisdom literature at least to some extent is indebted to the similar literature originating in surrounding cultures.

2. Other wisdom literature

The book of Proverbs shows similarities in form and content to other literature of the Old Testament and of the ancient Near East. Any study of the book needs to be informed by this dual context. Our primary interest is in Israelite literature, but an attempt will be made to relate also to non-Israelite material from neighbouring cultures which in all probability had some sort of exchange with Israel. Unfortunately the use of this comparative material in the present work is restricted by our reliance on secondary sources.

a. Defining wisdom

One problem with comparing the book of Proverbs to other Old Testament material and the literature from the surrounding cultures is the difficulty of defining what constitutes wisdom and wisdom literature.[106] We believe that such a definition will necessarily be broad because wisdom has to do with a particular approach to reality which takes within its scope a bewildering variety of life's possibilities and problems. In such a situation, no definite borderlines between wisdom thinking and other ways of approaching reality can be

---

[103] Kayatz (1966:75, 136). Cf. Kitchen (1977:84–86) who regards Prov 1–9 as the prologue of the first unit, Prov 1–24. By comparison with *Ahiqar* and *Onkhsheshonqy* he concludes that the use of long prologues is a phenomenon of the 1st millenium, but that the non-autobiographical style of Prov 1–9 puts it in an intermediate position between 3rd/2nd millenium works and those of the 1st millenium.

[104] Lang (1972:46–60). Lang's view is that the issue cannot be solved with certainty and that the only thing we know for sure is that the text originated during the period between the tenth and the third centuries B.C.

[105] Cf. Kitchen's conclusions (1977:97–102); Perdue (1983:84–85) concerning the Succession Narrative.

[106] See Crenshaw's (1976 A:3–5) overview of scholarly attempts to define wisdom.

clearly drawn. The most appropriate definition of wisdom we have found is that of Khanjian:

> Wisdom is concerned with the development of the skill of life; it is based upon experience, observation, insight into, and reflection on the various aspects of existence. It was used in different settings, as domestic instruction in the family or the tribe, as pertinent comment in a social circle by a friend or enemy, and as an academic subject and a tool for learning in the school.[107]

Fohrer notes that the root חכם, "to be wise, wisdom," occurs 180 times[108] in the books of Proverbs, Job and Qoheleth. It is found only 132 times in the other 36 books of the Old Testament.[109] This indicates that the wisdom literature is characterized by a certain vocabulary. It also shows, however, that since this vocabulary is not limited to pure wisdom texts, attempts to define criteria for identifying wisdom literature are not without problems.[110] Fohrer also demonstrates the difficulty in summarizing the meaning of and translating the term חכם because it is used in different parts of the Old Testament in different ways. In the wisdom books and the Psalms חכם mainly signifies a set of rules which are characterized by ethical and pious living; in the historical books, it refers to the skill and artistry of a craftsman; in the prophetic books, it points to different kinds of human knowledge and ability, e.g., the magicians of other peoples.[111] Compared to the use of the term in the wisdom books, the corresponding terminology in Mesopotamia[112] and Egypt[113] has less ethical connotations and is more related to the area of magic, which may explain some of the negative statements of the prophets against wisdom.

Von Rad questions the use of the term "wisdom," which has become increasingly unclear in the scholarly world and which he finds not directly rooted in the sources, and argues for a fresh, unprejudiced, study of the text material itself.[114] Von Rad certainly gives examples of such fresh study, but

---

[107] Khanjian (1973:26).

[108] Fohrer (1964:476). Cf. Sæbø (1971:558). Acc. to Sæbø the root is found 183 times in Job, Prov, and Eccl: the adjective 76 times and the singular noun 85 times.

[109] Fohrer (1964:476). Cf. Whybray (1974:76–82). Müller (1980:364–366) notes that the root occurs in Akkadian as a verb with the general meaning "know." In Ugarit it is exclusively associated with the high god El. For the semantic field of חכם, see synonyms-antonyms in Sæbø (1971:559, 562, 564) and Müller (1980:371–373).

[110] See Whybray (1974:74–76).

[111] Fohrer (1964:476). Cf. Preuss (1987:10–12), Sæbø's (1971:558–563) treatment of the verb, adjective and noun, and Fox's (1968:55) four-fold definition of the term: 1) Practical sagacity: general reasoning ability, statecraft, craftsmanship 2) ethical-religious wisdom 3) speculative wisdom 4) an intellectual technique for attaining this speculative wisdom a la Qoheleth. Fox points out that Proverbs represents ethical-religious wisdom and that the aim of this wisdom is primarily to teach and commend ethical behaviour and has little to do with knowledge and understanding of life and the universe in itself. This should not be stretched too far, but there is certainly a difference between the books of Proverbs and Qoheleth in this respect.

[112] Lambert (1960:1), Müller (1980:367–368).

[113] Krause (1980:368–370). On the role of magic in Egyptian religion, see Brunner (1961/2:541–542).

[114] Von Rad (1981:7–8).

his scepticism concerning the significance of the term wisdom for Israelite wisdom seems unnecessarily radical.[115]

Lambert points out that the term "wisdom" is, strictly speaking, a misnomer when used in connection with Babylonian literature. It belongs to Hebraic studies where it applies to the Old Testament wisdom books and has been extended to describe a group of texts "which correspond in subject-matter with the Hebrew wisdom books, and may be retained as a convenient short description."[116] It is, of course, difficult to define criteria for which Mesopotamian literature should be called wisdom; Lambert chooses to include in his collection material that might otherwise be labelled "philosophical" in the Greek sense of the word, literature that relates to ethics which gives practical advice on living and works dealing with intellectual problems inherent in what was then the current outlook on life. Fables, popular sayings and proverbs are also included.[117]

R. J. Williams notes that the term "wisdom" is not native to Egypt, but has been adopted from biblical studies to designate didactic texts with similar features as well as "speculative" works.[118] The didactic texts from Egypt are the so-called instructions while speculative works include laments or complaints as well as political propaganda.

b. Wisdom literature in the Old Testament
It may seem easy to define the extent of wisdom literature in the Old Testament, but the question has become increasingly protracted as different scholars have argued for the inclusion of a growing number of texts in the corpus.

Most scholars agree in defining the three books of Proverbs, Job and Ecclesiastes as wisdom literature. It should be noted, however, that these books contain major differences in style and content. While the book of Proverbs is made up of collections of sayings dealing with the two ways of life, the other two books are much more problem-centered. The book of Job is about a righteous man's struggle of faith in suffering, and the book consists almost exclusively of the speeches of Job, his "friends," and, finally, the

---

[115] Against von Rad see the statistics above for the root חכם in the OT! The richness of synonyms (von Rad [1981:53]) does not alter the fact that the root חכם seems to occupy a central position within the OT wisdom literature.

[116] Lambert (1960:1). The problem has also been noted by Bolle (1982) who discusses the difficulty of defining wisdom as well as the value of narrow versus broad definition. Buccellati (1981:35–47) is sceptical about defining any wisdom literature, but regards wisdom as an intellectual phenomenon in itself. The problem with such an approach is that what constitutes wisdom becomes a most subjective and abstract matter which is also evident in Buccelati's treatment of the subject.

[117] Lambert (1960:1).

[118] Williams (1981:1). The division into didactic-speculative texts is common in the evaluation of the biblical material as well as in the wider ANE context, cf. Rylaarsdam (1946:4) who uses the categories "prudential admonitions," commonly in proverbial form, and "reflective essays," often in a pessimistic vein.

Lord.[119] The book of Ecclesiastes, like the book of Proverbs, is made up of sayings about life in general, but is characterized by the radical scepticism of a man who looks in vain for a meaning in life.

The main discussion on the extent of wisdom literature within the Old Testament is whether or not to include other texts that have similar vocabularies, subject matter, ways of dealing with certain issues, etc. Among the texts suggested for inclusion are several psalms, certain prophets, parts of the Pentateuch and the historical writings as, e.g., the Joseph story, the Succession Narrative, the book of Deuteronomy and the book of Esther.[120] The on-going discussion involves which criteria that are to be used for defining the nature of wisdom and also what kind of "movement" wisdom represented in Israel and what its relationship was to the other sectors contemporary with it.

It is common for scholars to include at least some psalms within the wisdom corpus.[121] The problem lies in the lack of consensus as to *which* psalms should be included.[122] The usual presupposition is that "wisdom psalms" are non-cultic, stemming from a wisdom setting rather than the normal, predominantly cultic setting of the psalms.[123] If a psalm deals with certain issues, e.g., the problem of suffering, or includes a certain form, e.g., אשרי or acrostics, it is often on that basis assigned to the corpus of wisdom literature with an entirely different original setting than the other psalms.[124] Behind this type of reasoning lies a rigid compartmentalizing of Israelite society which needs to be reconsidered.[125] There is, e.g., reason to assume that an inter-relationship existed between the wisdom circles and the circles associated with the cult. If this is correct, there is no need to isolate the so-called wisdom psalms from the normal setting of the psalms. The use of motifs and forms in some psalms that to a large degree characterize wisdom can thus be explained as contingent upon the inter-relationship between the wisdom teachers and other groups in the society.

Whybray, who uses a terminological approach in his search for wisdom in the Old Testament, comes up with an impressive list of books and passages

---

[119] Westermann (1981: 1–14) reviews the discussion concerning the classification of the book, and himself defines it mainly as lament and consolation. See also Whybray (1989:238).

[120] See Emerton (1979:221–227) for an overview, and Preuss (1987:154–171) for a recent assessment of the wisdom thinking in different parts of the OT.

[121] E.g., Gese (1958:1) who includes Ps 1; 37; 49; 73; 78; 91; 111; 112; 119; 127; 133.

[122] See Murphy (1962:156–167), Crenshaw (1974 B:249–253), Perdue (1977:261–268), and Luyten (1979:59–81) for a review of the discussion. Luyten notes that more than a third of the Psalms have been called wisdom psalms by one scholar or another! Fichtner (1933:9) includes among the wisdom psalms: Ps 1; 19b; 32:8–11; 34:12–23; 37; 49; 73; 94:8ff; 111; 112; 119; 127; 128; 133, Eissfeldt (1965:124–127): Ps 1; (19); 37; 49; 73; 78; (90); 91; 105; 106; 112; (119); 128; 133; (139), Crenshaw (1976 A:15): Ps 1; 19; 33; 39; 49; 104; 127.

[123] Mowinckel (1955:205–206).

[124] See Kaiser (1978:133) for a list of common criteria.

[125] Brekelmans (1979:36–37). Cf. Mowinckel (1955:206–208).

influenced by what he calls the "intellectual tradition."[126] Whybray's approach assumes that there must be wisdom influence in other Old Testament texts since wisdom does not belong to a fixed setting, but is more of a movement administered within certain social groups. His investigation outlines the relationship that exists between what is usually called wisdom and other traditions of the old Testament.

Crenshaw has called attention to the need for sound criteria in identifying wisdom influence in other parts of the Old Testament.[127] Crenshaw emphasizes that "a distinction between wisdom literature, wisdom tradition, and wisdom thinking is essential."[128] The presence in other parts of the Old Testament of vocabulary, form, or subject matter which in a special way characterize wisdom traditions is not enough to categorize these texts as wisdom literature. It is necessary to take into account the common cultural stock shared by all of the traditions within Israel as well as to determine whether or not particular common elements are accorded the same meaning. We need also be open to the possibility of both indirect and direct influence between the different traditions within Israel. Such influences may explain the presence of wisdom thinking in other traditions of the Old Testament without any significant consequences for setting or interpretation.

Brekelmans, who refutes Weinfeld's thesis that the book of Deuteronomy originated in the scribal circles of Jerusalem by pointing out differences between the book and the wisdom literature, points to the common terminology and ideas of wisdom and other traditions:

> If wisdom was not the private property of the sages but the common property of all educated classes, it seems natural enough for at least some of its ideas and part of its terminology to be shared by other authors. Even the didactic style as such may have been common to wise men, preachers and others. Form-critical studies have accustomed us to accept one special life setting for each literary form. But the clear-cut conclusions of such an approach do not always do justice to the complexity of real life.[129]

The relationship between wisdom and the prophets turns out to be more complex than might be expected.[130] On the one hand, we have a strong criticism of wisdom especially in the books of Isaiah and Jeremiah. On the other hand, it has been argued that several of the prophets had close connections to the wisdom milieu.[131] The criticism of wisdom in Isaiah and Jeremiah seems in

---

[126] Whybray (1974:150–154): Gen 2–3; 37–50; Deut 1–4; 32; 2 Sam 9–20 and 1 Kings 1–2; 1 Kings 3–11; Ps 1; 19:8–15; 37; 49; 51; 73; 90; 92; 94; 104; 107; 111; 119, Isa 1–39 (gen. and add.); Jer; Ez 28; Dan; Hos 14:10; Mi 6:9.

[127] Crenshaw (1969:129–142).

[128] Crenshaw (1969:130).

[129] Brekelmans (1979:37).

[130] See Mogensen (1975) for an overview of the discussion. See also Morgan (1979) for literature and an interesting, though somewhat dubious, approach to a fuller understanding of wisdom in the OT.

[131] Fichtner (1976:429–438) for Isaiah, Wolff (1964) and Terrien (1962:108–115) for Amos. In a more general way Lindblom (1955:192–204) and Morgan (1979:209–244) discuss the relationship between the wise men and the prophets.

large measure to be due to 1) the magical, manticist and astrological connotations of the term which seem to have especially characterized non-Israelite wisdom,[132] and 2) the use of the term also for the kind of wisdom which is not coupled with piety and seeking the will of the Lord.[133] As argued above, there seems to be good reason to regard the connections especially between Isaiah, Amos and wisdom as due to a common stock of terminology and form as well as to a conceivable inter-relationship between the prophetic and wisdom traditions. The evidence does not warrant an understanding of either Isaiah or Amos as wisdom teachers.[134] It rather points at the influence of wisdom upon other traditions of the Old Testament and shows that "we ought not to think of priests, prophets, and sages in terms of watertight compartments and differentiate between them so sharply that all contact between them would have been impossible."[135]

Our view is that there is good reason to adopt a minimalistic approach when it comes to defining the extent of wisdom literature in the Old Testament. Similarities in subject matter, approach, style, and form elements that can be demonstrated outside the books of Proverbs, Job, and Ecclesiastes in the Old Testament are noteworthy and demonstrate that wisdom was not a strange and cloistered phenomenon in the world of the Old Testament.

c. Wisdom literature in the apocrypha and pseudepigrapha

It is interesting that Israelite wisdom compositions are to be found among the apocryphal and pseudepigraphic literature from the intertestamental period. These wisdom works are of a later date and exhibit several significant differences from those of the Old Testament. Nevertheless, they are of special interest since they exemplify later developments in the wisdom thinking that permeates the Old Testament books. Since our specific field of interest is the theological thinking characteristic of the book of Proverbs, which we take to be predominantly pre-exilic, the apocryphal and pseudepigraphic books are of limited value. The distinctive element in these books is that wisdom is to a large degree merged with Torah piety and also that there are clear signs of both Hellenistic influence and anti-Hellenistic polemics. The result of this is not only that wisdom has lost some of its significance, but also that it has become more influential by moving closer to the centre of Israelite faith.

The Hebrew book of Sirach[136] from the second century B.C.[137] is a good example of the way in which the wisdom and Israel's sacred traditions were

---

[132] Isa 19:1–15; 44:25–26; 47:9–13; Jer 50:35–36, see Müller (1980:376–377).

[133] Isa 29:13–16; 31:1–3, cf. 30:1–5.

[134] See Scott (1970:36–39) and Emerton (1979:223–226) for summaries of the arguments for and against a wisdom setting for some of the prophets.

[135] Brekelmans (1979:36), cf. Morgan (1979:228).

[136] See Fichtner (1933:9), von Rad (1981:240–262), Murphy (1981 B:23–24), Crenshaw (1982:149–173), Preuss (1987:138–147), with bibliographies.

[137] Crenshaw (1982:158–159), Preuss (1987:138–139).

merged[138] as well as of the identification of wisdom with the Torah.[139] A division of the book into two or three sections based on content can be defended,[140] but on the whole its arrangement does not appear to follow an organized scheme. One method apparently used to arrange the sayings in the book was grouping together proverbs with similar subject matter.[141] From the point of content, Sirach is close to the book of Proverbs. It exhibits a rich variety of forms dominated by the admonitory style.[142]

The Greek Wisdom of Solomon comes from the first century B.C.[143] It originated outside of Palestine, probably in Egypt or Syria,[144] and, like the book of Sirach, is directed towards Jews influenced by Hellenism. The book consists of three parts: the first part (chs. 1–5) is made up of parallelistic sayings advocating piety, wisdom and righteousness, the other two sections describe wisdom (chs. 6–9), and deal with the history of Israel and the supremacy of Israel's religion (chs. 10–19).[145] Hellenistic influence in the book is especially evident in the view of the human soul which is seen as eternal.[146] Here wisdom is not equated with the Torah as in Sirach, but rather with God's spirit which permeates and fully knows everything in creation.[147]

It is also possible to regard the Epistle of Aristeas,[148] the fourth book of Maccabees[149] and parts of the books of Tobit,[150] Baruch,[151] and 1 Esdras,[152] as wisdom literature. Often included in this category is the Mishnaic tractate The Wisdom of the Fathers which consists of wise sayings attributed to main teachers of Torah like Moses and Hillel.[153]

d. Wisdom literature among Israel's neighbours
In 1 Kings 5 the wisdom of Solomon is compared to the wisdom of the tribes of the east. The Old Testament also refers to the wisdom of Teman and

---

[138] See esp. chs. 44–50. Crenshaw (1982:149–158).

[139] See esp. ch. 24.

[140] Chs. 2–23; 24–50. Chs. 44–50 may be considered a separate section with its retrospect of Israel's history. Chs. 1; 51 are wisdom hymns that constitute a framework to the book. It seems probable that the wisdom hymn in ch. 24 intentionally divides the book in two nearly congruent sections. See Preuss (1987:139).

[141] Cf. the almost contemporary Egyptian text *Papyrus Insinger.*

[142] Crenshaw (1982:160–172), Preuss (1987:140–141).

[143] See Fichtner (1933:10–11), Murphy (1981 B:24–25), Crenshaw (1982:174–180) and Preuss (1987:147–151), with bibliographies.

[144] Preuss (1987:148).

[145] Preuss (1987:148–149).

[146] Wis 4:13–16; 9:15.

[147] 7:22–27; 9:17.

[148] Fichtner (1933:10), Preuss (1987:138).

[149] Fichtner (1933:11), Preuss (1987:138).

[150] Fichtner (1933:9–10), Preuss (1987:138).

[151] Fichtner (1933:10), Crenshaw (1982:187–188).

[152] Fichtner (1933:10), Crenshaw (1982:185–187).

[153] Fichtner (1933:11), Preuss (1987:151–153).

Edom.[154] The same is true of Phoenician wisdom.[155] Unfortunately, apart
from Egypt and Mesopotamia, hardly anything of wisdom literature from the
neighbouring cultures has been preserved.[156] The only exceptions are some
Akkadian texts from Ugarit.[157] Of special interest is, a text of the type *Ludlul*
bēl nēmeqi, which tells of the sufferings of a righteous man before his god
Marduk.[158] A fairly extensive instruction has also been found[159] as well as
some texts of proverbs.[160] Khanjian has attempted to demonstrate that there
are many points of contact between the sapiential traditions of Jerusalem and
Ugarit. The result is not very convincing and the examples Khanjian gives as
parallels in "content, a certain conceptual perspective, as well as a common
stock of phrases, formulae, and word pairs" are on the whole too general to
lead to any compelling conclusions concerning the relationship between
Israelite and Ugaritic wisdom.[161] At least one of the texts is not native to
Ugarit and must be regarded as dependent upon *Ludlul bēl nēmeqi*.[162]
Nevertheless, these texts are valuable as an indication of how wisdom and
wisdom texts were widely dispersed and well-known over the entire ancient
Near East at such an early period.

Archaeological discoveries in Mesopotamia have yielded a number of
ancient texts which exhibit significant parallels with Israelite wisdom.[163] The
problem is that "wisdom literature" is not a category that is completely appropriate for Mesopotamian literature. Therefore, when we refer to
"Mesopotamian wisdom literature," we mean texts which from the standpoint
of Israelite wisdom literature exhibit some degree of correspondence and
therefore can serve as points of comparison and help in the interpretation of
the Israelite material.

Gordon's *Sumerian Proverbs* from 1959 contains the two most well-known
Sumerian proverb collections—both from Nippur around 2000 B.C.[164] It is

---

[154] Ob 8; Jer 49:7; Job 2:11 relates that Eliphaz came from Teman.

[155] Ez 28:2–3, 17; Zech 9:2.

[156] Murphy (1981 A:11–12).

[157] Nougayrol (1968:265–300. See Khanjian (1973:139–206) for a presentation of the texts with
linguistic notes and commentary. Khanjian also includes (1973:207–208) a couple of short wisdom-like
sayings in Ugaritic from various literary and religious texts and letters.

[158] RS 25.460. See Nougayrol (1968:265–273), Khanjian (1973:191–206), (Wiseman (1977:83–85).

[159] RS 22.439. See Nougayrol (1968:273–290), Khanjian (1973:148–176), Wiseman (1977:85–86).

[160] Nougayrol (1968:291–300), Wiseman (1977:88).

[161] Khanjian (1975:373). Cf. Wiseman (1977:87). Murphy (1981 A:12) about RS 22.439: "Thus far,
the studies of the Ugaritic wisdom of Shube'awelum (RS 22.439) have yielded only modest results.
One finds wisdom sayings, admonitions, and exhortations; the work seems to be in the genre of the
Akkadian *Counsels of Wisdom*."

[162] Wiseman (1977:83)

[163] For suggestions concerning relevant texts, see Gordon's (1960) detailed survey, Fichtner (1933:6–
7), van Dijk (1953), Schmid (1966:223–239), Kitchen (1977:113–114), Crenshaw (1982:228–235)
and McKane (1985:151–208). Translations in Langdon (1923, Bab. mat.), Gordon (1959, Sum.
mat.), Lambert (1960, Bab. mat.), *ANET* (1969).

[164] See Alster (1978:97–112) for a list of Sumerian proverb collections and the text of another such
collection.

remarkable that very few of these proverbs contain theological references. The same is true of the Sumerian text *The Instructions of Suruppak,* attributed to the survivor of the great flood in Sumerian folklore, which consists mainly of short admonitions and demonstrates that parallelism was already used in the earliest times.[165] In his *Babylonian Wisdom Literature,* Lambert includes popular sayings, bilingual and monolingual Babylonian proverb collections from Babylonian and Assyrian times. In this group of texts as well theological references are comparatively rare. It is interesting that even though large amounts of Sumero-Akkadian material has been discovered, few Babylonian proverbs are to be found among them. Lambert's explanation is that the traditional status of the Sumerian material to a large extent excluded the acceptance of unilingual Akkadian material:

> Babylonian proverbs are not a genre in the traditional literature of the Babylonians and Assyrians. The reason can be suggested. The codifiers of traditional literature during the Cassite period were very academic scholars, who may well have frowned on proverbs which were passed around among the uneducated. These scholars already had a vast traditional genre of proverbs, Sumerian with Babylonian translations, which formed the proper study of the educated.[166]

There are several texts from ancient Mesopotamia that show similarities in content and form to the book of Job. The Sumerian *Man and His God,* which Kramer has called *A Sumerian Variation on the Job Motif,* is the lament of a suffering man and his plea to his personal god for restoration to health which is eventually granted.[167] The Babylonian *Ludlul bēl nēmeqi*[168] is likewise about a man who recounts his suffering. His inability to understand the reason for the sudden reversal of his fortune causes the desperate man to doubt his ability to please the gods. At last Marduk hears his pleas and, through different intermediaries, liberates the man from his afflictions. A recent analysis by Albertz concludes that the text is marked by personal "Mardukfrömmigkeit," the focal point of the text concentrates on Marduk's wrath and mercy while the framework highlights praise of Marduk.[169] According to this interpretation, the notion of the *innocent* suffering of a righteous man is not the main point of the text. Although Marduk is the central figure from the very beginning, the man's description of his affliction and his laments assert that he has been abandoned by his personal god and goddess and the relationship between these deities and Marduk is never made clear. *The Babylonian Theodicy*[170] is

---

[165] Alster (1974:34–51). An Akkadian fragment of the text from Middle Assyrian times is included in Lambert (1960:95) and *ANET* (1969:594–595).

[166] Lambert (1960:275–276).

[167] Kramer (1955:170–182), *ANET* (1969:589–591).

[168] Langdon (1923:1–66), Lambert (1960:21–62), *ANET* (1969:596–600). Wiseman (1980:104–107), Albertz (1988:25–53, transl. and comm.). Often called *I Will Praise the Lord of Wisdom* (transl.) or *The Poem of the Righteous Sufferer.*

[169] Albertz (1988:49–53).

[170] Lambert (1960:63–91), *ANET* (1969:601–604).

an acrostic poem consisting of a dialogue between a man stricken by tragedy and his friend. In the dialogue the friend seeks to console his friend with the traditional answers from what must have been conventional theology while the suffering man revolts against what he asserts is an undeserved fate. Here, too, we encounter complaints to the effect that the gods are inaccessible and inscrutable. The dialogue form and the suffering theme is also found in a fragmentary Akkadian text published by Nougayrol in 1952.[171]

There are a few other texts which contain a number of interesting features. The text that has been called *The Dialogue of Pessimism* or *A Pessimistic Dialogue between Master and Slave*[172] is another example of the dialogue form. Another work *A Dialogue about Human Misery*,[173] which also has been called *The Babylonian Ecclesiastes,* uses the dialogue form to explore the sorrowful state of man and life's injustices. *Counsels of Wisdom*[174] is a collection of moral exhortations[175] consisting of short sections, each dealing with one specific topic, and for the most part directed to a general audience.[176] When religious aspects are brought into the picture it is mainly Shamash and the personal god that are mentioned. *Counsels of a pessimist*[177] is a short tablet which may be an extract from a larger work exploring the problem of human transience and admonishing the reader not to cease fulfilling religious obligations toward "the god who created you" and the city goddess. *Advice to a Prince*[178] is of interest because of its "omen style" and its resemblance to royal instructions, being directed to the king to warn him of the dire consequences that will follow if he oppresses the citizens of Sippar, Nippur, and Babylon. Lambert includes in his *Babylonian Wisdom Literature* a work titled *A Bilingual Hymn to Ninurta*,[179] which contains several ethical injunctions, and *The Shamash Hymn*,[180] which exhibits certain parallels with Psalm 104 and the Egyptian Aton hymn, especially in the way that it refers to Shamash as a supreme, omnipresent and omnivisionary being who cares for all creatures and supervises justice in the world.

The Aramaic text *The Words of Ahiqar*[181] must also be mentioned. Speaking in first person the text tells the story of Ahiqar, the wise scribe and counsellor of the kings of Assyria, and contains a collection of about one

---

[171] Nougayrol (1952:239–250). Commented upon by van Dijk (1953:120–122), von Soden (1957:315–319; 1965:47–48), R. J. Williams (1956:14), Lambert (1960:10–11, n. 3).

[172] Langdon (1923:67–81), Lambert (1960:139–149), *ANET* (1969:600–601).

[173] *ANET* (1969:438–440).

[174] Lambert (1960:96–107), *ANET* (1969:595–596).

[175] For a concise discussion of content and form, see McKane (1985:153–156).

[176] Lambert (1960:96), cf. McKane (1985:151).

[177] Lambert (1960:107–109).

[178] Lambert (1960:110–115).

[179] Lambert (1960:118–120).

[180] Lambert (1960:121–138).

[181] *ANET* (1969:427–430), Lindenberger (1983, 1985:479–507).

hundred sayings arranged in a more or less haphazard manner. It closely resembles the genre and, to some extent, the content of the wisdom traditions of the Old Testament and apocrypha. Lindenberger dates the extant Aramaic form no later than the mid-sixth century B.C. allowing for the possibility that the wisdom sayings had a Syrian pre-history extending back as far as the earlier part of the first millenium—a setting and date that makes the book a potentially interesting close contemporary of the book of Proverbs.[182] The deities in this composition are the gods of Aram, Canaan and Mesopotamia who are depicted as the judges and protectors of humanity.[183] The text underscores the necessity of pleasing the gods in order to assure that one's accomplishments will be lasting.

This brief survey has mentioned the most important Mesopotamian texts for a comparative study to the Israelite wisdom literature. It is always difficult to decide precisely which works merit inclusion in such a survey, especially in the case of works whose relevance is marginal. Lambert and Pritchard also include among wisdom writings Akkadian fables[184] while Langdon takes up a text he calls *The Supposed Rules of Monthly Diet*,[185] but these texts have been deemed to be of minimal relevance for our study.

When we turn to Egyptian texts for comparative material, we find a number of texts that were categorized by the Egyptians themselves as belonging to a particular genre and signified by a specific term—instruction[186]—as well as some other texts that relate to wisdom in a broad sense.[187] R. J. Williams, in an article from 1981,[188] surveys the main instructions and "speculative works" available, which we list here in chronological order:

Old Kingdom	
Instructions:	*Speculative works:*
Teaching of Hardjedef	
Teaching of Kagemni	
Teaching of Ptahhotep	
First Intermediate period	
Instructions:	*Speculative works:*
Teaching of Merikare	Admonitions of Ipuwer
	Tale of the Eloquent Peasant
	Harper's Song(s)
	Dispute of a Man with His BAI

---

[182] Lindenberger (1985:482–484, 491).

[183] Lindenberger (1985:484).

[184] Lambert (1960:150–212), *ANET* (1969:410–411, 592–593).

[185] Langdon (1923:93–99).

[186] *sb3yt*. See Brunner (1980:964–968) for the meaning of the term.

[187] For suggestions of relevant texts see, e.g., Fichtner (1933:3–5), Kayatz (1966:17–24), Schmid (1966:202–223), McKane (1985: 51–150), Kitchen (1977:111–113; 1979:281–282), Crenshaw (1982:213–228) and Preuss (1987:13–20).

[188] R. J. Williams (1981:1).

Middle Kingdom
Instructions: *Speculative works:*
Teaching of Amenemhet I   Prophecies of Nepherty
Satire on Trades   Lament of Khakheperesonbe
Loyalist Teaching   Discourses of Sisobk
Teaching of a Man for His Son

New Kingdom
Instructions: *Speculative works:*
Teaching of Any
Teaching of Amenemope
Teaching of Amennakhte

Demotic Period
Instructions: *Speculative works:*
Teaching of Onkhsheshonqy
Papyrus Insinger

The most important instructions for our study are the teachings of *Ptahhotep*,[189] *Merikare*,[190] *Any*,[191] and *Amenemope*,[192] the others have little of theological importance to contribute. The Demotic instructions are quite interesting in several respects, e.g., form and theological content, and will be referred to later in this study but their late date places them in a secondary relationship to the book of Proverbs.[193]

Unfortunately, we have only fragmentary knowledge of the instructions of *Hardjedef* and *Kagemni*[194] from the Old Kingdom period. *The Instruction of Amenemhet*[195] from the Middle Kingdom which discusses regicide theme in the form of a first person account of the deceased pharaoh himself is unique but of little theological significance.[196] The same is true of *The Satire on Trades*,[197] which extols the scribal profession above all others,[198] *The Loyalist*

---

[189] *ANET* (1969:412–414), Lichtheim (1975:61–80).

[190] *ANET* (1969:414–418), Lichtheim (1975:97–109).

[191] *ANET* (1969:420–421), Lichtheim (1976:135–146).

[192] *ANET* (1969:421–425), Lichtheim (1976:146–163).

[193] Both works can be assigned to the Ptolemaic era with a possibility that *Onkhsheshonqy* is earlier, see Lichtheim (1980:159, 184). An interesting comparison between Proverbs and *Onkhsheshonqy* mainly with respect to form is made by Gemser (1960:102–128).

[194] *ANET* (1969:419–420), Lichtheim (1975:58–61).

[195] *ANET* (1969:418–419), Lichtheim (1975:135–139).

[196] Cf. *Merikare* (Perdue [1983:85, n. 44]). Williams (1981:3) points out that *Amenemhet* shows the close relationship between wisdom and biographical texts and that it could just as well be called an autobiography.

[197] *ANET* (1969:432–434), Lichtheim (1975:184–192). This text is also referred to as *The Instruction of Khety, son of Duauf/Dua-Khety* (for the name in different manuscripts, see Lichtheim (1975:192, n. 2).

[198] Cf. the text *In Praise of Learned Scribes/The Immortality of Writers* (*ANET* [1969:431–432]; Lichtheim [1976:175–178]) and *Papyrus Lansing* (Lichtheim [1976:168–175]; Caminos [1954:371–428]) on the same theme. The popularity of the theme is well attested in a number of hieratic texts from the New Kingdom (see Caminos [1954]).

Teaching,[199] which in a hymn-like manner prescribes correct conduct in relation to the divine king, and *The Instruction of a Man for His Son*[200] on the same theme.[201] *The Instruction of Amennakhte*[202] from the New Kingdom is a short incomplete text from a scribe to one of his disciples. It is typical of the instruction genre but sheds no further light on our subject.

The Egyptian speculative works enumerated by Williams are all from the First Intermediate and Middle Kingdom periods and relate only sporadically to our subject. *The Admonitions of Ipuwer*[203] describes either the actual or imagined disorder of disintegrating Egyptian society[204] in which all values are overturned. *The Tale of the Eloquent Peasant*[205] tells about a peasant who is robbed by a noble and who presents his complaint before the superiors with such eloquence that he finally receives justice. *Harper's Songs* are songs accompanied by the harp sung to the dead. Their main theme is death but the genre developed into songs urging enjoyment of life while it lasts.[206] The most well-known of them, *The Song from the Tomb of King Intef,*[207] is of interest for its scepticism concerning the reality of the after-life and the efficacy of tomb-building. The same scepticism is found in *The Dispute of a Man with His Ba,*[208] a difficult and fragmentary text which relates the discussion between a man weary of life and his soul, *ba,* which is threatening to leave him because he is longing for death. This action by the soul would mean total annihilation instead of resurrection and immortal bliss after death—a thought that fills the man with horror.[209] *The Prophecies of Nepherty*[210] is "a historical romance in pseudo-prophetic form"[211] which purports to tell how the sage Nepherty prophesies to king Snefru of the fourth dynasty about the downfall of the Old Kingdom and the redemption of the nation through king

---

[199] Part of the instruction is found on *The Stela of Sehetep-ib-re* (Lichtheim [1975:128], *ANET* [1969:431]). See Poser (1976) for the full text .

[200] Kitchen (1969:189–202). According to Poser (1979:307–316) the two texts *Counsels of prudence/Discretion* (Kitchen [1970:203–210]) and *Sagesse Inconnue* (Poser [1950:71–84]) may constitute the middle and end part of the work.

[201] The fragmentary text published by Barns (1968:71–76) and by Kitchen (1977:112) referred to as *Ashmolean Writing Board* seems to be a similar school text also advocating loyalty to the god-king, the shepherd and righteous judge of mankind.

[202] Poser (1955:61–72), Simpson (1973:341–342). *In Praise of Learned Scribes* may constitute the second part of this text (Kitchen [1979:281]).

[203] *ANET* (1969:441–444), Lichtheim (1975:149–163).

[204] The text is dated to Late Middle Kingdom by Lichtheim (1975:149), who interprets it as a late-comer of the same genre and character as *Nepherty* and *Khakheperesonbe* coming, as they did, from times of peace and prosperity, and certainly not from the disorder of the First Intermediary Period as they have been commonly interpreted since Gardiner.

[205] *ANET* (1969:407–410, partial only), Lichtheim (1975:169–184).

[206] See Williams (1981:4) concerning the interpretation of the songs.

[207] *ANET* (1969:467), Lichtheim (1975:194–197).

[208] *ANET* (1969:405–407, here called *A Dispute over Suicide*), Lichtheim (1975:163–169).

[209] Lichtheim (1975:163). See Williams (1981:4) concerning the interpretation of the text.

[210] *ANET* (1969:444–446), Lichtheim (1975:139–145).

[211] Lichtheim (1975:139).

Amenemhet I. *The Lament of Khakheperesonbe*[212] is similar to *The Admonitions of Ipuwer* in its pessimistic description of the effects of disorder on Egyptian society. *The Discourses of Sisobk*[213] which have a structure reminiscent of *Ahiqar* have a similar purpose. This work tells of the royal scribe Sisobk who is saved from mortal danger through the petition of a dancer. Following this introductory narrative, Sisobk's teachings on different subjects are given.

---

[212] Lichtheim (1975:145–149). This text is often referred to as an instruction, e.g., Preuss (1987:17), and indeed shares many of the features of this genre.
[213] Barns (1956:1–10). See also Kitchen (1979:239–240).

B. The book of Proverbs: its concept of God and theology

1. The portrayal of God in the wisdom literature

a. Introductory remarks

It is impossible to sketch a complete picture of the conceptions of God of either the sages or anyone else in the Old Testament context. From the very outset of our inquiry, our access to information about the theology of Old Testament times is restricted. Olsson differentiates between the mental concept of God and the express form in which this concept is communicated in, e.g., texts and images.[214] In biblical studies, we are restricted to dealing with the expressed form which by its very nature is always fragmentary. Information in the written sources may permit us to advance tentative inferences concerning the concepts present in the minds of the people, but no exhaustive reconstruction can ever be hoped for in a delicate, complex and nonconsistent issue such as that which we are investigating. The people who produced the book of Proverbs are unknown to us and lived over a period of several centuries. To give a comprehensive account of their mental concept of the deity is nothing less than impossible. The aim of this study, however, is to recognize and describe various qualities used to depict God in the book of Proverbs. These qualities reflect the way the sages viewed the relationship between God, themselves and the world. The extensive span of time and the differences in thought patterns which separate us from the ancient sage, coupled with the limitations in the available source material makes our task even more difficult. The methodology used in this study will be to first attempt to relate the theological statements in the book of Proverbs to other Old Testament material, primarily the other books of the wisdom tradition. Then we will proceed one step further to search for correspondences between our material and earlier or contemporary wisdom literature of the Ancient Near East. Israelite or non-Israelite texts of later date than Proverbs will considered to be only indirectly relevant here.

"Symbolic language is the mother tongue of faith" is a saying coined by Aulén[215] which implies that the object of the theological quest always remains inaccessible. We may assume that the theologians of the ancient world also experienced the elusiveness of the deity and therefore never claimed that their words, images, or other attempts to represent the deity were exhaustive, but

---

[214] Olsson (1983:91, 1985 B:42), Mettinger (1988:204–205; 1989:135). See also Geels (1983:83) for a similar differentiation, but more from the psychology of religion perspective.
[215] Aulén (1967: 151).

rather intended them to be understood as attempts to describe certain aspects
of the deity.[216]

Scholars have repeatedly pointed out that the Old Testament has no
systematic doctrine of God but describes him in relation to people. God is the
subject rather than the object in the Old Testament and this should be of great
importance for any attempt to reconstruct its theological thought patterns.[217]
The book of Proverbs is not a book characterized by theological reflection,
but a work of a primarily theological-ethical nature. This means that our
conclusions concerning the theological beliefs of the sages must be made with
extreme caution and due attention to the primary purpose of the texts we are
examining.

b. The uniqueness of the wisdom literature

Certain theological features of the wisdom literature are peculiar. Gnomic
literature, for example, deals with many important issues of life without a
single explicit reference to a deity. This applies especially to both the early
proverb collections from Sumer and the biblical book of Proverbs. This
phenomenon can be referred to as a secular tendency even though the absence
of explicit theological references in aphoristic treatments of everyday issues
does not necessarily indicate what we in our day mean by secularism.

Another characteristic of wisdom theology is the frequent preference for
generic or indeterminate expressions when referring to the deity. This is true
of the Egyptian instructions, which usually refers to the deity by using a
generic term. This feature is also to be found in Mesopotamian wisdom texts
which often contain only an indefinite reference to one's personal god, usually
"my god." In Ecclesiastes there seems to be a conscious effort to refer to and
describe the deity in very general terms. The depictions of the deity in the
book of Proverbs and in the speeches of the book of Job are not designed in
such a way that a Yahwistic interpretation is prompted, apart from the consistent use of the tetragrammaton in the book of Proverbs.

A third theological characteristic of the wisdom literature is its lack of
references to historical events.[218] This is especially noteworthy in Israelite
wisdom texts where, because of the importance of the historical traditions

---

[216] Hornung (1973:101–114) argues that the images of the Egyptian gods functioned meta-
linguistically which pointed towards the true God-representation. Cf. Brunner (1961/2:534–535) and,
on the phenomenon in general, Olsson (1985 A; 1985 B). Hornung (1973:113) maintains that "kein
denkender Ägypter wird sich vorgestellt haben, Amun sei in seiner wahren Gestalt ein Mensch mit
Widderkopf." See Jacobsen (1987:15–23) for a similar discussion concerning graven images in
Mesopotamia.

[217] Anderson (1962:417–418).

[218] Schmid (1966) attempts to show that the content of wisdom is related to the historical circumstances
surrounding its composition and is in that sense "historical." This may be the case, though the
possibility of recognizing such historical elements is virtually nil in the kind of material which makes up
the wisdom literature. Westermann (1981:108–122) and Kubina(1979:122, 144–146, 159–160) make
attempts to connect wisdom and salvation history, but the arguments are not convincing. Against
Kubina, see Habel (1985:528).

which are so often closely intertwined with theological thinking, one would expect such references. It is an astonishing fact, repeatedly pointed out by scholars that there are no references in the biblical wisdom books to historical accounts and traditions like those of the patriarchal narratives, the Exodus, Sinai, the law or the covenant.[219] This lack of references to history in the wisdom literature seems to be intentional and is probably, like the generality in its theological references, due to the specific intention of wisdom writers to express truths and deal with problems that are timeless and common to all peoples. Whether this is the result of a conscious internationalism or other considerations cannot be given a definitive answer until more evidence is available.

A fourth characteristic of most wisdom literature is a non-mythological depiction of the world and the deity. This finds its explanation in the theological perspective of the sages, but probably also in the character of the genres of the wisdom literature where especially the short units simply do not allow for lengthy descriptions. In the "speculative" works of wisdom, mythological imagery appears more frequently.[220]

A fifth characteristic of wisdom literature is a somewhat reserved attitude towards the cult.[221] This is especially valid for the books of Proverbs and Ecclesiastes, but is also the case with other wisdom compositions.

2. The theology of the book of Proverbs

a. God-references in the book of Proverbs
God is referred to by name[222] in ninety-four verses in the book of Proverbs: twenty-one verses in chapters 1–9,[223] fifty-seven verses in 10:1–22:16,[224] five verses in 22:17–24:34,[225] seven verses in chapters 25–29[226] and four verses in chapters 30–31.[227] About eleven verses in chapters 1–9 refer to God

---

[219] E.g., Zimmerli (1933:179), Fichtner (1951:145), Sæbø (1972:35).

[220] See, e.g., *Ludlul* where esp. the suffering man in the descriptions of his ill fortune makes use of mythological imagery (II 50ff, *ANET* [1969:597–598]).

[221] By this we mean that references to cultic matters are relatively few and that they tend to concentrate on the negative aspects of false cult and stress what is more important than cultic matters, see 15:8; 21:3, 27. This attitude is not unique in the Old Testament however, see, e.g., 1 Sam 15:22; Ps 4:6; 40:7–9; 50:9–14; 51:18–19; Isa 1:11–14; 58; Hos 6:6; Amos 5:21; Mic 6:7–8; Mal 1:10.

[222] Included are also constructs with the tetragrammaton.

[223] 1:7, 29; 2:5–6 (twice in verse 5), 17; 3:4–5, 7, 9, 11–12, 19, 26, 32–33; 5:21; 6:16; 8:13, 22, 35; 9:10 (twice).

[224] 10:3, 22, 27, 29; 11:1, 20; 12:2, 22; 14:2, 26, 27, 31; 15:3, 8, 9, 11, 16, 25, 26, 29, 33; 16:1, 2, 3, 4, 5, 6, 7, 9, 11, 20, 33; 17:3, 5, 15; 18:10, 22; 19:3, 14, 17, 21, 23; 20:10, 12, 22, 23, 24, 27; 21:1, 2, 3, 30, 31; 22:2, 4, 12, 14. Here 14:31 and 17:5 are included which refer to God by the epithet עשׂה, but not 21:27 and 22:11 where LXX supports a reading referring to the Lord.

[225] 22:19, 23; 23:17; 24:18, 21.

[226] 25:2, 22; 28:5, 25; 29:13, 25, 26.

[227] 30:3, 5, 9 (twice); 31:30 according to the MT text. The number of references to God depends on the way the text in 30:1–9 is interpreted and reconstructed.

anaphorically[228] as well as 23:11 and 24:12 which refer to God by other epithets.[229] In total, more than 100 verses in the book of Proverbs contain direct references to God. Since the book consists of 915 verses,[230] more than 10% of the verses contain direct theological references with the highest percentage in Proverbs 10:1–22:16 and the lowest in chapters 25–29 and 30–31.[231]

The frequency of God-references varies within the book as is demonstrated by the following table:

Chapter	God-references	Chapter	God-references
1	2	22:17–29	2
2	6	23	2
3	13	24	3
4	0		
5	1	25	2
6	1	26	0
7	0	27	0
8	9	28	2
9	2	29	3
10	4	30	4
11	2	31	1
12	2		
13	0		
14	4		
15	9		
16	11		
17	3		
18	2		
19	5		
20	6		
21	5		
22:1–16	4		

The direct theological references in chapters 25–27 are scarce and this fact has been widely used as an argument for the antiquity of these chapters and the original secularity of wisdom. However, it should be noted that chapters 4–7

---

[228] 2:7–8; 3:6, 20, 34; 8:26–31.

[229] There is also a possibility that צדיק in 21:12 refers to the Lord, see McKane (1985:561).

[230] 256 verses in Prov 1–9; 375 verses in 10:1–22:16; 82 in 22:17–24:34; 138 in 25–29; 33 in ch. 30; 31 in ch. 31.

[231] 12,5% in Prov 1–9; 15,2% in Prov 10:1–22:16; 8,5% in 22:17–24:34; 5,07% in ch. 25–29; 6,25% in chs. 30–31.

contain only two references to God and these chapters belong to the first section of the book which is commonly said to exemplify the theologization of wisdom. Instead of speculating about the stages of the putative theologization of wisdom, it is more fruitful to observe that certain passages within the book deal in a unique way with the theological aspects of life, primarily chapter 3 and chapters 15–16. There are passages where this aspect is almost totally absent as in the chapters mentioned above. The reason for this variation is not necessarily the different ages of the material, but might instead be due to factors like subject matter or the distinct background of individual units.

McKane classifies the sentences in Proverbs 10–29 one by one, regarding most of them as fairly early and characterized by an individualistic, utilitarian and secularist approach. Others he takes to be later theological reinterpretations of these earlier sentences, reinterpretations which are characterized by God-language and a moral concern that derives from Yahwistic piety.[232] This division of categories is not made purely on the basis of God-references but also on basis of linguistic evidence which McKane uses to attempt to describe the vocabulary of Yahwism in relation to earlier, mainly secular, wisdom. We will return to McKane's views later, for now let it suffice to say that even if McKane is right regarding the special connection between certain expressions and a distinctively religious interpretation, we do not on the whole find it feasible to make such distinctions between Yahwistic versus secularist terms and use them as grounds for dating the material.

b. The name of God in the book of Proverbs

It is remarkable, considering the probable complexity of the background of the material in the book of Proverbs, that the book refers to God almost exclusively by the name Yahweh.[233] Apart from the circumlocutions mentioned above, the only exceptions to this consistent Yahwism are in 2:5 and 9:10 where יראת יהוה is paralleled by דעת אלהים/דעת קדשים, 3:4 which has בעיני דעת אלהים ואדם, 2:17 where ברית אלהיה probably is to be understood as a general designation of the sacral character of the marriage and 25:2 which has כבד אלהים. 30:1–9 has Yahweh only once, containing in its place several other designations[234] which appears to have been a deliberate way of indicating the different origin of this passage.

Delekat has observed that the targum of the book of Proverbs has אלהים instead of יהוה eight times out of nine and that the Septuagint also contains a higher percentage of אלהים. His view is that the consistent use of the tetra-

---

[232] McKane (1985:10–22).

[233] Cf. Eccl. and Job 3–37 where Yahweh is never used (exception in Job 12:9 which is usually regarded as a "lapsus calami" for אלוה for which there is manuscript evidence). Qoheleth uses consistently אלהים and the even more general האלהים, while in Job אלוה, אל, and שדי are employed most of the time.

[234] דעת קדשים (v 3), אמרת אלוה (v 5), יהוה and שם אלהי (v 9).

grammaton in the Masoretic text is due to late redactions and that אלהים was
retained only when it could not be replaced by יהוה for a variety of reasons.[235]

The view that the consistent use of the tetragrammaton in the Masoretic text
is due to redactional work, or, we might say, belongs to the collection stage,
and is not original in every instance seems reasonable in view of the probable
composite background of the sayings. What surprises us is the consistency
with which this redactional activity was carried through in this book while not
in others.[236]

c. Theologization or original theology?

One crucial issue for the theology of the book of Proverbs and wisdom literature is the relationship between sayings which contain explicit theological
content and those that do not. The assumption that explicit theological content
is an indication that an earlier, more or less secular saying has later been
theologized is still widespread among scholars.[237] This assumption determines
one's understanding of the over-all perspective of the book of Proverbs since
it views the theological statements separately from the rest of the book.
Furthermore, secondary additions tend to be regarded as a species of distor-
tion. Thus one's understanding of the theological thinking reflected in the
book of Proverbs depends in large measure on whether the theological
statements are regarded as standing in harmonious unity with the remaining
ninety percent of the book or to be isolated from the rest of the book and
regarded as a corrupting element.

The separation of secular and theological thinking seems suspiciously
modern[238] and there is reason to doubt that anything like secular thinking ever
existed in the biblical world.[239] While the book of Proverbs demonstrates that
many issues could be considered without explicit appeal to divine ordinances,
this is far from proof of a secular mindset. Appeals to reason, tradition, and
common sense do not need to be understood as standing in opposition to theological thinking. Indeed, throughout the Masoretic text's arrangement of the
book of Proverbs, theological and non-theological statements are found side by
side. It is quite probable that ancient thought was in this sense holistic and

---

[235] Delekat (1971:48–51). The reason why אלהים is retained in 3:4 and 25:2 is that here it is not a
name but bears the meaning "gods." In 2:5 it is a name but is retained as a parallel to יהוה. Delekat is of
the opinion that 2:17 originally had בעלה where בעל according to practice was exchanged which yielded
אלהיה. Delekat gives no explicit reason for retaining אלוה and אלהי in chapter 30, he merely notes that
the latter is read אלה in the targum.

[236] Fichtner (1933:98): "Aus diesem Tatbestand ersieht man, dass die älteste isr. Wsht den
Gottesnamen יהו als den gebräuchlichen völlig unreflektiert verwendet, während sich in den jüngeren
Stücken die Tendenz bemerkbar macht, den Eigennamen Gottes durch Appellativa zu ersetzen."

[237] E.g., Whybray (1965 A:72), McKane (1985:1–22). See Kaiser (1978:143, n. 41).

[238] Noted by, e.g., Sæbø (1972:46). See also von Rad (1981:61).

[239] See Skehan (1971 A:23) and Priest (1963:278). The best example of something which might
arguably be "secular" are the early proverb collections from Sumer, which are very mundane in their
outlook and contain few references to any deity.

without tension between belief in man's own capabilities and belief in divine intervention.[240] This also applies to the relationship between the Israelite sages and non-Israelite wisdom. Murphy correctly argues that since distinctions like religious versus secular and experience versus revelation were probably foreign to the Israelite mind, the borrowing and inclusion of non-Israelite wisdom material by Israelite compositions was not considered a problem.[241]

McKane's main argument for his notion of reinterpretation is the divergent use of vocabulary within the book of Proverbs.[242] McKane presents what he calls "some of the more telling linguistic details" pointing out the varying use of terms like מזמה,[243] תחבלות,[244] מחשבה,[245] לב,[246] בינה,[247] חכם בעיניך.[248] It can hardly be regarded as remarkable that terms like these in the book of Proverbs are used in different contexts with different meanings.[249] A term like תחבלות can signify the steering guidance of good counsellors as well as the deceitful designs of the wicked. In a sentence like 19:21, it is not necessary to understand "the many plans of a man's heart" in a pejorative sense because of their transitoriness in relation to the counsel of the Lord. The examples McKane supplies do not prove that these usages are temporally distant from one another, nor do they demonstrate that such thoughts must be derived from two completely different world-views originating in different groups of people. We agree that they are examples of different approaches to certain issues—an openness which may well be a trait of wisdom from the very beginning and not only at a later redactional stage. The same holds for McKane's example of a substitution, 13:14 and 14:27.[250] In the first sentence it is the instruction of the wise man that is the fountain of life; in the second it is the fear of the Lord. The two sentences certainly exemplify different approaches, but these are not mutually exclusive nor does one need to postulate that their origins are separated by a considerable period of time. Neither do we find it necessary to attribute them to completely different world-views.

Fox follows Whybray[251] to a large degree when he describes the development of religiosity traceable in the book of Proverbs in three stages: the

---

[240] Pedersen (IV/1959:486–491), von Rad (1981:61–64), Skehan (1971 A:23), Nel (1982:84), Murphy (1987:450).

[241] Murphy (1969:298). For an interesting discussion of the probable processes that were part of the incorporation of Egyptian material into Israelite wisdom and Proverbs, see Bryce (1979).

[242] McKane (1985:17–18).

[243] 8:12b; 12:2b.

[244] 11:14a; 12:5.

[245] 12:5; 19:21.

[246] 19:21.

[247] 3:5; 20:24; 21:30.

[248] 3:7; 26:5, 12, 16; 28:11.

[249] See Wilson's (1987:320–327) detailed and convincing critique of McKane's views.

[250] McKane (1985:18).

[251] Whybray (1965 A).

"Egyptian," the "Yahwistic" and the "theological" stage.[252] The religiosity of the "Egyptian" stage is virtually identical to that encountered in Egyptian instructions, with the main emphasis on a concept of order and a remote deity only indirectly involved in the world of men. The "Yahwistic" stage is characterized by the introduction of Yahweh as the source of wisdom, by the identification of wisdom with the "fear of Yahweh," by Yahweh's liberation from the world order and the description of him as being in control of man's fate, and, finally, by the call for trust in Yahweh. The "theological" stage represents an elaboration on the divine origin of wisdom and is found in the passages which personify wisdom.

Fox makes several noteworthy observations concerning the theological thinking of Proverbs, but there is reason to be sceptical towards the kind of approach which he and Whybray use when it comes to the chronological development of the theological thinking in the book of Proverbs.[253] Fox's three stages highlight the different characteristics used to depict the Lord in the book of Proverbs, but nevertheless his portrayal of the putative development from impersonal deity to Yahwism and then to personification is neither convincing nor necessary. A development from impersonal deity emphasizing world order to a more personal concept of the deity may be relevant to a certain degree to Egyptian wisdom, but this development predates the emergence of Israel as a nation and there is therefore no reason to postulate a similar development in Israel and impose it upon the Israelite material. The fact that we have such a development in Egyptian wisdom indicates that within the wisdom traditions that influenced Israel, there were already depictions of the deity that exhibited these variations. This makes it quite probable that Israelite wisdom, at least to some degree, would have absorbed some of these features.

Fox argues that the "Yahwistic" stage was "a serious attempt to harmonize the God-concept of wisdom circles with the God-concept of normative Israelite religion."[254] If so, it is remarkable that much of what is usually considered normative Israelite religion is still missing from the book of Proverbs. In the book of Sirach such a harmonization is evident, but the Yahwism of the book of Proverbs does not appear to be designed as a bridge between an "Egyptian style" of religion and Israelite faith. We believe that the religiosity of the book is better explained as a Yahwistic species of wisdom as it originated in Israel, presumably when different wisdom traditions were moulded together and were interpreted in a Yahwistic manner.

Several prominent scholars maintain that although early Israelite wisdom was not entirely devoid of theological thinking it was, in fact, marked by a

---

[252] Fox (1968:55–69).
[253] Fox (1968:56–57) refrains from an attempt to date the different stages absolutely. This is attempted by Whybray (1965 A:105–106) who dates his two stages of additions to the time of the pre-exilic prophets and the post-exilic Persian period.
[254] Fox (1968:64).

belief in the concept of order coupled with a concept of the deity that had close parallels in the wisdom circles of the surrounding cultures.[255] This issue will be further discussed in chapter three. Suffice it to say here that the view seems to be too much determined by a desire to adapt the wisdom thinking of Israel and its development to fit the Egyptian model.

The so-called Yahwistic redaction of the book of Proverbs has been eminently discussed by Wilson in a recent article where he delineates the main scholarly views on the issue and their presuppositions[256] as well as presents his own view:

> In rejecting the thesis of a Yahwistic reinterpretation of mundane wisdom, the present study has alternatively suggested that theological wisdom in the book of Proverbs evinces a complementary and reciprocal relation with mundane wisdom, thereby affirming the value of mundane wisdom while also elaborating its theological dimensions.[257]

Wilson's point concerning reciprocity is that it makes a difference in our view of the over-all content of the book if we accept the reinterpretation view. If, as we maintain, there is from the beginning a close connection in Israel between this kind of mundane wisdom and theological wisdom, this has important implications for our understanding of Old Testament theology as a whole.

The Yahwistic sayings do not deviate in form from the non-Yahwistic sayings, which implies a common origin. Furthermore, the Yahwistic sayings are spread throughout the book and its different sections. This indicates that a secondary inclusion of Yahweh-sayings cannot be explained except by a rather substantial reworking of the entire book.[258] This becomes even more evident when we also take into account the "vocabulary expressive of a moralism which derives from Yahwistic piety."[259] Such moralism is difficult to define, which means that the extent of such vocabulary and language to a large degree becomes a matter of individual interpretation. In McKane's calculations, a third of the sentences in Proverbs 10:1–22:16 are part of the reinterpretive stage of this section.[260] What is left of the different sections of the book after the reinterpretation analysis[261] are rather hypothetical entities, determined to a large degree by the preconceptions of their reconstructors.

---

[255] Schmid (1966:144–149), Preuss (1972; 1987:50–60), Würthwein (1976). Murphy (1987:449) discusses the "ma'atizing" of wisdom.

[256] Wilson (1987:313–334).

[257] Wilson (1987:328).

[258] See Whybray's attempt (1979:153–165) to relate the Yahweh-sayings to their context. The result may be used as an argument in favour of an original, rational plan for the structure of the collections rather than as evidence for reinterpretation.

[259] McKane (1985:11).

[260] McKane (1985:12).

[261] See Whybray (1965 A) for chapters 1–9 and McKane (1985) for 10:1–22:16; 25–29.

d. Tension between Yahwism and wisdom?

An interesting observation that can be made in the study of the sentences in the book of Proverbs is that an explicit connection is never made between Yahweh and wisdom.[262] The only time the root חכם is related to Yahweh is in 21:30. This sentence exemplifies a kind of juxtaposition[263] where three wisdom terms are set in contrast to the Lord:

> 21:30. No wisdom, no understanding, no counsel
> against the Lord.[264]

It is not necessary to interpret this sentence as maintaining a pejorative stance towards wisdom. Its limitations and subordination to Yahwism should be considered together with similar sentences which lay special stress on God's sovereignty.[265] But it is noteworthy that this one instance where wisdom and the Lord are directly related to each other in a sentence, points to the gap between wisdom and God. This may imply a tension between wisdom and Yahwism in Israel, something that has been suggested by several scholars. Noth observes that there seems to be a hesitancy about using the attribution "wise" in relation to the Lord in the Old Testament.[266] The reason may well be, as Noth suggests, that the connotations of the term are too closely associated with human skills.[267] Another possible reason is the frequent use of the adjective as an epithet for El and other deities in the surrounding cultures.[268] The point of Isaiah 31:2, one of the two texts where the Lord is called wise in the Old Testament,[269] may be that, knowing that the gods of other nations evidently were considered wise, the prophet now ascertains that this epithet applies to the Lord as well.[270] It seems probable that at least one of the reasons for the cautious use of the term in Israel was its association with other deities and its allusions to magical beliefs and practices in these contexts.[271]

---

[262] Cf. 2:6 and less directly 1:7 and 9:10

[263] On juxtaposition as a stylistic device in the sentences, see J. G. Williams (1980:40–44).

[264] Our own translation. The form is different and cannot be described as the usual kind of antithetical parallelism. The terms חכמה, תבונה, and עצה are used elsewhere in close connection and must be regarded as synonyms here, together denoting the totality of wisdom claims. לנגד may also be translated less adversatively by "in comparison with" (Toy [1977:412]).

[265] See below, ch. 3.

[266] Noth (1955:232).

[267] Noth (1955:233), cf. Murphy (1981 C:342–343) who argues that wisdom could be seen as divine first after it had "failed" as human wisdom.

[268] For references, see Fohrer (1969:263), Zerafa (1978:186–188).

[269] Also Job 9:4. Note the ironical flavour of both passages!

[270] It is also possible that the non-stated party of the contrast is the politicians of the day to whom the words are directed, so, e.g., Fohrer (1969:263).

[271] Murphy (1981 C:342) questions the view that the characterization of El as wise in the Ugaritic texts constituted the reason for the rare attribution of wisdom to the Lord. This may be right, esp. since Proverbs does not yield any other evidence of a tension between El and Yahweh, but the argument is based not only on El as wise, but also other gods, as well as the fact that magic and mantic practices played a role in what was referred to as wisdom in these contexts.

Von Rad points out that in Proverbs 10–29 the acquisition and practice of wisdom is described as a human activity. He then applies this fact to his own unique view of the Solomonic era.[272] Perhaps the best reason to view von Rad's Solomonic enlightenment theory with scepticism[273] is to be found in his remarks on the understanding of reality that is reflected in the book of Proverbs. We may say that the approach of the book of Proverbs is more anthropocentric than theocentric, at least in the way it is formulated. In this respect no major difference exists between the different collections of the book. This anthropocentric approach to reality may explain a certain scepticism towards wisdom that can be traced within the Old Testament as well as in its history of interpretation.

e. The theology of the book of Proverbs in relation to other Old Testament books and traditions

It is not difficult to point out divergences in the approach to reality manifested, on the one hand, in the book of Proverbs and the other wisdom books and, on the other hand, in the general thrust of the main historic, prophetic and cultic traditions of the Old Testament.[274] First, Proverbs shows an absence of references to Israel's history; second, nationalism is lacking in favour of an international orientation; third, there is no apparent interest in cultic issues; and fourth, there is a strong anthropocentric tendency towards individualism that focuses on a wide range of everyday life issues.

The relationship between the theology of the wisdom literature and that of the rest of the Old Testament has been discussed extensively by scholars.[275] To a significant degree the issue hinges upon decisions one makes about several key issues in Old Testament theology, e.g., what constitutes "Yahwism"[276] and what was the relationship between Israelite faith and religions of the surrounding cultures. Toombs hits the nail on the head in an article from 1955:

> As long as Old Testament theology is represented exclusively in terms of the history, institutions and cultus of the Hebrew people it will exclude the wisdom literature by definition.[277]

---

[272] Von Rad (1981:57–65).

[273] See Whybray (1982:13–26).

[274] See, e.g., Goldingay (1979:194).

[275] For an overview see Scott (1970:39–41), Nel (1982:101–115), Scobie (1984:43–48).

[276] This point is crucial to Preuss' reservations towards early wisdom (1970:393–417; 1972:117–145). Preuss' definition of Yahwism is derived from a salvation-historical standpoint. He does not find this concept of God in the OT wisdom books, but instead regards every parallel in non-Israelite wisdom literature as evidence for the non-Israelite context of OT wisdom. For criticism of Preuss, see Murphy (1975:123–124), Nel (1982:104–106).

[277] Toombs (1955:195–196).

The same point is made by Murphy:

> Moreover, when Old Testament theology is reduced to the divine intervention and the prophetic interpretation, there seems to be little room for a literature that primarily analyzes human experience.[278]

Murphy argues that to do justice to the wisdom literature "we must move into theological anthropology"—the study of man in his relationship to the world with his concrete personal experiences in the Old Testament context where the Lord is his saviour, creator and sustainer.[279] In a later article Murphy again deals with the issue and ingeniously turns the tables by advocating a broader understanding of Israelite religion:

> Hence, one may ask: By what right is Yahwism defined exclusively by the action of God in history: The patriarchal promises, the Exodus and Sinai events, etc.? This is a correct base, because it captures what is distinctive of Israel. But it may also be too narrow, when one considers the total religious experience of the Israelite, or at least, of the biblical record. Instead of inserting wisdom into Yahwism, with Yahwism as a kind of implicit determinant of orthodoxy, one might rather turn the question around: How is Yahwism to be inserted into wisdom, into what was the daily experience of the Israelite? The wisdom literature constitutes a significant index to this concrete experience of the worshipper of Yahweh, and it deserves to be heard, just as much as the liturgical kerygma.[280]

A number of attempts have been made to define the theological centre of the Old Testament.[281] Such a theological centre would have a significant bearing on the possibility of integrating wisdom literature within Old Testament theology. Zimmerli argues that the theological centre of the Old Testament is to be found in the name and person of Yahweh, to which salvation history as well as creation faith are related, and that from this starting point everything from prophetism to wisdom can be included in Old Testament theology.[282]

The move towards identifying large parts of the Old Testament as wisdom means that the gap between the wisdom books and other parts of the Old Testament to a large extent has been bridged. Similarities in themes, approach, vocabulary, etc, between wisdom and other Old Testament material indicate that there were contacts between the groups and milieus where the different traditions originated and were fostered.

The relationship between the world view of the wisdom traditions in the Old Testament and the historical traditions is discussed by Rendtorff in an article where he relates to the life-work of von Rad.[283] Rendtorff's view is

---

[278] Murphy (1969:289).

[279] Murphy (1969:292–293).

[280] Murphy (1975:119–120).

[281] For a short overview see Zimmerli (1974:28–30), Sæbø (1976/77:200).

[282] Zimmerli (1974:27–54). Cf. Sæbø (1976/77:201–205) who from a similar view of centre goes on to define three main theological approaches within the Old Testament: 1) Salvation theology with its historical-theological depiction, 2) cultic theology stressing God's presence, 3) theology of order depicting God as the creator and upholder of creation.

[283] Rendtorff (1977:344–353).

that the difference between the two is not as stark as has often been argued. The historical traditions are marked by an attempt to describe reality in terms of rules and regularity; Wisdom thinking is highly conscious of God's ultimate freedom and sovereignty. Rendtorff explains the differences in approach between the two traditions by their different Sitz im Leben and different foci—addressing the individual or the nation as a whole.[284]

The different theological perspectives of salvation history versus wisdom are also discussed by Goldingay.[285] He finds that their relationship is tied to the close, complementary relationship between redemption and creation.[286] Since wisdom focuses "more on everyday life than history, more on the regular than the unique, more on the individual (though not outside of his social relationships) than the nation, more on personal experience than sacred tradition,"[287] it may be legitimate to subordinate wisdom to "creation" if the latter concept is defined in its widest sense. Wisdom deals with the way man is to live in the world in which he is placed and given a position of authority and responsibility by the creator. In this way the perspectives of wisdom and salvation history are complementary with the latter supplying what is "missing" in the former, viz. the focus on God's redemptive acts and his demands upon the nation in certain settings. We agree with Wilson that "the problem with wisdom is not whether wisdom is in part secular, but whether the theology of wisdom contradicts or complements and supplements other dimensions of Hebrew theology."[288] Even if the salvation history perspective does dominate the Old Testament and the history of its interpretation, it does not mean that other perspectives are unimportant, irrelevant, or irreconcilable to it. The international character of wisdom thinking makes it less unique in the world of the ancient Near East but the inclusion of the wisdom traditions alongside of the other Old Testament traditions indicates that it played an important role in the Israelite community. The fact that wisdom in the post-exilic period more or less merged with law and salvation-history might have contributed to its eventual canonical status, but it also deprived it of some of its peculiarity.

A similar way of approaching the question is found in Nel's study of the wisdom admonitions in Proverbs and their ethos. Nel detects a relationship between wisdom and creation and argues that wisdom constitutes "the knowledge of the created order and of God himself"—a knowledge that is not without religious foundation and that fully harmonizes with revelation.[289]

---

[284] Rendtorff (1977:352).
[285] Goldingay (1979:194–207).
[286] Goldingay (1979:201–207).
[287] Goldingay (1979:194).
[288] Wilson (1987:328).
[289] Nel (1982:115).

Our view is that stark antitheses between empirical knowledge and revelation, between salvation-history and everyday experience, between wisdom traditions and others, do not exist in the Old Testament. While one can certainly see both lines of connection and tension between the different traditions, the very fact that the book of Proverbs and other wisdom books played a part in the Israelite community and were eventually included in the Old Testament canon together with other traditions is the best evidence for their reciprocity and individual value in the minds of the ancient Israelites.

f. Wisdom, monotheism and the Ancient Near East context

The book of Proverbs appears to be a truly monotheistic work.[290] In the sayings there is no mention of other gods or powers which might be understood as competing with the Lord. This monotheistic setting is emphasized by the consistent use of the tetragrammaton for the deity, making it clear beyond the shadow of a doubt that the God in question was the Lord of the Israelites.[291] Even though correspondences can be established between the content of the book of Proverbs and that of the surrounding cultures, the creative link forged between these adopted teachings and Israel's Lord in the biblical book merits careful consideration. It indicates that the other books of the Old Testament constitute the primary theological context for understanding what is said about God and his relationship to the world in the book of Proverbs.

There are important differences between the clear references to the Lord in the book of Proverbs and the frequently generic and indeterminate references to deities in the wisdom literature of Egypt and Mesopotamia.[292] In these polytheistic contexts[293] the wisdom books often contain intentional ambiguities in their references to the deity. There is a preference for referring to the deity by a generic term instead of by a proper name. This phenomenon has been used as an argument for the influence of monotheistic tendencies, especially in Egypt, but, as Hornung and others have demonstrated, this is not correct. The reason for the use of the generic term for the deity which is so common in wisdom texts, is rather that the specification intentionally is left

---

[290] Lang (1986:126–131) argues that the depiction of wisdom, esp. in ch. 8, indicates that חכמה originally was a female deity, demythologized by later editors to make it possible to include the book in the biblical canon.

[291] Fichtner (1933:122). Fichtner also notes that it is in the post-canonical works that we first find a debate with polytheism.

[292] See Schmid (1966:24–25, 106, 125). In this respect Job and Ecclesiastes stand closer to the non-Israelite wisdom books than Proverbs.

[293] A monotheistic tendency, usually termed henotheism, can also be traced in the surrounding cultures, even if it is not explicitly present in the wisdom books. It finds its clearest expression in Akhenaten's reform in Egypt in the 14th century, but can also be demonstrated from Mesopotamian and Ugaritic sources from the same time period. See Hornung (1973:240–246), Assmann (1983), de Moor (1983:8–46; 1986:1–20), Hutter (1987:25–39), Sommerfeld (1989:7:360–370).

open to the reader and to the situation.[294] These generic designations of god functioned in a way parallel to a blank space in a liturgical text which is to be filled in with the appropriate expression by the supplicant.

There is no great difference between the active depiction of the deity in Israelite and that of non-Israelite wisdom. However, the important issue here is not so much a question of vast differences in mode of expression but the small but key differences in intended religious contexts for interpretation. A shift in interpretive context from, say, Mesopotamia to Israel can easily produce quite different results from similar theological statements.[295] The monotheistic setting of Israelite wisdom has a significant bearing on the way the knowledge and trustworthiness in character of the deity would be perceived. Though a reflective monotheistic faith inevitably faces serious theological problems like that of theodicy, the struggle with such issues may also serve as a catalyst for the formulation of a coherent theology. While the gods of the polytheistic religions around Israel were to a large degree depicted mythically and anthropomorphically running the whole gamut of human weaknesses and shortcomings, the monotheistic and predominantly non-mythological Israelite faith was able to produce a concept of deity with more unified characteristics of integrity and perfection.[296] It goes without saying that such a difference in the concept of deity would have deeply influenced the interpretation of the wisdom literature. To a certain degree it seems possible to agree with Fichtner:

> Weiter ist der Gott der isr.-jüd. Wsht—wie der Gott des A.T. überhaupt—dadurch gekennzeichnet, dass er den Charakter absoluter heiliger Gerechtigkeit trägt, was in der ausserisr. Wsht durchaus nicht in dem gleichen Masse der Fall ist....[297]

---

[294] Hornung (1973:30–49), Frankfort (1961:67), Fox (1980:123–126). Cf. Otto's conclusion (1971:20) concerning the identity of what he terms "Helfergott."

[295] E.g., when Marduk is called "The Lord of wisdom" this does not have the same meaning as similar statements in Israel.

[296] According to Hornung (1973:244) one consequence of Akhenaten's monotheistic reform was the removal of mythical imagery. See de Moor's remarks about the myths of Ugarit and the "pantheon of disillusion" (1986:6-7). Roberts (1976:1-13) argues against the common generalizations concerning the relationship between Israelite religion and that of her neighbours, but admits that there are differences, e.g., he seems to agree that to a larger degree myth characterizes Mesopotamian religion. See also Lambert (1972:65-72, esp. 65-66, 71). Cf. Saggs (1978:92), van der Toorn (1985:4-5).

[297] Fichtner (1933:123; cf. 1951:145).

Part one

Theology of creation and order

Chapter two

The book of Proverbs and creation theology

Introduction

This chapter is devoted to the role of creation in the book of Proverbs, with a special focus upon what valid inferences the contents of the book allow concerning the concept of God when understood within the context of the circles associated with wisdom in ancient Israel. It is essential to recognize from the outset that no part of the book of Proverbs can be called theological in the strictest sense. It is not the aim of the discourses and sayings of the book to present a theology *per se*. God is, in fact, only made conspicuous by his absence in parts of the material. Therefore the use of the term "creation theology" in the title of this chapter is potentially misleading and requires a word of explanation. Our primary purpose is to investigate the way the creation motif[1] is used in the book of Proverbs, and, if possible, describe the concept of God among people associated with the traditions preserved in the book. One important though tentative assumption of this kind of study is that as the ancient Israelites composed, collected, took over, rewrote or revised wisdom material, their own views would have left marks on the finished product. Specifically, one would expect that the world view and the main theological positions of the sages who assembled this material will be reflected in the selection, presentation, content or arrangement of the material.

Some notable scholars have maintained that creation theology is to be considered the underlying theology of the wisdom literature,[2] and even of the Old Testament as a whole.[3] We hope that, through a careful consideration of the texts relating to creation from the book of Proverbs, this chapter will enhance our ability to evaluate this position.

---

[1] The term "creation motif" will be used in the following to refer to the concept of creation and the activity of God as its creator in general. This motif manifests itself in Proverbs and elsewhere in two themes: 1)the creation of the world, and, 2) the creation of man.

[2] Zimmerli (1964:147–148), Sæbø (1979:154–155), Hermisson (1978:43–57).

[3] Schmid (1973:1).

A. Analysis of text material related to creation in the book of Proverbs

The book of Proverbs does not contain very many explicit statements on creation.[4] Even if we direct our attention just toward the "God-sayings," i.e. the sayings explicitly mentioning God, the creation motif is by no means dominant.

In the first section of Proverbs, chapters 1–9, we find the creation motif in a short poem (3:19–20) as well as in a longer (8:22–31). In the second section (10:1–22:16), we find the motif in a few proverbs: 14:31; 16:4, 11; 17:5; 22:2, and also in a somewhat different way in 20:12. No such direct references occur in either 22:17–24:22 or the short collection 24:23–24:34. In chapters 25–29 only one reference to creation is found (29:13). This is, in fact, the last reference to creation in the book. These are the only direct references in the book linking God with creation. It is obvious that when scholars state that creation theology should be considered the theological foundation of wisdom and of this book in particular, their view is not based on the frequency of sayings relating to creation. In the following chapter we will analyze these sayings and attempt to provide a rationale for understanding them within the context of the various wisdom traditions reflected in the book of Proverbs. Our analysis will, therefore, devote special attention to the identification of which theological views in all likelihood may have influenced these wisdom traditions.

Proverbs 3:19–20

> 3:19. Yahweh by wisdom founded the earth,
> By understanding established the heavens.
> 20. By his knowledge the waters well forth,
> and the clouds drop down dew.[5]

Even if these verses originally constituted a separate poem, they should be seen here in connection with their context, especially with the preceding verses 13–18. Von Rad has pointed out the similarities between the structure of 3:13–26 and the other passage on creation in chapters 1–9. Both in chapter 8 and this text one encounters the praise of wisdom (vv 13–18), a retrospective of the role of wisdom at the beginning of time (vv 19–20) and an appeal to follow

---

[4] Noted by Hermisson (1978:43).
[5] Toy (1977:66).

her (vv 21–26).[6] Scott considers verses 13–18 and verses 19–20 to be two separate poems and the rest of the chapter to be the fourth discourse under the heading "The Security and Obligations of the Wise."[7] This brings about an unnecessary separation of verses 19–20 from the surrounding verses.[8] A comparison of the structure of this passage with the structure of chapter 8, indicates that it is more plausible to follow von Rad's view that verses 13–26 constitute a single redactional unit. Taking this view of the text, however, does not exclude the possibility that verses 13–18 and verses 19–20 originally constituted separate poems. In fact the original distinctiveness of these units may well lie behind the shift in thought between verses 18 and 19. Verses 13–18 deal with the infinite value of wisdom and the character of her providence for humankind. Verses 19–20 deal with God's creation of the world and the role of wisdom and knowledge in that process. Whether this shift was both intentional and original or whether it is the result of later stages of compilation is difficult to determine.

In the structure of 3:19–20 the first verse constitutes a synonymous bicolon where "by wisdom," בחכמה, and "by understanding," בתבונה, are synonymous while earth and heaven signify the totality of creation. The verbs used are common in relation to God and creation[9] with the meaning of "to found, establish,"[10] and "to set up, establish."[11] Verse 20 is a continuation of verse 19 with , "by his knowledge, בדעתו, related to both parallel cola of the verse. Here also the interest lies with what is below and above—the subterranean waters and the waters above were designed to water the earth.[12] It is not clear whether the verbs should be translated in the past or the present, nor is it clear

---

[6] Von Rad (1981:151, n.4).

[7] Scott (1982:45–46).

[8] Doll (1985:48–49, n. 27) argues that vv 21–35 should not be considered a "Lehrrede" and regards instead vv 27–35 as "eine kleine Sammlung von Einzelnmahnungen (zu sozialem Verhalten) und von Einzelspruchen." According to him v 21 cannot be an introduction to an instruction since the common appeal to adhere to the fathers' instruction is not found here, but only the more general exhortation to strive for wisdom.

[9] יסד in qal is also used in Ps 24:2; 102:26; 104:5, 8; Isa 48:13; כון in polel used in Ps 8:4; 119:90; Isa 45:18. Toy (1977:71): "The expressions *founded* and *established* belong to the old-Hebrew cosmogonical ideas. The earth was conceived of as a solid plane, resting on an ocean (Ps 24:2; 136:6), as having foundations (Isa 51:13; Ps 104:5; Pr 8:29) and as supported by pillars (Job 9:6; Ps 75:3[4])."

[10] BDB (1980:413).

[11] BDB(1980:466). See also McCarthy (1984:78).

[12] The terms used, deep waters, תהומות, which were cleft, בקע (ni), indicates a mythological view of creation, commonly referred to as the *Chaoskampf* myth, traces of which can be found elsewhere in the Old Testament using the same vocabulary, Gen 1; 7:11; Ps 104:5–13; Prov 8:22–29; Job 38:8–16, 30; Ps 33:6–9. A dominant feature of this non-Israelite myth was the subjugation of the hostile deep waters in primeval times, see Gunkel (1984:25–52) for what has become the conventional exposition of the myth and its relation to the OT. In Prov 3:20 the waters are significantly referred to, but here they are just part of a language which brings an echo of this mythological view of creation.

whether the reference is to actions pertaining to a past original creation or to the on-going sustaining of the creation of the present.[13]

One important issue in this connection is the correct understanding of בחכמה, בתבונה and בדעתו.[14]   These expressions are evidently used in a synonymous and interchangeable way here[15] although it is probably significant that חכמה occurs first as it also does in verse 13 and 24:3–4.[16] The translation of the preposition generally adopted is the instrumental: The Lord by wisdom...; by understanding...; by his knowledge....[17] From a theological point of view, it is most important to come to grips with the distinction governing the relationship between the subject of the action, the action, and wisdom/understanding/knowledge employed in carrying out the action of creation. Is wisdom to be understood as an agent carrying out the Lord's action, or is the reference to wisdom to be understood as impersonal, as a way of characterizing the manner in which the Lord acted?[18] If one considers the verses apart from their present context in chapters 1–9, a case might be made for the second alternative, but given this particular context some variation of the first appears more favourable. An additional question arises concerning the possibility that this agent/instrument of creative action may have been regarded within the wisdom traditions as a being independent of the Lord. Was wisdom/understanding/ knowledge viewed as an attribute of the Lord or perhaps understood as personified or even hypostatized in these verses? We will deal with these distinctions further in the treatment of chapter 8. For now, it should suffice to point out that in these verses there is no need to assume a specific personification or hypostatization to grasp the sense of the text.[19]   The most natural way to interpret the passage is to take

---

[13] Toy (1977:71) argues that the verbs are better understood as present, saying: "v 19 deals with the creation of the world, here we pass to its present guidance; if the verbs be rendered as past, the reference will be to the original arrangement." McKane (1985:215), translates in the present tense and comments (1985:297): "Verse 20 refers to two fertilizing agencies, rain or dew which falls from above, and the springs which well up from beneath," while Scott (1982:48) remarks that in the first part of the verse there is "an echo of Gen 7:11 where the water which submerged the world in the days of Noah is said to have surged up like a tide from the subterranean ocean and fallen from sluices in the sky." Hermisson (1978:49) makes a point of noting the presence of the past tense of יסד and עשה in the similar text Ps 104:5, 19 and regards them as indicating that Yahweh's creation is seen as once and for all.

[14] Note the parallel use of בחכמה in Ps 104:24 and בכח/בחכמה/בתבונה in Jer 10:12.

[15] Becker (1965:219).

[16] Ps 104:24 has only בחכמה which may indicate that חכמה had a more prominent position compared to its parallels. Against is the fact that Ps 136:5 has only בתבונה.

[17] E.g., RSV. Scott (1982:45) translates "through."

[18] Von Rad (1981:155) notes that the expression "in wisdom" can be understood as an attribute of the earth rather than a divine attribute: "Creation was raised by God to a state of wisdom or understanding." This rendering seems less probable.

[19] Toy (1977:71): "Wisdom here seems to be simply an attribute, with no approach to hypostatization." Stecher (1953:425): "Es sei nun nicht gut möglich, von diesen drei Ausdrücken nur *chokma(h)* als

wisdom/understanding/knowledge as definite attributes or qualities of the Lord which can be referred to individually and which the Lord makes use of in acts of creation.

The position of בחכמה and בתבונה in verse 19 right after the subject and at the conclusion of the verse indicates their significance in relation to the subject. In the next sentence, the subject is represented only by the personal suffix appended to דעת. This indicates that the main message of the verses is not about creation as such nor about the Lord, but about the role of wisdom in the world. Wisdom is regarded as closely associated with the Lord and one of his major acts—creation. In this way wisdom is given an enhanced status of supreme importance and is also closely connected with Yahwism.[20] The statement that wisdom played an active role in creation together with the Lord must have been of highest importance within the wisdom traditions. Wisdom was conceived of as having played an important role even before the cosmos came into existence and as standing in a special relation to the created world of men.[21] Wisdom literature emphasizes the indispensability of wisdom for understanding the world of man, as essential in the search for a world view which helps man cope with his present reality.

Proverbs 8:22–31

8:22. Yahweh formed me as the beginning of his creation,
The first of his works, in days of yore;
23. In the primeval time was I fashioned,
In the beginning, at the origin of the earth.

24. When there were no depths was I brought into being,
No fountains full of water;
25. Before the mountains were sunk,
Before the hills was I brought into being,
26. When he had not yet made the earth, [ ]
Nor the first of the clods of the world.

Person zu verstehen." Stecher (1953:425–426) also points out that in the preceding verses no clear personification is to be found and that the interpretation of 3:19–20 ought to be done in view of the parallels in Ps 104:24, 136:5, Jer 10:12.

[20] McKane (1985:296–297): "The most significant thing about vv 19f., in my view, is that they furnish another demonstration of the integration of wisdom with Yahwism."

[21] Von Rad (1981:155–156) compares with the expression in Sir 1:9 that God has "poured wisdom out upon all his works," Job 28, and the statement in Isa 6:3 about the glory of the Lord which "fills" the earth, and concludes that wisdom was seen as something which in a mysterious way was bestowed on all creation. In line with this is von Rad's (1981:148) statement that: "This wisdom is to be found somewhere in the world; it is there, but incapable of being grasped....On the other hand—and this is admittedly remarkable—it is also again something separate from the works of creation. This 'wisdom', this 'understanding' must, therefore, signify something like the 'meaning' implanted by God in creation, the divine mystery of creation."

27. When he established the heavens I was there,
When he marked off the vault on the face of the deep,
28. When he made firm the clouds above,
'fixed fast' the fountains of the deep,
29. When he set bounds to the sea, [ ]
When he laid the foundations of the earth.

30. And I was at his side, as his 'ward,'
full of delight day by day,
Sporting in his presence continually,
31. Sporting in his world. [ ][22]

There are some indications that this whole chapter may constitute a carefully composed original unit. Verses 1–11 and 22–31 each contain twenty-two lines, as do verses 12–21 in the Septuagint, and the peroration, verses 32–36, contains eleven lines.[23] In light of this, one might draw the conclusion that one and the same author is responsible for the different parts of the chapter.[24] Regardless of whether or not this argument is convincing, verses 22–31 cited above should be considered in relation to the rest of the chapter.[25] Verses 1–3 represent wisdom in a way similar to 1:20–21 where she acts like a wisdom teacher roaming the public places calling men to hear and follow her instructions.[26] There are similarities between the way wisdom in this section and the prophets address men in public in order to demand attention to their message.[27] In a conventional way, verses 4–21 point out the importance and high value of wisdom's message and the function she serves in the highest circles of power. Verses 22–31 break off from this more conventional presentation which relates wisdom to the prudent behaviour of individuals and the policies of statesmen.[28] This line of thought is broken by tracing wisdom's

---

[22] Toy's translation (1977:172–173). Toy (1977:175–179) emends מחוצות from v 26 and the second colon of vv 29 and 31.

[23] Noted by Scott (1982:71)who also finds this structural form elsewhere in chs. 1–9.

[24] Scott (1965:71) extends this argument by pointing out the similarities in language between vv 32–36 and what he identifies as the ten discourses of chs. 1–9 and then arguing that this similarity point in the direction of common authorship for the discourses and the poems in chs. 1 and 8.

[25] See von Rad's comments cited above in relation to 3:13–26, pp. 48–49. Toy (1977:159) regards the chapter as a separate discourse "consisting of two closely related sections (vv 4–21 and vv 22–31) with introduction and conclusion." Cf. Kaiser (1978:143) whose division of the chapter is structured according to three themes: wisdom's excellence (vv 1–21), wisdom's origins (vv 22–31), wisdom's blessings (vv 32–36).

[26] This was hardly the conventional way wisdom teachers recruited disciples. It rather emphasizes the urgency of wisdom's address to man.

[27] McKane (1985:342) correctly notes, however, that it is the teaching of a sage rather than the preaching of a prophet which is in view.

[28] McKane (1985:344) remarks that ch. 8 is firmly anchored in the ethos of old wisdom and that vv 22–31 perhaps should "be regarded as a speculative superstructure which is raised on the foundations of the empirical givenness and effectiveness of wisdom, and which tries to fill out the meaning of these

existence back to the earliest times in order to further enhance its value. One further observation applies to the whole of chapter 8, apart from the first three introductory verses: Wisdom presents herself in the first person. This phenomenon, which is also found in chapter 1, is a form of expression which carried with it all of the trappings of authority.[29] Wisdom possesses the authority to claim in verse 35: "He who finds me finds life." This is a remarkable statement even when immediately followed by: "And obtains favour from Yahweh."[30] The most reasonable way to understand these statements is to see them as an emphatic way of expressing the close relationship between the Lord and wisdom.[31] Of course, the same evidence has also been used to support the view that wisdom was a divinity not identical to Yahweh.[32]

The structure of verses 22–31 is somewhat repetitive, containing a number of terms which emphasize the wisdom's existence before creation, several negative temporal clauses to the same effect which affirm that wisdom existed before anything else was created and positive temporal clauses which describe the sequence of the acts of creation climaxed by verses 30–31 stressing wisdom's presence with God during the process of creation. It has been pointed out that the main focus of verses 22–31 is not the creator or acts of creation, but the presence of wisdom in the creation process.[33] In contrast to Proverbs 3:10–20, wisdom in this text has no part in the actions of creation, the main point instead being the presence of wisdom at creation in close

---

phenomena by tracing the history of wisdom beyond the phenomenal world to a supra-historical *locus*, thereby supplying a theological explanation for the empirical dominance of wisdom."

[29] Terrien (1981:134) calls 8:22–31 "an aretalogy of wisdom, in the 'I-am form'," and comments that (1981:149, n.43): "the term 'aretalogy' has been used for the Hellenistic poems on Isis, but the *Ich-bin Gattung* is undoubtedly much older than the IVth century B.C, a characteristic of the pattern of theophany in Mesopotamia, Egypt and Israel."

[30] 8:35 (Toy's translation [1977:179]). Cf. 1:30–33, 3:18. Von Rad (1981:163) points out that the verse goes beyond the claims that any prophet could make for himself.

[31] A parallel might be seen in the מלאך יהוה who at times appears to be identified with the Lord and is able to address men in the first person in an authoritative manner, see Gen 22:11–12.

[32] This is the view of Lang (1986:55–58) who argues that in this chapter wisdom takes on a much more important role than that of a teacher, in vv 12–35 introducing herself as a patroness of high-ranking state officials and kings. Lang's observations are most significant, even though his main thesis—that wisdom is to be understood against the polytheistic background of most Israelites in pre-exilic times and that in the original setting of vv 12–35 she was a goddess related to the creator god El—is not entirely convincing (1986:126–131). The shift, according to Lang, from the role of teacher in vv 4–11 to that of goddess and patroness of wisdom in vv 12ff., could as well be explained as the shift between the two settings of school and court, two settings most probably associated with the wisdom traditions in Proverbs.

[33] Doll (1985:54–55): "Das Motiv hat also nicht eine Aussage über die Weltschöpfung, sondern über die Weisheit zum Ziel." Lang (1986:66): "Wisdom, not the Creator and his work, is the central theme and focus of the poem." Whybray (1965 B:509): "The temporal clauses do not refer to the *Creator's* priority over other gods or over matter; they refer to the *relative* priority of one of his creatures, wisdom, over the others."

relationship to the creator. This notion of the presence of wisdom with God from the very beginning of time is basic to the belief world of the wisdom traditions. One inference that was frequently made from this view was that only through wisdom was one able to discern the secrets of the created world and live in accordance with them.[34] Therefore, the function of verses 22–31 is not merely to provide an additional rationale for heeding wisdom's call by referring to her longevity, but rather to emphasize the primacy and importance of wisdom based on her status as the sole eyewitness to creation available to man.[35]   Through wisdom, man had the key to the correct understanding of the world.

A key issue in the identification of wisdom is the interpretation of the terms קנני in verse 22 and אמון in v 30. The verb קנה is used in twelve other passages in the book of Proverbs, all with the usual meaning "to acquire, possess what has been acquired."[36]   But most translations follow the Septuagint in translating קנני "created me" in this particular passage. Support for translating "create" is found in the use of the term in other passages of the Old Testament[37] and the occurrence of a cognate root bearing this meaning in Ugarit,[38] also in the phrase "El, creator of the world."[39]   The most significant argument supporting the translation "create" here is the vocabulary of the immediate context, especially the parallel verbs נסך (ni) and חול (polal) of verses 23 and 24, and the extensive usage of temporal phrases which indicate that at the very beginning of time something occurred in relation to wisdom, which "acquire" does not convey with sufficient force.[40]

---

[34] Prov 1:7; 2:6–15; 3:13–26; 7:1–5; 8:1–36; 9:1–6; 13:14; 16:23; 30:2–3. This is what is pointed out in negated form to Job in chapter 38—that he was not present at creation and because of this does not have the insight and understanding in the deep mysteries of the world. This theme of wisdom's presence at creation is picked up and expanded in Wis 9:9–11.

[35] This is pointed out by Lang (1986:70): "Among the sages of Israel, age does indeed matter, but what counts even more is wisdom gained by observation and application of the intellect."

[36] Scott (1982:71).

[37] Westermann (1974 B:395) advocates this meaning in Gen 4:1 and finds the same meaning in Gen 14:19, 22; Exod 15:16; Deut 32:6; Ps 78:54; Ps 139:13 and Prov 8:22.

[38] Vawter (1980:205–216) argues against the translation of קנה as "create" maintaining that the root never bears this meaning in the Old Testament or in Ugaritic texts. He emphasizes that procreation must be distinguished from creation and finds other possibilities to translate the passages referred to by Westermann bearing the meaning "create." He concedes that there are difficulties in explaining Ps 139:13, where we also have סכך (pu), parallel to נסך (ni) in Prov 8:23, which render his case not entirely convincing. De Moor (1980:171–187) investigates the creation motif in the Ugaritic texts and points out that *qny* describes procreation but also has connotations of creative activity and that creation and procreation in Ugarit are closely related.

[39] For references and a discussion of the phrase see Schmidt (1964:28, n. 2) and Vawter (1980:210).

[40] Kaiser (1978:144) notes that these three verbs describe the way wisdom came into existence and that ten words in vv 22–26 stress the temporal priority of wisdom.

The meaning of אמון in v 30 has been disputed by a number of scholars. Scott enumerates five possibilities, all having some support in the ancient versions and the history of interpretation and all more or less making sense in the context.[41] McKane mentions several more.[42] The main alternatives are to translate אמון as "infant, nursling, one brought up, cherished" describing wisdom; or as "master builder" referring to God.[43] The immediate context, where שעשעים indicates delight[44] and שחק (pi) bears the sense of play and amusement before God,[45] as well as the larger context where wisdom is "created/born" at the beginning of time, favour the former understanding.

Terrien[46] notes the peculiar structure of verses 30–31 with its significant use of word couplets. This use of couplets, which is not usually reflected in the translations, can be illustrated in the following way:

8:30. *And I was* beside him as a child,
And I was **(his) delight** daily,
Playing before him continually,
31. *Playing* in the world of his earth,
and **my delight** was with mankind.[47]

This arrangement clearly shows that there is a dual relationship between 1) wisdom and the Lord, on the one hand, and 2) wisdom and creation and mankind on the other.[48] Wisdom plays before the Lord and is his delight, but she also plays on his earth, the abode of mankind, and her delight is mankind. In a sense, wisdom functions as an intermediary between God and man, between God and his world.

---

[41] Scott (1960:213–223). Scott himself finds a generalized meaning of the qal active participle form meaning "binding, uniting, fashioning" to be the most probable original meaning. "Wisdom is then seen as personifying the principle of coherence and order in the world which Yahweh is creating" (1960:219). Scott's method (1960:221) for solving the puzzle of the five possible interpretations is to regard each of them in turn "on the supposition that it was the author's meaning, to see how the alternative explanations could have arisen from it." The method is ingenious but involves a high degree of subjectivity and is hardly suitable as the main criterion for a choice.

[42] McKane (1985:356–358). McKane asserts that it is probable that the word is connected with its Akkadian cognate and that it is the court expert close to the king who is alluded to in this representation of wisdom.

[43] As noted by Keel (1974:25) and Lang (1986:65), the latter translation, if adopted, must be regarded in apposition to the pronominal suffix in אצלו and be a reference to the Lord, since the translation "master builder, architect" does not fit as a description of wisdom in this context.

[44] Toy (1977:173, 178).

[45] For this understanding of the word, see Stecher (1953:429–430). Keel (1974:31–68) points out interesting parallels to this phenomenon in Egyptian iconography, e.g., with Ma'at and Hathor entertaining God. A parallel is found in the OT when David and all Israel play, שחק (pi), before the Lord when the ark is brought to Jerusalem (2 Sam 6:5, 21).

[46] Terrien (1981:134).

[47] Our own translation.

[48] Toy (1977:179) regards the second clause of verse 31 as secondary since it involves the relationship of wisdom to man, not previously referred to in vv 22–31.

The description of wisdom in chapter 8 raises the question of personification or hypostatization of wisdom in Proverbs. Personification in a broad sense is not rare in the Old Testament.[49] Referring to an impersonal object figuratively as though it were a personal being is a common feature in the Old Testament.[50] In chapter 8, wisdom is clearly characterized as a person, a practice which is followed elsewhere in Proverbs 1–9.[51] She stands in contrast to the personification of folly (9:13–18)[52] who is seen as more or less directly related to the multiple descriptions of seductive women in the preceding chapters.[53]

The issue of whether we should call the presentation of wisdom in Proverbs a hypostatization or personification is still being debated. To a large degree the matter is an issue of the definition of terms. Ringgren's wide definition of hypostasis as "a quasi-personification of certain attributes proper to God, occupying an intermediate position between personalities and abstract beings,"[54] enables him to point out many examples of hypostasis in the Old Testament. According to Mowinckel's widely recognized definition, "hypostasis" is the name given to "eine halb selbständige, halb als Offenbarungsform einer höheren Gottheit betrachtete Göttliche Wesenheit, die eine Personifizierung einer Eigenschaft, einer Wirksamkeit, eines Gliedes usw. einer höheren Gottheit darstellt."[55] Since Mowinckel the meaning has been more closely defined to signify "...eine Grösse, die teilhat am Wesen einer

---

[49] Kitchen (1977:103) notes "the ubiquitous attestation of such personification throughout the biblical Near East in the 3rd, 2nd, and 1st millenia alike, up to 15 centuries before the birth of Solomon."

[50] Lang (1986:132–134, 173, n. 15–18) mentions as examples of personification: Job 11:14; Jer 22:13; Isa 55:7; Prov 28:22; Zech 2:14; Isa 52:9; Ps 96:11ff; 85:10; 89:14; Prov 20:1; Judg 9:8ff; Ez 16; 23; Isa 47:11ff; 51:17ff; Zech 11:1–5. Further examples: Exod 23:27; Job 25:2; Ps 43:3; 78:49; 85:11–12, 14; 89:15; 96:6; Isa 58:8; 59:14; 63:5; Amos 5:7.

[51] Cf.1:20ff; 4:5–9; 7:4; 9:1–4.

[52] If the personification of folly is primary, it might be argued that the main reason for the extensive use of the personification of wisdom in chs. 1–9 is to serve as a lively competitor for the attentions of men. The preeminence of folly must be considered a possibility since the personification of folly must be regarded in relationship to the repeated descriptions and warnings against seductive women, a well-known motif in Egyptian instructions from earliest times, see, e.g., *Any* (Lichtheim [1976:137]): "Beware of the woman who is a stranger, One not known in her town," and also elsewhere in the Old Testament. Most commentators, however, consider the personification of folly secondary to that of wisdom, see, e.g., Plöger (1984:106). Murphy (1966:8) asks why wisdom is personified as a woman, and answers "it is very tempting to see her as a balance to the emphasis that is laid by the sage on avoiding the 'strange woman' or adulteress."

[53] McKane (1985:312) points out that warnings against "the seductive and alluring woman is a stock one in the international Instruction, and it is improbable that its appearance in the biblical book of Proverbs requires the specialized interpretation which Boström advances." Regarding the personification of folly we have a double significance. On the one hand the personification of folly contrasts with wisdom, on the other hand the passages issue concrete warnings against seductive women, harlots. In chs. 1–9 these two aspects are intertwined, esp. evident in the description and language of 9:13–18.

[54] Ringgren (1947:8).

[55] Mowinckel (1928:2065).

Gottheit, die durch sie handelnd in die Welt eingreift, ohne dass sich ihr Wesen im Wirken dieser Hypostase erschöpft."[56] Along with these definitions of hypostasis, Stecher's definition of personification ought to be noted:

> Von einer Personifikation (Prosopopoiia) sprechen wir in der Literatur dann, wenn einem Unpersönlichen, Seelenlosen die Merkmale der Persönlichkeit verliehen, ihm Eigenschaften, Gedanken, Handlungen, Gefühle, und Bestrebungen zugeschrieben werden, die sonst nur einer beseelten menschlichen oder göttlichen Persönlichkeit zukommen.[57]

We agree with von Rad that the interests of understanding of the texts are not served by first establishing crystal clear definitions and then imposing them upon the texts.[58] It seems more sensible to proceed in the reverse order, examining the texts first and then, if possible, formulating a descriptive definition of the phenomenon. The texts depict wisdom as a person who addresses men, who is "created/born," and who is in close fellowship with the Lord. Thus it seems correct to apply the term personification to wisdom, but only as a loose designation which does not force a narrow interpretation on texts in question. Clearly there is no attempt in the texts to lead the reader to the conclusion that wisdom is "identical to" or "part of" the Lord. Wisdom is personified separately from the Lord, "at his side" in 8:30.[59] Therefore, the precis nature of the relationship between wisdom and the Lord must be determined by carefully examining the allusions in the texts, their context, and the general theological frame of reference of the wisdom traditions.

A few observations from our analysis of the texts may help to resolve the question. First, it is important to note the airs of authority with which wisdom speaks, which is prominently displayed in the "I" of chapters 1 and 8. In form wisdom's first person speech resembles the way the Lord speaks in other parts of the Old Testament. This indicates a parallel portrayal of wisdom and the Lord, perhaps even the identification of their character. Second, a comparison of the two texts which explicitly take up the theme of creation in Proverbs 1–9

---

[56] Pfeifer (1967:15).

[57] Stecher (1953:442).

[58] Von Rad (1981:147, n. 3).

[59] Lang takes this fact all the way and argues that wisdom in fact originally was completely separate from the Lord and that the high position given her in the texts is to be explained by the fact that she was a goddess worshipped alongside Yahweh during the polytheistic times of pre-exilic Israel. Later the texts were revised in a monotheistic direction, and wisdom was "demoted" to a personification of the Lord. Of course, the weight of this theory must be considered in relationship to the complex study of religion in pre-exilic times. Lang (1986:115): "I am, however, insisting that an interpretation only makes sense in the context of a comprehensive reconstruction of ancient Israelite religious history or, more specifically, a plausible view of the origins and development of monotheism." Considering here the portrait of wisdom in Proverbs, we do not find Lang's reconstruction of the religious history of ancient Israel the only way to make sense of the text. We leave to others the task of evaluating the theory in general terms.

is fruitful. In Proverbs 3:19–20 wisdom is referred to as a mere instrument of God without any hint regarding her independence. When wisdom is depicted separately from the Lord in Proverbs 8, there is no reason to assume that a thoroughly reworked concept of wisdom is being introduced. This argument becomes more convincing when we consider the structural similarities between these two passages. It seems reasonable to argue that similar concepts and thought patterns underlie the passages—that they belong to a common tradition. Third, it is quite possible that one of the main reasons for presenting wisdom in personified form was as a literary and moral counterbalance to Lady Folly who is associated with seductive women and a self-destructive life-style. If this is the main reason for the personification of wisdom in these passages, then one should be extremely careful not to inject too much theological content into what may well be a purely literary phenomenon. What we have before us may be a vivid way of characterizing the two moral paths laid before man.[60] Fourth, it does not seem probable that anything like hypostatization could have been in the mind of the redactors who embedded chapter 8 in the book, since the book is so consistently monotheistic, indeed Yahwistic.[61] The relative paucity of mythological traits found in the book[62] supports this conclusion. The hints of mythological traits which remain, are by and large demythologized[63] and hardly more than features of vivid style.[64] Fifth, the common discrepancy between the way something is

---

[60] The theme of the two alternative ways open to man is an important theme in the whole book of Proverbs and is frequently referred to in chs. 1–9, see: 1:8–19; 2:8–22; 3:23; 4:10–19; 5:5–6, 21; 9:6, 15. In fact, this theme is so dominant that one might even claim that the the whole message of the book centres around it, even when it is not explicitly referred to. The ethical dualism of mankind is referred to in many different ways, always making a sharp distinction between right and wrong and their respective outcome. McKane (1985:306) comments that the metaphor of the "road" plays an important part in the instructions and is not necessarily bound up with what he terms "Yahwistic reinterpretation." The prominence of this theme has also been noted by Stecher (1953:413–414).

[61] Stecher (1953:439): "Die erste Folge hätte für den überzeugten Monotheisten eine Auseinandersetzung mit der bisher gültigen Gottesvorstellung sein müssen. Irgendwie hätte sich der Verfasser doch die Frage stellen müssen, wie sich diese neuauftauchende Zweiheit zu dem Glauben an den einen Gott verhalte."

[62] E.g., 1:12; 2:18; 3:18; 7:27; 8:22–31; 9:18; 10:11; 11:30; 13:14; 14:27; 15:11; 16:22; 21:16; 27:20.

[63] See McKane's comments (1985) on the passages mentioned in the preceding note and also his arguments against Boström's cultic-mythological interpretation of the אשה זרה/נכריה in 2:16–19; ch. 5; 6:20–35; ch. 7; 9:13–18. That demythologization applies not only to the wisdom texts is convincingly argued by McCarthy who analyzes the use of Chaoskampf imagery in what are considered the most ancient texts of the Old Testament and concludes (1984:84–85): "there was little feeling of a religious reality behind it. Rather it was simply a convenient source of tropes." Further: "Thus the evidence hardly indicates a need for demythologizing.... The evidence is that such 'demythologization' was there from the first...."

[64] Gordon (1965:94): "The Ugarit tablets confront us with so many striking literary parallels to the Hebrew Bible that it is universally recognized that the two literatures are variants of one Canaanite tradition. To the Hebrew writers, however, the mythology is often little more than a literary background on which to draw for poetic imagery."

described and the way it is actually conceived needs to be kept in mind, especially when a poetic text is analyzed.

Proverbs 14:31

14:31. He who oppresses the poor reviles his Maker,
He honours him who has mercy on the needy.[65]

In this short antithetical saying, God is referred to as the creator of man, and as we move into the second main part of the book of Proverbs there is a thematic transition from the creation of the world to the creation of man. The negative behaviour condemned in 14:31 is the oppression[66] of the "poor"[67] and the positive behaviour enjoined by the text is kindness toward the "needy".[68] The usage of the singular form refers collectively to the poor and needy. The verb translated "revile," (pi), has the meaning "to say sharp things against, reproach, taunt, despise."[69] The verb is repeatedly used when the Assyrian king Sennacherib is said to "insult, mock" the Lord by sending his messenger to proclaim that the Lord is not able to deliver Jerusalem from the Assyrians.[70] It is used in an extended sense in Isaiah 65:7 which equates idolatry with reviling the Lord. The meaning of the word in these passages seems to be that, by means of the words and behaviour referred to, God's name and reputation are impugned. The opposite of "revile," חרף, is behaviour which honours and accords importance, כבד (pi), to the Lord.

Special interest in the situation of the poor is attested elsewhere in Prov 10–31[71] as well as in the other books of Old Testament.[72] God's particular

---

[65] Toy's translation (1977:298).

[66] עשק means "oppress, wrong, extort" and is used esp. in contexts referring to the poor and the defenceless (BDB [1980:798]).

[67] דל is esp. common in the wisdom traditions, which are generally held to be older, as well as in early poetry in parallel to needy, אביון, oppressed, עני, orphan, יתום, and in contrast to rich, הון, עשיר. דל is used by Amos, commonly in parallel with אביון and עני, but after the time of Amos the word is rarely used. In Proverbs the root is found 15 times in the collection 10:1–22:16, 7 times in chs. 25–29, and twice in 22:22. See 10:15; 19:4, 17; 21:13; 22:9, 16 (דל); 22:22; 28:3 (דלים עשק), 8, 11, 15; 29:7, 14. It is difficult to give a precise identification of who דל refers to, but the references in Proverbs make it clear that דלים are people from the lower echelons of society, perhaps small property owners, those who are "weak" and cannot defend themselves from oppression and injustice. See Fabry (1978:208–230), Malchow (1982:122-123), Pleins (1987:63–72) concerning the use of terminology.

[68] אביון means someone in need, want, who is poor. The word is very common in the psalms and occurs also in Proverbs 30:14; 31:9, 20, all three times parallel to עני. The early identification with צדיק in Amos 2:6; 5:12 is interesting. The term in Exod 23:11 is used in contrast land owners and non-land owners. A closer identification is not possible because of the general character of the designation.

[69] BDB (1980:357).

[70] Isa 37:4, 17, 23, 24 (2 Kings 19:4, 16, 22, 23). Cf. 1 Sam 17:10, 25–26, 36, 45.

[71] See Prov 22:22; 23:10–11; 28:27; 31:9, 20. Of the 42 occurrences in the book of the different words signifying poor (אביון, דל, רש, ענו/עני), 33 are found in the collections 10:1–22:16 and chs. 25–29. Significant is the prominent position of the motif in 22:22 and 23:10–11. 22:22 is the first of the

concern for the poor and needy is stressed throughout the Old Testament and in Proverbs 10–31 several such sayings are connected to creation.

The reference to God as "his Maker," עשהו, is of special interest.[73] The pronominal suffix may refer to either the oppressor or the poor. In the light of the emphasis on God's particular concern for the poor in the wisdom traditions, it is more probable that the pronoun refers to the poor man. Because the Lord is his maker and intends for the poor to have a good life, acting in opposition to this ideal is tantamount to reviling the Lord. Showing mercy to the poor, on the other hand, is an action in accordance with God's purpose and therefore gives honour to God, the poor man's maker.

The concept of God's creation of man is the presupposed basis here. Grounded in the common knowledge that one and the same Lord is the creator of all men, the saying becomes understandable and forceful.[74] Creation functions as the philosophical basis for social ethics.

Proverbs 16:4

16:4. Yahweh has made everything for its own end,
Yea, even the wicked for the evil day.[75]

This is a most interesting verse in several respects. The parallelism is synonymous with the second half-verse specifying what was generally stated in the first. The verb used in reference to the Lord is פעל, a very general term for "to do, make" which is not normally used in the OT to refer to creation.[76]

The meaning of the expression "for its own end," למענהו, is somewhat problematic since it is not clear whether the suffix refers back to the Lord or to "everything." The ambiguity of the phrase is further exacerbated by the fact that this noun can be understood to signify either "goal, purpose, design"

---

thirty sayings in 22:17–24:22, which gives it a certain emphasis, and 23:10–11 concludes the part of the section which exhibits more or less direct connections to *The Instruction of Amenemope*. The occurrence of the motif in the introduction and conclusion of this section is significant and the first motive clause of theological nature is without parallel in the Egyptian text.

[72] E.g., Lev 19:10; Deut 15:7; 24:12; Job 31:13–23; Ps 12:6; 35:10; 40:18; 107:41; Isa 3:14–15; 10:2; Jer 20:13; 22:16; Amos 2:6; 4:1; 5:12; 8:4.

[73] Cf. *Amenemope* xxiv 13–14 (Lichtheim [1976:160]): "Man is clay and straw, The god is his builder." For the significance and syntactical meaning of participial ascriptions to the Lord, see Stuhlmueller (1970:48–56).

[74] Cf. Job 10:3, 8–11, 18–19; 31:15; 33:4–6; 34:19; 36:3; Ps 22:10–11; 71:6; Mal 2:10a. Scott comments to Prov 17:5 (1982:110): "In the wisdom writings, belief in retribution rests on the thought of God as the Creator of all...."

[75] Toy's translation (1977:319).

[76] Elihu refers to God by פעלי in Job 36:3 (cf.עשה in Prov 14:31, 17:5) and passages like Ps 74:12ff., Ex 15:17 may suggest some form of creation. For פעל elsewhere, see Humbert (1953:35–44), Wildberger (1963:94–98), Stuhlmueller (1970:219–220).

or "counterpart, answer." The latter alternatives are favoured by McKane who interprets the sentence accordingly :

> The sentence 'Yahweh has made everything in relation to its counterpart' suggests a self-contained, self-regulating order rather than theodicy in the strict sense, i.e., a government which is enforced by repeated forensic interventions made by Yahweh either to 'justify' or 'condemn'.[77]

This interpretation introduces the broader theological issue of the concept of order in the wisdom literature, an issue which cannot be dealt with fully at present. For now, let it suffice to note that scholarly assertions to the effect that this verse expresses the theological view that the created order is autonomous and that, consequently, the active involvement of the Lord is impossible, appear to have been hastily deduced from a hypothetical translation of an unclear expression. The most common interpretation of the first line runs something like this: "The Lord has made everything for its purpose."[78] It seems reasonable to conclude that the proverb is an answer to the question of why evil exists in God's creation or perhaps why the wicked prevail, the "theodicy problem."[79] In line with other creation traditions preserved in the Old Testament, this verse states that everything, including the wicked man, is created by the Lord. But the structure of the sentence places the emphasis on כל and למענהו, which are most plausibly interpreted to mean: everything God created is for a definite purpose, goal, or end. This notion is in line with the second colon of the sentence which does not specify any counterpart for the wicked man, but states that for the wicked man, as for everything else, an appropriate end is awaiting—in the case of the wicked, the evil day. Furthermore, the suggested reading "counterpart," which is derived from "answer," is misleading since it is doubtful whether the word מענה signifies a member of a pair. Because this understanding of מענה is rather doubtful, it can hardly be used to support the view that this is a reference to a built-in order in creation.[80] The agent of the action is the Lord and there is nothing to indicate that he has retired from the arena. The point is rather that the Lord ensures that the ways of the criminal will not prevail because as creator he continues to be actively involved in his creation. The saying does not provide an unequivocal statement of the reasons for the existence of evil, but nevertheless

---

[77] McKane (1985:497).

[78] So, e.g., RSV.

[79] See Hermisson (1978:46).

[80] The view of creation as consisting of complementary pairs of good and evil is later employed by Sirach as one of his answers to attacks upon divine justice, see Sir 42:24, "all things go in pairs, one the opposite of the other; he has made nothing incomplete" (NEB), and also 33:14–15. There is no evidence that this view of creation was held in OT times.

it serves as an example that the wisdom traditions associated with the book of Proverbs did indeed wrestle with the problem.[81]

Our conclusion is that the suffix in למענהו refers to "everything" and not to the Lord, while the preferable understanding of מענה is "goal, purpose." What the sentence reveals concerning the concept of creation in the wisdom traditions is that there was a firm belief that everything belonged to God's creation and worked according to his will. In addition, questions concerning the existence of evil and wickedness in creation were the subject of debate within wisdom circles.

Proverbs 16:11

> 16:11. The balance and true scales are Yahweh's concern,
> All the weights in the bag are his affair.[82]

This sentence is in synonymous parallelism. It is not primarily concerned with creation, even though it refers to the weights as the Lord's "work," מעשה, a noun based on the root עשה which elsewhere denotes creation. The point of the sentence is well indicated by the word "concern" in the first line, which is a circumlocution for the preposition ל. The theme of this sentence relates to the ethics of the marketplace. The subject of scales and weights occurs no less than four times in the Yahweh-sayings of the book;[83] the other three occasions being statements to the effect that false weights are an abomination to the Lord, תועבת יהוה. The subject also comes up in the Holiness Code, Deuteronomy and the prophets[84] and seems to have been important in the ethical codes of the Israelites. Several of these texts forge a close link between fairness in the marketplace and social justice and concern for the poor. This theme is also frequently taken up in the traditions of Egypt, Sumer and Babylon.[85] In particular, chapter 16–17 of *Amenemope* relates how the god Thoth invented the weights and the measurements and that cheating is an abhorrence to him.[86] It is possible that the condemnation of false measurements is a subject which found its way to Israel through the wisdom traditions. The discussion of the topic in the book of Amos implies an early date for the sentences on this theme.

---

[81] This question is also dealt with in other material related to Israelite wisdom, see, e.g., Job, Eccl, Ps 37, 73. The answer supplied in Ps 37:1–2; 73:18–19, 27 is similar to our interpretation of Prov 16:4.

[82] McKane's translation (1985:235).

[83] Also 11:1, 20:10, 23.

[84] Lev 19:35–36; Deut 25:13–16 (here also תועבת יהוה expresses the Lord's disfavour); Ez 45:10–12; Hos 12:7; Amos 8:5; Mic 6:10–11.

[85] For references see Scott (1982:87).

[86] *Amenemope* xvii 18–xix 9, Lichtheim (1976:156–157).

Proverbs 17:5

> 17:5. He who mocks the poor reproaches his Maker,
> He who is glad at calamity will not go unpunished.[87]

Proverbs 17:5 is a sentence, probably to be regarded as in synthetical parallelism,[88] with close similarities to 14:31 especially in the use of the identical forceful statement חרף עשהו. Compared to 14:31, there is a more obvious connection in this verse between the person's action and the way it affects God. While 14:31 has "oppresses the poor," 17:5 instead has "mocks the poor"[89] which better corresponds to the shared continuation "reproaches his Maker."[90]   In this saying it is made clear that action against the poor[91] is tantamount to action against the creator.

The first part of 17:5b must be interpreted in relation to 17:5a. Calamity, איד, is a general term often used to describe the fate of the wicked. Here it refers to the unfortunate situation of the poor man who is without friends and financial surety and in his helplessness he is exposed to every conceivable threat to human existence. Toy points out that "the second clause, taken by itself, might refer to the punishment of heartlessness through the operation of natural laws,"[92] but the close connection with 17:5a makes it clear that the punishment will be meted out by God.

---

[87] Toy's translation (1977:337).

[88] Doll (1985:17) shares this opinion and argues that the second colon with its reference to punishment takes the thought further than the first. It is also possible to simply regard the parallelism as synonymous without any significant progression in thought.

[89] לעג means "mock, deride" (BDB [1980:541]) and can be understood as the expression of an attitude of superiority and contempt.

[90] We do not follow Doll (1985:18) who concludes that "Spr 14,31 greift auf die Überlieferungen des Sprichwortes 17,5a zurück." It is true that the connection between the two parts in 17:5a is closer and more logical than in 14:31a and that חרף in 14:31 is used in a quite general sense. But it is the case in many sayings in Proverbs that the different parts of a saying do not exhibit a completely logical correspondence. To say that the more logically constructed sayings are original is a simplistic way of handling the very complex background for the diverse sayings in the book. Interesting to note is that LXX many times rewrites the proverbs to bring out the parallelism more clearly (see Gerleman [1956:22–26]). Doll's attempt to relate the sayings to a particular socio-historical background is interesting, even though it must be noted that attempts of this kind must be undertaken with great caution when it comes to proverbial sayings. Phenomena like oppression of the poor are general phenomena to be found during almost any time period. In this case, however, the vocabulary employed implies that an early date, probably around the time of Amos, is feasible.

[91] רש signifies someone "in want, poor," and is a term occurring almost exclusively in Proverbs to designate the poor (רש נבר in Proverbs 28:3 is probably to be understood as ראש נבר, see McKane [1985:629]). The designations used for the poor in 14:31 and 17:5 are general in character and give no clear indication of a social setting, but both רש and דל may point to an early date for the sentences, since these terms are almost extinct in later passages referring to the poor.

[92] Toy (1977:337).

Proverbs 20:12

> 20:12. The hearing ear, the seeing eye—
> Yahweh has made them both[93]

This saying is different in form from the other sayings referring to creation.
It is cast in the form of a statement, beginning with the introduction of
object(s) by means of a subordinate clause which is then followed in the second
line by the main clause. The form may be considered reminiscent of the
numerical sayings[94] which occur elsewhere in the book.[95] The verb indicating
creative activity is עשה, a root which we have already observed elsewhere as
signifying God's creative activity. There are different opinions concerning the
main point of the saying. Is it that eye and ear can be trusted, that their
reliability is guaranteed by their maker[96] or does it convey the hortatory sense
that eye and ear are to be used according to their divine purpose, in obedience
to the Lord?[97] We have already noted in our discussions of other creation
sayings in Proverbs that sayings referring to creation usually bear a
significance beyond merely stating that the Lord is creator. The sayings
concerning the creation of man, for example, do not purport to state facts
about human origins but also give prescriptions and recommendations for
human behaviour and coexistence in society. In light of this multiplicity of
purpose, the assertion that the main sense of this text is a qualitative evaluation
of the accuracy and trustworthiness of the human senses is all the more dubious. It is much more likely that the emphasis here is on the normative
dimension, on the extension of a call to the proper use of these organs. Doll
relates this saying to Exod 4:11[98] where the context is the authoritative
command given by the Lord to Moses to approach Pharaoh and eventually lead
the people out of Egypt—a mission Moses is by no means anxious to lead. The
Lord's reply to the reluctant Moses is: I gave man the organs of speech and
perception and "I will be with your mouth," עם־פיך אנכי אהיה , and "teach you
what to say," והורתיך אשר תדבר. The implication is that man should use what is
given to him for the Lord's purposes. In this particular case it is explicitly
stated that the Lord will empower him to that end.

It is probable that the point made in Proverbs 20:12 is that man is given his
senses with a particular—or at least an ethically limited—use in mind. Moses'

---

[93] Toy's translation (1977:388).
[94] Nel (1981:134).
[95] Prov 6:16–19; ch. 30.
[96] McKane (1985:547).
[97] Toy (1977:388).
[98] Doll (1985:34).

case, of course, appears to be an exceptional instance of being equipped for a very special mission. In more general terms, the prescription for the proper use of the sensory organs was probably seen mainly in its relationship to society and the everyday life of man, with particular concern for the educational setting.[99] Eyes and ears are given to man to be used in ways which promote the well-being both of man himself and society. Supporting this interpretation is the fact that listening and observing were evidently considered especially important qualities in the wisdom traditions and are regularly the subject of exhortations and advice.[100]

This subject, though rare, gives explicit prominence to the fact that God created the sensory and speech organs and is echoed in at least two other passages.[101]

Proverbs 22:2

22:2. The rich and the poor stand side by side
Yahweh is the maker of them all.[102]

Toy defines this saying as a sentence with suggested antithesis, but it is also possible to regard it as a synthetic parallelism.[103] The first half-verse simply states that the "rich," עָשִׁיר, and the "poor," רָשׁ, meet, probably with the sense that they exist side by side in society. The second half-verse states that the Lord is the Maker, עֹשֶׂה,[104] of them both, using the same participle as in 14:31 and 17:5.

As in 16:4, the saying emphasizes that the Lord is the creator of all things, but its further implications are difficult to grasp. One possibility is to view it as a monotheistic statement which, by stating that the Lord created both the rich and the poor, stresses that he has designed the universe with these built-in contrasts and counterparts. Another possibility is to take the sentence as an

---

[99] Shupak (1987:113–116) discusses the references to the ear in Egyptian sources and in Israelite wisdom literature, primarily the book of Proverbs, and regards the parallels as one piece of evidence for the existence of schools in ancient Israel. He demonstrates that references to the ear in both cultures appear to indicate a setting in the field of education.

[100] See, e.g., Prov 2:2; 4:20, 25; 5:1, 13; 6:6; 8:32–34; 15:31; 18:15; 20:13b; 22:17; 23:12;.25:12. Cf. *Amenemope* iii 9–10. One aspect of the characterization of the fool/wicked person is precisely that he neither hears nor adheres to admonition, see, e.g., 12:1; 13:1; 23:9; 28:9.

[101] Ps 94:9, Sir 17:6.

[102] Toy's translation (1977:413). "Stand side by side" is literally "meet one another," פֻּגַשׁ (ni).

[103] Doll (1985:18).

[104] Schmidt (1964:165–166) comments concerning the use of this root in Gen 1: "Zwar gibt schon עשה 'machen' keine Auskunft über die Art und Weise der Durchführung, stellt aber die Schöpfung in Analogie zum menschlichen Tun eines Handwerkers dar (vgl. etwa Hos 8:6; Jer 18:4; Jes 44:13; 45:9; Ex 25:8ff)." Schmidt concludes that the usage of עשה in relation to creation is late and that "keine alte unde feste Tradition einer עשה-Schöpfung herausschälen lässt" (1964:166, n.1). He also notes the absence of ברא in the wisdom literature.

antithetically parallel bicolon which by means of a stark contrast portrays the actual disparity in the position of the rich and the poor in society with the more egalitarian ideals of the created order. If this were the case, the second clause would have to be regarded as a reminder directed not just at the rich and the poor, but as a general axiom for all to the effect that every person has rights and intrinsic value. The actual wording of the saying takes the form of a simple statement of fact: the rich and the poor meet, the Lord is the maker of them both. The interpretation is left to the reader. In reconstructing the probable meaning of this saying, it is important to relate it to the actual features of the wisdom traditions known to us. In this saying, one might well expect some further qualification rather than the bare statement that the Lord has created both the rich and the poor. While there is no tendency in the wisdom traditions to strive for the abolition of social class differences, the concerns expressed for the welfare of the poor in these traditions are significant. This verse should probably be interpreted in light of this general concern for the poor in in the wisdom traditions. The Lord is the maker of the poor and the rich alike, even though the latter is the one given honour in society. The saying reminds both parties of the fact that they are God's creation and as such have both rights and responsibilities.[105] The rich are thus seen as responsible participants, in accordance with the will of God, in the process of ensuring that the life of the poor is not a burden.

It has been noted that this saying might be viewed against the legal background of the city gate where the poor and the rich met in order to settle their disputes.[106] Within the wisdom traditions we certainly find an expression of special concern for the disenfranchised.[107] Even if the concern expressed by the verse is probably broader, the legal setting certainly gives special prominence to the content.

Proverbs 29:13

29:13. The poor and the oppressor meet together,
Yahweh gives light to the eyes of both.[108]

The construction of this verse is the same as in 22:2 using the verb פגשׁ (ni) to express the presence of both categories of people in society. Here the contrast between the categories is emphasized, the poor man, רשׁ, as in 22:2, is contrasted with the man of oppression or violence, אישׁ תככים. It is not

---

[105] Doll (1985:19): "Der Spruch macht den Armen Mut und zeigt zugleich den Reichen ihre Grenzen."
[106] Doll (1985:18–19).
[107] See, e.g., Prov 22:17; 23:11.
[108] Toy's translation (1977:510).

explicitly stated who is the unfortunate recipient of oppression meted out by the latter but the poor man is the obvious candidate as is implied in most translations. The use of the singular form refers here, as elsewhere, to the groups or classes within society. These categories must have been selected to reflect the powerful contrast between these two social groups, whose relations are normally characterized by tension. The second clause should be understood as a more poetic way of expressing the same notion as "the Lord has made them both" of 22:2.

Again, the question of the message of the saying must be addressed. We find it difficult to follow McKane's view that both this saying and 22:2 contain nothing more than a simple observation of the polarities existing within the order created and upheld by the Lord.[109] Though the terminology used is different, the man of violence and oppression is referred to elsewhere in Proverbs and there is always an ethical dimension to these sayings.[110] If this saying is compared with 14:31 and 17:5, for example, it appears quite probable that a strong moral tone is implied. Even though the moral entailments of the saying are not explicitly stated, a moralistic interpretation must have been unavoidable since concern for the poor and the denunciation of oppression and violence were such dominant features in the wisdom traditions from the earliest times on.[111]

Our conclusion is that a double message is detectable in this saying; on the one hand there is a simple expression of concern for the poor, while on the other hand, there is a denunciation of the behaviour of the oppressor.

This sentence, like 16:4, is thematically related to the theodicy issues. The assertion that the Lord created both good and evil was not without difficulties and, even in the book of Proverbs, there are indications that the sages were challenged by this issue.

---

[109] McKane (1985:640). Hermisson (1978:45) is more to the point: "The sentence about the poor man and the oppressor seems to be the most scandalous: is this said out of cynicism or resignation in the face of reality? Perhaps it is indicative that creation is not explicitly mentioned here. 'The Lord gives light to their eyes' does mean the granting of existence, to be sure, but it also signifies the dependence and limitation of the oppressor—certainly not his justification."

[110] 1:10–19; 11:17; 12:10; 14:31; 17:5, 11; 21:7; 22:22–23; 24:1–2, 15–16; 28:3, 24; 30:14. See also above our comments to 16:4.

[111] The moralistic note is also present in the Egyptian creation text from the Middle Kingdom *All Men Created Equal in Opportunity* (see below, p. 71) where it is stated that all men were created equal, and it was not intended for they to do evil, but their hearts, their free will, violated their original purpose.

B. The creation motif in the book of Proverbs in relation to other creation traditions

Scholars have observed that there is a variety of traditions relating to creation in the Old Testament, each with its own background and emphasis.[112] Anderson finds the creation motif related to the creation of a people in the Mosaic covenant tradition, to cosmic and social order in the royal covenant tradition,[113] to a harmonious world order which is established and upheld by the Lord in the wisdom traditions, to cosmic order and origins in the priestly circle, to expectations of a new creation in Second Isaiah—with all of these traditions making use of the same mythopoeic language.[114] We will attempt to relate creation in the book of Proverbs to various features of the different creation traditions which are significant for our study.

1. Creation of man and creation of the world

Of greatest significance is the difference in the use of the creation motif in the two main parts of the book of Proverbs. In chapters 1–9 the creation of the world is in focus while in chapters 10–31 it is the creation of man. The view that these two traditions are of separate origin and were used in different settings has been put forward by Westermann[115] while Albertz applied this distinction to Deutero-Isaiah, the Psalms, the book of Job[116] and to Mesopotamian and Israelite religion in general.[117] This theological distinction has also recently been applied to wisdom literature by Doll.[118] He asserts that there is a clear distinction between these two traditions which coincides with the division between the two main genres in the book of Proverbs—instruction and sentences. The only passages that are less clearly associated with the appropriate tradition are 16:4 and 20:12 with their reference to correct scales and the organs of perception as the Lord's creation. In our view the interpretation of both passages point towards ethical implications which indicate their close relationship to the other sayings on the creation of man.

---

[112] E.g., Gaster (1962:702–709), Westermann (1967:238–244), Kapelrud (1979:159–170), Sæbø (1979:138–165), Anderson (1984:1–24).

[113] Acc. to Anderson (1984:7) the royal covenant tradition stresses the correspondence between the cosmic order and the social order and is a theological perspective grounded "primarily in the election of the Davidic king and the choice of Zion as the divine dwelling place."

[114] Anderson (1984:1–24).

[115] Westermann (1967:243; 1974 A:32–60; 1974 B:31–34). See Albertz (1974:54-55).

[116] Albertz (1974).

[117] Albertz (1978).

[118] Doll (1985).

a. The creation of man

The theme of the creation of man never has the mere description of the circumstances surrounding man's creation as its primary purpose. Instead, the theme is uniformly used to corroborate a point or strengthen an argument. It serves as the basis—assumed to command universal assent—for exhortations to ethical social behaviour and especially to just treatment of the poor and needy in society. Albertz' view that the theme of the creation of man is part of a rather general and popular aspect of religion which differs from the posture of official religion is interesting. Albertz calls this aspect of religion "persönliche Frömmigkeit" and regards it as related to the individual and the family.[119] Even if there is uncertainty regarding the Sitz im Leben of wisdom, it is probable that wisdom, especially the "proverbial type," to some extent had its roots in this setting of the family, the clan and everyday life situations. And it is in this genre of wisdom, the form that can be called "Aussagewort"[120] and is usually regarded as the most original, that we find creation references which relate to society and the relationships between the different groups in society. It seems that the content, genre and probable setting of the sayings relating to the creation of man support Albertz' argument for a "non-official" setting for certain Old Testament traditions.

While Albertz' conclusions concerning the setting of this theme in the psalms are in line with what can be assumed in the case of the sentences, there are differences in the function and use of the theme. Albertz concludes that the theme of the creation of man is used in individual lament psalms and "Heilsorakel," none of which are "Gattungen" found in the book of Proverbs. Still one might argue for a correspondence between the function of the sentences and the function of the "Heilsorakel." Most of the sentences deal with the situation of groups of people in difficult circumstances and imply an exhortation to assist and help them. In one sense some of the sentences constitute a non-cultic parallel to the literary form "Heilsorakel" where the individual is assured help from his creator as the answer to his appeal for assistance. There is also a parallel to the psalms of individual lament in the fact that God's "Mit-Sein" to the man in need, which marks these psalms,[121] is similar to what is implied about the Lord in these creation-sayings.

---

[119] Albertz (1978:92). Albertz characterizes this personal piety in contrast to official religion: "Das bedeutet zweitens, dass sich diese persönliche Frömmigkeit charakteristisch von der Jahwereligion des Volkes und seiner offiziellen Institutionen unterscheidet. Das Fehlen der israelitischen 'Heilsgeschichte' in den Klagen des Einzelnen setzt sich fort in dem Fehlen der grossen Heilstraditionen in der Namengebung und findet seine Entsprechung in der Differenz zwischen der Väterreligion und der Jahwereligion der Stämme."

[120] See Westermann (1971:73–85) concerning the form and its Sitz im Leben.

[121] Albertz (1978:32–37, 93).

With regard to the function of the theme, a possible relationship to the Yahwistic account of creation must be considered. God's creation of man is clearly the key ingredient in Genesis 2, while the creation of the earth is merely a prerequisite.[122] Other significant features of the Yahwistic creation tradition are the absence of struggle, the craftsman-like description of God,[123] his closeness to man and the prominence given to man in creation. It gives an account of the creation of man in which man is given regnal authority and responsibility for the maintenance of order in God's world, an authority and responsibility which can also be misused. This creation tradition may well provide us with a more precisely defined backdrop against which the relation of social ethics to the theme of the creation of man in Proverbs 10–29 may be seen. Man, in his own right as a responsible created being in close relation to God, is given the task to maintain the harmony established by God in creation.

The non-Israelite accounts of the creation of man may give us some insight into the function of the theme of the creation of man. The conclusion that these other creation accounts show at least some degree of relationship to the Israelite account seems inescapable. E.g., the view that man is created from clay seems to be a general idea as well as the statement in Genesis 1 that man is made in the image of God.[124] Pettinato answers the question as to why, according to texts from Mesopotamia, man was created:

> Auf die Frage 'Weshalb wurde der Mensch erschaffen', geben die keilschriftlichen Texte eine einheitliche und klare Antwort: 'Der Mensch wurde erschaffen, um zu arbeiten, und zwar um die Götter von ihrer schweren Arbeit zu entlasten'.[125]

Pettinato also notes the contrast between the Sumerian and Akkadian texts where the gods are both in close relationship to and dependent upon man and the situation portrayed in Genesis 1.[126] This close relationship to man, while not emphasized in the Genesis 1 account of the creation of the world, is however paralleled in Genesis 2 and the creation of man passages in Proverbs. In Egypt a central conception is that man was made from the tears of the god. This is a play on the Egyptian words for "tear" and "man" and expresses a close relationship between the deity and mankind.[127] The same thought occurs when it is stated that man, the cattle of the god, was created in his image:

---

[122] Westermann (1967:243), Kapelrud (1979:162).

[123] That man is modelled from clay by a god is an idea found in Egypt, Babylonia and probably also to be deduced from Ugaritic texts, see de Moor (1980:180) for references.

[124] Westermann (1967:243). For a survey of OT scholarship on the issue of extra-biblical parallels, see Jónsson (1988:200–201).

[125] Pettinato (1971:21).

[126] Pettinato (1971:22).

[127] Assmann (1984:681).

Well tended is mankind—god's cattle,
He made sky and earth for their sake,
He subdued the water monster,
He made breath for their noses to live.
They are his images, who came from his body,
He shines in the sky for their sake;
He made for them plants and cattle,....[128]

In Egypt anthropogony and theogony generally precede cosmogony and there is an emphasis on the suitability of the world for mankind. This is especially clear in the creation hymn ending *The Instruction of Merikare* where it is emphasized that everything in creation was made by the god for the well-being of man.[129] Another interesting text is the coffin text that has been given the title *All Men Created Equal in Opportunity* where the emphasis on the equality of men parallels the theme of the creation of man in Proverbs 10–31. The All-Lord proclaims his four good deeds:

I did four good deeds within the portal of lightland:
I made the four winds that every man might breathe in his time. This is one of the deeds.
I made the great inundation that the humble might benefit by it like the great.
This is one of the deeds.
I made every man like his fellow; and I did not command that they do wrong.
It is their hearts that disobey what I had said. This is one of the deeds.
I made that their hearts are not disposed to forget the West, in order that sacred offerings be made to the gods of the nomes. This is one of the deeds.
I have created the gods from my sweat, and the people from the tears of my eye.[130]

The reference to evil in man's heart and man's responsibility for evil are noteworthy. Here is a parallel to Genesis 3 and Proverbs 16:4, texts which also deal with the presence of disobedience and evil in the world of man. None are sophisticated treatments of the issue, but they point to an awareness of the problem of disharmony in creation.

b. The creation of the world

References to the creation of the world are restricted to the first section of the book of Proverbs. Both passages relating to creation are of a poetic nature and are clearly of a different form than the material in the surrounding context. It appears that the theme of the creation of the world shows a special affinity

---

[128] *The Instruction of Merikare*, Lichtheim (1975:106).
[129] See Lichtheim (1975:106). The relations between certain features in the conclusion of this text dealing with creation and Genesis 1 has been expounded by Herrmann (1961:413–424) who names the text a "kleinen ägyptischen Genesis."
[130] Lichtheim (1975:131–132). Also in *ANET* (1969:7–8), Beyerlin (1975:34–35).

with the hymn genre[131] as, for example, when the theme is introduced in chapters 3 and 8 in the context of instruction. This difference in genre affinities between the creation of man and the creation of the world is also of importance in determining the original setting. While the creation of man is at home within the sphere of personal religion, the theme of the creation of the world belongs to the official religion and its cult.

Psalm 104 is the outstanding example of a wisdom creation psalm.[132] Among its interesting features is an emphasis on a cosmic order established by the Lord, with an enumeration of details in creation which like Job 38–39, Psalm 148 and Sirach 43, has a certain resemblance to onomastica.[133] In these texts man is referred to as merely one creature among others! As in Proverbs 3 and 8, creation has to do with the main cosmological components—heaven, earth, the deep, springs, hills, etc.—and the way that the Lord masters and orders the whole. Proverbs 3 and 8 make use of the same hymnic language and imagery as Psalm 104, but in Proverbs God's creation of the world is not the central issue but serves as the backdrop against which wisdom is accorded prominence and authority. While the creation of the world in Psalm 104 praises the Lord, the theme in Proverbs is used to exalt wisdom by placing wisdom side by side with the Lord. This wisdom in Proverbs is accessible to man and the value of searching after it is emphasized. This is also the case in Sirach 24[134] while Job 28 handles the theme in a slightly different fashion proclaiming that wisdom is known and accessible only to God.[135]

We observed that hymn is the primary literary form in which the theme of the creation of the world is cast. According to Albertz the function of this theme was to exalt the Lord, but we find that in the book of Proverbs this function is altered and the object of exaltation is wisdom. The creation of the world is employed here to serve a particular purpose which might be thought of as an extension of its original purpose.

Originally, Genesis 1 was probably an independent account of the creation of the world into which the creation of man was secondarily inserted.[136] The chapter is marked by precise expression when it relates the creative acts that

---

[131] Ps 33:6–9; 74:13–17; 89:9–15; 95:3–7; 104; 115:15–16; 136; 148; Isa 44:24; 45:5–8, 11–12, 18; 48:12–13; Sir 16:24–17:14; 39:15–35; 42:15–43:33. Albertz (1974:173): "Die Weltschöpfung gehört in das beschreibende Lob, sie dient dazu, die weltüberlegende Macht Jahwes zu preisen." Cf. Hermisson (1978:47).

[132] Hermisson (1978:47), Anderson (1984:11–14).

[133] Sæbø (1979:150). Sæbø (1979:156) also connects this form to the enumeration of God's creative acts in Gen 1.

[134] In Sirach, wisdom seems to be generally accessible within Israel, which is where wisdom settled. This is a nationalized interpretation, but still on the line of accessibility to all. Cf. Bar 3:36–37.

[135] Nielsen (1976/77:160–162). Cf. Bar 3:31–32; Wis 9:9–11.

[136] See Albertz (1974:54).

produce order in creation. This feature has a counterpart in Proverbs 8:22–29, though Genesis 1 constitutes a more clear-cut creation account and is more extensive, while Proverbs 8 sketches out the acts of creation as a background for its main purpose of enhancing wisdom. Kapelrud regards Genesis 1 as an answer to the ideological competition which was created by creation accounts like *Enūma elish*. Because of this competition, he argues, the two main features "Ordnung" and "Trennung" found in *Enūma elish* are also given prominence in Genesis 1 while absent in the earlier account of Genesis 2.[137] While this may be a correct reconstruction, it should also be noted that these two features are found in the book of Proverbs as well as in Psalm 104, a fact which may suggest a more diversified background. There are further similarities between Genesis 1 and *Enūma elish,* but, as has been pointed out by several scholars, the relationship between these documents is much more intricate than mere direct borrowing.[138]

Whybray carried out an interesting comparative study of Proverbs 8, several Egyptian and Babylonian creation poems which had been proposed as possible prototypes, and Genesis 1–2.[139] Whybray concludes:

> ...these texts are of various kinds and hardly comparable one with another except for the simple facts that they all refer to the creation of the world and that in doing this they (in most cases at least) employ similar grammatical constructions: negative temporal clauses. Neither in their general purpose nor in the function of these temporal clauses can any strong similarities be found. This raises the question whether we can speak here of a common tradition or prototype at all.[140]

There are features in the description of the creation of the world in Proverbs 8 which are in line with a common cosmological tradition in Israel,

---

[137] Kapelrud (1979:164).

[138] Westermann (1967:240): "Die Zeit der Versuche, das Verhältnis der biblischen Schöpfungsaussagen zu ausserisraelitischen durch die Annahme literarischer Abhängigkeit auf der Ebene literarkritischer Vergleichung zu bestimmen, ist vorbei....Es ist heute z. B. unmöglich geworden, Gen 1 mit dem Abschnitt von der Weltschöpfung durch Marduk in Enūma eliš zu vergleichen, ohne auf die breite und verzweigte Vorgeschichte dieses babylonischen Textes einzugehen." Anderson (1984:2) remarks that Gunkel only perceived the tip of an iceberg and that since his time further finds of mythological literature has widened our horizons to the point where it no longer is possible to view the *Chaoskampf* motif solely from a Babylonian perspective, since this motif "touches the depths of mythical apprehension of reality found in 'archaic' societies." Schmidt (1964:30–31) points out several striking similarities between Gen 1 and *Enūma elish* but still argues against a direct borrowing: "Zwar ist im israelitischen Raum sicher mit einer Bekanntschaft babylonischer Mythen zu rechnen, trotzdem bleibt eine unmittelbare Abhängigkeit der priesterlichen Schöpfungsgeschichte von dem babylonischen Schöpfungsepos ausgeschlossen; dazu reichen die gegenseitigen Beziehungen bei so gewichtigen Unterschieden nicht aus."

[139] Whybray (1965 B:504–514). The prototypes, suggested by Gemser and Ringgren, included in the study are: the Egyptian Book of the Apophis, Enūma elish, and a bilingual account of the creation of the world by Marduk.

[140] Whybray (1965 B:512).

Mesopotamia, and probably the whole Ancient Near East.[141] But Whybray
points out that "we must constantly pay due attention to the possibility of
coincidence. Any account of the creation of the world is likely, in view of the
nature of the subject, to have some points of resemblance with others—e.g.,
one would expect references to heaven, earth, plants, living creatures, man,
etc."[142] Whybray adds further weight to this argument by citing the Brahmin
Rigveda and the Japanese *Nihongi* which contain similar descriptions of
creation.

c. Common features of the creation traditions in the book of Proverbs
Two common features of the two different creation traditions in the book of
Proverbs are of some importance to our study. The first is the feature of
demythologization. This is especially remarkable in the references to the
creation of the world which make use of mythological language and motifs,[143]
but also apply to the theme of the creation of man. It seems clear that non-
Israelite mythological material was known and used in Israel; the interesting
question is the degree to which Israel remoulded this material. It is especially
striking in the wisdom literature that when mythological motifs occur they do
not refer to mythological realities, but are merely employed figuratively.[144]
This feature of demythologization is to some degree relevant for the use of
mythological traits in the Old Testament on the whole, but it is especially
prominent in wisdom texts. In Psalm 104 Leviathan is demythologized to the
level of what might be called a "zoological curiosity,"[145] one of the Lord's
playthings. Such demythologization can also be detected in parts of the book
of Proverbs which are not closely connected with the theme of creation.[146] On
the whole it seems possible to say that the wisdom traditions were marked by a
non-mythological concept of reality.[147]

The second common feature of the creation traditions in the book of
Proverbs is the description of creation as an act of the Lord occurring in the

---

[141] Schmidt (1964:29): "Die Vorstellung , dass die Welt zu Beginn nur Wasser oder die Erde von
Wasser bedeckt war, hat Gen 1 mit dem ganzen alten Orient, sowohl dem Zweistromland als auch
Ägypten, gemeinsam; ja, sie ist wie der Trennungsmythos eine der weit verbreiteten Grundtypen
kosmogonischer Vorstellungen überhaupt."

[142] Whybray (1965 B:513).

[143] The "Trennung" motif and the primeval waters are present in both Prov 3:20 and 8:27–29.

[144] Gordon (1965:94), Hermisson (1978:54), McCarthy (1984:84–85).

[145] The expression from Anderson (1984:13).

[146] See 1:12; 2:18; 3:18; 7:27; 9:18; 10:11; 11:30; 13:14; 14:27; 15:11; 16:22; 21:16; 27:20.

[147] Von Rad (1981:304). Schmidt (1964:46) suggests that the process of demythologization evident in
Gen 1 may have been supported by influences from wisdom traditions.

past and establishing the world once and for all.[148] There are allusions to the sustenance of creation,[149] but never to a need for a continual re-creation.[150] This definitive character of the acts of creation is highlighted by the reference to the sea's "limit", חק, in Proverbs 8:29, which by the Lord's command eliminates the threat previously posed by the turbulent waters. The same idea appears in other wisdom texts.[151] This notion of security in a world established by the Lord through his initial creation acts is a main belief within the wisdom traditions. Trust in the Lord thus merges with confidence in his creation. The only thing which might threaten creation is that the Lord withdraws the חק and lets the chaotic powers loose again. Although this was, in light of biblical traditions, more than a mere possibility,[152] the wisdom traditions express a strong confidence in the belief that the Lord guarantees the establishment of order in his creation.

2. Creation as Chaoskampf

The *Chaoskampf* motif has already been referred to in relation to several issues in this investigation. This motif is associated with the creation of the world in the broader cultural context of the ancient Near East.[153] In the book of Proverbs it is in the creation of the world texts that we find the allusions to the *Chaoskampf*.

This motif must have been well known in Israel and is employed in a variety of ways in the Old Testament, not just with reference to the creation of the world.[154] It can be argued that the use of the *Chaoskampf* motif within the wisdom traditions is restricted primarily to the use of language without actual

---

[148] 3:19. See Hermisson (1978:49) regarding Ps 104:5, 19. Cf. RS 25.130:18'–21',40'–43' (Nougayrol [1968:293–295], Khanjian [1973:187]).

[149] See our comments on Prov 3:20. The emphasis on social order can be viewed as an interest in sustaining the creation by living according to the intentions of the creator and his devices.

[150] The psalms of the Jerusalem cult may serve as a contrast by reflecting a world view where again and again the world had to be steered away from chaos. It appears that wisdom instead viewed chaos as fundamentally eliminated from this world once and for all (Hermisson (1978:51). Anderson (1984:13): "Whereas hymns in the Zion tradition (e.g. Ps 93) tend to speak of Yahweh's creative action as being repeated in the present, as the divine King overcomes the powers of chaos, in Psalm 104 statements like 'Yahweh has founded the earth'(v 4) or 'Yahweh has made the moon' (v 19) refer to 'basic data of the past....' "

[151] Job 38:8–11; Jer 5:22 (it may well be that Jeremiah here employs an idea usually associated with wisdom), Ps 104:9 (the same idea expressed by נבול). Job 14:5 is notable for its use of the same expressions. However, these occur in the context of the theme of the creation of man and are employed by Job to designate life-span which is predetermined by God, which is a חק and cannot be overturned. In Job 28:26 חק also refers to water—the rain.

[152] Gen 7.

[153] Schmidt (1964:29–31).

[154] Anderson (1984:5) notes that the motif in Ex 15 is related to the creation of the people. See also McCarthy (1984:74–89, esp. 84–85).

belief in the mythological reality which such language originally described. In fact, it is this lack of belief in the reality of these myths, that made it possible for their imagery and language to be adopted and used in such an extensive and free way without creating theological problems.[155]

We have also observed the significance of the fact that the waters are pushed back and confined within limits in Proverbs 8. A potential dualism is suppressed here.[156] Creation is secure and is being upheld by the power and authority of the Lord. What may disturb the order in creation is not evil powers or gods, but man through his actions.[157] Here is a connection to the creation of man sayings and a point where the different traditions might be connected.

Crenshaw argues that the tension between creation and chaos constitutes an important motif in the wisdom traditions, even though it should not be related to the annual threats of a certain ritual conception.[158] This may be correct, but only if we accept a broad definition of the concept of chaos which includes *any* threat to order in the world of men. Crenshaw argues that the threat of chaos lies in the realms of human perversion, human ignorance and the divine hiddenness. This accords to some extent with our conclusion that the main threat to harmony in creation according to the book of Proverbs is man, but it must be noted that there is no immediate connection between this threat and the hostile powers of chaos. The problems of social justice and theodicy were matters of interest in the circles associated with wisdom traditions, problems dealt with extensively in the books of Job and Ecclesiastes. But these areas of disturbance cannot be easily identified with the connotations of chaos which is associated with the primeval waters and their mythological background.[159]

3. Creation of El type and of Baal type

Of special interest both in the days of the Old Testament and in the world of present Old Testament research is the relationship between Israel and

---

[155] This is the view of McCarthy (1984:84) concerning the *Chaoskampf* motif in the OT as a whole. While his view may not be of equal validity in relation to each of the different traditions of the OT, it is certainly in line with the use of the *Chaoskampf* motif in the wisdom traditions.

[156] The existence of dualism within the OT and esp. the Israelite wisdom literature is a matter of dispute. Hermisson (1984:54): "On the basis of its traditions, wisdom incorporated the myth of the chaos struggle in thorough accordance with Yahwistic faith, that is, in such a way that every dualistic overtone was excluded." This seems to be an oversimplification, see Keel (1978:156–158), Kubina (1979:86–106), Lindström (1983:151–157).

[157] See the context of Jer 5:22.

[158] Crenshaw (1976 A:26–31). Cf. Hermisson (1978:51,53).

[159] The matter turns out somewhat different in Job where the theodicy problem is the central issue for Job. To Job everything is chaos (ch. 3) since he cannot trust God any longer.

Canaanite culture. Perhaps the most disappointing lack of evidence when it comes to creation is that no Canaanite creation account has yet been found.[160] Still several scholars postulate that El was most likely the Canaanite creator god,[161] citing as evidence Genesis 14:22 and appellative expressions like "father of mankind," "creator of the earth,"[162] and the thematic connection between procreation and creation.

The expressions "creation of El type" and "creation of Baal type" are adopted from Fisher's study where he uses them for creation in the sense of origination and the broad sense of bringing order in the world, respectively.[163]

However, the phrase "creation of Baal type" may be a misleading designation since nothing in the texts is said concerning Baal that can be applied to creation in the common meaning of bringing something into being.[164] In the Babylonian *Enūma elish* it is explicitly stated that Marduk, after having slain Tiamat, created heaven and earth including man.[165] If we compare the "creation of the world" passages in Proverbs to Fisher's rather general description of what constitutes "creation of Baal type," the differences are prominent. In Proverbs, though the main interest is not in origins, the questions of beginnings as well as ordering do come into play. The "Trennung" motif, which is absent in the Baal-Yamm account, is emphasized in both Proverbs 3 and 8.

---

[160] McCarthy (1984:74). Pope (1955:49–50): "There is hardly anything that could be called a creation story or any clear allusion to cosmic creativity in the Ugaritic texts so far exhumed...It is altogether probable that El was a creator God, but the Ugaritic evidence is by no means explicit. All the Ugaritic allusions to El's creativity are in terms of generation and paternity." See also Kapelrud (1981:79–85).

[161] De Moor (1980:171–187) regards El as the deity who created at least the gods and man, and probably also the world. His view is that El must have served this function in Ugarit since Baal did not and since it is hardly imaginable that a minor deity would have been the creator god.

[162] "Creator of the earth" is not found in Ugarit but in inscriptional material from several other sites in the Canaanite-Phoenician context dating from before the 12th century down to the 8th. See Miller (1980:43–46) for references and discussion of this expression from the Jewish Quarter in Jerusalem. Miller concludes that El, the Creator of the Earth was the ancient god of Jerusalem who later was fully identified with Yahweh. This connection of El to a creation deity to Jerusalem is of interest to us, since Jerusalem was the centre of the wisdom traditions and El was the patron of wisdom in Canaanite culture.

[163] Fisher (1965:313–324) finds the conflict between Baal and Yamm related to kingship, order and temple building, which all relate to a larger thematic complex of creation in the sense of bringing order in the world. He terms this "creation of Baal type," in contrast with "creation of El type." Concerning "creation of Baal type," see further Grønbæk (1985:27–44).

[164] Fisher (1965:315), McCarthy (1984:74–75), Grønbæk (1985:28–29) warn against defining creation too narrowly, as solely creatio *ex nihilo*. On the other hand, we believe that the definition of "creation" is too wide if it is thought of as identical to the bringing of order into the world.

[165] O. Kaiser (1959:76): "Der Kampf zwischen Marduk und Tiamat erfolgt vor der Schöpfung der Welt. Der Kampf zwischen Baal und Jam setzt offensichtlich die Welt selbst bereits voraus." The reference to the making of the earth from the second part of Tiamat's carcass in Enūma elish is missing, but is regarded as having been there originally. Also, it is Ea who takes over the initiative and creates man (*ANET* [1969:67–68]).

It is not entirely clear what Fisher includes in "creation of El type." It seems to be confined to issues related to ultimate origins and he does not find this creation type attested in the Old Testament[166] and he argues that it was rejected by the Hebrews.[167] Even if concern with origins is not a prominent feature of the creation traditions, it is present by implication in a number of Old Testament passages, especially in Genesis 1[168] and also to some extent elsewhere, e.g. in Proverbs 8.[169]

The prominent feature of "creation of El type" is the absence of struggle, *Chaoskampf*.[170] This is in harmony with Genesis 2 and the creation of man theme in Proverbs and also with the view of the creation of the world in the book of Proverbs. In both Proverbs 3 and 8 we find traces of *Chaoskampf* language and imagery, though no real struggle is implied.

Another fact which indicates a relationship between "creation of El type" and creation in the book of Proverbs is the association of wisdom with El. Although the wisdom of El is not explicitly connected to creation in any of the extant texts, wisdom is associated with El in ways that are parallel to the depiction of the Lord in the first section of the book of Proverbs, the section that deals with the creation of the world.

Another possible point of contact can be seen in El's lofty, non-cultic status, which is in harmony with the lack of cultic emphasis in the wisdom traditions. El dwells at the source of the rivers, to be compared to the Mesopotamian creator god Ea who is a god of wisdom and lives in the *apsû*.[171] It has been suggested that El "dwelt at this remote point of the cosmos exactly because he

---

[166] Fisher (1965:321, n. 4) indicates that there may be a few traditions, e.g., Gen 14 that preserve creation of the El type.

[167] When Fisher refers to this rejection, "creation of El type" seems to be the same as procreation: "They were concerned about the problems that a parent-god, who spewed out other gods, would give them" (1965:321). True, the sexual connotations associated with El as the father of other gods, must have been a problem in the understanding of El as the creator, but, as the struggles outlined in the OT make perfectly clear, adopting the features of Baal into Hebrew traditions was not the least bit unproblematic either. Fisher's arguments seem somewhat strained in view of the fact that El's importance was receding during OT times and his function something like the nominal head of the pantheon (Kapelrud 1981:79–85) Instead Baal came to play the prominent role in the cult. It must have been less problematic to take over and modify traits of the El type than it was to adopt those associated with Baal. This is also the picture we discern in, for example, the early prophets who strongly oppose Baal syncretism.

[168] So Eichrodt (1962:1–11) and Anderson (1984:14–18).

[169] Whybray (1965 B:507–508) observes a difference between Prov 8:22–31 and its supposed prototypes in the former's use of temporal clauses, which give an orderly and detailed presentation of the events of creation, and "constitute an ordered statement of the actual creative process." This is at least close to origination.

[170] The absence of this feature is observed by Brandon (1963:63, 86) in Egyptian and Sumerian cosmogonies where the primeval ocean is present but does not constitute a threat. This warns against making the *Chaoskampf* motif too dominant in reconstructions of ANE cosmogonies.

[171] See Brandon (1963:119).

had to maintain the order he had created. This would explain why El never leaves his abode in the Ugaritic texts."[172] This may be a Canaanite parallel to the description of the elevated position of the Lord in many of the psalms and implied in the wisdom texts. He is in heaven and from there controls and maintains order in the the world.

Lastly, the generally amicable perception of the connection between El and the Lord in Israel can be brought into the picture. The use of El as a designation for God in Israelite religion, contrasts starkly with the refusal to use Baal as an appellative or proper name for God. Habel makes an interesting comparison between the designation of the deity in Genesis 14, "El Elyon, creator of heaven and earth," and the similar formula using Yahweh in some psalms.[173] His conclusion is that when this formula is applied to the Lord, it is derived from the context of blessings from the early Israelite El cult. This formula is later used in a more general way as a reference to the creator of the world.

Comparisons with Canaanite theologies of creation thus turn out to be problematic because of the limited material available. The most acceptable view of the connections between Canaanite and Israelite wisdom theologies is that the god El who appears to have played the role of creator and who was the patron of wisdom was of such significance in the Canaanite pantheon that a relationship was possible while the influence of other deities, e.g. Baal, is at most minimal. The fact that El and Yahweh in Israelite religion were identified supports this view.

---

[172] De Moor (1980:183).
[173] Habel (1972:321–337).

C. Conclusions

1. Frequency and position of the creation sayings

Creation is referred to in two poems in chapters 1–9 and in seven sayings in
the rest of the book of Proverbs. Chapters 2–3 can be called the theological
centre of Proverbs 1–9 and it is here we find the first poem on the theme of
the creation of the world. The second poem occurs in chapter 8, also
significantly, near the conclusion of the first section of the book.

In Proverbs 10–31 God is referred to around seventy times. One tenth of
these references are linked to the idea of creation. It is especially in 10:1–
22:16 that we find references to creation, five sentences in 16:1–22:16 while
only one occurs in the first six chapters of the section which are dominated by
the antithesis form. In 22:17–24:34 there is no reference to creation.

Thus, we conclude that notion of creation cannot, at least in terms of its
frequency of occurrence, be said to play a dominant role in the book of
Proverbs. It does not even play a dominating role within the "God-sayings."
The position of the "creation of the world" passages in Proverbs 1–9 ascribes
to the creation of the world theme some prominence. However, it is not
possible to ascribe any special importance to the creation of man theme in
Proverbs 10–31 from the position of the passages.

2. Dating the creation passages

Giving defensible suggestions concerning the dating of the creation passages in
the book of Proverbs is difficult for several reasons. To begin with, a
consensus has not yet emerged from the on-going scholarly discussion of the
dating of other creation traditions in Old Testament. This is related to the
issue of whether creation is to be considered as a subject in its own right
within the traditions of ancient Israel or whether it is a later phenomenon
which should be both historically and thematically subordinated to some other
theological topic, e.g. salvation history. In addition, the debate within wisdom
literature research is still heavily influenced by the view that "theologized
wisdom" represents a later stage in the development of a wisdom that was
originally secular. If one adopts this point of view, the very subject matter of
these verses—the Lord's work of creation—automatically rules out an early
date.

The main spokesman for the subordination of the creation motif was von
Rad who argued that it should be regarded as subservient to the doctrine of

redemption.[174] This was based on his understanding of Yahwism as primarily concerned with redemption and his observation that the notion of creation is never used in isolation but always had an ancillary function in the Old Testament. Only in the wisdom literature does von Rad find the doctrine of creation to be independent. This leads him to suggest that this type of view of creation is of Egyptian origin. However, von Rad's view suffers from an excessively narrow definition of Yahwism which rules out the notion of creation from the outset. In addition, his view also misinterprets the use of the creation motif in the wisdom traditions. Our investigation has demonstrated that creation in the book of Proverbs does not function as an independent motif. Instead, the different creation themes are used in the argumentation of the sages to provide the premises for conclusions which are to be drawn on the moral plane. Thus wisdom literature cannot serve as an example of the independence of the doctrine of creation. It is important to note that the disparate use of creation themes within different traditions renders the argument for subordinating the doctrine of creation under some other doctrine irrelevant. It rather demonstrates the existence of "independent" creation traditions which were generally known and could be employed freely for different purposes. This disparate use of creation traditions, however, compounds the difficulty of tracing their history and date.

The practice of assigning a late date to wisdom passages on the basis of the presence of a particular theological element has been discussed in our introductory chapter. In our view, it is not possible to establish a late date for the creation sayings solely on this basis, in spite of the fact that scholars still tend to use this theological element as a criterion for a late date.

While it might be simply assumed that the creation themes have a history reaching far back in time, it is no easy task to find clear textual support for this view. The main "creation accounts" available to us are considered late, at least in their extant versions. Sæbø points out that in the oldest texts of the Old Testament there are no traces of creation theology while in the pre-exilic prophets there are only few allusions. However, Sæbø finds early references in Genesis 14:19–22; 24:3 and Psalms 8; 19A; 33; 104.[175] Westermann argues that the creation accounts are products of long development that stretches back into Israel's pre-history[176] and that a reconstruction of the development of the creation traditions in general indicates that the tradition of the creation of man is older than that of the creation of the world.[177]

---

174 Von Rad (1984:53–64).

175 Sæbø (1979:139–142). Cf. Schmidt's discussion (1982:69).

176 Westermann (1967:241).

177 Westermann (1967:243).

Albertz concludes that both the traditions concerning the creation of man and of the world are to be traced back to pre-exilic times. He is confident that Israelite traditions of the creation of the world extend back to the times of the early kings. Based on a dating of the texts in question, he suggests an eighth century date for the extant form of the tradition of the creation of man, though he regards an earlier date for the tradition itself as probable. From the time of Deutero-Isaiah, and even perhaps earlier, it was possible to relate the two creation traditions, but this was done only in a limited way and the two traditions were maintained as separate traditions, though with a certain degree of interconnection.[178]

Our study of the texts and the two traditions indicates that the "creation of man" tradition goes back at least to the eighth century.[179] This is in line with the conclusions of Albertz. When it comes to the creation of the world passages, no direct indications have been observed. Doll regards the whole of Proverbs 1–9 as an example of late "Theologisierung der Weisheit" constituting the third stage after "Volkssprichwörtern" and the collecting and reworking of these into "Kunstsprüche."[180] The form of the creation of the world theme is the hymn, which has been employed to enhance wisdom's status instead of giving primary emphasis to the Lord himself and his acts in relationship to the nation. But it is by no means necessary to postulate that this use of the hymn motif is a late development transferred to post-exilic times, as argued by Doll:

> Man kann sich die Entstehung in nachexilischer Zeit sehr gut innerhalb eines Kreises der Jerusalemer Priesterschaft vorstellen, dem ausser der Betreuung des offiziellen Kultes am Tempel auch die Tätigkeit der theologischen Weisheitslehrers an einer Tempelschule zufiel.[181]

But if the institutions and bearers of the hymn and wisdom traditions were close to each other at this stage one would expect Proverbs 1–9 to reveal at least some signs of the influences of a theology marked by interest in the Torah and the cult—which is precisely what happens in the type of wisdom found in the books of Sirach and Wisdom of Solomon. Since the instruction genre by no means needs to be regarded as later than the sentences, there is no need for the presupposition that Proverbs 1–9 is post-exilic. Considering the diversified use of the creation of the world theme in the Old Testament and the background of the creation of the world traditions in the ancient Near East as a

---

[178] Albertz (1974:160–164).
[179] Primarily the use of רש and דל. See comments above on 14:31, 17:5.
[180] Doll (1985:9, 78–79).
[181] Doll (1985:78).

whole, it seems probable that wisdom texts dealing with the creation of the world are to be dated to pre-exilic times, close in date to the psalms which make use of the same theme,[182] at least some of which must be regarded as relatively early.

3. The function of the creation themes

The references to creation in the book of Proverbs relate to two main traditions—the creation of the world and creation of man. These traditions are kept separate in the book of Proverbs; references to the creation of the world are found in the main section of the book which is in the genre of instruction, while references to the creation of man occur in sections which are in the sentence genre.

Our study has demonstrated that the creation of the world theme is employed to enhance the status of wisdom by portraying is as closely associated with the Lord as an instrument in, or a unique witness of, his creation. In this fashion, the creation motif itself turns out to be secondary, though at the same time it conveys a number of ideas and views of creation which were part of the theology cherished within the wisdom traditions. Enhancing wisdom's status by giving it a role in creation is accomplished by means of the use of the hymnic form, which was natural since the theme of the creation of the world was primarily expressed in the form of a hymn to the creator. There is nothing in the poetry on the creation of the world in the book of Proverbs that supplies explicit evidence to relate it to official religion and cult, for the theme is employed in the context of instruction, which points instead to an educational setting. However, there are some indirect hints of such a relationship by means of the association of the creation of the world theme with official religion. The use of the hymn genre, with its connections to the official religion and its cult, may also be a sign that the two settings of the temple and of the centre of learning were interrelated.[183] The function of this theme is undoubtedly to relate wisdom both to creation and to the creator, to "theologize" wisdom and point to the wisdom inherent in creation. Wisdom is nearly identical with the Lord in terms of authority in the context of Proverbs 1–9, and in the creation passages wisdom is closely associated with the Lord, both as his "instrument" and as his "companion."

In the tradition of the creation of man, the creation motif primarily serves a social-ethical function, frequently used as an encouragement to recognize the

---

[182] See Albertz (1974:91–117) concerning creation of the world in the psalms.

[183] See Doll (1985:78) who argues similarly, but with another view concerning the development of wisdom.

value of the poor and weak in society and promote their welfare. This is also brought into relief through the use of divine appellatives, e.g., "Maker" which twice refers to the Lord as the poor man's creator. Thus, the use of this theme might be called "man-centered" or anthropocentric. God and creation function as motifs and background for statements concerning man and his world, while references to cultic obligations or nature are lacking. To a certain degree, this non-cultic trait marks the book of Proverbs and the Old Testament wisdom literature as a whole.[184] The absence of references to nature is a trait of the creation of man tradition while there are naturally many references to nature in the traditions of the creation of the world.

One may wonder why the motivating function of the creation motif was not more frequently used or extended in scope. Certainly many exhortations and statements could have been forcefully supported by the rationale that "this was the way the Lord created things to be." The fact that the idea of the creation of man was seen to have specific implications for the social sphere may indicate that the creation of man theme was a solid tradition in Israel. It is also possible that this relationship between the creation of man tradition and social ethics should be explained by reference to a common original setting in the tribal and family circle. It should be noted, however, that the explicit connection between social issues and creation appears to be peculiar to the wisdom traditions. It is also possible that it may be derived from a heightened interest in human life and its conditions which seems to have been cultivated especially in these circles. This general interest in the fate and circumstances of man can be detected throughout Proverbs 10–29 which deal with a variety of subjects relating to the behaviour, attitudes and destiny of man.

4. The significance of the creation motif

The creation motif does not seem to have been very important in the ancient Near East, for the number of creation accounts preserved is by no means great.[185] Kapelrud demonstrates that, while it may be correct to claim that creation was an important issue in Assyro-Babylonian religion, the same cannot be said of the religions of Sumer and Egypt.[186] References to creation in the Canaanite context, if they exist at all, are few and vague in character.

Bearing this in mind, we may be less than surprised to find a limited number of clear-cut references to creation in the book of Proverbs, in other

---

[184] Perdue (1977]) demonstrates that cult was not a foreign element to wisdom and that no tension should be presupposed between the two.

[185] Against, e.g., von Rad (1962:136) who argues that the religious atmosphere in the environment of Canaan was "saturated with creation myths."

[186] Kapelrud (1979:159).

parts of the wisdom literature and in most parts of the Old Testament. The creation texts in the book of Proverbs probably assumed something like their present shape during the monarchic period, but the pre-history of these traditions may extend back to a time before Israel's existence. In view of the diversified use of the creation motif in the Old Testament, we conclude that traditions of the creation of man and of the world existed separately in Israel, and that they were of great importance in the Israelite world of theological thought.[187]

Crenshaw has observed that references to creation are rare in the book of Proverbs and argues that one cannot speak of creation faith in the book since creation theology is subordinated to wisdom speculation. He concludes that "creation theology plays a minor role in early Proverbs, a slightly greater role in Job, and a significant one in Sirach" and notes that Qoheleth in this regard is closer to Proverbs than to his near contemporary Sirach.[188] It is certainly the case that creation is referred to extensively in the book of Sirach.[189] But the differences between the use of creation traditions in the book of Sirach and their use in the Old Testament books must be noted. In Sirach the creation of man and the creation of the world are fused together and the creation of man tradition loses its distinctive social implications. The notion of creation itself is also altered through the identification of wisdom with the Torah.[190] Sirach employs the fused themes of creation in relation to a variety of predestination doctrine and as the basis for praise of the God of Israel and his works in nature.[191]

The different use of the creation motif by the different characters in the book of Job is most interesting. Job refers to the creation of the world in several hymn-like passages,[192] but also to the creation of man in a form resembling the psalms of individual lament.[193] The friends refer to man's inferiority[194] in a way that appears to be derived from one aspect of the creation of man theme, and to God's majesty revealed in the created world.[195] Chapter 28 must be regarded as a separate composition, perhaps introduced as

---

[187] See, e.g., the extensive use of the creation motif in Deutero-Isaiah, Ez 21:30; 28:13, 15; Amos 4:13; 5:8; 9:6; Mal 2:10, 15.

[188] Crenshaw (1974 A:32).

[189] Doll (1985:59) concerning the apocryphal wisdom books: "Das Reden von Schöpfung erfährt hier regelrecht eine Inflation."

[190] Sir 24:23, see also Bar 4:1.

[191] Doll (1985:66–68, 72).

[192] Job 9:4–10; 12:7–25; 26:5–14.

[193] Job 3; 7:17–18 (echoes Ps 8:5–7); 10:8–12; 14:1–3.

[194] Job 4:17–19; 15:7–8, 14–16; 25:4–6.

[195] Job 5:8–16; 25:2–3.

a critique of the theology of the friends[196] who indirectly claim to posses
wisdom that allows them insight into things which are known only to God and
are intended to remain a mystery to man.[197]   Elihu refers to God as "my
Maker"[198] in his introductory words and proceeds to say that the spirit of God
has "made him"[199] and that he, like Job, is formed from a piece of clay.[200]
The major point in his speech is that man is not sufficiently wise to dispute or
call into question God's perfect justice and rule of the world.   There is no
great difference between the theological position of Elihu and that of the
friends, but it may be correct to attribute his speech to a later form of
"fromme Naturbetrachtung" closer to what is found in the book of Sirach.[201]
Lastly, the book of Job includes the speeches of God which constitute long lists
enumerating God's creative acts in the past and present. The point here must
be, as in the hymns, to declare the power and majesty of God. The difference
lies in the questionnaire and self-presentation form. A noteworthy fact in this
impressive list of creatures is the absence of man—typical for the creation of
the world accounts.   Clearly here is a version of the creation of the world
which, one may assume, serves the main purpose of emphasizing the majesty
of God and evoking a response of subordination and adoration from the
listener.

    We agree with Crenshaw that the creation traditions play a more prominent
role in the book of Job, since they consistently run through the whole book and
are related to its main issue in a more direct way than in the book of Proverbs.
But the creation traditions appear to be of significance in the book of Proverbs
as well. The creation of the world theme is connected to the value of wisdom
and provides a theological basis for the enhancement of wisdom's position and
also relates this wisdom intimately to the world of man and creation itself. Its
position in chapters 3 and 9 indicates that it is "brought in" as a supportive
argument for the ethical-theological kind of wisdom found in this section of
the book. Comparison to Egyptian instructions reveals that there is no need to
regard the theological aspect of Proverbs 1–9 as a foreign element.   The
creation of the world passages and especially the more extensive one in chapter 8, elaborate this theological aspect and provide it with further significance.

---

[196] Doll (1985:57).

[197] See Job 28:20–28.

[198] Job 36:3, פעלי; Job 32:22, עשני. Cf. Prov 14:31 and 17:5.

[199] Job 33:4, עשתני.

[200] Job 33:6, מחמר קרצתי. See above, p. 70, n. 124. Cf. Atrahasis I 256ff., Lambert-Millard
(1969:61–62), Gilgamesh I ii 34f., *ANET* (1969:74).

[201] Doll (1985:64).

The creation of man theme provides a theological rationale for action in an area that was important for the well-being of society. Since this argumentation relates to the very being of man by giving him intrinsic value and responsibility, it must have been of importance also in in all areas of wisdom teaching. Since motivation clauses are not that common in the sentences, those employed become all the more significant, especially when the reason given is a higher principle and not based solely on the success of the particular practice under discussion. In general, references to the Lord seem to have served the function of providing a fundamental principle which was of great importance in the wisdom traditions. Again, even when this theological argumentation was not explicitly expressed, there is reason to believe that it was more or less presupposed as part of the general philosophical background for ethical behaviour.

We conclude therefore that the creation motif was of great importance to the wisdom traditions represented in the book of Proverbs. This does not mean, however, that there are grounds for referring to creation faith as the single underlying theology of the whole book, for the direct references to creation are few and the creation themes are employed in too limited a fashion to support such a conclusion. There is certainly a case for a pre-supposed creation theology,[202] especially when it is closely associated with a concept of world order. This may strengthen the case for the importance of creation theology, but cannot be extended to the point that it is equivalent with the thesis that creation theology is *the* theology of Old Testament wisdom.[203] A description of the theology of the sages needs to be informed by the totality of theological statements present in the wisdom traditions. Our view is that "creation theology" does constitute one important component of the theological understanding reflected in the wisdom traditions and the book of Proverbs, but not the only one.

5. The concept of God as creator

At this point it is appropriate to attempt to draw a few conclusions concerning the concept of God in the wisdom traditions based on our investigation of creation in the book of Proverbs.

God appears consistently as Yahweh in the book of Proverbs. Of the few exceptions, two are found in relation to creation, where God twice is referred to as the poor man's "Maker." It is evident, however, that this particular manifestation of Yahwistic emphasis differs from what is conventionally

---

[202] See Hermisson (1978:43–44).
[203] Against Zimmerli (1964:148).

referred to as Yahwism. Here there is no reference to salvation history, to God's acting for his chosen people, covenant, etc.[204] Rather, the description of the Lord is quite general without significant historical references or allusions.

The probable explanation for this phenomenon is that the wisdom circles deliberately approached issues of concern from a more universal standpoint. The reason may well be connected to wisdom's international context and the fact that some of the material was taken more or less directly from non-Israelite sources. As we have noted above, this conclusion does not necessarily indicate a late date for the books. This international influence and general approach may well go back to the men of Hezekiah or even the times of Solomon. In fact, a comparison with the approach of the apocryphal wisdom books implies that it is less problematic to ascribe this "non-Yahwistic" and international approach to pre-exilic times.

It is possible that parts of the material in the book of Proverbs originally used other designations for God and that the consistent Yahwism should be associated with a time when these teachings were being collected for use in an Israelite milieu, for example in a school setting. The employment in chapter 30, obviously known to be of non-Israelite origin, of other God-designations supports this theory. But even if Yahwism were not original to all the material in the book of Proverbs, it must be observed that it is very difficult to discern any traits of a concept of God which can be regarded as inconsistent with Israelite traditions concerning God's nature and *modus operandi*. This argues for a view of the Israelite wisdom traditions which regards them as being firmly established within the Yahwistic faith while at the same time being universal.

When we consider the underlying concept of God in the creation of the world passages, it seems clear that the concept of the Lord as the sole and sovereign creator and ruler of the universe is presupposed. Only by assuming this, does the association of wisdom with God and creation become a meaningful feature. One may say that the hymnic praise of the creator of the world is the theological throne upon which wisdom is elevated.

A demythologized view of creation and a distinctive use of the *Chaoskampf* motif implies an established monotheism, which appears to have been a prominent feature of the wisdom traditions in Israel. The fact that no other gods are referred to in these contexts is significant,[205] but so also is the

---

[204] Noted as a striking fact by Rylaarsdam (1946:20), who regards most of the canonized wisdom literature as post-exilic.

[205] Esp. when we consider the use of the *Chaoskampf* motif elsewhere, it is significant that no other gods or powers take part, since this motif in itself is polytheistic.

insistence on the Lord's supremacy over all great powers in the world.[206] This may be the basis for the optimistic and confident approach to the world and its complex reality which is so characteristic of wisdom in the book of Proverbs.

In the creation of man passages a view of God marked by both distance and closeness can be detected. On the one hand, God, in his role as creator and judge, is completely beyond man. On the other hand he is concerned about the "details" of his creation: the harm inflicted on men is taken as though it were directed against him. The mystery of God and the deeper problems of creation theology are hinted at in Proverbs 16:4, 22:2 and 29:13, but are, at least for the moment, covered by the affirmation that God has created all men and has a purpose for all things. As in the creation of the world passages, one can detect in the sentences a sense of confidence and security which finds its basis in the belief that the Lord governs the world in righteousness and sovereignty. The Lord has given man freedom and responsibility in the world—this is made evident by the references to misbehaviour which, at least for the time being, will be permitted to continue, but for which man will be held responsible.

We have observed a connection between the theme of man creation and the Yahwistic traditions in Genesis 2. Also the possible background to the worship of the Lord as world creator in an El cult. Concerning both the Yahwistic traditions and the El cult there are indications for an early setting in Jerusalem.[207] This is interesting, since, regardless of which view is held concerning the original Sitz im Leben of wisdom, it is clear that Jerusalem early became a centre for the wisdom traditions.

---

[206] Ps 104; Job 40–41.

[207] Richter (1966 B:96–105) argues for a connection between the Yahwist and Jerusalem and cites a number of facts which argue for this opinion. Concerning the Jerusalemite El cult, see above n. 162.

Chapter three

God, retribution and order in the book of Proverbs

Introduction

The primary interest of this dissertation is to give a descriptive definition of the concept of God reflected in Israelite wisdom texts, particularly in the book of Proverbs. In the first part of our study we concentrate on the examination of four concepts: creation, the character-consequence relationship, order and retribution. These concepts are all related to the way in which God's involvement in the world was perceived by the sages. In this second chapter, we put the question: how did the fundamental belief in the Lord as creator of the world influence views regarding God's relationship to the world of man maintained in wisdom circles? Did the sages found their view of reality upon the understanding that God directly determined all things in universe including their own situation, or did they also believe that other factors were significant in the maintenance of justice and governing man's destiny in life?

The examination of the creation texts in the preceding chapter demonstrated that the notion of God as Creator of the world and mankind constitute important facets of the concept of God in the book of Proverbs. Though the conclusion that the theology of the wisdom literature can be termed creation theology without further ado was rejected, our analysis of text connected with the notion of creation made it clear that in the thinking of the wisdom circles the notion of God as creator was of great importance and served as a basis for ethics and as a rationale for the pursuit of wisdom. The acknowledgement of the specific significance of this belief in the Lord as creator and upholder of the world brings our investigation to the primary question of this chapter.

In this chapter the focus will be on the way the sages perceived God's activity in relation to man's conduct and fate. One of the dominant thought patterns in the book of Proverbs is that quality of life runs closely parallel to conduct. This view, which is often referred to as "the act-consequence relationship,"[1] is in our opinion more accurately designated by "the character-consequence relationship" since the relationship reflected in the texts pertains more to life-style

---

[1] Koch (1955:1–42), Gese (1958:33–45), von Rad (1981:124–128).

than to individual actions.[2] It is of particular interest to try and determine what role God was seen as playing in this relationship and what conclusions can be drawn from this concerning the sages' concept of God. In order to draw valid conclusions on this question, it must be clarified whether the frequent affirmation of the character-consequence relationship was brought about by a rigid belief in its universal applicability or if other factors may have influenced its dominant role in the teaching of the sages.

In recent years the concept of order has become a familiar conception in scholarly works dealing with the wisdom literature[3] and today it is regarded as almost axiomatic that the concept of world order is essential to any attempt to grasp the underlying thought and theology of the wisdom literature of the Old Testament.[4] The problem is that the concept is referred to by scholars in different ways, at times vaguely as simply designating a view of the world as orderly rather than chaotic. The term is also employed to refer to a world view in which everything works strictly according to a metaphysical principle of order to which even God seems to be subjected.[5] Another matter of interest in this chapter will be to examine the textual material in order to evaluate the adequacy of the view that the sages founded their teachings on a concept of world order, and, if this view proves correct, to define this concept of order more precisely.

One's understanding of both the act/character-consequence relationship and the concept of order directly influences one's overall interpretation of the world view of wisdom. The introduction of a concept of order as well as the view that actions and their consequences are inseparable, both imply an understanding of God as remote and uninvolved in the world, a view bordering on deism. The questions which we are attempting to answer run something like this: In which sense did the sages mean that a man brought destruction or success upon himself? Did they believe that the consequences of actions or attitudes were determined by an impersonal power or by intrinsic necessity, that reality was designed in such a way that consequences "automatically" followed upon behaviour? Or did they attribute the consequences to the Lord's direct response to a man's way of life? The answers to these questions are crucial for our attempt to reconstruct the theology of wisdom. Either God's involvement in relation to his created world is unnecessary except as some kind of superin-

---

[2] Cf. Skladny (1962:8, 72) who at least for certain sections finds the term "Haltung-Schicksal-Zusammenhang" to be more appropriate, since a connection is seldom made to specific actions.

[3] Zimmerli (1933; 1964), Gese (1958), Schmid (1966; 1968; 1973), von Rad (1981), Hermisson (1978).

[4] E.g., Crenshaw in *IDBSup* (1976 B:954): "The fundamental premise of wisdom is belief in order. Implicit is a world view of reality as subject to laws established by the Creator, to governing principles discernible by use of reason." See Blenkinsopp (1983:41-73) for an overview of how "moral order" more or less pervades all Israelite traditions.

[5] Preuss (1972:120–128).

tendent, or it is absolutely central to the process of justice and orderliness in the world.

This chapter will also deal with the concept of retribution. God's retributive role in the Old Testament has been under discussion in recent decades and text material from the book of Proverbs has played a prominent role in this discussion. Nevertheless, scholarly conclusions on the question of retribution in the book of Proverbs have to a large degree been dependent upon preconceived notions of retribution.

The concept of retribution highlights the role of God in the process of bringing reward and punishment to man. If it can be established that the Lord was associated with retributive action towards the sinner, then it is clear that his level of involvement in the world of man is viewed as quite high. But if retribution is a later theological construct without a firm foundation in the biblical texts, the traditional understanding of the so general view of the role of God in relation to justice is thrown into doubt.

Zimmerli and Hermisson refer to world order as intrinsic to the concept of creation.[6] Creation theology is the theological basis of the wisdom literature, not predominantly because of its explicit references to creation, but more due to the fact that its teaching is founded upon a presupposed concept of world order. This order is inherent in creation, since the Lord created the world in wisdom.[7] In old wisdom everything is regarded as a product of this order and serves a purpose in the world according to this order. This interpretation of the teaching of the sages may be criticized by noting that the connection between creation and the concept of order is not by any means explicit in the texts, but derived from the texts' general awareness of orderliness in the world. In addition, when a protest is registered against the traditional teaching of wisdom, as especially in the book of Job, the reaction is against God as ruler of the world, responsible for justice and order in it, not against the world order *per se*.[8]

Drawing a close parallel to Egyptian *ma'at,* Gese portrays the concept of order as the underlying thought-pattern of the sentences.

> Vielmehr wird hier in der Weisheit auf Grund der Erkenntnis *einer der Welt innewohnenden Ordnung* gesagt, dass der Fleissige durch sein Tun reich, der Faule arm wird; und ebenso

---

[6] Zimmerli (1964:146–158), Hermisson (1978:44–47).

[7] Hermisson (1978:44–47).

[8] Job 3 makes it clear that the words of the despairing Job allude to Genesis 1, expressing the desire that the order of creation be returned to primal chaos (see Cox [1973:37-49], Fishbane [1971:153], Lindström [1983:148-149]). But it is evident from the subsequent dialogue that this order is not an entity in and of itself, for Job holds God responsible for the injustice he experiences. There is a certain order established by God in creation—this is also the message of chs. 38–39. But this order is intimately connected with God and his rule of the world. Therefore the primary reaction in the book of Job is against God and not against any world order *per se.*

wird der Gerechte Erfolg, der Ungerechte Misserfolg davontragen. Wir können fast von einer naturgesetzlichen Weise sprechen, in der sich die Folge aus der Tat ergibt.[9]

This order, like Egyptian *ma'at,* permeates every facet of existence, sociological as well as cosmological. Gese points out, however, as "Sondergut" in Israelite wisdom some sentences in the book of Proverbs which he interprets as indicating a view of the Lord as free to act apart from this order, e.g. Proverbs 16:9:[10]

16:9. Man devises his way,
but Yahweh directs his steps.[11]

It might be objected that, contrary to Gese's view, it is not altogether clear that Israelite wisdom shared the world view of the Egyptians characterized by an impersonal concept of order as the governing principle.[12] Rather, there is reason to argue that Israelite wisdom had from the very beginning a religious raison d´etre for its teachings based on the Lord as creator and ruler of the earth. Furthermore, this comparison with Egyptian *ma'at* can be questioned from the Egyptian side as well. The view of the role of *ma'at* in the Egyptian instructions maintained by Egyptologists at present is somewhat different than the views proposed during the heyday of comparisons with the book of Proverbs.[13]

Schmid has made a serious attempt to specify what the concept of order signified in Israel. His view is that there is a common "altorientalische Weltordnungsdenken" which can be observed in Egypt, Mesopotamia, Canaan and Israel. This ancient oriental concept of world order was very broad in the scope of its application, including the areas of law, wisdom, nature, war, cult and kingship, and is designated by the root צדק in the Old Testament[14] which "scheint in ihrem kanaanäischen Hintergrund diesem Vorstellungsbereich einer umfassenden Weltordnung anzugehören."[15]

Schmid's case has been criticized by Halbe who raises the matter of content of the term "world order."[16] Almost any world view, Halbe argues, has elements of a concept of order. The components of this universal phenomenon must be distinguished from the particular view of world order held in the ancient Orient in order to lend any validity to Schmid's argument. The main feature of this latter concept of order—the act-consequence relationship—is of

---

[9] Gese (1958:34–35).
[10] Gese (1958:45–50).
[11] Toy's translation (1977:320).
[12] See White (1987:299–311). This objection is relevant even more for the views of Preuss (1970; 1972; 1987) and Würtwein (1976) who regard the wisdom represented at least in Proverbs 10:1–22:16 and 25–29 as next to identical with Egyptian wisdom.
[13] See below pp. 95–96.
[14] Schmid (1968:14–23, 65). Against Schmid, see Römheld (1989:121–122).
[15] Schmid (1968:66).
[16] Halbe (1979:381–418, esp. 385-395).

such a general character that parallels can be found in most cultures, which indicates that the presence of this feature in two neighbouring cultures does not constitute evidence of borrowing.

Schmid's interpretation of the root צדק can also be disputed. His attempt to provide examples from the Old Testament which demonstrate that the root relates to a particular concept of order in each of six areas of life is not convincing,[17] and neither is his idea that the root צדק constitutes terminology for a particular world order.[18] Schmid regards the book of Proverbs as late and consequently asserts that it has little to contribute to his discussion of the meaning of the root צדק:

> Die israelitische Spruchweisheit bietet allerdings eine spezifische (weisheitsgeschichtliche Spät-)Form von Weisheit, die sich auf dem Weg dazu befindet, eine Weisheitsdogmatik zu entwerfen, deren zentrales Anliegen ist, den ungebrochenen und möglichst immer sichtbar aufweisbaren Zusammenhang von Tat und Ergehen zu behaupten.[19]

In this dogmatic form of wisdom Schmid observes a more generalized use of the root צדק which is characterized by both reduced concreteness and the lack of a specific application to particular situations. The most Schmid is able to bring forward from the book of Proverbs to support his view that the term does in fact signify the world order is a series of examples where the root occurs and which in a general way demonstrate the "Zusammenhang von Tat und Ergehen."[20]

Koch discusses the theme of retribution in the Old Testament, building his arguments mainly on the basis of texts from Proverbs 25–29, Hosea and the Psalms.[21] Koch's view is that there is no such thing as a doctrine of retribution in the Old Testament and that instead "each deed is like a seed which produces a sphere of influence for good or for ill and each deed of man will in the end yield its own fruit."[22] The sages did not regard the role of the Lord as that of a judge in this process, but rather as that of a midwife who brings to completion the outcome of man's actions.

Koch has been criticized by several scholars[23] who, while agreeing with his view that the Old Testament texts contain one layer in which this impersonal, magical, principle of retribution is observable, they argue that the primitive notion of retribution was replaced early in Israel's history by the concept of

---

[17] Schmid is not able to demonstrate the broader meaning of the term in the biblical texts and concludes that the root צדק in Israel became restricted to the three areas of law, wisdom and kingship (1968:171).

[18] As indicated above Schmid is forced to assume a Canaanite background for the root which carries this particular meaning, but which is more difficult to detect in the OT material.

[19] Schmid, (1968:157).

[20] Schmid (1968:158–159).

[21] Koch (1955:1–42).

[22] Gammie's (1970:1) formulation of Koch's view.

[23] See Gammie (1970:2–5) for details. See also the careful discussion of the issue by Miller (1982:121–137).

the Lord as judge and agent of retribution.[24] Pax has also pointed out that Koch fails to provide a precise definition of the term retribution but builds his line of argument upon a legal understanding of the term involving the meting out of punishment by a judge.[25] If retribution is instead defined as "die lohnende und strafende *Reaktion Gottes* auf die guten und slechten Taten der Menschen"[26] or as "the repayment of someone according to that person's just merits or deserts" in religious literature usually by God,[27] it can hardly be denied that the term expresses the stand-point upon which the Old Testament in the main builds its view of the act-consequence relationship. It will be the aim of this chapter to determine whether or not this view of retribution also pertains to the book of Proverbs.

The view that Israelite wisdom was built upon a concept of order relies upon a comparison with Egyptian literature and the function of *ma'at* in Egyptian instructions. The common view is that *ma'at* appears in these instructions as an impersonal principle according to which all things in the world are ordered. Biblical scholars have extended this Egyptian phenomenon to explain the fact that the consequences of behaviour in the biblical sentence literature are usually impersonally formulated as well. The evidence for a historical relationship between Egyptian and Israelite wisdom literature[28] has strengthened the force of this argument, as well as the "secular" character of the sentences, i.e. the large number that contain no reference to God. In the last several years there has been a shift in consensus among Egyptologists on the nature of *ma'at* which has not yet had significant impact on the world of biblical scholarship.[29] Several leading Egyptologists[30] point out that the concept of *ma'at* in Egyptian religion was not an unchangeable one. Over time, this concept changed from a belief in the *principle of ma'at* as the dominant factor to an emphasis on the *will and power of the god*. Brunner broke the ground for this new view in 1963 with his seminal article "Der freie Wille Gottes in der ägyptischen Weisheit" where he points to the fact that from the 18th dynasty onward there is a shift in Egyptian wisdom literature from the conventional view of *ma'at* towards an emphasis on human piety and the free

---

[24] This is in line with the observation by Rankin (1964:59) that literature of a later date may preserve e.g. traces of magical thinking from a much earlier period and that this "is consistent with the fact that religions outgrow and transform, but seldom entirely abandon, former modes of expression and belief."

[25] Pax (1960:62).

[26] Pax (1960:62).

[27] Towner (1976:742).

[28] The similarities between Proverbs 22:17–24:22 and *The Instruction of Amenemope*, in matters of form as well as certain themes of content, constitute the main evidence for these relationships.

[29] Römheld's recent monograph is an exception.(1989:131–150). Römheld finds *Amenemope* to be the prime example of personal piety but arrives at the remarkable conclusion (1989:183) that paradoxically the younger text Prov 22:17–24:22 in terms of content appears to be the older, because it contains no indications of personal piety.

[30] Morenz (1963:70; 1964:42–47), Brunner (1963:103–120; 1980:966–967), Hornung (1973:191), Assmann (1979:12–15).

will of the god. It is interesting to note that the text of Amenemope is referred to as a primary example of this shift in emphasis, since it can be clearly demonstrated that, contrary to the earlier scholarly analysis, it is not *ma'at* which plays the significant role in this text but instead human piety and the free will of the god to act towards the pious which dominate the picture. It should be noted that during the same period *ma'at* acquires personal characteristics, including depiction as a goddess, and receives her own temple and cult.[31]

These more current Egyptological views render inadequate the view that Israelite wisdom took over the concept of order from Egyptian instructions. The Israelite material is of a later date and the shift in emphasis in Egypt would have already been an accomplished fact well before the time of any such influence. It is especially noteworthy that *The Instruction of Amenemope* is singled out by Egyptologists as a prime example of this new emphasis since this text is central to the issue of the relationship between Israelite and Egyptian wisdom texts. In addition, recent archaeological discoveries have pushed the dating of the origin of this text back to a time well before the emergence of the monarchy in Israel[32] and certainly before the production of any wisdom text in Israel.

---

[31] Bonnet (1952:432–434), Kayatz (1966:93–98), Helck (1980:1114–1115). Frankfort (1961:76) regards the notion of an impersonal force as modern and points out that *ma'at* was referred to as a personal god.
[32] Williams (1975:242; 1981:10), Ruffle (1977:33–34).

A. Retribution and order in the God-sayings

Our investigation will begin with an examination of the God-sayings in the book of Proverbs. An attempt will be made to determine which particular relationships between God, man's conduct and the outcome of man's actions are reflected by these sayings. In order to keep the discussion relatively brief, we will restrict our discussion to those God-sayings that are found to be particularly pertinent to the subject.

1. Proverbs 1–9

A main feature of the Yahwistic sayings in chapters 1–9 is the expression "fear of the Lord," יראת יהוה,[33] alternatively יראָ־אֵת יהוה,[34] which refers to the attitude of the wise man towards God and the world.[35] This expression which is approximately equivalent to "piety" appears in the book of Proverbs as a set phrase denoting the totality of the righteous man's life-style. The importance of the expression is evident in its prominent inclusion in the introduction (1:7) and conclusion (9:10) of the entire section.[36]

The use of the expression in 1:29 and 2:5 is also significant. יראת יהוה is paralleled by דעת (אלהים) in contexts which deal with the respective fates of the man who lives according to יראת יהוה and he who does not. Especially in chapter 1, this formulation indicates that the impending doom of the fool is the inevitable outcome of unwillingness to heed wisdom, to receive knowledge and יראת יהוה. They reap "the fruit of their own conduct" (1:31), and "the indifference of the insensate will slay them, the careless ease of fools will destroy them" (1:32)[37]. The passage emphatically places the blame on the individuals themselves and demonstrates what may be called an axiom of the wisdom literature–that man himself determines his destiny in life. The sense of 2:5 is somewhat different. Here it is stated that wisdom from the Lord protects whoever seeks it, emphasizing wisdom's ability to safeguard all who respond to her call. 2:21–22 sketch out the respective fates associated with each of the two ways. It is of interest that verse 22 employs the passive form, "the wicked shall be cut from the land,"[38] to describe the fate of the רשעים in contrast to the ישרים/תמימים in verse 21. The activity of the Lord and personified wisdom in helping those who heed is stressed in this context,[39] while the undesirable fate of the wicked is expressed in an impersonal way.

---

[33] 1:7, 29; 2:5; 8:13; 9:10.

[34] 3:7.

[35] For a comprehensive study on "Fear of God in the Old Testament," see Becker (1965).

[36] Lang (1986:88–89).

[37] Toy's translation (1977:21).

[38] יסח in the second clause must be taken as indefinite or passive to fit the parallelism (Toy [1977:53–54]).

[39] Cf. 3:21–26.

Representative of the instruction genre in Proverbs 1–9 are 3:5–10:

> 3:5. Trust to Yahweh with all thy heart,
> And lean not on thine own understanding;
> 6. In all thy ways acknowledge him,
> And he will smooth thy paths.
> 7. Be not wise in thine own eyes–
> Fear Yahweh, and turn away from sin—
> 8. Then will there be health to thy 'body'
> And refreshment to thy bones.
> 9. Honor Yahweh with thy wealth,
> With the best of all thy revenue—
> 10. Then will thy barns be filled with 'corn'
> And thy vats will overflow with must.[40]

Verses 5–6 portray the Lord as the one who smooths the paths of those who heed his admonition. In the following verses the outcome is expressed in more impersonal terms, "it [fearing the Lord and departing from evil] will be healing to your body and refreshment to your bones."[41] In our opinion this variation in the mode of expression should not be seen as a clear indication of differing viewpoints on the act-consequence relationship. Rather, the existence of these divergent modes of expression only demonstrates a certain latitude in expressive style in the wisdom circles. It seems probable that the two statements were viewed as next to identical by the sages. It is the Lord who both straightens man's way (v 6) and acts as the healer and refresher (v 8) of the God-fearing person. There is a slight difference in emphasis between the verses. While verses 7–10 could be termed anthropocentric with their stress on the positive results of a pious life-style, verses 5–6 are theocentric and built up somewhat differently with the last clause forming a climax assuring that the Lord rewards those who trust in him.

Proverbs 3:32–34 are noteworthy in several respects. In particular verse 34, at least in the first colon, expresses a view which is very close to strict retribution, even using the same root to describe the behaviour condemned and the way in which the Lord will react

> 3:32. For a bad man is an abomination to Yahweh,
> But between him and the upright there is friendship.
> 33. The curse of Yahweh is on the house of the wicked,
> But the habitation of the righteous he blesses.
> 34. Scoffers he scoffs at,
> But to the pious he shows favour.[42]

Verse 34 underscores the teaching of the preceding verses by specifying the nature of the Lord's reaction. Verse 32 simply describes the Lord's attitude towards the two different types. In verse 33 we again observe the tendency to

---

[40] Toy's translation (1977:56).

[41] Reading שׁאֵרְךָ or בִּשְׂרְךָ instead of MT שָׁרֶּךָ, "your navel."

[42] Toy's translation (1977:79–80) reading in v 34 אִם־לֵצִים and Q עֲנָוִים.

express especially negative results by means of impersonal formulations: "The curse of Yahweh is on the house of the wicked."

Proverbs 5:21 is a rather interesting verse, even though it says nothing explicit concerning the activity of God in relation to man's conduct. The fact is that this verse is followed by two verses which give classical expression to the so-called "synthetische Lebensauffassung,"[43] that every act has built-in consequences for its performer, that sin and punishment in the Old Testament are inseparable.

> 5:21. For the ways of a man are before the eyes of Yahweh,
> and he weighs all his paths.
> 22. His iniquities shall catch him [ ],
> and in the net of his sins he shall be taken.
> 23. He shall die for lack of instruction,
> and 'perish' through the greatness of his folly.[44]

The sense of פלס (pi) is "to make even" or "weigh." If the former alternative is to be preferred here as in 4:26, which also has מעגל, the saying clearly refers to an active involvement of the Lord in the affairs of men.[45] The somewhat abrupt shift between verse 21 and verse 22 argues against this alternative. Furthermore, "the wicked," את־הרשע, which is usually regarded a secondary expansion, would be necessary to specify to whom reference is made if this alternative is the correct one. The reference to the all-seeing eyes of Yahweh in verse 21a and the context of verses 22–23 indicate that verse 21 refers instead to actions which the Lord takes in his capacity as judge.[46]

Proverbs 5:21–23 are often viewed as a secondary, interpolated conclusion which was added to the preceding instruction-like passage[47] or which should be transferred to the end of chapter four.[48] The combination of statements concerning the omnivision of the Lord and the impersonal way of expressing who is responsible for the final result of man's evil acts should be noted. The two ways of expression are combined in a natural way in this passage presumably on the basis of what must have been a common theological inference—that the Lord was not only observing the ways of men, he was actively engaged holding men responsible for their deeds.

---

[43] The term introduced by Fahlgren (1972:126–129) and adopted by, among others, Koch (1955:26–27) and Otto (1977:371–400), designating a view of reality where act and consequence are inseparable and comprehended as one totality.

[44] Toy's translation (1977:116). Toy leaves out the explanatory את־הרשע ending v 22 and finds the parallelism to require a translation of שׁנה as "perish" in the the second clause of v 23.

[45] LXX has "observed." The parallelism and the general sense of the verses imply an understanding in this direction. But the parallelism in Proverbs is not always exact and the Greek version sometimes adapts the text to make the parallelism more to the point.

[46] Cf. 15:3, 11 and our discussion below in chapter 4 of 5:21 together with 16:2; 21:2; 24:12.

[47] McKane (1985:313) regards it as a reinterpretative expansion with a Yahwistic note which is absent from the rest of the chapter.

[48] Scott (1982:14, 51).

The wisdom poem in Proverbs 8:22–31 expresses something which could be termed "creation order." The most striking reference is 8:29 which is one of a series of temporal clauses proclaiming the antiquity of wisdom. Its immediate context in verses 27–29 follows a series of negative temporal clauses and refer to the basic acts of creation: the establishing of the heaven and earth.

> 8:27. When he established the heavens, there was I,
> when he fixed a disc on the surface of the deep;
> 28. when he strengthened the clouds above,
> when he contained the springs of the deep;
> 29. when he assigned to the sea its limit
> —and the waters do not transgress his word—
> when he fixed the foundations of the earth,
> 30. I was beside him....[49]

The word translated "limit" in verse 29 is חק, also used in verbal form in verse 27 and again in the last clause of verse 29. The idea conveyed is that the Lord in a decisive way held back the waters, something which is further emphasized by the following "and the waters do not transgress his word." It has been noted in our chapter on creation theology that this term and idea is also found elsewhere in the wisdom texts.[50] There may be an allusion to the same idea in Proverbs 30:4 where Agur poses a number of questions:

> 30:4. Who has ascended to heaven and descended,
> Gathered the wind in his fist,
> Bound the waters in a garment,
> Fixed the boundaries of the earth?
> What is his name, and what his son's name
> Surely thou knowest.[51]

The interpretation of the words of Agur is debated.[52] For the purposes of the present work, it will suffice to put forward the suggestion that 30:4 is similar in thought to Proverbs 8:27–29. It seems probable that the binding of the waters expresses something similar to the חק-idea, that the Lord restricts and holds back the waters. This notion is also found in a similar connection in the *Enūma elish* where Marduk, in creating heaven and earth from the dead body of Tiamat, sees to it that the waters are held back.[53] There is good reason to believe that such references to the holding back of waters are rooted in a widespread and general idea of the creation of the world in the Ancient Near East. While it might be appropriate to refer to this common cultural heritage under the rubric of world order, there is nothing in the texts that imply that here is a

---

[49] McKane's translation (1985:223).

[50] Job 26:7–10; 28:24–27; 38:4–11; Jer 5:22; Ps 104:9 (נבול instead of חק). See Sæbø (1979:145–146).

[51] Toy's translation (1977:521).

[52] See McKane (1985:643–647) for a survey, and Crenshaw's article (1980:1–19) presenting Agur as the most radical sceptic in the Bible.

[53] IV 137–140 (*ANET* [1969:67]).

reference to a comprehensive order which relates to all areas of life in the world, e.g., the relationship between act and consequence in man's life. The notion of God's holding back the waters is restricted to the domain of the creation of the world and constitutes a theologically based assurance to man that the world in which he lives is stable.

Our observations on the text of Proverbs 1–9 can be summarized in the following way: there are clear statements that the Lord directs the outcome of man's actions and that he, or alternatively his wisdom, protects the righteous man from evil. There is also a tendency to express especially the consequences of man's evil actions in impersonal terms which highlights man's responsibility for his own fate. 5:21–23 may serve as an illustration of the fact that the two different ways of expressing the character-consequence relationship were sometimes used alongside one another and that they were not perceived as mutually exclusive. A concept of world order can be detected in 8:22–31 which provides a theological rationale for confidence in the stability of world.

2. Proverbs 10:1–22:16

In Proverbs 10:1–22:16 there are a number of תועבה-sentences[54] stating what is displeasing to the Lord, often found in parallel to an antithetical notion which is declared to be pleasing to him, i.e. his רצון.[55] Characteristic of these sentences is that they simply specify abominations to the Lord, e.g., the use of false measurements (11:1; 20:10, 23), falsehood and scheming (12:22; 15:26), sacrifice without true piety (15:8), pride (16:5) and juridical prejudice (17:15). Nothing is stated concerning the consequences of the attitudes and behaviours mentioned with the exception of a passive formulation in 16:5 which asserts that the proud will not go unpunished. It is evident that the focus of interest in these sentences is not on the consequences *per se*, but upon the theological facets of man's actions—תועבה expressing emphatically the Lord's displeasure with the object of the clause. תועבה is often used elsewhere in the Old Testament to refer to cultic phenomena,[56] though in Proverbs it consistently has an ethical meaning. However, the presence of the term in 15:8 should be noted since this sentences is one of the few references to cultic praxis in the book.

There are sentences in these chapters which more or less clearly state that the Lord is actively involved in supplying the needs of righteous people and in the destruction of the wicked. In 10:3 it is stated that the Lord will not allow the righteous man to starve, while he thwarts the wicked's cravings. The

---

[54] 11:1, 20; 12:22; 15:8, 9, 26; 16:5; 17:15; 20:10, 23.

[55] 11:1, 20; 12:22; 15:8.

[56] Toy (1977:80). McKane (1985:439) refers to similar formulations in *Amenemope* and suggests that the phrase תועבת יהוה "represents a modification of an expression which is derived from international wisdom."

portrayal of the Lord as taking an active part in the process of retribution is even more pronounced in 15:25:

> 15:25. Yahweh uproots the house of the proud,
> But establishes the border of the widow.[57]

In 12:2 it is stated that the schemer is condemned by the Lord and in 22:12 that he overthrows the words of the liar. These sentences reflect a view of the Lord as the agent of retribution. 16:7 emphasizes the element of the Lord's action in rewarding wise behaviour:

> 16:7. When a man's ways please Yahweh,
> He makes even his enemies to be at peace with him.[58]

In these sentences, the Lord is portrayed as a supreme being and ruler, who opposes evil men and their plans while he actively provides for the success and well-being of the righteous. The notion of divine reward is also pronounced in 19:17, but on this occasion it is closely related to a certain class of wise behaviour:

> 19:17. He who has pity on the poor lends to Yahweh,
> And he will repay him his deed.[59]

Standing in apparent contrast to this is the recurring teaching of the wisdom literature that man himself is responsible for and causes his destiny. While the sentences in general stress that it is man's conduct that brings good or evil upon him, a number of God-sayings assign this role to the Lord. This tension is ingeniously alluded to in 19:3:

> 19:3. It is a man's own stupidity which ruins his life,
> Yet he is bitter against the Lord[60]

Part of man's stupidity is precisely his inability to understand that his fate is his own fault, that his manner of life is the reason that the Lord has brought ruin upon him, i.e. that the Lord is the *agent* but not the *cause* of his trouble.

A number of God-sentences in 10:1–22:16 express the confidence that the Lord protects the righteous person and that piety leads to safety, honour and happiness.[61] The way in which these rewards are realized is not specified and neither are their negative counterparts. Again we notice a certain preponderance of impersonal formulations by means of idiomatic expressions like יראת יהוה[62] and שׁם יהוה.[63] Though God indirectly appears in these sentences, they are

---

[57] Toy's translation (1977:314).

[58] Toy's translation (1977:319).

[59] Toy's translation (1977:375). Note the relationship of שׁלם (pi) to נגמול!

[60] Scott's translation (1982:115).

[61] 10:27, 29; 14:26, 27; 15:16, 33; 16:6, 20; 18:10; 19:23.

[62] 10:27; 14:26, 27; 15:16, 33; 16:6; 19:23; 22:4; ירא יהוה in 14:2.

[63] 18:10.

anthropocentric in their approach since the focus is on the character of man and its consequences, e.g., 14:26:

14:26. He who fears Yahweh has strong ground of confidence,
And his children will have a refuge[64]

It is inherent in the aim and structure of sentences like this to avoid specifying how the consequences will be realized. It may be presumed that, if the sages had consciously dealt with this issue, they could have justified their teaching in different ways. They could refer to their belief in the Lord who rules and directs everything and who rewards piety and righteous living,[65] but also to every man's responsibility to reject unrighteous lifestyles and the company of evil men[66] which inevitably leads to destruction. A further probable line of thought among the sages was their conviction concerning the way society works. At least in the long run, society will acknowledge the righteous person while unrighteousness will face spite, repulsion and judgement.[67] This view has been argued by Keller in an interesting article:

In vorliegenden Beitrag möchten wir die These verteidigen, dass der Glaube an den Zusammenhang von Rechttun und Glück, wie von schlechtem Handeln und Unglück, nicht primär auf weltanschaulichen Prämissen (wie "Weltordnung" oder "Schicksalswirkende Tatsphäre") beruht. Vielmehr is er Formulierung und Bewusstwerdung bestimmter Sozialer Prozesse.... Im gesellschaftlichen Leben *ist es nämlich so*, dass der "Gerechte" Erfolg hat, ja es muss so sein, und das nicht aufgrund irgendeiner Weltordnung, sondern als Folge richtiger Handhabung der gesellschaftlichen Spielregeln.[68]

A considerable portion of the God-sentences in this part of the book of Proverbs place their emphasis on the omnipotence and omniscience of the Lord who directs everything according to his purposes. In our chapter on creation we arrived at the conclusion that the theme of creation in the sentence literature primarily functions as a basis for social ethics, but it may also be said that these passages[69] underscore the belief in the Lord as supreme ruler of the world.

That the knowledge and vision of the Lord are viewed as unlimited,[70] extending even to the underworld, שאול and אבדון, is made clear by 15:3, 11. The mythological background is evident[71] and the verse constitutes a signifi-

---

[64] Toy's translation (1977:297).

[65] E.g., 10:3; 16:7; 22:12.

[66] E.g., 1:10–19; 24:21–22.

[67] This interpretation seems especially adequate for sayings describing malevolent behaviour, e.g., 6:12–15; 10:10; 26:26; 28:25, though it may be applied even further, see 25:6–10. Cf. *Counsels of Wisdom* 127–134 (Lambert [1960:104–105]). The problem is that it is hard to provide clear evidence from the text for the plausibility of the interpretation, see our comments to 11:24–26; 18:7, 20–21; 28:25 and 29:25.

[68] Keller (1977:225). See also Römheld (1989:119–120.

[69] 14:31; 16:4, 11; 17:5; 20:12; 22:2; 29:13.

[70] 20:27 may be similar in meaning, though the sense of the sentence is somewhat problematic and the reading keeper, נצר, is suggested instead of נר.

[71] See Scott (1982:38), McKane (1985:269–270).

cant acknowledgement of the all-encompassing power and influence of the Lord. No other powers are able to restrict his activities.

Gese classifies a number of sentences which he views as incompatible with the act-consequence relationship as "Sondergut" in relation to the wisdom literature of the surrounding cultures,[72] e.g., 16:9:

16:9. Man devises his way,
But Yahweh directs his steps.[73]

The remarkable thing about these sentences, according to Gese, is that they depict the Lord as acting against the plans of men and independently of men's actions bringing out his purposes.[74] The focus is on the distinction between the Lord and man—most emphatically expressed in 21:30:[75]

21:30. There is no wisdom nor understanding
Nor counsel against Yahweh.[76]

This sentence is interesting from several different points of view. At this juncture, it should be sufficient to note that the entire realm of wisdom is regarded as being subordinated to Yahwism. The accent is on the sovereignty of the Lord which in turn implies the relative incapacity of man.

One understanding of God manifested in the wisdom literature is characterized by a strong belief in the Lord as supreme ruler and director of the world. Even if he was regarded as responsible for the correspondence between a man's life and his fate, we also note an emphasis on God's freedom to work out his purposes. This awareness of the inscrutability and sovereignty of the Lord must have constituted a safeguard against the transformation of the basic belief in the character-consequence relationship into a dogma.[77]

A distinction between the retributive action of man and of the Lord is made in 20:22, one of the few admonitory sayings in this part of the book:

20:22. Say not: "I will take revenge for wrong";
Trust to Yahweh and he will save thee.[78]

Repaying evil one way or the other constitutes a basic human need which in Israel was expressed in the Mosaic law. Scott regards this substitution of personal revenge with divine retribution as one step further in the advance

---

[72] 10:22; 16:1, 9, 33; 20:24; 21:31. Gese (1958:45–50).

[73] Toy's translation (1977:320).

[74] Gese (1958:47).

[75] See also 16:2; 19:21; 21:2.

[76] Toy's translation (1977:412).

[77] We may say that while Job defends God's sovereignty, esp. in the prologue, his friends build their arguments upon a belief in a coherent system which also includes God.

[78] Toy's translation (1977:392). This verse along with 19:17 which was treated above, p. 102, illustrate the difficulties in following Koch's view (1955:1–42) that שלם (pi) means "vollenden," "In-Kraft-setzen" without any retributive aspect. Here the verb refers to man's activity and the view that he will bring the other person's activity to completion or function as a "midwife" does not fit in. See Scharbert (1972:300–324) for a study of the verb in the OT and a critique of Koch.

towards "non-resistance and love as the most effective response to a wrong suffered." The final stage in this development he detects in, e.g., 25:22.[79] Even if this chronological development is doubtful, it is to be noted that the book of Proverbs contains diverse views on the punishment of evil. The admonition to leave vengeance to the Lord is built upon the belief that he repays all men according to their deeds, that he—rather than man—is active in dispensing justice in his world. 20:22 has parallels in 24:29 (though it lacks reference to God) and in Egyptian instructions, e.g., the somewhat cryptic words of *The Instruction of Amenemope* xxii 1–8:

> Do not say: "Find me a strong superior,
> For a man in your town has injured me";
> Do not say: "Find me a protector,
> For one who hates me has injured me."
> Indeed you do not know the plans of god,
> And should not weep for tomorrow;
> Settle in the arms of the god,
> Your silence will overthrow them.[80]

Our observations on Proverbs 10:1–22:16 can be summarized by concluding that there is great diversity in the God-sayings of the section. Quite a number ought to be labelled theocentric. These say nothing about how the results of man's actions will be brought about, but instead focus on the attitude of the Lord towards certain behaviours and characters. Other sayings simply give the assurance that the Lord will protect the pious. Some sentences were designated anthropocentric because of their concentration upon the character of the pious man and the positive end he will experience without specifying how. It was noted that the sentences primarily make man responsible for his fortune or misfortune in life. There are some sentences which clearly make the Lord the agent of man's destiny, where the term retribution is appropriate with the Lord being understood as the one who brings about both the negative and positive consequences of human actions. Several of the God-sayings stress the omnivision, omnipotence and omniscience of the Lord in relation to man and point towards a concept of God as supreme ruler and director of the world. 20:22 is special in form and content with its admonition to abstain from personal revenge and leave such matters to God. The relationship between divine retribution and personal revenge is seldom referred to in the wisdom literature, thus it may be supposed that they were usually viewed as complementary rather than mutually exclusive.

---

[79] Scott (1982:122).

[80] Lichtheim (1976:159). Cf *Any* viii 14–16; *Amenemope* v 10–19; *Onkhsheshonqy* xii 16; *Papyrus Insinger* xxiii 6; xxxiii 1–xxxv 15; *Counsels of Wisdom* 31–48.

3. Proverbs 22:17–24:22

Like Proverbs 1–9, the section 22:17–24:22 is mainly in the instruction genre characterized by direct address, the imperative mood and a frequent use of motivation clauses. The frequency of God-references is similar to Proverbs 10–29.[81]

22:22–23 are interesting for several reasons. They are part of the unit, 22:17–23:11, which is closely paralleled by *The Instruction of Amenemope* as is illustrated by the following:

Amenemope iv 4–7:	*Proverbs* 22:22–23:
Beware of robbing	Rob not the poor
a wretch,	because he is poor
Of attacking	and oppress not the
a cripple;	lowly in the gate.
Don't stretch out your hand	For Yahweh will plead
to touch an old man,	their cause
Nor open your mouth	And rob their robbers
to an elder.[82]	of life[83]

The Yahwistic theological foundation of the argument supplied in the Proverbs text is without parallel in *Amenemope*.[84] If, as it appears, there exists a relationship between these two documents,[85] it is noteworthy that Proverbs already from the start inserts a method of reasoning which depicts the Lord as closely involved in the case of the poor and lowly. The references to the gate and to the Lord's ריב ריבם both here and in 23:10–11 carry with them the connotation of legal proceedings. The Lord is not depicted as a judge, but as a גאל—a friend or relative who takes up the cause of the helpless to see to it that he receives his rights.[86] The last clause of 22:23 is a pun on the word קבע and may be interpreted as expressing something similar to the doctrine of retribution, maintaining that the Lord will act towards evil-doers in a way which corresponds exactly to their actions.[87] 23:10–11 ends the part of the section which is characterized by a close relationship to the sayings in *Amenemope*.

---

[81] 22:19, 23; (23:11), 23:17; 24:18, 21.

[82] Lichtheim (1976:150).

[83] Toy's translation (1977:425).

[84] *Amenemope* has many theological references and exemplifies the way piety and the free will of the god have replaced the more "automatic" concept of order in the earlier instructions, see Brunner (1963:107–108; 1980:967), Assmann (1979:15).

[85] In an extensive article, Ruffle surveys the scholarly discussion of the Egyptian parallel material where he concludes that the agreement between the documents is not close enough to indicate a direct borrowing, rather: "The sort of relationship that can be demonstrated can be adequately explained by the suggestion that this passage was contributed by an Egyptian scribe working at the court of Solomon based on his memories of a text that he had heard and, may be, used in his scribal training."(1977:65).

[86] McKane (1985:379–380): "The *gō'ēl* is the one who accepts social responsibility for his nearest kinsman and who shields him in his defencelessness." See ch. 5, p. 200. Cf Job 19:25 where Job expresses his confidence that a kinsman, probably the Lord, will appear on his side after all his nearest has abandoned him.

[87] McKane (1985:245) brings this out vividly in the translation "[Yahweh will] beat to death those who beat him [i.e. the poor man]."

The theological reference found in this text, therefore, may be especially significant because of its position in the section. Nevertheless, it should be noted that in this case there is theological foundation of the argument in *Amenemope* as well:

Amenemope viii 11–12	*Proverbs* 23:10–11
One pleases god with the might of the Lord	Remove not the landmark of the 'widow,'
When one discerns the border of fields.[88]	Into the field of the orphan enter not;
	For their redeemer is mighty,
	He will plead their cause against thee.[89]

The idea put forward in 23:17–18, that the fear of the Lord rather than the apparent good fortune of sinners is the proper object of envy is somewhat difficult:

> 23:17. Do not envy sinners,
> but fear thou Yahweh always,
> 18. for there is a future,
> and thy hope will not come to naught.[90]

The admonition not to envy sinners must be an allusion to the problem that at times evil men prosper and not the righteous. Again we find an allusion to the awareness among the sages of the complexity in the relationship between life-style and fate. The basic belief in the character-consequence relationship was neither unproblematic nor completely optimistic.[91] The meaning of the second clause—literally: "but rather (envy) the fear of the Lord,"—is problematic because the verb, קנא (pi), must do double duty in both clauses. The problem is that the verb in this kind of construction normally has a negative connotation[92] and that the verbless clause needs an insertion to make sense: *envy those who live a life characterized by* the fear of the Lord. Another possibility which yields a similar result is to regard יראת as a collective term for a concrete subject, equivalent to יראי, as the antithesis of חטאים in the first clause.[93] A third possibility is to make an emendation to ירא את־יהוה, "fear thou Yahweh."[94] The possibility cannot be excluded, however, that the MT should be retained with "the fear of the Lord" standing both as an antithesis to the life-style of the sinner,[95] and specifying the object, the goal, to be pursued above all else. This sort of usage would be in line with the use of the idiom

---

[88] Lichtheim (1976:152).

[89] Toy (1977:431). Cf. 24:19–20. MT has נבול עולם, ancient landmark, in 23:10a, but the parallelism as well as the correspondence to *Amenemope* favours נבול אלמנה, though it should be noted that the MT alternative occurs in the identical 22:28a.

[90] Toy's translation (1977:434).

[91] "Optimism" is used in scholarly literature on wisdom to designate a world governed by reason and morality, which can be understood and trusted, see, e.g., Rylaarsdam (1946:47).

[92] Toy (1977:434).

[93] See McKane (1985:387).

[94] Toy (1977:434).

[95] See Plöger (1984:274) on the verb קנא.

elsewhere to denote piety and the totality of a pious life in contrast to wickedness and foolishness. Verse 18 indicates that the life of the sinner will be cut
off while there is an אחרית, a future, for the pious. אחרית is paralleled by תקוה,
hope, both signifying a good end in life. Even if at a certain point the pious
man may experience trouble and doubt the value of his manner of life, he is
assured that the ultimate outcome will be to his advantage. The character-
consequence relationship is affirmed in such instances, but it should be noted
that the argument is built upon a knowledge and awareness that one's situation
in life does not always corresponds to what one might expect on the basis of
manner of life. Here, as elsewhere in the book, it is clear that the character-
consequence relationship, at least in a short perspective, did not constitute an
unquestionable dogma in wisdom but was, in fact, qualified by an awareness of
the complexity of the issues and phenomena involved.[96]

The most feasible interpretation of 24:11–12 is that they describe innocent
people who have been unjustly condemned to death[97] and that the saying therefore contains thematic parallels to 22:22–23. Thus man's action, not the
Lord's, is the main focus of these verses. The point of the saying is that the
omniscient Lord is not fooled by the man who shuts his eyes and tries to argue
that he was not aware of the injustice. The Lord will repay, שוב (hi), him for
his sins of omission.

> 24:11. Deliver those who are taken to death,
> Save those who are tottering to slaughter.
> 12. If thou say: "'I' did not know this,"
> He who weighs hearts, does he not perceive?
> He who observes thy soul, does he not know?
> And will he not requite every man according to his deeds?[98]

The subject of requite, שוב (hi),[99] can be none other than the Lord and the verb
expresses his active dealings with passive observers of the injustice. While
22:22–23 and 23:10–11 emphasized the active role of the Lord himself for the
sake of the weak party, the passage before us now is a theological argument
for human involvement. Again, the active concern of the Lord over the injustices of his world and the awareness that justice is not always accomplished are

---

[96] See, e.g., 10:24–25; 13:7; 14:12 (=16:25); 14:31; 16:2, 4–5; 17:5; 19:1; 20:9, 15, 22; 21:2, 6;
24:11–12, 16; 28:6, 29:2. See Gladson (1978:156–261).

[97] Toy (1977:445), McKane (1985:401–402). See below pp. 147, 197–198, 200.

[98] Toy's translation (1977:445–446).

[99] This verb and שלם (pi) are discussed by Koch (1955:5, 9), who is of the opinion that none of them
signify divine retribution, but rather that the built-in consequences of actions return upon the doer.
There is some truth in the latter part since the whole book is more or less based upon a close relationship
between act/character and consequence. In this passage it is explicitly stated that man will be requited
according to his deeds; note, however, the indefiniteness of the plural. Nevertheless, it is difficult to
deny the active role of the Lord in this process. The two former questions climax in the third with an
emphasis that makes it highly improbable that the role of the Lord can be reduced to that of a "midwife"
(Koch [1955:5]).

noteworthy. The depiction of God is characterized by closeness and involvement, especially in the situation of the weak and helpless.

24:17–18 are also of interest for our discussion. The stated reason for not gloating at the fall of the enemy is somewhat remarkable—it is not out of compassion for the enemy, but out of fear that the Lord will be displeased by the gloating and turn, שוב (hi), his anger from the enemy. The ethical implications of such a statement may disturb the modern reader, but the idea that the Lord disapproves of such malicious joy is the key here. There may even be an indication that the Lord will turn his anger against the gloater.[100] Even if this is not the case, there is reason to believe that this prohibition is grounded in an awareness of human corruptibility and the view that humility is quintessential to the character of the wise.[101] It should be noted that this saying brings the sovereignty and free will of the Lord into relief. He is depicted as free to impart destruction on man or rescue him from it, sometimes in a manner which, at least to modern man, appears arbitrary.

It is remarkable that in this short section there are at least five sayings that have a distinctive bearing on the subject of our investigation. The concept of the Lord found in these sayings is characterized by involvement, concern and activity in relation to man's destiny in life. These sayings also disclose a deep awareness of the complexity of the character-consequence relationship. Without diverging from this basic "order" of understanding, several sayings demonstrate the consciousness that man's situation may not always correspond to his manner of life.

4. Proverbs 25–29

Proverbs 25–29 are of special interest in relation to the concepts of order and retribution since these chapters are generally supposed to be the oldest section in the book. They are also supposed to contain the clearest evidence of a secular stand-point and a concept of order which is used where we might otherwise expect references to Yahwism as the theological foundation for the arguments. It is also from these chapters that Koch draws examples which he claims indicate the presence of a concept of actions with built-in consequences instead of divine retribution.[102] The variance in form between chapters 25–27 and chapters 28–29 has been noted above and may be an indication of the originally heterogeneous character of this section. The God-references in Proverbs 25–29 may be few, but they are of special significance in the attempt to provide a more accurate interpretation of such a hotly debated key corpus in the wisdom literature.

---

[100] Toy (1977:448), who argues that the full form of the expression is that the Lord will turn, שוב (hi), his anger from the enemy *to you*, i.e. the gloater.

[101] See, e.g., 11:31; 15:33; 20:9.

[102] Koch (1955:2–10).

Scott's view that 25:21–22 represents the final step towards a view where non-resistance and love constitute the most effective response to a wrong suffered has been mentioned.[103]

> 25:21. If thine enemy be hungry, give him to eat,
> And if he be thirsty, give him to drink;
> 22. For thou wilt heap coals of fire on his head,
> and Yahweh will reward thee.[104]

The longer unit stands out from the context.[105] The main crux is how to interpret the metaphor of heaping hot embers on the head of one's enemy, i.e. the person who hates you," שׂנַאֲךָ. There are three possible alternatives. "Hot embers" may refer to future punishment, and in this case showing kindness towards an enemy is perhaps a way of liberating oneself from the desire for vengeance by leaving the issue of punishment in the hands of the Lord. The second alternative is that "hot embers" refers to the psychological character of the feelings of remorse and contrition which an enemy will naturally experience in the face of kindness. In addition, this psychological reaction could lead to the healing of the relationship.[106] The third alternative is a variant of the former—that this metaphor is derived from an Egyptian repentance ritual which was known to signify repentance in Israel as well.[107]

It seems probable that this sentence constitutes a parallel to 20:22, the main point of both passages being that retribution is the Lord's prerogative. While showing kindness towards a hateful person may evoke contrition and reconciliation, it nevertheless seems doubtful that the figure of hot embers would be associated with pains of remorse.[108] Furthermore, the idea of acting in a way calculated to evoke an enemy's remorse is not attested elsewhere in the book and would be unique in the sentence literature.[109] The hot embers may instead signify the intensification of the enemy's hatred when provocation is met with kindness, and the consequent, heightened guilt when his unwillingness to be reconciled is demonstrated. The main, twofold point of this sentence appears to be the promotion of a conciliatory behaviour and the affirmation that the Lord rewards, שׁלם (pi), him who refrains from seeking vengeance by even repaying good with evil. In which way the other party will react or be punished for his attitude is veiled in the ambiguous figure of the hot embers.

---

[103] See above, pp. 104–105.

[104] Toy's translation (1977:468).

[105] Longer sentences consisting of more than two members exist in the sentence literature in limited numbers. The structure of 25:21–22 is comprised of two conditional clauses followed by imperatives which in turn are followed by two motive clauses.

[106] Toy (1977:468), McKane (1985:591–592). Cf. *Ptahhotep*, maxim 33 (Lichtheim [1975:72]), *Amenemope* v 1–6 (Lichtheim [1976:150], *Counsels of Wisdom* 41–42 (Lambert [1960:100–101]).

[107] Morenz (1953:187–192), Klassen (1962-3) 343–344, Scott (1982:156).

[108] See Ps 140:11.

[109] Cf 1 Sam 24:17–20 where David's goodness calls forth feelings of remorse in Saul. Also Ex 23:4–5 though nothing is indicated concerning the enemy's reaction.

The understanding of God alluded to here, as in 20:22, is one which depicts him as in supreme control of the situation, who knows and rewards wise behaviour.

Similar antithetical clauses are also found as the second members of the sentences in 28:25 and 29:25. These expressions are formulated in the passive: the person who trusts in the Lord will be protected or satisfied. These descriptions of the wise and righteous person's manner of life and its consequences are contrasted to the problems of the greedy person and the "man-fearer." The passive construction following the description of the wise man in idiomatic expressions, in this case בוטח על/ב יהוה, has been observed previously. The emphasis of the clause is not on how or by whom the outcome will be accomplished, but rather on the totality of alternate life-styles and their ultimate ends. It is of interest to observe the first clause of each sentence, especially 28:25: "A greedy man stirs up strife."[110] This exemplifies the way that a certain manner of life produces a reaction from society, from people who surround the greedy man. In a sense, the attitude of greed has built-in consequences, it evokes contention from others. Here is an observation of the particular way in which society reacts to certain behaviours, what might be termed the social aspect of the concept of order. The same interpretation can be applied to 29:25.

The legal connotations are prominent in the depiction of the Lord in 29:26 where he appears in the garb of a judge pronouncing justice, משפט:

29:26. Many court a ruler's favour,
but it is from Yahweh that one gets justice[111]

This sentence is to be understood as antithetical, expressing the moral contrast between a ruler and the Lord, without giving specific, practical advice to repudiate the court proceedings of the royal palace. The antithetical relationship is between the *limitation* of the worldly ruler and the *sovereignty* of the Lord, the one who has the power to ensure that משפט is carried out. 21:1 can be referred to as a possible parallel:

21:1. Like watercourses is a king's heart in the hands of Yahweh–
Whither he will he turns it.[112]

These two sentences emphasize the Lord's supremacy with the implication that he is able to work out his purposes through or even despite his worldly representative. This view corresponds with Humphreys' conclusions on the royal sayings in Proverbs 10–29—that in Israel one did not immediately infer that the king's and the Lord's will were identical.[113]

---

[110] Toy's translation (1977:505).
[111] McKane's translation (1985:257).
[112] Toy's translation (1977:398).
[113] Humphreys (1978:186–187). See also Gese's comments (1958:48–49) to 21:1 and 25:2.

Proverbs 25–29 contain a limited number of God-references. We have noted that 25:21–22, like 20:22 in our previous discussion, is significant for its expression of profound confidence in the justice and power of the Lord in retribution. In 28:25 and 29:25 the Yahwistic elements are idiomatic expressions which serve to specify piety which means that these sayings are more anthropocentric than theological. One passage where juridical imagery is used to describe God is 29:26. In this case, the Lord is depicted as the sovereign judge elevated beyond comparison to any worldly ruler.

5. Conclusions concerning retribution and order in the God-sayings

Our investigation of the God-sayings in the book of Proverbs in relation to the concepts of order and retribution and divine involvement, demonstrates that the material is not uniform. These sayings at times refer very specifically to the Lord executing retribution, punishing and rewarding men on the basis of their life-style. But a large number of the sayings do not specify the way the outcome of a person's life-style will be brought about; it just states or implies what the end result will be.

The observation was made that especially the negative consequences of man's actions tend to be formulated in the passive without specifying any agent or detailing a course of events. This sort of practice may have been an attempt to deliberately leave open the question of specifically how such retribution would befall the evil or ignorant. Part of the reason may also be that these sentences intentionally emphasize the present importance of making a *choice* between the alternative life-styles, rather than the *processes* which brings about their respective outcomes. The difference in outcome was included mainly for pedagogical reasons.

In the sections characterized by the instruction genre we noted several passages expressing the complexities of the act-consequence relationship. Among these, there are several especially noteworthy examples in the short section 22:17–24:22. Part of the explanation for the special character of these passages may be potentiality of the genre. The shorter sentence genre is by nature more limited to the expression of "simple" truths while longer units allow more extended discussion of the complex issues of life. The instruction genre was a more appropriate and powerful means for presenting subtle or detailed philosophical discussions. The sentence genre was to a higher degree suited to pithy statements and the formulation of the "rules" which in effect give a general application to observations, traditions, and, to a lesser extent, philosophical reasoning.

A number of the God-sayings, especially in the sentence literature, express the sovereignty of the Lord—his omnivision, his omnipotence, his omniscience and his ability to direct everything according to his purposes. Nothing is usually said about his activity, but there is good reason to assume that these sayings played an important role in providing the confidence that ultimately justice would be done and men rewarded according to their life-style.

The conclusion to be drawn in relation to the question before us is that the God-sayings underline the assertion of the wisdom literature that there is a close relationship between life-style and fate in the world of men. The God-sayings contribute to this emphasis by stressing the Lord's active role in ascertaining and carrying out justice and retribution.

B. Retribution and order in other sayings of the book

We will now continue our investigation with a treatment of the concepts of order and retribution in the sayings of the book of Proverbs which contain no direct theological reference. Since most of the sentences (ca 90 %) in the book are of this type, our discussion will have to be restricted to a number of representative sayings that in some way relate to the character-consequence relationship and play a primary role in the scholarly discussion on the subject.

1. Proverbs 1–9

The discussion on the concept of order has mainly been concentrated on the sentence literature of the book of Proverbs which has been regarded by scholars as older, mainly secular in character and representing an early tradition of wisdom in Israel, which built its teachings consistently upon a concept of order. The longer units in Proverbs 1–9 have been seen as later, less "original," and representing in theology as well as form a later development of the sentence literature.[114] However, since there is no longer any unequivocal reason for considering this part of the book to be younger than the subsequent chapters, it is certainly relevant to examine these chapters for an understanding of the concepts of order and retribution in the book of Proverbs.

The first instruction constitutes a warning against fraternizing with violent and evil men and concludes with the statement that these men will suffer the same fate that they inflicted upon others. The correspondence is made clear by the use of the same verbs in verses 11 and 18. Those who lay an ambush for blood and waylay the innocent (v 11), unknowingly lay an ambush for their own blood and waylay their own lives (v 18). The teaching is summarized in verse 19:

> 1:19. Such is the 'fate' of all who by violence seek gain:
> It destroys the lives of its possessors.[115]

Verse 19 is a typical example of the way in which the close relationship between act and consequence was discussed in Hebrew wisdom teaching. No indication is given of the way the destruction will come about.

The description of evil men in 1:8–19 has a parallel in 2:12–15[116] which is followed by the characterization of the "strange woman," אשה זרה/נכריה,[117]

---

[114] See, e.g., Scott (1982:XXV–XL).

[115] Toy's translation (1977:13). "Fate" corresponds to MT ארחות, ways, which can be emended to אחרית, end.

[116] See also 4:14–17, 22:24–25.

[117] See McKane (1985:285–288 and following pertinent passages) for a balanced discussion of the identity of the woman.

whose company also is to be avoided since it brings nothing but death.[118] In chapter 2 the Lord's wisdom plays an active role in saving those who keep away from bad company. The passive description of the fate of the wicked has been observed previously. The same sense is brought out in the passive descriptions in 2:22 and 1:32 as well as in 1:18–19 which stresses the self-destructiveness of violence and greed. The evil-doers bring upon themselves destruction—the question left open is how wisdom teachers thought the destruction would take place. The Lord and his wisdom can save from destruction, but where does the destruction come from?

In 3:21–26 it is stated that the person who gives heed to instruction will be safe in every circumstance. Before the God-reference in verse 26 we find the following assurance to that effect:

3:25. Thou wilt not fear the calamity that befalls the 'foolish,'
Nor the storm that strikes the wicked;....[119]

The idea is that terror and destruction will befall the wicked[120] while again it is stressed that the wise and righteous will be protected. These sayings reflect a view of the world as dangerous and frightening, where wisdom and a righteous life are needed to safe-guard man from the ever-present threats to life. In this connection we should note the absence in Hebrew wisdom of a magical thought pattern, which could have been expected with this view of the world as full of threats and dangers. The common role of wisdom and the Lord as protectors of the wise from destruction merits consideration here as well. The very fact that the wise stand in need of protection demonstrates that the world-view of wisdom was not naive in its optimism. In a world full of threats and danger the wise man is able to live in security and safety from the terror of evil,[121] but only because he is protected. Underlying such assurances we catch a glimpse of the insecurity and instability which marked a small country where disasters of war, famine, wild animals, etc, continually threatened the existence of its inhabitants. Under these circumstances security and safety were of primary importance and a natural part of religion.

In chapter 6 there are several passages that relate to our subject. One is the pericope on the ant and the lazy man (vv 6–11) which implicitly asserts that the lazy man bears sole responsibility for his impending doom expressed in the words that poverty will suddenly fall upon him like a runner or a warrior. No other cause needs to be inferred, the man's lack of action necessarily leads to

---

[118] Cf the similarity in vocabulary with 5:5–6 where the woman is called זרה, with 7:27 which is the conclusion of a passage where she is simply called אשה, and 9:18 which concludes the description of Lady Folly's invitation, setting it into contrast with Lady Wisdom's invitation. Cf also 23:26–28.

[119] Toy's translation (1977:73). Toy emends MT פחד פתאם, sudden terror, to פחד פתאים, terror of the foolish, which is possible, but not necessary even if 1:22, 26–27 are taken into account.

[120] See 1:26–27 for similar imagery.

[121] Cf., e.g., 1:33.

his poverty. This passage poignantly and humorously illustrates the emphasis the sages did place on the responsibility of an individual for his own fate.

Another passage in chapter 6 describes a mischief-maker, 6:12–15, a person who makes a nuisance of himself by sowing discord and treacherous scheming. His end is described with the following words:

> 6:15. Therefore of a sudden shall calamity strike him,
> Suddenly shall he be crushed, and that without remedy.[122]

Again no indication is given of how the calamity will come about. In this case one should probably assume that the text contains a veiled warning to the effect that this kind of behaviour will provoke a reaction in the community with dire consequences for the mischief-maker, but nothing in the text proves this assumption.

Of prime interest for our study are the passages warning against adultery (esp. 6:20–35). These warnings are motivated in a number of different ways. In chapter 2, it is pointed out that adultery leads to death, in chapter 5 that it brings poverty.[123] In 6:29 it is simply stated in the passive voice that adulterers will not go unpunished, while verse 34 refers to the terrifying vengeance of the husband. Thus even within this one text different methods are used to refer to the destruction which descends upon the unwise and the wrong-doer. It may well be that these different ways of expression all lay within a range of alternatives concerning the outcome for the wrong-doer. The important matter for the sages was to affirm the view that men are responsible for their way of life and must face the consequences. We find that the firm belief in the close relationship between act/character and consequence and its frequent assertion was built upon several factors, such as experience and observation,[124] traditional norms,[125] God's will and involvement, and, lastly, the didactic function of the sayings to advocate the ethics of the sages.

Proverbs 1–9 contains several intriguing passages that are relevant to our investigation of the concepts of retribution and order in the book. These sayings indicate that causation of the destruction of the wrong-doer was viewed in a variety of ways. The relationship between life-style and fate was indeed regarded as close, but the predisposition for the passive formulation of especially the negative judgements neither necessitates nor justifies the introduction of an impersonal concept of order or of a strict causal nexus between actions and consequences. Our view is that the passive formulation was favoured because it left every possibility open for the impending destruction of the wicked. The positive side of the same coin was the belief that wisdom, equiva-

---

[122] Toy's translation (1977:125).

[123] Cf 27:13; 29:3.

[124] Cf. Zimmerli (1964:149–154) and Crenshaw (1981:58–62) who stress the activeness of wisdom search for a structure in the multitude of phenomena in the world.

[125] The traditional aspect of wisdom is evidenced in various ways, e.g., by the construction with "my son" attested in Proverbs and Egyptian instructions.

lent to the function of the Lord in the God-sayings, protects the wise and righteous man from the terror which befalls the unwise and evil man.

2. Proverbs 10:1–22:16

One of the examples provided by Gese[126] as evidence for a concept of order in wisdom is 10:4:

10:4. A slack hand makes poor,
A diligent hand makes rich.[127]

Gese warns against a eudaemonistic interpretation built upon our modern dichotomy between the inner and outer dimensions of an act, and he finds the sentence to be based upon an understanding of the world as permeated by order.[128] Gese's conclusions are to a large degree built upon his understanding of Egyptian *ma'at* and his aspiration to demonstrate that this concept is key for the interpretation of the Israelite material. These two facets of his view, however, may be debated from several points of view.[129] A *ma'at*-like built-in world order is not necessary in order to interpret Proverbs 10:4. We have previously suggested that its parallel, 6:6–11, can be explained as a simple observation of the way a man causes his own destiny.[130] Thus reference to a higher order of any specific kind is not necessary to the point of the saying. The knowledge that man lives from the work of his hands is of such a basic nature that the sense of the term "order," if employed, is so general that comparisons to, e.g., Egyptian material prove nothing.

A considerable share of the sentences resemble 10:4 in simply being statements of what must have been regarded as common sense truisms which were accepted without further ado.[131] To introduce a concept of order as the background of such statements is misleading, since the most probable interpretation is that they express traditional values and simple observations without reference to any over-arching principle. In this large corpus of sentences there are very few hints of a reliance upon the character-consequence relationship, but rather outlines of condemnations or recommendations of certain types of behaviour.

Anti-social, malevolent behaviour is depicted in 10:10 as in 6:12–15, and we may assume in this case as well that society was seen as playing a role in the destruction of a person characterized by such traits. Of course, "destruction" is a non-specific term. We assume that it signified, e.g., loss of rank and position, rejection by friends and kinsmen, or worse. If the MT is retained and

---

[126] Gese (1958:34). Other examples provided by Gese: 10:2, 15, 30; 11:21; 12:11, 14; 13:25.
[127] Toy's translation (1977:200).
[128] See the quotation from Gese above on pp. 92–93.
[129] See the discussion on the concept of *ma'at* in the introduction to this chapter.
[130] Cf 12:24; 13:4; 20:4; 23:19–21, etc.
[131] 10:5, 7, 11, 12, 13, 14, 15, 16, 17, 18, 19, 20, 23, 26, etc.

interpreted as signifying the disclosure of crooked ways by one's fellow-men, 10:9 may easily be harmonized with the interpretation of the following verse.[132]

One of Preuss' examples of "das Ordnungsdenken, d. h. der enge und notwendige Zusammenhang von Tun und Ergehen, von Tat und Tatfolge"[133] is 10:24:

> 10:24. What the wicked fears will befall him,
> But the desire of the righteous will be granted.[134]

This sentence corresponds to our conclusions from Proverbs 1–9 that the sages viewed the world as full of threats and terror, at least to the wicked, who lacked divine protection. The same world view is detected in 10:25 which probably is placed next to verse 24 intentionally. The point of these sentences is not to be found in the correspondence between certain acts and their consequences, but rather in the way in which they contrast the shaky position of the wicked with the safety of the righteous. McKane argues for a Yahwistic interpretation of the second clause by regarding the Lord as the subject of "grant," יתן,[135] which is possible and would contrast with the deliberately vague formulation concerning the way the evil and good outcomes will be achieved.

A survey of Proverbs 10–22:16 shows that sentences, e.g., 10:2, 3, 6, 16, 24, 25, 28, 30, etc., which use the roots צדק and רשע contrastively are often particularly relevant to a proper understanding of the character-consequence relationship. This antithesis usually depicts a twofold outcome with reward and destruction being received by the appropriate characters. This contrasting pair figures repeatedly in the God-sayings and the designations צדק and רשע seem to have a religious dimension. McKane argues that the antithesis of צדק–רשע constitutes an example of the Yahwistic reinterpretation of old wisdom.[136] This line of reasoning seems doubtful, if nothing else, for the simple reason that the sentences containing this construction are so plentiful and appear to be part of the main stock of sentences in the book. Thus it is preferable to regard this word-pair as original to wisdom and as consistently carrying with it a more or less religious sense.

Taken as a group, these sentences outline the characteristics of righteousness and wisdom on the one hand, and wickedness and foolishness on the other,

---

[132] The last word can be emended to ירוע (cf. 11:15), suffer, to suit the parallelism. McKane (1985:423) retains the MT but interprets it as referring to the Lord who will seek out and punish the man who's ways are crooked.

[133] Preuss (1987:39). Other examples provided by Preuss: 10:17, 30; 11:2, 3f., 6, 17f.; 12:14, 21, 24, 28; 14:27; 15:9, 24; 16:5, 7, 9, 18; 17:13; 18:10, etc.

[134] Toy's translation (1977:214). Toy notes that the second line can be translated "the desire of the righteous he will grant" with reference to the Lord, but prefers a passive reading.

[135] McKane (1985:426).

[136] McKane (1985:15).

employing conventional language to a high degree.[137] This means that care must be taken not to make too much of the formulations used in individual sentences. We have already made the observation that especially the negative consequences are often left unspecified. Usually there is no specification of when or how "destruction" will befall the evil, neither is there any indication of who will cause it. Our suggestion is that this vagueness was intentional since the sages assumed that an outcome could be brought about in the variety of ways which only the breadth and indefiniteness of passive formulations could encompass.

Koch suggests that 11:5–6 demonstrate that there is no trace of divine retribution in the book of Proverbs but instead that actions and their consequences are inseparable in Hebrew thinking:[138]

11:5. The righteousness of the perfect smooths his path,
But the wicked will fall by his wickedness.
6. The righteousness of the upright will save them,
But the wicked are caught in their own desire.[139]

The main emphasis in these two sentences is the contrast between different character types and the consequences of their behaviour. The implication is that man has a choice between these two alternatives and that the outcome is included in this choice as part of each alternative. But we hesitate in adopting Koch's view of the inseparability of actions and their consequences. Sentences like these contain an anthropocentric emphasis on the responsibility of man for his manner of life and the natural, or, to the sages appropriate, consequences of each alternative are included in the presentation to reinforce the importance of the choice. It is undeniable that the sages maintained that evil-doers somehow bring evil upon themselves, but the idea that the sages believed that the character-consequence relationship functioned like clockwork is an ossified, exaggerated version of the more fluid view of the matter that one observes in the texts. In our view a proper interpretation of passages like 11:5–6 does not argue for a doctrine of a comprehensive world order nor does it indicate the presence of the view that actions contain built-in consequences. Statements like "the wicked will fall by his wickedness" or "the righteousness of the upright will save them" are better interpreted as general expressions of traditional views which serve a hortatory function, thus promoting the practical outworking of the ethical righteousness of the sages with all its implications. There are indications in the book of Proverbs that statements like these stand in need of

---

[137] By "conventional language" we mean idioms and phraseology intrinsic to the language of wisdom and religion to such an extent that their content did not have to be interpreted literally. One illustration of this phenomenon is seen in the reiteration of identical clauses in different sentences, see 10:10b cf. 10:8b and 10:11b cf. 10:6b, which do not always result in proper parallelisms.

[138] Koch (1955:6) provides several examples in Proverbs 11 to demonstrate the correctness of his view: 11:1, 3–6, 17–21, 27, 30–31.

[139] Toy's translation (1977:221).

qualification in their practical application. The sentence genre, in particular, seems to have been employed mainly to give expression to useful "generalizations" and the promotion of traditional points of view.

Gese provides by 11:10–11 an example that "diese Ordnung ist in erster Linie die soziale Ordnung."[140] The social aspect of the ethos of wisdom needs to be emphasized and 11:10–11 demonstrates that the outlook of the sentences is not entirely individualistic.

> 11:10. When it goes well with the righteous the city rejoices,
> And when the wicked perish there is shouting.
> 11. By the blessing of the upright the city is exalted,
> But by the mouth of the wicked it is overthrown.[141]

The character-consequence relationship is here depicted as relating not only to the individual, but also to the community. Even if passages with this approach are scarce, we may assume that this idea was a consistent and integral component of the total outlook of wisdom, since it is not probable that an individualistic outlook ever became totally dominant in Israel, even in post-exilic times.

One probable example of intentional juxtaposition is 11:24–26. The case for this becomes stronger when it is observed that verse 25 contains synonymous parallelism,[142] which is rare in Proverbs 10–15, and the verse seems to have been placed here precisely because it is related in content to the previous and following sentences.

> 11:24. There is the man who disburses his wealth freely and yet is always getting richer,
> there is another whose miserliness leads only to want.
> 25. He who creates prosperity is himself prosperous,
> and he who satisfies others is himself satisfied.
> 26. A community curses one who withholds grain,
> but there is a blessing on the head of one who sells it.[143]

The above verses have an important relationship to the issues of retribution and order. The first two sentences leave it open concerning the way generosity brings about prosperity, while the last sentence speaks very specifically on a particular feature of the answer to the character-consequence relationship. Verse 26 makes explicit reference to society's reaction to individual behaviour and attitudes. Cursing and blessing one's fellow-men was thought to have a real impact on another person's life, and this sentence demonstrates the role of society in the process of retribution.[144]

The close relationship between action and consequence is expressed in 11:27, especially in the second line where the use of evil, רעה, in a distinct

---

[140] Gese (1958:35).
[141] Toy's translation (1977:226).
[142] 25b can be regarded as antithetical by reading מארר and יואר, curse.
[143] McKane's translation (1985:228).
[144] Cf. 22:9.

formulation communicates both what the person seeks on behalf of others and what will overtake him:

> 11:27. He who seeks good 'wins' favour,
> He who seeks evil, it will overtake him.[145]

The second line must be interpreted as stating that the person who seeks to inflict evil upon others will experience it himself.[146] If this were thought to be a strictly defined doctrine, one might rightly call it an exact "eye for an eye" type of retribution. But it seems more adequate to understand this saying in a way parallel to our comments on 6:20–35 and 11:5–6 and take it as expressing a "tentative" belief in the maintenance of justice in the world based on a complex of ideas: God's involvement, community's role, the good and evil influences of others, ethics, etc. To these suggestions could perhaps be added a psychological perspective which viewed the wicked as persons who were addicted to evil and caught up in its destructive cycle until they were eventually destroyed. All such ideas ought to be included in the concept of "order." But instead of "order," a more general term like "world-view" would be a more accurate designation for this cluster of beliefs, since "order" is associated with a strict view of causation which the texts provide no support for even though the world-view in question is to a large degree characterized by regularity, justice and orderliness.

Another sentence related to the retribution problem and referred to by Koch[147] is 11:31:

> 11:31. Behold, the righteous will be punished on earth—
> How much more the wicked and the sinner![148]

The correct understanding of שׁלם (pu) is essential to the interpretation of this text. First, it should be noted that no reference is made to any actions performed but only to people. This complicates Koch's interpretation of the verb as signifying the bringing of the act-consequence relationship to fruition. The point is that men will be rewarded in accordance with the totality of their life-style, individual actions are seldom specified in the sentences. The repayment of the righteous in this case is probably not to be understood in a positive sense since the point of the sentence seems to be the progression from the smaller to the greater. This is underlined by the structure of the sentence with the same verb qualifying both clauses. The point is that if the righteous man,

---

[145] Toy's translation (1977:236). Toy observes that רצון nowhere else in the OT is preceded by בקשׁ (pi) and understands it to mean "win favour." McKane (1985:228) translates: "He who strives after good seeks to win approval" signifying the attempt to "win the goodwill and esteem of the community" (1985:434). McKane's interpretation seems correct especially since the community has been in focus in the preceding verses.

[146] Cf 12:12 (if the MT is retained), 13; 14:22; 17:13.

[147] Koch (1955:6).

[148] Toy's translation (1977:239). Toy defines the parallelism as progressive—an advance from the lesser to the greater.

who was by no means seen as perfect, is to be punished for his minor inadequacies, the same will apply to an even greater degree to the wicked and the sinner.[149]

This sentence serves the function of underlining the surety of punishment for wickedness and the ultimate triumph of justice. The way this will be accomplished is left open, but in this case it seems improbable that a theological dimension is to be excluded even though this is not specifically indicated. But there is good reason to assume that the belief in the Lord as world ruler and guarantor of justice formed the basis for the belief in retribution and ultimate justice. The most probable interpretation of a sentence like 11:31 implies a background which contains a belief in some kind of comprehensive power or principle. In our view, the Yahwism expressed elsewhere in the book is the only plausible alternative if one takes into consideration both the saying and the broader context of its occurrence in the book of Proverbs.

The security of the righteous in contrast to the wicked is affirmed in 12:21:

12:21. No mischief befalls the righteous,
But the wicked are full of misfortune.[150]

This sentence is in line with others on the security of the righteous, but its radicalness is remarkable. To claim that no calamity befalls the righteous is certainly a controversial statement and may be seen as approaching the dogmatism represented by Job's friends.[151] This radical expression of assurance is unique in the book of Proverbs and the sentence serves as an example of the function of sentences as a means of reinforcing a certain point of view essential to the general thrust of the text, a function which can be actualized through the use of radicalization and exaggeration. Regardless of which interpretative approach one adopts, it is difficult to imagine how this sentence could have been interpreted literally in light of the fact that its radicalness is not strongly represented in the totality of the teaching of the sentences.[152] Instead, it serves as an example of the radicalization of views and statements found elsewhere in the book,[153] a radicalization which during the Old Testament period was moderated by other tendencies in the material and therefore never attained the status of general rule or doctrine.[154]

---

[149] The use of the designation "sinner", חוטא, parallel to רשע, is to be noted. It occurs now and then in the sentences in a mainly non-religious sense, e.g., 13:22; 14:21; 19:2; 20:2.

[150] Toy's translation (1977:254).

[151] For almost identical statements from the Egyptian texts, see Brunner (1983:109, 113).

[152] Another such radical statement that could hardly have been taken literally is 13:8 where the MT can be understood to state that the poor man will never feel threatened.

[153] E.g., 14:11 which is less radical because it avoids stating that the upright will be saved from *all* calamity, guaranteeing only that the dwelling of the upright will ultimately flourish in contrast to the wicked.

[154] The development towards a doctrine of retribution is demonstrated in the apocrypha and the post-biblical era, see Rankin (1964:98–123).

A small collection of royal sentences is found in 16:10–15. Verses 10 and 12 are of relevance to our subject:

> 16:10. A right decision is on the lips of a king,
> in giving a verdict his speech does not err.
> 12. Evil-doing is loathed by kings,
> for a throne is established by righteousness.[155]

The word here translated "right decision" is קסם, a word used elsewhere in the Old Testament to refer pejoratively to pagan divination.[156] In this context, it appears to denote the king's legal judgements and presents the words of the king as infallible, perhaps even divine. We have previously made the observation that the king in Israel was never identified with the Lord. But he is accorded great authority and high status, and to a significant degree the royal sayings employ the same vocabulary in reference to the king which is used elsewhere of the Lord. Schmid emphasizes the function of the king in Israel and the ancient Orient as the representative of the deity and as the upholder of the divine world order.[157] While no identification is made between the words or activities of the Israelite kings and those of the Lord, there is a correspondence[158] which supports the view that also in Israel the king was regarded as the divine representative. Gese says concerning these verses and other "Königssprüche": "Man ist erstaunt, dass über den König in einer Weise gesprochen werden kann, die der gleicht, in der man über Jahwä spricht."[159]

In Egyptian imagery *ma'at* is depicted as the throne of Pharaoh.[160] It seems possible that such imagery have influenced the description in 16:12, but one must be careful not to read too much into that similarity.[161] The statement here that doing evil is תועבת מלכים[162] and that the king's throne is established by righteousness, בצדקה, together with the general ideology of the royal sayings, indicates that the supreme position of the king was intrinsic to the world-view of the sages, that the view of the king as the representative of the Lord was basic to the structure of the world at least in certain strands of the wisdom traditions.[163]

---

[155] McKane's translation (1985:235).

[156] McKane (1985:499). See Deut 18:10; 1 Sam 15:23; 2 Kings 17:17; Jer 14:14; Hes 13:6, 23; 21:26–27. The word is also used in relation to Balaam, Num 22:7; 23:23.

[157] Schmid (1968:83–89; 1974:100–101).

[158] See, e.g., 20:8, 26 where the king executes judgement upon the wicked, in a manner which corresponds to sentences about the Lord's displeasure with the wicked, see 10:3; 15:8–9, 29; 16:4, etc.

[159] Gese (1958:36). Other "Königssprüche" listed by Gese: 14:35; 16:13–15, 19:12; 20:2, 8, 26.

[160] Brunner.(1958:426–428). Cf Ps 89:15; 97:2, and Prov 20:28 where LXX reads בצדק in the second clause which makes it closely parallel to 16:12. Cf. also 25:5; 29:14.

[161] See McKane's discussion (1985:492–493).

[162] Cf. the following 16:13 which begins רצון מלכים.

[163] The royal sayings are not evenly spread out in Proverbs, 8:15; 14:28,35; 16:10, 12–15; 19:12; 20:2, 8, 26, 28; 21:1; 22:11, 29; 25:2, 3, 5, 6; 29:4, 14; 30:27–28, 31; 31:4. It is remarkable that there

The matter of speech is the subject of a number of sayings, e.g., 18:7:

18:7. A fool's mouth is his ruin,
And his lips a snare to him.[164]

The power of the tongue and one's responsibility for what one says constitute major themes in wisdom literature,[165] further stressed by verses 20–21 in the same chapter. In the sayings on this theme it can be inferred that society was conceived of as playing a major role in inflicting the consequences of a person's speech upon himself. Through their ill considered speech and arbitrary pronouncements the fool and the wicked expose their true character, ruining their position in society, exposing the evil character of their intentions and placing their life in jeopardy.[166] Ruin, destruction and similar destinies are given in these sentences as a general outcome for evil, but what these terms signify in individual cases is deliberately left unspecified. The main point of the sentences is the self-disclosure of man through his words and the assertion that his end will be in accordance with his character.

The Hebrew text of 21:12 is difficult. Toy suggests the following translation:

21:12. The righteous considers the house of the wicked man,
overturns the wicked to misfortune.[167]

The main problems are the identity of the righteous, צדיק, and the meaning of משכיל, here translated "considers." The latter can hardly refer to instruction as in the preceding verse but must convey something like "look at, give attention to, consider," "act wisely towards,"[168] or "control."[169] צדיק stands for either the righteous in general, as elsewhere in the book, or is an eponym for the Lord. The problem posed by accepting the normal reference of צדיק here is that צדיק is the subject of the second clause where the character of the action exceeds one's expectations for righteous man. Nowhere else in the book do we have a statement that the righteous man acts against the wicked man. On the other hand, nowhere else in the book, or in the Old Testament for that matter, does צדיק occur as a God-designation.[170] Of the two alternatives we believe that in light of the characterization of the Lord elsewhere in the book, e.g., 22:12 and 15:3, it is preferable to view צדיק as a God-designation and משכיל as

---

is only one royal reference in Proverbs 1–9 (8:15) which in terms of genre is similar to the Egyptian texts where royal references are frequent.

[164] Toy's translation (1977:358).

[165] 10:8, 11, 19–21, 31; 11:9; 12:6, 14, 17–19; 13:2–3; 14:3, 5, 25; 15:1–2, 4, 7, 23, 28; 16:23–24; 17:4, 7, etc. See also, e.g., *Ptahhotep*, maxim 8, 12, 23–25, *Amenemope*, ch. 9, *Counsels of Admonition*, lines 21–30.

[166] See 10:14; 12:13; 13:3; 16:28; 17:20, etc.

[167] Toy (1977:402).

[168] Toy (1977:403).

[169] McKane (1965:68, 1985:561).

[170] McKane refers to Job 34:17b but there צדיק is further specified by כביר which indicates that it is a God-designation.

signifying "give attention to, consider." Taken in this way, the message of the sentence accords with the views of retribution and of the Lord's omnivision and control which are found in the rest of the book.

The close relationship between character and consequence is expressed by means of agricultural imagery in 22:8:

22:8. He who sows iniquity will reap calamity,
And 'the produce of his work' will come to naught.[171]

"Iniquity," עולה, and "calamity," און, in the first clause are close in meaning. עולה is fairly rare in the Old Testament and is only attested this one time in Proverbs while it occurs several times in Job.[172] It signifies injustice[173] but Toy is probably correct in regarding its use here as a term for "moral badness in general."[174] און occurs elsewhere in the book[175] as a designation for the wicked person and his activities, and also, as here, signifying his ruin. This term serves as an illustration of the way in which a word in the Hebrew could signify both act and consequence, thus indicating their close relationship. But this does not prove that acts and consequences were thought of as inseparable and there are only a few examples where it can in fact be demonstrated that a single term conveys both sides of this relationship.

This sentence illustrates once more the sages' belief in and emphasis on the inevitability of the destruction of the evil person. The use of agricultural imagery and non-specific terminology underlines the general character of the sentence, which is formulated in such a way that it is applicable in a wide range of cases and situations.

The sentences in Proverbs 10:1–22:16 provide many examples that point to the sages' belief in the close relationship between the character and acts of a person and his fate in life. It should be noted that this fate is an expected future development, for is not in the nature of these sentences to simply report facts. The beliefs of the sages, as expressed in these sentences, appear to be based mainly on traditional views and observations and serve the purpose of transmitting and affirming these traditional beliefs to a broader group. These credos in the form of short sentences tend to be one-sided, indefinite, sometimes radical and even exaggerated. Because these statements are designed for application to a whole range of situations their vocabulary consists to a large degree of idiomatic expressions and terminology of a very general nature. We

---

[171] Toy (1977:416). Toy reads in the second clause עברה, "work," instead of עברה, "wrath," and reads שבר, grain, instead of שבט, rod. This extends the agricultural theme and gives good sense, but it may still be that the MT is to be preserved referring to man's *hubris* (Gemser [1963:82]). Emendation of the final verb to יכהו improves the sense of the clause, but is not necessary since כלה has a broader sense of meaning indicating end or destruction.

[172] Job 5:16; 6:29–30; 11:14 (in parallel with און); 13:7; 15:16; 22:23; 24:20; 27:4; 36:23. In Job the word is often related to speech, which is one of its common uses.

[173] BDB (1980:732).

[174] Toy (1977:410).

[175] 6:12, 18; 12:21; 17:4, 30:20.

have also made the observation that the sentences as well as the longer sayings in Proverbs 1–9 have a predisposition for indefinite formulations, especially in describing the end of the wicked. Our view is that the passive and impersonal constructions are employed intentionally for the sake of leaving all alternatives open concerning the way the consequences of a person's character and activities will be realized. In addition to the theological side of the way this end was envisaged, we have suggested that society, the individual himself, as well as the psychological-influential aspect of evil may have been thought to play a role in this process. The combination of these facets provides a wide spectrum of options by means of which individual cases could be squared with the act/character-consequence relationship. While our suggestions may not cover the totality of alternatives, the important point is the observation that a variety of factors were understood to form a part of the sages' assertions and beliefs concerning retribution and order. We have also pointed out the importance of the belief in the character-consequence relationship for the ethical teachings of the wisdom traditions. The assertion of this relationship was used to support the ethics of the sages by specifying the rewards of heeding their instruction or the dangers of ignoring and disobeying it. We suggest that this function of the character-consequence relationship influenced the radical, at times even exaggerated, formulations of the sentences. Exceptions to the rule and doubts concerning the absoluteness of these radical statements form the natural background for the discussion of act/character-consequence relationship in the books of Job and Ecclesiastes.

3. Proverbs 22:17–24:34

There is an interesting saying in 24:15–16 which indicates that the righteous also experience troubles, but in contrast to calamities of the wicked they are only temporary set-backs:

> 24:15. Lie not in wait [ ] for the home of the just,
> And assault not his dwelling-place.
> 16. For seven times the just man falls and rises,
> But the wicked are overthrown by calamity.[176]

The explicit acknowledgement that the righteous man may encounter serious troubles is rare in the book. This saying defines the difference between the righteous and the wicked not so much in terms of their fortune in life but in terms of their respective abilities to recuperate and endure. The term for "fall," נפל,[177] is morally neutral carrying no negative implications *per se* con-

---

[176] Toy's translation (1977:447). Toy removes רשע from the text, regarding it as stylistically out of place, a gloss that disturbs the rhythm of the saying. That רשע has been introduced here to define the addressee of the saying is perfectly understandable since the content of the admonition presupposes an addressee other than the "son" in the rest of the section.
[177] In 24:17 also parallel to כשל.

cerning the character of the affected person. Here it must be related to the hardships of life which both the righteous person and the wicked may experience. Verse 15 indicates that the righteous person may be reduced to a position of such weakness that he becomes vulnerable to exploitation and oppression. The formulation of the fate of the wicked is in the passive and similar to what has been observed elsewhere.[178] They are overthrown or, more literally, made to stumble in or by calamity.

The significance of this saying lies in the acknowledgement of the fact that the righteous man also experiences misfortune and trouble. The distinctiveness of the position of the wicked is that they are left to perish while the righteous man has the ability to rise again and ultimately persevere.

A similar line of reasoning is followed in 24:19–20:

24:19. Fret not thyself because of evil-doers,
envy not the wicked;
20. For there will be no (happy) end for the bad man,
The lamp of the wicked will be put out.[179]

Two observations on these sentences relate directly to our subject. First, the saying indicates that there were situations when the state of the wicked appeared enviable.[180] This implies a certain acquiescence to the fact that at times consequences do not correspond to character, at least not in the short term. The second observation has to do with the term אחרית, which is also attested in the parallel sayings 23:17–18 and 24:14. One of the connotations of this term is that there is a future, an end, when things will be set aright, when the wicked will be punished and the righteous rewarded. But this end is not a present reality but something which the saying delegates to an indefinite future. The saying demonstrates the way the destruction of the sinner could be affirmed even when reality stood in contrast to it. This lack of a strict realism served as an encouragement to persevere and to hold fast to the ethical standpoint of wisdom.

As we concluded in the treatment of the God-sayings of this section, Proverbs 22:17–24:22 contains several noteworthy examples of a profound awareness of the complexity of the character-consequence relationship. The parallels to *Amenemope* do not indicate that this awareness derives from the Egyptian tradition. The only conclusion which seems possible is that this short

---

[178] Cf 2:22; 4:19; 5:22.

[179] Toy's translation (1977:449).

[180] The element of envy is not present in the first verb, but the vexation might be understood as caused not only by the acts of the evil-doers but by their prosperity as well. The resultant parallelism is adequate and the sense of envy in קנא (pi) can be retained, cf 3:31; 23:17; 24:1. It should be noted that three of the occurrences of the verb are in this section of the book and that the fourth also occurs in an instruction context. There is no parallel to 24:19 in *Amenemope*, but the verse is identical to Ps 37:1 though there the following motivation makes use of another kind of imagery. All four examples with the root קנא occur in the form of double sentences where the second sentence supplies a rationale for the first.

section originated in circumstances where this matter was thought through more thoroughly than elsewhere.

It should be noted that the short section 24:23–34 contains several sayings related in different ways to the character-consequence relationship: verses 23–25, 29, 30–34. No particular conclusions can be drawn from this fact and our interpretation of these sayings is in line with observations made elsewhere.[181]

4. Proverbs 25–29

The importance of Proverbs 25–29 for the exposition of the character-consequence relationship in relation to the concept of order and divine retribution has been noted in our treatment of the God-sayings of this section.

The material in Proverbs 25–27 shows a considerable variation in both form and content. Many of the similes and sentences simply state facts where any relation to a belief in a character-consequence relationship or a concept of built-in consequences is very difficult to demonstrate.[182] It is probably significant that Koch includes only a few examples from these chapters while texts from chapters 28–29 are much more important to his argument.[183] If a low frequency of God-references is not accepted as a criterion for an early date there is nothing in Proverbs 25–27 which indicates that these chapters pre-date the other sentences. This variation in form and content might instead be used as an argument for the opposite view.

There are more similarities between Proverbs 28–29 and 10:1–22:16. The frequency of God-references in Proverbs 28–29 is the same as in chapters 11–13 and 17–18. It is of interest to note in terms of dating that McKane regards almost everything in chapter 28 and a large part of chapter 29 as consisting of late vocabulary expressive of a moralism which derives from Yahwistic piety.[184] The criteria for identifying late vocabulary can be debated, but McKane's view demonstrates that it is by no means clear that these chapters represent the earliest strand of wisdom in the book.

The formulation of the admonition against gossip in 25:9–10 is somewhat different, especially its argumentation, when compared to statements of a more general character that has been observed elsewhere:

> 25:9. Discuss the matter with thy neighbour (in private),
> And reveal not his secret 'to' another.

---

[181] 24:23–25 corresponds to 11:26 in its use of curse and blessing, but the context is somewhat different. The original formulation that he who shows partiality will be cursed by peoples and nations is interesting—a rather odd expression in relation to partiality in singular cases of legal decisions. 24:29 should be understood in light of 20:22 as an admonition to abstain from vengeance, here without reference to the Lord as punisher. The latter part of 24:30–34 is identical to 6:6–11 and a parallel to 10:4 on the consequences of laziness.

[182] 25:2, 3, 6–7, 8, 11, 12, etc.

[183] Koch (1955:2–4). Koch's examples from Proverbs are: 25:19, 21–22; 26:27–28; 28:1, 10, 16b, 17, 18, 25b; 29:6, 23, 25.

[184] McKane (1985:620, 632).

10. Lest he who hears put thee to shame,
And thine ill-repute pass not away.[185]

The consequences of gossip are concretely specified and affects the person's position in society. The expression of such social repercussions is attested elsewhere in these chapters[186] and provides an interesting point of comparison with the more conventional formulations in other passages.

The consequences of entrusting a fool with something of importance is dealt with in 26:6:

26:6. *A man who cuts off his feet, who drinks violence,*
one who sends a message by a fool.[187]

The imagery of the verse is somewhat difficult,[188] but it is clear that it describes the awful result of unwise behaviour. No other explanation is needed except to take note of the general untrustworthiness of the fool.

The most noteworthy sentence in Proverbs 25–27 in relation to our subject is 26:27 which has an interesting parallel in 28:10:

26:27. He who digs a pit will fall into it,
And he who rolls a stone, it will come back on him.
28:10. He who seduces the upright to evil
Will fall into his own pit. [ ][189]

The parallelism in 28:10 is weak even when translated more correctly "He who leads the upright astray into an evil way...." There is good reason to regard the addition of the third clause in the Hebrew, "and the perfect will inherit good," as a subsequent attempt to improve the sentence.

McKane concludes that "the figure in 26:27 amounts to an empirical observation that aggressive anti-social behaviour is self-destructive."[190] This is certainly a plausible interpretation of the sentence though it does not provide a detailed picture of the underlying thought-pattern. Thus a number of important questions must still be addressed, such as: In what way did the sages re-

---

[185] Toy's translation (1977:460). Toy notes the forensic language, ריבך ריב but chooses to interpret it as referring to a private discussion. McKane (1985:581–582) points out the problem posed by 9a in relation to 9b if a legal process is in view here. He concludes that the verse instead encourages "direct and honourable confrontation" with the neighbour or friend.

[186] 25:6–7, 8, 17; 26:26.

[187] McKane's translation (1985:252). The italics indicate McKane's understanding of the difficult MT text.

[188] The imagery of the first part of the simile is understandable—to send a message by a fool is to cut off one's own feet which could have done the job. The second part , "who drinks violence," חמס שתה, is more difficult, and may best be understood as generally referring to the experience of "hardship" (Plöger (1984:306, 310).

[189] Toy's translation (1977:479, 499). Toy omits the MT's ending for 28:10: "And the perfect will inherit (or, possess) good" as a gloss reminiscent of such passages as 2:21; Ps 37:4, 9, 11, 22, 29. McKane (1985:622) finds it possible that 28:10c is a gloss but regards it as a correct exegesis of the preceding part of the verse, which he interprets as an illustration of "the dogma that those who are morally blameless will inherit what is good."

[190] McKane (1985:622).

gard anti-social behaviour as self-destructive? Which factors were thought to
bring about the destruction?

This sentence is applicable to a wide range of life situations stating that he
who schemes evil against others will find himself suffering from precisely that
which he had inflicted on others. The crucial question here is: What would the
sages have regarded as the cause of this consequence? We do not believe that it
is possible to arrive at a definite answer to this question. Furthermore, the
danger of forcing the complex reality of the more flexible statements of the
texts into a rigid, systematized interpretive framework which is entirely
foreign to the thinking of the wisdom traditions is all too real. We have suggested that the affirmation and belief in the character-consequence relationship
had a composite background of several factors. We agree with McKane that a
belief in the self-destructiveness of evil may have played a part. We noted
earlier that the admonitions not to associate with the wicked may have been
based partly on the belief that evil *per se* is contagious in the human community,[191] a belief which could have implications also for the interpretation of,
e.g., 26:27 and 28:10. If there was such a view of evil the contrary may have
also been held to be true. However, the notion that goodness and righteousness
are catching is even more difficult to trace in the texts. This belief in good
and evil as entities of influence has implications for both the concept of order
and the notion that actions have built-in consequences, though the extent of
these influences should not be exaggerated.[192] If relevant at all, this view of
good and evil constituted a mere fragment of the world-view of the sages, for
the textual material does not give any indication that it dominated the picture.
The texts do not warn against evil as an autonomous entity, but against people
which are characterized by evil behaviour.

The discussion of Koch's views by Reventlow and others have arrived at the
conclusion that the inseparability of acts and consequences constituted an early,
primitive-magical view of reality which has left enduring traces in the biblical
material.[193] While the interpretation of a sentence like 26:27 may have this
background, one cannot exclude the possibility that its formulation is built
upon a combination of theology, observation, tradition, proverbial and didactic
function.

Another example of the close relationship between action and consequences
is 27:18:

> 27:18. He who tends a fig tree will eat its fruit,
> And he who has due regard to his master will be honour.[194]

---

[191] See our comments on 11:5–6, 27, pp. 119–121.

[192] See Murphy (1975:122).

[193] Reventlow (1960:311–327), Gammie (1970:1–12).

[194] Toy's translation (1977:489).

The verse serves as another illustration that the consequences of certain acts were viewed as "natural" with no need of any other explanation than the fact that a particular kind of action leads to certain consequences. The level of specificity varies within this saying. The short statement in the first clause is specific but with potential application to a number of different situations. The second clause, on the other hand, may be regarded as a practical application of the principle expressed in the first. That the person will be honour has to do with his position in society and serves as one more parallel to the kind of consequences noted in 25:9–10 and elsewhere in these chapters.

Koch refers to 28:18 which expresses the end of contrasting life-styles:

28:18. He who lives blamelessly will be kept in safety,
But a man of vicious life will fall [ ].[195]

The vocabulary is somewhat unusual among the sentences. "He who lives blamelessly," הולך תמים, is only attested here and in Ps 15:2 where it is part of a temple entrance liturgy, while "a man of vicious life," עקש (ni), is common in the book. The use of עשׁי (ni) is attested only in a few other sentences[196] and again is reminiscent of the language of the psalms. This difference in vocabulary is paralleled in other sentences of chapters 28–29[197] and indicates for these chapters the correctness of the statement in 25:1 that the following section consists of a separate redaction of wisdom material.

The parallels to the thought world of the Psalms makes a theological interpretation of the sentence appear promising. However, the meaning of the sentence might also be that the blameless are kept in safety by refraining from evil while the person who is perverse in his ways leads himself into trouble through bad company and self-destructive behaviour. We agree with Koch that this sentence does not entail a belief in divine retribution even though its strong relationship to the theological world of the Psalms argues for the plausibility of such an interpretation. However, against Koch's position it should be noted that sentences like this by no means prove the existence of the concept that actions have built-in consequences. The two characters are not depicted in terms of particular actions but in terms of their total life-style. The omission of an explanation concerning the way that these respective outcomes will be achieved does not necessarily indicate a comprehensive, impersonal principle of order, but is most cogently explained by imputing to the sages a deep appreciation of the complexity of the issue.

---

[195] Toy's translation (1977:502). Toy deletes דרכים and באחת. דרכים also occurs in v 6 and a slight emendation yields the more probable דרכי. באחת is more difficult, but may be kept or changed to בשחת in line with 26:27.

[196] The root occurs in 20:22; 21:31 with reference to the Lord and in 11:14; 24:6 in more general sense.

[197] See McKane (1985:619–642).

Another verse used by Koch in his argument is 29:6:

> 29:6. There is a snare in an evil man's wrong-doing,
> but a righteous man *runs on* rejoicing.[198]

The term מוקש, snare, is a favourite metaphor for the fate of the wicked in the sentences.[199] The sense of this trope seems to be that the person is lured into something which turns out to be his destruction. For the wicked man the attraction to—and fleeting satisfaction in—transgression is alluring, but to his great surprise and consternation the whole thing turns out to be an unyielding trap. It is not far-fetched to assume that this saying to large degree is based upon observation. The notion that the wicked man himself will experience evil and that it will befall him suddenly and unexpectedly is recurrent in the whole book and we may assume that every generation had an ample stock of illustrations of the correctness of this belief. Again, it seems probable that the exact manner in which "justice" was carried out was unspecified since allowance was made for a variety of causes and since the key point was the affirmation of this belief as a support for the ethical teachings of the sages.

Proverbs 25–29 provides a number of sentences that have a bearing on our subject. It is possible that 26:27 and 28:10 as well as 29:6 implies something about the way evil was thought about by the sages, but, in our opinion, they must be considered together with other sayings that point to other features in the retribution system. The notion that the person who associates with evil will be overcome by it may be called a theme of the book. The vocabulary of 28:18 indicates a closeness to the world of Psalms and points toward a theological interpretation.

5. Conclusions concerning retribution and order in other sayings of the book

The investigation of a sample of relevant sayings in addition to the God-sayings has demonstrated the heterogeneous character of the material. It is hardly possible to apply any single concept to the corpus as an all-inclusive interpretative tool. A large number of the sentences state well-known facts or opinions from which no conclusions can be drawn concerning world-view or religious faith. A large number of sayings describe the consequences of certain actions, especially negative actions, using passive or impersonal constructions which allow the reader freer reign to interpret the probable means by which it will be actualized. In general the pertinent text material appears to contain only general statements with few indications of any doubts or problems related to

---

[198] McKane's translation (1985:256). "Runs on" is arrived at through a perhaps unnecessary emendation of ירון to ירוץ. McKane (1985:639) regards the verse as a reference to the evil man's attempts to snare the righteous man, but parallel uses of מוקש indicate that it is the evil man himself who is snared by his wrong-doing.

[199] See 12:13; 13:14; 14:27; 18:7; 20:25; 22:25, 29:25.

the character-consequence relationship. One exception is the section 22:17–24:22 where several sayings indicate an awareness of the complexity of the issue.

We have observed that not just the consequences are unspecified and expressed in conventional language, but that the other side of the character-consequence relationship is described in a similar way. In fact, in the text material related to our issue specific acts are only rarely mentioned and instead the consequences are tied to character traits, descriptions of different attitudes and life-styles. Of course, the character of a person was thought of as expressing itself in action, but it is noteworthy that these sayings do not emphasize individual acts, but rather the totality of a person's life-style. This indicates that the consequences outlined did not function in order to cause people to refrain from certain actions as much as they did to vivify the importance of the choice between life-styles, to promote wisdom and righteousness in contrast to foolishness and wickedness.

In the course of this investigation we have made several observations and suggestions concerning how and through whom consequences were thought to come about. It is evident that the sages were not as keenly interested in this issue as their modern interpreters. Our view is that they understood that the consequences could be realized in different ways and that the individual himself, his fellow-men, society and God could all take part. It was also suggested that the sages may have thought of evil and good as almost contagious, as something that automatically had an influence upon any person who came into close contact with it.

C. Conclusions

1. The formulation of consequences

a. The general rule

Our study of a representative sample of sayings from the book of Proverbs related to the concepts of order, retribution and God's activity has led us to draw the conclusion that as a rule the sentences as well as the longer units show little interest in specifying the exact consequences of actions and their causation, even though these consequences are referred to repeatedly. Especially when outcome of evil behaviour is under consideration, there is a clear predilection for use of impersonal or passive formulations employing conventional language, but this observation pertains as well to the reward to the wise and pious man, though less frequently.[200]

b. Specified consequences

There are exceptions to this general rule, examples of sayings where it is indicated how the consequences will be brought about. Some make it clear that the Lord will execute justice, e.g., 15:25, others make the consequences fully dependent on the action of the individual himself, e.g., 6:6–11 and 10:4. There is one example where a person exacting vengeance is the agent of the destruction, 6:34. In other instances fellow-men were seen as playing an active role in the realization of the consequences of certain types of behaviour, e.g., 25:9–10. A number of sayings stress the fact that the wise and righteous in contrast to the fool and the wicked are protected by the Lord or by wisdom from the terrors of life in an uncertain world, e.g., 2:12–17 and 3:26. It is possible that traces of a belief that saw evil, and perhaps also good, as *per se* having an influence on its environment have remained from an earlier stage. It is possible that this remnant of an earlier belief played a role in sayings which warned against bad company, e.g., 1:10–19, and perhaps also to some extent in a larger number of sayings which state that evil acts or intentions will eventually turn back upon those who commit them, e.g., 26:27. Such a view corresponds to some extent with Koch's view of actions with built-in consequences. However, we detect the influence of such a view only in a limited number of sayings and never in contrast to belief in the Lord and retribution. Lastly, we have noted that a large number of sayings in the book, especially among the sentences, are best interpreted as simple expressions of common sense built on observation and traditional views, e.g., 10:5, 7; 25:3, 11. We hesitate in imposing any systematic structure upon sayings of this kind because they must be regarded as diverse in both character and background and they

---

[200] Koch (1955:17) points out that in the Psalms the Lord's activity is much more frequently related to positive actions. This applies to some extent to Proverbs as well. However, the majority of sayings make no mention of God and express both negative and positive actions impersonally.

express viewpoints which hardly can be reduced into one, solitary concept, see, e.g., 11:16; 26:4–5.

c. An intentional openness

It is our view that the impersonal and passive formulations of consequences are a species of deliberate ambiguity with the express purpose of leaving particular cases open for spontaneous interpretation. The variety of alternatives and contributing factors mentioned above, indicate that the sages thought that the outcome of attitudes and behaviour might be materialized in a variety of different ways. An example of this was detected in the warnings against adultery which indicate that consequences can be realized in several different ways.

d. Genre and anthropocentric approach

The implications of genre and the anthropocentric approach of the book in general should also be weighed carefully when drawing conclusions concerning the predilection for impersonal and passive constructions. In particular, the material in the sentence genre exemplifies the lack of specification of the causal connections in the character-consequence relationship. The longer units in the instruction genre—though they make use of the same types of constructions—often provide a more diverse and arguably fuller picture. The sentence genre is inevitably more limited in its range and was employed in order to draw its focus on one particular aspect of an issue, in this case predominantly the advocacy or condemnation of certain behaviour and attitudes of man.[201] The longer sayings in the instruction genre function very much the same way, but the extended context often makes possible the inclusion of details which supply information concerning other aspects of this issue as well.

2. The relationship between the God-sayings and other sayings

A crucial issue in any conclusions concerning the character-consequence relationship and the activity of God, is the relationship between the God-sayings and the rest of the material in the book.[202] If all theological statements are considered to be late additions or reinterpretations of an originally secular corpus, the explanation of the impersonal and passive constructions is restricted to non-theological solutions, and even though the text material contains several such alternatives for individual sayings, the interpreter will also search for an underlying basic concept which serves as an explanation for the totality of the statements of the book. Our view is that the religious understanding of the world in the God-sayings is the best candidate for such an underlying basic concept. To imagine a tradition in Israel or in the ancient

---

[201] See Collins' (1980:5–6) comments concerning the "generalization" of proverbs.
[202] For a general discussion of the issue, see ch. 1, pp. 36–39.

world that was devoid of a religious aspect is not historically credible.
Though the large number of sayings in the book do not contain explicit theological references, this does not necessarily indicate that the world-view of the
sages was secular. It is more plausible that the God-sayings should be
regarded as an intrinsic part of the wisdom tradition and that they provide us
with a quintessential aspect of the world-view of wisdom.

The close relationship between the God-sayings and the rest of the book is
underscored by Gese's observation that no essential difference exists between
the God-sentences and others except for the Yahwistic references made in the
former. Gese mentions 12:2–3 as an example and gives two reasons for not
separating the sentences that contain a reference to the Lord from those who
do not. First there is a "formale Ähnlichkeit" between the two groups, and,
second, the fact that for Israelites there was no alternative to the Lord "der
diese 'Vergeltungsordnung' setzt und erhält."[203]

3. The active role of the Lord

Against Koch's and Fahlgren's view we have argued that a number of God-
sayings explicitly express the active role of the Lord in the process of retribution, e.g., 23:10–11, 24:11–12 and 29:26, though these are not numerically
dominant and the primary function of the Yahwistic references in the book
cannot be restricted to sayings on retribution. In fact, the name of the Lord is
used as often in descriptions of the character of the righteous person, e.g., 1:29
and 28:25. Furthermore several sayings express his satisfaction or disapproval
of men's attitudes or acts while avoiding going so far as to state that he takes
part in the retribution process, even though this must be implied, see, e.g.,
3:32 and 12:22. A number of sayings are significant in their emphasis on the
sovereignty of the Lord in relation to man and the world. The God-sayings as
a whole point towards a belief in the Lord as ruler and director of the world
where his active role in the retributional process constitutes *one* facet.

4. The concept of order

a. An orderly world
The term "order" is appropriate as a designation of the world-view of the
sages. The book of Proverbs in the main believes in a world which is characterized by regularity, order and harmony.[204] The correspondence between
character and consequence underline this world-view and is an indication of
the confidence that the world of men was regarded as being marked by justice,
although the very fact that this is constantly asserted in the book argues that
these statements had a predominantly normative force. We have suggested that

---

[203] Gese (1958:37).
[204] See, however, our comments above to, e.g., 3:21–26, p. 115.

the belief in the character-consequence relationship, though forcefully asserted, was to a certain extent "tentative"[205] and not without vacillation, even though this rarely comes to expression in the book.[206]

b. A problematic term

The problem with using the term "order" to designate the world-view of the sages lies in the connotations: it designates a particular world-view (suggested by, e.g., Preuss) in which "order" is regarded as an impersonal principle governing all things in the world. Thus this view countenances a kind of deism in which justice and order are inherent in the structure of the world, rendering God's continued involvement redundant. However, it should be noted that one could hardly find a view which was more contrary to what we know of the mindset of the sages or the textual material. If one is to make use of the term "order" to signify the world-view of Israelite wisdom, it must first be qualified theologically as the order which the Lord has established and upholds in the world.[207] But there is reason to be hesitant in applying to the material a term which is not represented in wisdom's own vocabulary and which usually is understood as signifying an independent entity which acts on its own. Von Rad's words seize the essence of the issue:

> In view of all this, one must therefore be cautious in one's use of the term "order" which we, too, have felt unable to dispense with in our discussion. Can one really say that the teachers were searching for a world order? Our findings, especially the discussion of the Yahweh-proverbs, suggested, rather, that one can in no sense speak of a world order as really existing between God and man. What could be determined was, rather, that the statements of the teachers move in a dialectic which is fundamentally incapable of resolution, speaking on the one hand of valid rules and, on the other, of *ad hoc* divine actions.[208]

It should be noted that a number of scholars make use of the concept of order in their interpretation of the wisdom literature with the reservation that the Lord is above or independent of this order.[209]

5. Anthropocentricity

In the course of our investigation of the pertinent passages in the book of Proverbs we have suggested that the concept of order or, better, the world-view of the sages was founded upon a number of different premises. Fortune in life and individual destiny were not related exclusively to the belief in the Lord as the upholder of justice and order in his world. In fact the main thrust of these views was anthropocentric, that man's own behaviour and attitudes led

---

[205] Cf. White (1987::299) who refers to a "tentative" order among Israelite sages.

[206] See comments above to, e.g., 23:17–18, 24:16.

[207] See Nel (1982:111–112), Jenks (1985:44).

[208] Von Rad (1981:106–107). Cf. White (1987:305).

[209] Gese (1958:45–50), Kayatz (1966:136), Crenshaw (1976 A:23–24), Fohrer (1969:271–272), Rendtorff (1977:349), Nel (1982:103–115).

to certain consequences. This anthropocentricity is especially pronounced in the wisdom literature but need not be placed in contrast to theocentricity. The important point is that man is depicted as a responsible being who has the freedom to choose between the alternatives of wisdom and righteousness on the one side and foolishness and wickedness on the other side. The stress is on the fact that man, by his own choice, brings about the predictable consequences. The book of Proverbs exhibits little interest in the processes bringing about these consequences, but our investigation has suggested that the sages regarded different factors as being involved in these processes. Man's behaviour, his company, the community, the intrinsic power of good and evil—all these aspects along with the theological angle seem to have been regarded as playing a role in the realization of the consequences appropriate to each individual.

6. Acts and consequences

The close relationship between man's acts and their consequences is in line with this anthropocentricity. Nevertheless, the view that actions were regarded as having built-in consequences, which according to Koch rules out the concept of divine retribution in the Old Testament, is contradicted by the general way that consequences are described as well as by our analysis of the passages that are usually taken as referring to retribution.

a. Character-consequence

The consequences mentioned in the book of Proverbs do not relate primarily to particular acts performed but rather to the total life-style and disposition of the person.[210] For the book of Proverbs as a whole we have suggested that the term "character-consequence" is more appropriate than act-consequence, since individual acts are seldom referred to. Both sides of the character-consequence relationship are in most cases formulated in such a general way, using idioms and conventional language, that any conclusions concerning their precise relationship must remain tentative.

b. The Lord's involvement

The analysis of passages on retribution which make use of the terms שלם (pi) and שוב (hi) is significant. Koch's view that these terms do not signify retribution, and that the role of the Lord is that of a midwife who brings to completion the act-consequence relationship, simply does not convince and must be regarded as according too much importance to the comprehensive theory and not enough to the texts, e.g., 24:12; 25:21–22. Scharbert has convincingly demonstrated the incorrectness of Koch's interpretation of שלם (pi) in the Old Testament and also pointed out that the function of the Lord is not so much

---

[210] Skladny (1962:71–79) and Schmid (1966:162–164) postulate the development from a belief in actions with built-in consequences to moral attitudes that bring about certain results.

that of a judge as that of a kinsman who is affected by men's attitudes and interrelationships.[211]

> Wenn das AT ślm Pi auf Gott überträgt, dann spricht es von ihm als dem Freund und Wohltäter, der durch menschliches Verhalten seinerseits zu einer gnädigen Wohltat bewogen wird oder aber, bitter enttäuscht, dem Sünder "mit gleicher Münze heimzahlt". Hinter dieser Ausdrucksweise steckt also die Vorstellung, dass Gott durch sittlich relevante Taten des Menschen direkt berührt wird und darauf entsprechend reagiert, und ferner das natürliche Gerechtigkeitsempfinden, das für eine "Leistung" oder "Missleistung" einen entsprechenden, angemessenen "Lohn" fordert. Die Feststellung mag bei allzu spiritualistisch denkenden Theologen Unbehagen auslösen, aber sie ist, wenn man unbefangen auf das Wort der Schrift hört, doch wohl aufweisbar: Nach der Lehre des Alten Testaments "bezahlt" Gott menschliche "Leistung" bzw Missleistung.[212]

7. The concept of God

a. Involvement and activity

Our investigation on "God, Retribution and Order in the book of Proverbs" has led us to the conclusion that the world view of the sages was neither built upon a concept of an impersonal order nor of actions with "automatic," built-in consequences, but on the active participation of the Lord in the affairs of men in conjunction with man's own responsibility. The concept of God was characterized by belief in his close involvement with his creation, especially with the weak and mistreated in society. This belief was so basic that many God-sayings in the book simply state that certain attitudes or behaviours affect the Lord negatively or positively, or that the Lord watches all things, with the obvious implication that he will deal with the people referred to in an appropriate way. At times he is depicted as both judge and agent in the process of retribution, but also as a נאל to man. The main emphasis in the minds of the sages seems to have been on the sovereignty of the Lord, that he controls and directs his world towards justice, harmony and order. At the same time, the sayings of the book, and even many of the God-sayings, present an anthropocentric approach to reality. This approach emphasizes the freedom of man to choose his way of life while at the same time making it crystal clear that he will be held responsible for this choice. The tension between the anthropocentric and theocentric approach is dealt with in some sayings which point out the sovereignty of the Lord who works out his purposes independently of man's plans and activities. The remarkable thing about the book of Proverbs is that the anthropocentric approach never collides with the theocentric. The probable explanation is that the sages regarded the two as complementary and not mutually exclusive.

---

[211] Cf. Gamper (1966:216–218, 241).
[212] Scharbert (1972:322–323).

b. *Complementarity of approaches*

Throughout the book, the anthropocentric approach to the issues of life and the theocentric appear side by side. The results of our investigation do not indicate that the sentence genre is predominantly anthropocentric, while the instruction genre is predominantly theocentric. In both genres a fairly even representation from throughout the spectrum is found. Our view is that the anthropocentric material always had a complementary relationship to the theological approach to reality. Even when dealing with statements of common sense, we can assume a world-view which is not devoid of religious aspects, even though the religious dimension has neither the chance nor any reason to appear in the formulations of such statements.[213]

This chapter has indicated both the closeness of the Lord to his world and his distance from it in the eyes of the ancient sage. These traits characterize the concept of God in the wisdom literature and will be further pursued in part two of this study.

---

[213]See Blenkinsopp (1983:42) who correctly argues that the "monotonous contrast" between the fate of the righteous and the wicked is based on specifically religious premisses and can not have arisen out of observation and experience alone.

Part two

God's relationship to the world

Chapter four

The Lord as supreme God in the book of Proverbs

Introduction

The book of Proverbs consistently depicts the Lord as supreme God of the world. There is always a fundamental differentiation between the Lord and man and there is no indication of a belief in the existence of competing divinities. The differentiation between the Lord and man is a twofold distinction relating to both nature and scope of activity. Nature—since God is viewed as infinite and transcendent while man is limited and "earthly." Scope of activity—since God's power and abilities are never depicted as subject to any limitations, while there is clearly an awareness of the incompleteness of man's understanding and potential. The anthropocentric approach of the book ascribes great powers and abilities to man, but at the same time there is a consciousness of God as man's superior and man's consequent dependence upon him always shows through these ascriptions. The contrast between God and man is so profound that one may say that they belong to different worlds. Man exists within the limits of this world while the Lord does not appear to be bound by its limitations. God belongs to a reality separate from and unknown to man at the same time as he is actively involved in the world of men.

Most religions manifest some form of belief in divine beings with certain characteristics which can be termed "supreme beings"[1] or "Hochgötter"[2]—in English often translated "high gods." Research attempting to define the nature of this kind of divine being has found that in the pantheon of most religions there is such a "supreme being" associated with the sky or the astral bodies.[3] This "Hoch-gott" often takes the form of a *deus otiosus* who has withdrawn from active engagement in the world.[4] Pettazoni, in his study of the historical forms of supreme beings, has made clear the ambivalent structure of a supreme being who may also function as the "all-knowing God,"[5] as an

---

[1] Sullivan's (1987:166–181) terminology.
[2] Widengren (1969:46–92).
[3] Pettazoni (1956:5–12).
[4] Sullivan (1987:170).
[5] The title of Pettazoni's 1956 monograph: *The All-knowing God: Researches into Early Religion and Culture.*

extremely dynamic overseer of the moral order, actively involved in maintaining justice on earth.[6] Widengren describes the relationship between the high gods and man by stating that "...die Hochgötter prinzipiell als Schicksalsgötter zu betrachten sind, d. h. als absolute Beherrscher des Schicksals aller irdischen Geschöpfe."[7]

Several of the characteristics of these supreme beings correspond to aspects of the depiction of the Lord in the wisdom literature and the book of Proverbs, e.g., 1) their non-mythological and non-cultic character, 2) the roles of creator, sustainer of creation and guarantor of good order and 3) a transcendental and infinite nature characterized by omnipresence, omniscience and omnipotence.[8] The characteristics of high gods exhibit some variance and it is not our goal to show that the depiction of the Lord in the book of Proverbs is in every detail parallel to this general description of the nature of high gods. Still, recognizing the widespread manifestation of the idea of supreme beings in other religions, including the religions of Israel's neighbours,[9] serves as a suggestive background to this chapter which seeks to define the elements used in certain passages in the book of Proverbs which depict the Lord as the supreme God of the world.

An attempt will be made to compare our observations on the book of Proverbs to other parts of the Old Testament as well as wisdom texts from the surrounding cultures in order to gain a broader basis for interpretation as well as to determine the similarities and differences between these blocks of literature. Such a comparative study should help us to see more clearly the relationship between Old Testament wisdom, the other theological traditions in the Old Testament and non-Israelite wisdom.

---

[6] Pettazoni (1956:20–26). See also Sullivan (1987:179) on Pettazoni.

[7] Widengren (1938:2; see also 1969:83).

[8] See Sullivan's survey of the general features of supreme beings (1987:166–167).

[9] See Widengren (1938), Pettazoni (1956:49–117).

A. The transcendent God

The book of Proverbs is about man and his life situation. It exhibits even less of a tendency to take up "theoretical" issues such as definitions of the nature of God than most of the other books of the Old Testament. This means that one can only make limited inferences concerning the book's concept of the nature of God by investigating the way God is referred to in the texts, the attributes he is given and the relationships that he is assumed to have with man and the world. Intrinsic to the view of the Lord as supreme God was the belief in his transcendent nature. In the first section of this chapter we will try to describe this aspect of the sages' understanding of God by concentrating on three concepts which imply the transcendence of the Lord: 1) his function as the one responsible for justice and retribution in the world, 2) the view of him as sole creator of all things and 3) the lack of direct communication between God and man with the peculiar role of wisdom as a representative of the Lord before man.

1. Definition of transcendence

A simple distinction between immanence and transcendence might be maintained by asserting that the former designates presence *within* and the latter presence *above and beyond* a particular sphere.[10] However, the two terms have been used in various ways in philosophy and theology to such an extent that it is often difficult to establish their meaning in a particular context. The concept of transcendence "geht von der Vorstellung einer Grenze des Gegebenen und Verfügbaren aus."[11] We will use the term here in relation to the nature of God to signify that which to its essence is not bound by, or limited to, this world and its boundaries. When we say that God by nature was viewed as transcendent, this does not necessarily contradict the belief that he was seen as active and present in the world. God can act and reveal himself in the world of man, but he is not bound by its spatial and temporal limitations. Thus it is quite appropriate to say that he is transcendent.[12] The presence and activity of God brings into the world of men a reality and potentialities which exceed that which would otherwise be the case. We believe that this theological understanding is adequate in a reconstruction of the world view of Israelite wisdom literature.

---

[10] Rodhe (1957:935).

[11] Blumenberg (1962:989).

[12] An example of this kind of thinking in other Old Testament traditions is the prayer of Solomon at the inauguration ceremony of the temple, 1 Kings 8:27, which asserts the differentiation between the Lord and the world—here the temple, the point of connection between heaven and earth. Cf. Weinfeld (1972:190–209), Mettinger (1982:38–79).

2. The Lord as transcendent in the book of Proverbs

In his excellent monograph from 1933, Fichtner notes that anthropomorphisms are almost completely lacking in Israelite wisdom literature and that "...die Geistigkeit und Transzendenz der Gottheit ist als selbstverständlich vorausgesetzt."[13] We agree with Fichtner that a lack of anthropomorphisms certainly does characterize the book of Proverbs. The primary explanation for this may be found in the genres and type of material in the book, but because certain Old Testament traditions appear to avoid anthropomorphisms for theological reasons,[14] there is good reason to believe that the motivation behind this practice is the same for the book of Proverbs.

a. The Lord as responsible for justice and retribution
In chapter three we concluded that an important feature in the characterization of the Lord in the book of Proverbs is the depiction of him as supreme judge and guarantor of justice in the world. Fichtner, who regards God's transcendence and spiritual nature as the sages' fundamental assumption in their understanding of God, remarks:

> Ebenso deutlich und allgemein anerkannt ist aber, dass dieser transzendente Gott das immanente Sein entscheidend bestimmt; denn Gott ist für den Weisen in erster Linie der *vergeltende* Gott, der Bürge für die Durchführung der Vergeltung, an die er glaubt.[15]

The teaching of a number of the passages dealt with in the preceding chapter,[16] was based on the view that the Lord sees, knows and governs his world in a way that provides justice for the individual. This firm belief of the sages in the Lord as the upholder of justice and order must have been connected to the conviction that he was the supreme God, above the limitations and deficiencies of men. Only a transcendent God can be entrusted with the "impossible" task of dispensing justice to each individual and situation!

Since the Lord oversees justice and retribution, the passages in the book stressing that the Lord knows everything that happens in the world are of importance. The fact that the Lord's eyes are present everywhere, that he observes everything[17] and even knows a person's innermost thoughts, is stated a number of times and seems to have constituted an important premiss in the

---

[13] Fichtner (1933:105).
[14] Anderson (1962:423).
[15] Fichtner (1933:105).
[16] 3:33–34; 5:21; 10:3; 12:2; 15:25; 16:7; 20:22; 22:12, 22–23; 23:10–11; 24:11–12, 17–18; 25:21–22; 28:25; 29:25, 26.
[17] 5:21; 15:3, 11; 22:12; 24:12.

sages' understanding of God, indicating his exalted position in relation to the world. In 17:3 this view is formulated in the following way:

> 17:3. The fining-pot is for silver, and the furnace for gold,
> and Yahweh is the trier of hearts.[18]

The first clause which refers to the process of testing and refining metals, a well-known motif in the prophetic tradition,[19] is duplicated in 27:21. The point of the comparison between the fining-pot, the furnace and the Lord must be that God alone can fully know what is inside a man—man may know it to some extent, but never fully.

A representative example of the assertion of the omnivision of the Lord is found in 5:21, significantly followed by verses that tell how the wicked person will be snared by his iniquities:

> 5:21. For the ways of a man are before the eyes of Yahweh,
> And he weighs all his paths.[20]

"The ways of a man" is a way of referring to a person's style of living in general[21] while the fact that the Lord weighs his paths puts stress on the fact that the Lord has complete insight into a every individual's manner of life. Nothing escapes his eyes and man is fully responsible to him down to the last detail. The connection between the notion of the Lord as observer and his function as the guarantor of justice in the world of men is here brought out by the connection with verses 22–23, but is implied also by the imagery of the sentence itself, especially by the expression "weighing his paths."[22]

The text and translation of 22:12 involves some problems, but McKane's translation conveys the probable sense of it:

> 22:12. The eyes of Yahweh guard knowledge,
> he subverts the words of the liar.[23]

---

[18] Toy's translation (1977:336).

[19] Isa 1:25; 48:10; Jer 6:29–30; Ez 22:17–22; Dan 12:10; Mal 3:3.

[20] Toy's translation (1977:116). Toy translates the piel participle of פלס as "weigh" and finds it to be favour by the parallelism. The meaning "make plane" from 4:26 hardly fits here since the theme is not the freedom of man to run his course, but rather the Lord's role as overseer or judge. Toy's translation is supported by *BDB* (1980:814) which renders the piel verb the meaning "weigh out" or "make level." The parallel to Egyptian thought here is of interest. Scott (1982:106) regards the idiom "to weigh the heart" as ultimately derived from Egyptian religious belief, in which "judgment after death followed the weighing of a man's heart against Truth, in the balances of the supreme god Re...." This view seems esp. relevant for 21:2 and 24:12 where the verb תכן determines "heart" which better corresponds to the Egyptian imagery than רוח in 16:2 and מעגלה here in 5:21.

[21] Cf. 16:2, 7.

[22] See above n. 20.

[23] McKane (1985:245). The crucial matter is whether דעת is an abstract for "the person who has knowledge" or an allusion to the Lord's superior knowledge. Toy (1977:418) maintains that the "OT. usage [does not] permit the interpretation of this term as =*him who has knowledge*." Plöger (1984:255–256) and McKane (1985:570–571) favour the alternative that here is an allusion to the superior knowledge of the Lord.

This sentence clearly relates the Lord's omnivision to his vigilance and active involvement in providing justice for man. We have noticed that the negative side of this coin—that the Lord sees evil acts and punishes them accordingly—is especially relevant. This correlates with Pettazoni's conclusion concerning the all-knowing god: "Most frequently, it is bad actions which are the object of Divine omniscience."[24]

An example of the demythologizing in the book of Proverbs[25] can be seen in 15:11:

15:11. Sheol and Abaddon lie open before Yahweh,
How much more the hearts of men![26]

The assertion that even the underworld is open before the Lord must be interpreted as a sublime confession of his supremacy. Not even the mysterious abodes of the dead are beyond his reach. Sheol and Abaddon are not represented as autonomous powers or rival deities capable of challenging the Lord.

That God knows even the inner thoughts of an individual is made clear by 24:11–12.[27] The passage demonstrates at the same time that the sages were aware of the problem of innocent suffering, the existence of which implied that justice and order were not always established. The point here seems to be that the Lord who knows all things will hold even the passive spectator who has done "nothing" responsible. This saying has interesting implications concerning the freedom of man and the extent of the Lord's involvement in the world. Man is in a position where he must choose between involvement and passivity. God is aware of injustice and will bring judgment upon the passive spectator and, we must add on the basis of parallel sayings,[28] upon those who pervert justice. Despite these statements of the Lord's active engagement in the judgement of unjust action, it is important to note that nothing is said about the Lord intervening to save the innocent person whom everyone else has abandoned.[29] This saying is an example of the sages' awareness that at times injustice prevails in the world of men. Nevertheless, it ought to be noted that the main thrust of the saying is the assertion that the Lord is aware of the situation and holds all men responsible, even the spectator who, while he was not actively involved, nevertheless failed to come to the aid of a person he must have known was regarded as innocent.

---

[24] Pettazoni (1956:15)

[25] See ch. 2, pp. 58, 74.

[26] Toy (1977:307).

[27] See our discussion of the passage in ch. 3, pp. 108–109 and in ch. 5, pp. 197–198, 200.

[28] 17:15; 21:3; 22:22–23; 23:10–11; 29:26.

[29] Cf., e.g., 23:10–11 where the Lord intervenes for the weak party.

b. The Lord as creator

Another feature of the characterization of God in the book of Proverbs which indicates his supremacy and transcendent nature is the reference to him as creator. In chapter two it was observed that the traditions of the Lord as creator of the world and of man are distinct traditions and used in different ways in the book of Proverbs, though both are employed to fortify the teachings of the sages. The idea that the Lord created everything was an accepted belief which needed no argumentation; it was a commonplace assumption that could be used as a premiss in support of arguments relating to other issues.

A survey of the references to creation in the book of Proverbs shows that the texts always starkly differentiate between the Lord as creator on the one hand and on the other hand the creation. This strict subject-object distinction indicates that the sages regarded the Lord as transcendent, he was never regarded as immanent in creation.

Proverbs 8:22–31 refers to a time before anything was created and to the time when the Lord established the heavens and laid the foundations of the earth. The main point of this text is its affirmation of the preexistence of wisdom, but the text also contains a distinctive portrayal of the creator. Everything in the world, from שמים to תהמות,[30] was fashioned by the Lord who as a matter of course is regarded as predating it all. The issue at stake is the antiquity of wisdom while the existence of the transcendent Lord, which seems to have been regarded as extending beyond time, is so much beyond doubt that it is never taken up for discussion.

Proverbs 16:4 and 29:13 relate to the problems of theodicy[31] in their claim that the Lord is the creator of everything, even the wicked, and that there is an appropriate purpose or end for them as well. Both sentences leave many questions unanswered but are important in that they assert that the Lord is the one and only creator. Thus the problems of theodicy are in a sense brushed aside by a shift of focus to the supremacy of the Lord. As a result God is portrayed as inscrutable and beyond the reach of man, who is unable to understand the deep secrets of the world. The discussion of the problems of theodicy are used to widen the perceived chasm between the transcendent God and earth-bound man.

c. The absence of divine direct address and wisdom as God's representative

A notable fact concerning the God-man relationship in the book of Proverbs is that the Lord never directly addresses man. While this may not be so surprising for the parts of the book that are in the sentence genre, one might expect the parts in the instruction genre to take up a more direct form of

---

[30] 8:27 seems to presuppose the existence of תהום, but 8:24 refers back to a time when there were no תהמות which means that they were regarded as part of creation.

[31] See our discussion of the passages in ch. 2, pp. 60–62, 66–67.

address, especially Proverbs 1–9 which has several sections which one could imagine as coming from the mouth of the Lord. However, the direct form of address is completely lacking. What we encounter instead in Proverbs 1–9 is the personification of wisdom who functions as God's representative before man. She, instead of God, speaks to man in the authoritative first person singular and lays before man a choice of either life or death based on man's obedience or disobedience to her words.

The primary texts where wisdom appears in this role are 1:20–33, chapter 8, and 9:1–6. In 1:20–33 wisdom makes a public appearance in the city in the places where many people normally congregate. Speaking in the style of a public preacher or prophet, she invites the people to repent (vv 22–23), but suddenly her tone changes to a stinging denunciation of the unrepentant (vv 24–32) as though the people had refused to accept her invitation. The vocabulary is to a large extent that of a wisdom teacher though the situation reminds of the prophet.[32]

When we consider the content of the sermon, it is remarkable that wisdom is the one who invites man to relationship throughout the poem. One's relationship to wisdom and to her message means life or death; it is to her that the unrepentant will call for help when destruction descends upon them. Only once in 1:20–33 is God mentioned and then indirectly by means of an established idiom—it is said that the unrepentant did not choose "the fear of the Lord," which stands in parallel to "knowledge," דעת, "wisdom's counsel", עצה, and "reproof," תוכחת. While the prophets transmit the message of the Lord in the first person singular, laying before man life or death, wisdom speaks on her own authority with a similar force. It is the relationship with wisdom which is emphasized and God has in a sense withdrawn to a more remote position in relation to man. While both wisdom and the prophet function as God's representatives before man, wisdom is endowed with her own authority to address and challenge man. God and wisdom are portrayed as nearly identical, while the relationship between a prophet and the Lord is always strictly that of messenger and master.

This ascription of a close relationship between God and wisdom also applies to chapter eight where wisdom again appears in public, addresses men and speaks in first person. Her speech, however, differs from chapter one in its more uniformly persuasive and positive tone. Its content corresponds to normal wisdom teaching[33] and consists primarily of a commendation of wisdom buttressed by a description of the benefits of adhering to her advice. Again, one's relationship to wisdom determines whether one's fate will be life

---

[32] See Kayatz (1966:119–134) and McKane (1985:272–277) for a discussion of the depiction of wisdom in relation to the wisdom teacher and the prophet.

[33] McKane (1985:342–343).

or death. God is mentioned in verse 35 which points to the close relationship between wisdom and the Lord:

> 8:35. For he who finds me finds life,
> And obtains favour from Yahweh[34]

"Life" and "favour from Yahweh" are synonymous, both being consequences of finding wisdom. Wisdom plays the primary role in relation to man, but the fact that favour from the Lord results from finding her is of theological importance. These interconnections affirm both the interrelationship of wisdom and the Lord and the distance between God and man. Favour from the Lord is obtained through wisdom. Wisdom's representative and intermediary functions are two-sided in representing finite men before God and the transcendent God before men.

Two invitations are given in chapter 9—to come and participate in the feast that wisdom has arranged, or respond to the seductive invitation of folly. The outcome of the first is life, while the second leads those who respond to a destination they never anticipated, namely Sheol. The chapter ends the first part of the book by dramatically emphasizing the choice between wisdom and folly which has been constantly in focus. The identification of wisdom and the Lord is less clear in this text if it is regarded in isolation from the other two, but implicit in wisdom's authority is the ability to reward her adherents with the gift of life.[35]

3. Comparisons between the book of Proverbs and other Old Testament traditions

Our primary interest is to relate our observations concerning the features of transcendence in the depiction of God to other wisdom books of the Old Testament. An attempt will also be made to broaden the field to include other relevant Old Testament traditions as well.

a. The wisdom traditions

It is easy to see that the Lord's responsibility for justice and retribution also constitutes a major theme in the conception of God in other wisdom books. A legal pattern can be traced throughout the book of Job,[36] built upon the question whether or not the Lord is just and righteous. Neither Job nor his friends ever doubt that Job's sufferings come from God who in his supremacy rules and executes justice in the world. The problem for Job is that he does not find the severity of his "punishment" to be appropriate to the gravity of his shortcomings.

---

[34] Toy's translation (1977:179).

[35] וחיה must be understood as consecutive of the preceding "forsake folly" ("folly" is obtained by reading פְּתָיוּת instead of MT פְּתָאיִם).

[36] See Müller's survey of juridical interpretations (1978 A:94–98) and Habel (1985:54–57).

Ecclesiastes differs in being more negative to the belief in God's justice. He debates whether there is any justice in the world; at times he appears to assent to the traditional belief in God as the guarantor of justice but in the next moment the observations he chronicles contradict it.[37] Nevertheless, there is no essential difference in the view that God is responsible for justice; the difference is that Ecclesiastes analyzes the empirical evidence and finds it to be insufficient.[38] In the end Ecclesiastes does not draw any unorthodox conclusions concerning the nature of God or man's relation to him. God is still the supreme and transcendent God who carries out justice in the world, but to Ecclesiastes he and his ways are totally inscrutable and hidden to man.[39] All man can do is to appreciate and receive the joy that life and its toil bestows on him as a gift from God.

We find that the legal aspect of God's activity, with its implications concerning God's transcendence, permeates the wisdom traditions of the Old Testament. This also holds true for several of the so-called wisdom psalms, e.g., Psalms 37, 49 and 73.

The emphasis on God as creator of all things with its implications concerning his transcendent nature, is a prominent motif in Old Testament wisdom traditions . This motif occurs throughout the book of Job. Already in Job's introductory lament (ch. 3) where he states his wish that the whole world would revert to chaos,[40] it becomes evident that confidence in God's preservation of the order in creation is one of the crucial questions for Job. The speeches of Job, which to a large extent are delivered in the form of individual lament, also include this genre's occasional reference to the creation of man where God is "reminded" that the one lamenting is his creation. However, the situation in Job is distinct in that this assertion does not constitute the basis for the expression of trust or for a humble plea for help.[41] The main texts related to creation in the book are the speeches of the Lord which are somewhat reminiscent of onomastica in their enumeration of a large number of phenomena in the world, even though here the enumerations occur in the form of rhetorical questions. Despite the fact that the two speeches do not specifically deal with Job's personal situation, they nevertheless constitute an answer to Job by pointing out that God as creator is in control and that chaos does not have the upper hand. All these rhetorical questions and the way the Lord reveals himself certainly serve to emphasize the immense difference between God's power and man's limited capabilities. Man's perspective is so limited that he can gain neither a complete understanding of the complicated

---

[37] E.g., Eccl 8:10–15; 9:1–6.

[38] Cf. Gese (1963:145) who maintains that in Qoheleth the automatic act-consequence relationship of older wisdom has been replaced by the model of God's legal recompense.

[39] Wright (1968:334) finds the idea of the incomprehensibility of God's actions to constitute not only *a* theme but *the* theme of the book.

[40] See ch. 3, p. 92, n. 8.

[41] Job 10:8–22, cf. Ps 22:10–11; 71:6.

structure of the world nor the power to control it. Again we notice that
theodicy widens the gap between transcendent God and man in his limitation.

Rylaarsdam notes that Genesis 1–3 are used by Ecclesiastes in his argument
for the vanity of life—man is created like the animals, dies like them, he is
taken from the dust and returns to dust.[42] Crenshaw remarks that though
Ecclesiastes 3:11 opens with an affirmation of the goodness of creation
reminiscent of Genesis 1, this statement is immediately qualified in such a way
that it gives no solace to man.[43] The book of Ecclesiastes is to a high degree
centred around the belief in God as creator and the problems presented by a
lack of order and justice in this creation. Irrespective of these inconsistencies
in his creation, God is still the supreme creator. Ecclesiastes' conclusion is
that most things in the world are incomprehensible, precisely because God has
designed the world that way.[44] The tone here is radically different from the
optimistic search for knowledge which permeates the book of Proverbs. The
problems and inconsistencies of the world lead on the one hand to resignation
and passivity, on the other hand they put emphasis on the transcendence and
incomprehensibility of God and his work.[45]

Among the so-called wisdom psalms, Psalm 104 is of particular interest
here.[46] The interesting features in this psalm are the emphasis on the Lord's
on-going work of creation in maintaining harmony and order in his world and
also the majestic depiction of the Lord against whom neither the waters nor
Leviathan has any power. God is not only thought of as the supreme creator
of the distant past, for if he did not uphold creation in the present everything
would die and disappear. This depiction makes him clearly supreme in
relation to everything in creation.

The third feature in the depiction of God which we have discussed in
relation to his transcendent nature, is the fact that the Lord never establishes
direct contact with men in the book of Proverbs. Instead, this function is
fulfilled by personified wisdom in Proverbs 1–9. There is a prominent
example of divine direct address—the appearance of the Lord in the book of
Job.[47] But no parallels to the intermediary function are found in the other
wisdom books. In the book of Ecclesiastes, which is characterized by the
"remoteness" of God, there is never any attempt to bridge the chasm between
God and man. Neither is there any close parallel in the book of Job, though it
should be noted that Job several times refers to "someone" who is on his side

---

[42] Rylaarsdam (1946:25).

[43] Crenshaw (1974 A:28–30; 1982:134). Cf. Müller (1978 B:242–243).

[44] Eccl 3:11.

[45] Cf. Müller (1968:507–521; 1978 B:238–264) who refers to the religion of Qoheleth as a kind of
"Urheberreligion."

[46] See our comments in ch. 2, pp. 72, 74.

[47] See Preuss (1977:338–339; 1987:88).

and will function as an intermediary and judge between him and the God who is beyond his reach.[48]

We conclude that a sense of transcendence and remoteness characterizes the concept of God in the Old Testament wisdom traditions. In the book of Proverbs this is partially mitigated by the personification of wisdom, in the book of Job by the revelation of the Lord and in the Psalms by the expression of faith and trust. The remoteness of God in the book of Ecclesiastes, however, is imbued with a pristine, uncompromising starkness mainly because of its philosophical nature and its strong empirical-critical approach.

b. Other traditions of the Old Testament

The relationship between our observations concerning the transcendent nature of the Lord in the book of Proverbs and the other Old Testament traditions cannot be dealt with exhaustively in the present study. We will therefore restrict ourselves to a survey of the more important points.

The view that God is responsible for justice and retribution is not exclusive to the wisdom traditions even though it may be argued that it is of grand importance there.[49] This understanding of God may be regarded as basic to the prophetic tradition as well. Würthwein states:

> For them [i.e. the prophets] the holy God is in basic antithesis to every sinful creature. This means that the annihilating judgment of divine retribution must fall wherever sin reigns.[50]

The entirety of the preaching of the prophets is built upon the belief in God as supreme judge and retributor. The prophets deliver direct messages from the God who holds men responsible for their manner of life, not only in the religious realm but also in the socio-ethical and political. In addition, the Lord's sphere of activity is not limited to Israel but extends to other people and lands as well, as is made clear by the repeated pronouncements of judgment over Israel's neighbours. The Lord is God over all the earth and brings punishment and justice to all nations.[51]

The Deuteronomistic tradition is also of interest in this respect. Here the concept of retribution is clearly two-sided, involving either blessing or curse in accordance with man's faithfulness to the Lord.[52] The Deuteronomistic tradition even makes this belief in two-sided retribution a key for the interpretation of the history of Israel as a whole. The Deuteronomistic history serves to emphasize God's righteousness in executing justice as well as to

---

[48] מוכיח 9:33, עד 16:19–21, גאל 19:25–27. The idea is picked up by Elihu (33:23–24) who refers to an angel, an advocate, מליץ; see Habel (1985:469–470).

[49] Cf. Würthwein (1967:711).

[50] Würthwein (1967:708).

[51] See, e.g., Isa 24, esp. vv 1, 21.

[52] Blenkinsopp (1983:41–42) notes 1 Kings 8:31–32 as an example of the divine moral order. Since good and bad actions are not always followed by appropriate consequences, the moral order demands the intervention of the Lord as judge.

explain the fluctuation in the fortunes of the nation from the standpoint of their obedience to the Lord.

These two examples demonstrate that the belief in God as responsible for justice and retribution is in line with other major traditions of the Old Testament and that the wisdom traditions shares common ground at this point with at least large parts of the Old Testament. What is peculiar to wisdom is the dominantly individualistic application of the retribution scheme, but it must be kept in mind that individualism is a characteristic of the wisdom literature as a whole, not just a facet of its handling of the problem of retribution. It should also be noted that an individualistic approach is foreign neither to the prophets[53] nor the deuteronomists.[54]

References to the Lord as creator which imply his transcendence, relate to other texts in the Old Testament. The texts on the creation of world in the book of Proverbs exhibit the same tendencies to eschew anthropomorphism and mythology which are found in the creation story of Genesis 1,[55] since in both cases the main point is to recount the establishment and organization of the world as a suitable place for life. The references to the Lord as the creator of man which serve as basis for ethics have no direct parallels in other Old Testament traditions. In Isaiah 40–55 the creation of the world and of man have merged with a nationalistic, salvationist approach and the double creation motif becomes for the most part a basis for trust and encouragement.[56] Of special interest are 45:7 and 54:16; both seem to assert that God's creational activity is all-encompassing and includes even the negative side of the created order, and therefore should be mentioned as parallels to Proverbs 16:4 and 29:13.

The function of the creation motif in Isaiah 40–55 is to emphasize God's supremacy and greatness. That God is the creator serves as a basis for confidence in his ability and disposition to act on behalf of his people in the present, while in Proverbs 10–29 the same motif serves as the basis for individual ethics. The more strict creation account in Genesis 1 has as its primary theological purpose the proclamation that the Lord is the sole creator of all things. The uses of the creation motif in Isaiah 45:7, 54:16, Proverbs 16:4 and 29:13 have a parallel purpose. Here an immense disparity between God the creator and the created world is indicated, implying a different theological understanding than that found in the mythological creation accounts that often depicted creation as a struggle between conflicting powers.

The last feature in the depiction of the Lord in the book of Proverbs which indicates his transcendence is the lack of direct communication between God

---

[53] See, e.g., Ez 18; Jer 31:29–30.

[54] The depiction of the kings in the deuteronomistic history is full of details which reveal a lively interest in the individual behind the kingly office.

[55] See Landes (1974:279–293) for both divergencies and similarities of the two texts.

[56] Jes 40:27–28; 43:1–7, 19–21; 44:2, 21–28; 45:9–19; 49:1–7; 51:9–16; 54:4–10.

and man and the key role played by personified wisdom as God's representative. The Lord's use of an intermediary is not unique in the Old Testament. This is the function of the prophets who both speak in God's name in first person singular and also represent the people before God. Moses stands in an intermediary position between God and man with both parties making their will known to the other party through him. But it is not only men who can fulfil this intermediary function. The most intriguing figure playing this role in the Old Testament is the "angel of the Lord," מלאך יהוה, who through his authoritative speech and closeness to the Lord seems—just like personified wisdom—to be almost identified with him at the same time as he is depicted as a separate being.[57] The function of the angel of the Lord seems to be the same as that of wisdom in the book of Proverbs—to bridge the gap between transcendent God and man on earth. The angel of the Lord represents the Lord and has the authority to pronounce the same kind of promises as the Lord himself.[58]

Our conclusion is that the features of the depiction of the Lord in the book of Proverbs which tend to emphasize his transcendence are all paralleled to some degree in other Old Testament traditions.

4. Comparisons between the book of Proverbs and non-Israelite wisdom

The next step in our study is to compare our observations concerning the transcendent nature of the Lord in the book of Proverbs to the concepts of deity in the extant wisdom literature of the surrounding cultures.

a. Egypt

The primary comparative material to the book of Proverbs from Egypt is in the instruction genre. The extant texts are of various dates ranging from the time of the Old Kingdom until the Ptolemaic age.

The first thing to note in connection with the portrayal of deities in these texts is the peculiar fact that the gods in the instructions usually appear anonymously under the generic designation god, *nṯr*. For example, *The Instruction of Amenemope* specifically refers to deities by name only a few times though there are numerous theological references in this text. As in the book of Proverbs, the instructions never engage themselves in explicit discussions of the nature of the deity. The deity is regularly referred to as the

---

[57] See, e.g., Gen 16:7–14; 21:17.
[58] Cf. Gen 15:5 and 16:10.

object of man's trust and confidence;[59] he is clearly above man and directs the destiny of man:

> Man is clay and straw,
> The god is his builder.
> He tears down, he builds up daily,
> He makes a thousand poor by his will,
> He makes a thousand men into chiefs,
> When he is in his hour of life.[60]

Morenz calls the eighteenth chapter of *Amenemope* "das Hohelied des transzendenten Gottes":[61]

> Do not lie down in fear of tomorrow:
> "Comes day, how will tomorrow be?"
> Man ignores how tomorrow will be;
> God is ever in his perfection,
> Man is ever in his failure.
> The words men say are one thing,
> The deeds of the god are another.
> Do not say: "I have done no wrong,"
> And then strain to seek a quarrel;
> The wrong belongs to the god,
> He seals (the verdict) with his finger.
> There is no perfection before the god,
> But there is failure before him;
> If one strains to seek perfection,
> In a moment he has marred it.
> Keep firm your heart, steady your heart,
> Do not steer with your tongue;
> If a man's tongue is the boat's rudder,
> The Lord of All is yet its pilot.[62]

Here the wide chasm between the god of perfection and fallible man is quite visible, though Hornung takes special note of the fact that this passage which emphasizes "die Überlegenheit Gottes über den Menschen" ends with an assertion of their common situation:

> ...die berühmten bildkräftigen Schlussverse... zeigen beide, Gott und Mensch, im gleichen Boot. Dieses Boot ist—um im Bilde zu bleiben!—die Nusschale des Seins auf dem Ozean des Nichtseins, den es gemeinsam zu bestehen gilt.[63]

The view of the god as responsible for justice and retribution to a certain degree also pertains to the Egyptian wisdom tradition. Pettazoni points out

---

[59] *Amenemope* ix 5; xiv 1.

[60] *Amenemope* xxiv 13–18, Lichtheim (1976:160). The last line probably means that the sun-god acts through the gods who are assigned to each hour of the day (Lichtheim [1976:163, n 27]).

[61] Morenz (1964:47).

[62] xix 11–xx 6, Lichtheim's translation (1976:157–158). In order to achieve a logical flow in the text, Lichtheim (1976:163, n. 17) emends xix 23 to read "But there is failure before him" instead of "But there is no failure before him" (*ANET* [1969:423]).

[63] Hornung (1973:191).

that several of the great gods in Egypt—Re, Thoth, Horus, Amun and also the king as Re's or Thoth's son—are described as having omnivision and knowledge about men's activities, especially their evil deeds.   Among the instructions *The Instruction Addressed to King Merikare* gives particular prominence to this view of the god, even though it is also implied elsewhere:

> For god knows the treason plotters,
> God smites the rebels in blood.[64]

> While generation succeeds generation,
> God who knows characters is hidden;
> One can not oppose the lord of the hand,
> He reaches all that the eyes can see.[65]

> It is the god who judges the righteous,
> His fate comes and takes him away.[66]

> When the people raise their hands the god knows it.
> He knows the impious man who thinks of evil.
> He knows the godly man and that he has the greatness of the god in his heart.
> Before the tongue has been questioned the god knows its answers.[67]

Pettazoni concludes: "The notion of divine omniscience is thus expressed primitively in Egypt as a by-form of universal vision, regarded as an attribute of a supreme sky god, whose eyes are the sun and moon...."[68]

The Instruction of Ptahhotep from the Old Kingdom points out over and over again that it is the god who gives success, wealth and advancement to a person.[69]   There is little that indicates the reasons for this, but a few passages seem to connect success, wealth and advancement to behaviour and character. It is also stated that the god punishes people for scheming against others.[70] *The Instruction of Merikare* refers to a posthumous judgment when a man's deeds will be reviewed and judged in his presence,[71] asserts that the deity prefers right action to right offerings[72] and also puts forward views which closely resemble a retribution doctrine:

> For it is evil to destroy,
> Useless to restore what one has damaged,
> To rebuild what one has demolished.

---

[64] *The Instruction Addressed to King Merikare*, Lichtheim (1975:100).

[65] *The Instruction Addressed to King Merikare*, Lichtheim (1975:105).

[66] *The Instruction of Any*, Lichtheim (1976:141). The second clause refers according to Lichtheim (1976:146, n. 12) to the punishment of the aggressor.

[67] *The Instruction of Papyrus Insinger* xxxi 2–5, Lichtheim (1980:209).

[68] Pettazoni (1956:63).

[69] *Ptahhotep*, maxim 9, 10, 13, 22, 30, Lichtheim (1975:66–67, 69, 71).

[70] *Ptahhotep*, maxim 6, Lichtheim (1975:64), cf. *Kagemni* ii 4–5, Lichtheim (1975:60) where the point is not to be boastful since "One knows not what may happen, What god does when he punishes."

[71] Lichtheim (1975:101).

[72] Lichtheim (1975:106).

Beware of it! A blow is repaid by its like,
To every action there is a response[73]

In the *Instruction of Amenemope* ethical instruction is given additional force by reference to the will and pleasure of the god.[74] That the god holds men responsible for their actions is not expressly stated but must be regarded as a presupposition.

Papyrus Insinger from the latter part of the Ptolemaic period uses—with some minor variations—as a recurring refrain at the end of each section, "The fate and fortune that come, it is the god who determines them," and clearly views the god as the just retributor:

He who dies (or, has died) in the middle of life, the god knows what he has done.
The god does not forget the punishment for any crime.[75]

Indications of belief in the deity as responsible for justice and retribution is found in the instructions at all periods though it is not until the late period that it is emphasized, e.g., in Papyrus Insinger where the deterministic view of life is pronounced. Everything is decreed by the god and it is up to man alone to humbly accept whatever life has to bring.

In some instructions an element of arbitrariness can be discerned in the god's actions against or on behalf of man. One example is *Amenemope* xxiv 13–18, quoted above, which tells that the god tears down and builds up daily, makes a thousand poor and a thousand into chiefs.[76] The thrust of passages like these is to highlight the free will and sovereignty of the god, but they also indicate a certain amount of arbitrariness in the nature of the god. However, this element in the description does not alter the view of the god as transcendent and supreme in his way of acting in the world. Emphasizing the incomprehensibility of the god's actions in fact rather strengthens the notion that the deity is transcendent and above man.

The second characteristic of God, namely that he is supreme creator and the connected notion that he is transcendent, has an interesting parallel in the *Instruction of Merikare* which includes a hymn to the creator-god.[77] The hymn recounts how the god has fashioned everything in creation for man's sake and created man in his own image, from his body, and ends by asserting that "god knows every name."[78] The function of the creation hymn within this instruction seems to be to focus on the establishment of good and helpful things

---

[73] Lichtheim (1973:105).

[74] *Amenemope* v 7–8; viii 11–12, xxvi 13–14.

[75] *Insinger* xx 10–11, Lichtheim (1980:201).

[76] See also, e.g., *Amenemope* xxi 5–6, *Kagemni* ii 4–5.

[77] The late Demotic text *Papyrus Insinger* includes a creation hymn to the god (xxxi 23–xxxii 17, Lichtheim [1980:210–211]) with the main message that the god has made all things which keep the world going. The hymn follows as an answer to questions like: "How do the sun and moon go and come in the sky? Whence go and come water, fire and wind? Through whom do amulet and spell become remedies?" (xxxi 20–22).

[78] Lichtheim (1975:106).

in creation for the sake of man: plants and cattle to eat, the shrine of the god assuring his presence, rulers to assist the weak, magic to ward off evil—all this as well as the god's active presence in maintaining order guarantees a world which merits confidence.[79]

The reference to the creation of man in relation to ethics is paralleled in *Amenemope* by the lines preceding the text cited above about man as clay and straw and the god as his builder:

> Do not laugh at a blind man,
> Nor tease a dwarf,
> Nor cause hardship for the lame.
> Don't tease a man who is in the hand of the god,
> Nor be angry with him for his failings.
> Man is clay and straw,....[80]

The assertion that the god is the creator of the world and mankind stresses the fundamental difference between him and creation. The god is the designer who, belonging to a realm above and beyond the world of man, creates everything with a definite purpose, a purpose that sometimes escapes man's attention. Thus man stands in need of wisdom instruction based on tradition, experience and theological reasoning in order to live harmoniously in this world.

When it comes to the lack of direct communication between God and man and the role of wisdom in the book of Proverbs as intermediary, we find that the Egyptian instructions also lack direct communication between the god and man. The form of the instruction is consistently that of a man who gives advice to his son, or a teacher to his pupil and never a divine "I." As in Proverbs 1–9 other material can be inserted, like the creation hymn in *The Instruction of Merikare,* but we do not have any evidence from the instructions that, e.g., *ma' at* played a role as communicator of the divine will to man.[81]

If we broaden the scope of our inquiry to include Egyptian literature beyond the instruction genre, a few further observations can be made. The first is that there are no extant law codes from Egypt.[82] This may be explained by reference to the role of the pharaoh in Egypt, who was regarded as a god and whose word was divine.[83] This fact may have influenced the concept of the gods in Egypt, contributing to the tendency to describe their decrees not so much with legal language, as in terms of their will or pleasure.

A second general observation is that almost all gods in Egypt could be referred to as creator-gods, but also that they themselves were regarded as

---

[79] Assmann (1975:44) explains the hymn as a theodicy from the chaotic first intermediary period with the function of acquitting the god of responsibility for the prevailing disorder.

[80] *Amenemope* xxiv 8–13, Lichtheim (1976:160).

[81] The king in Egypt had an intermediary role with access to the sphere of the gods as well as the human realm, see Morenz (1960 B:42–43), Assmann (1975:18).

[82] Crenshaw (1982:229).

[83] Hornung (1973:129).

part of creation to a higher degree than was the case in Israel. Hornung debates whether it can be said that the gods in Egypt are transcendent in the true sense of the word.[84]

> Die ägyptischen Götter haben einen Anfang in der Zeit und ein Ende in ihr. Sie werden geboren oder geschaffen, sie wandeln sich in der Zeit, sie altern und sterben, und sie werden eines Tages nicht mehr sein.[85]

The Egyptians seem to have believed in a primeval God, that in the very beginning one god existed[86] who created the other gods, and in this sense Ptah, Re, Amun, Atum or any other creator god could be referred to as the father of the gods.

Hornung also argues that the Egyptian gods usually were viewed as limited both to a geographical sphere of influence and in terms of capacity;[87] however in the New Kingdom at least the sun-god was given universal attributes.[88] If Hornung is right in his view of the gods, it becomes possible to explain the almost total absence of attention to the problems of theodicy in Egyptian texts by means of factors internal to the Egyptian religious conceptuality.[89] Since the gods like man are limited and evil preceded their creation, they cannot be regarded as responsible for unrighteousness and evil in the world, but must rather be seen as fighting against evil together with man.[90]

A third general observation on Egyptian religion has to do with the role of *ma'at*. *Ma'at* represents the order and harmony in creation which is constantly threatened and in need of reestablishment. The interesting question in the present context is whether the background for the depiction of personified wisdom in the book of Proverbs is to be found in the figure of *ma'at* or elsewhere. Christa Kayatz concludes her study of Proverbs 1–9 by saying:

> Die überwiegende Mehrzahl der in Proverbien 1–9 vorkommenden Formtypen hat ihr Vorbild in den ägyptischen Weisheitslehren. Für die reden in Ich-Stil finden sich weitgehende Entsprechungen in den ägyptischen Götterreden. Mehrere Einzelmotive wurzeln in ägyptischen Vorstellungen. Vor allem lassen sich wesentliche Züge der personifizierten Weisheit von der ägyptischen Maatgestalt herleiten: Die Weisheit als vor Jahwe speilender "Liebling", ihre Prä-existenz vor der Schöpfung als Ausdruck ihrer

---

[84] Hornung (1973:186).

[85] Hornung (1973:134).

[86] Hornung points out (1973:168) that the names of the sun-god indicate that the Egyptians believed that this god had at one point been self-created. Cf. Assmann (1977:757–758, 771–772).

[87] Hornung (1973:160–164).

[88] Hornung (1973:161).

[89] Williams (1956:18) explains the lack of theodicy in Egypt by the absence of written laws in Egypt and therefore also of the conception of justice as a right. A second reason, according to Williams, is "the characteristic Egyptian belief in immortality" which made injustice in this life a less vital concern. Cf. von Soden (1965:42–44) concerning the religious prerequisites for a discussion of theodicy. The Middle Kingdom text *All Men Created Equal in Opportunity* (*ANET* [1969:7–8]) relates to theodicy and is reminiscent of Eccl 7:29 and Gen 3 in blaming evil on man's heart and his disobedience and not on the creator: "I made every man like his fellow. I did not command that they do evil, (but) it was their hearts which violated what I had said." See also Assmann's (1975:44) interpretation of the creation hymn in *Merikare*.

Würde und Autorität, die Weisheit als Geliebte, ihre Liebe zu den ihr gehorsamen Menschen, die Weisheit als Leben- und Schutzspenderin, die Weisheit in ihrer Beziehung zum König.[91]

The similarities between *ma'at* and personified wisdom are no doubt highly interesting, but it is important to note that they can be evaluated in different ways. Lang does not agree with Kayatz' contention that there is in, e.g., Proverbs 8 a structural pattern parallel to that of Egyptian divine speech, and concludes: "Nothing more than a general affinity of self-presentation, self-predication, etc. between the Egyptian divine speeches and Prov. 8 can be detected."[92]

Lang also points out: "...at the decisive point, the parallelism of *hokmah* and Maat breaks down: The notion that Maat would actually speak to human beings is foreign to the Egyptians."[93] This fact that *ma'at* never addresses human beings proves to be decisive evidence against *ma'at* as the specific background for the depiction of wisdom as a preacher/teacher of the highest authority in the book of Proverbs.

b. Mesopotamia

In the group of texts that can be called "reflective essays," references to the personal god and goddess are the dominant type of theological statements. In the proverb collections available which are characterized by a low percentage of god-references, references to individual gods like Utu/Shamash, Ningishzida or Inanna are found, but just as often it is the "anonymous" personal god who appears.

Our first feature indicating the transcendence of the Lord in the book of Proverbs is paralleled to a certain degree in Mesopotamian wisdom when it is stated that the gods are responsible for justice and retribution. A number of the great gods are ascribed omnivision and omniscience in the sense that they have superhuman knowledge of man's activities. Pettazoni enumerates a number of examples from Babylonia: Anu, Enlil, Ea, Sin, Shamash, Marduk and some less prominent deities.[94] The view of the omniscient deity who observes and knows about each person's activities is connected with the legal aspect of that deity's rule and function.

It is especially the sun god, Utu/Shamash, who is responsible for justice and equity.[95] Two Sumerian proverbs illustrate the way Utu brings about justice:

A boat bent on honest pursuits sailed downstream with the wind;
Utu has sought out honest pursuits for it.

---

[90] Hornung (1973:208–209).

[91] Kayatz (1966:135).

[92] Lang (1986:163, n. 5).

[93] Lang (1986:144).

[94] Pettazoni (1956:77–88).

A boat bent on fraudulent pursuits sailed downstream with the wind;
he (i.e., Utu) will wreck (?) it on the beaches.[96]

In the later fragmentary proverb collections from Mesopotamia little is found
to support the view that the gods were regarded as responsible for justice even
though there are indications that at this time as well the gods were viewed as
possessing omnivision and as holding men responsible for their actions.[97]

Several of the reflective essays deal with the problems connected with belief
in justice and retribution in the world. The Sumerian text *Man and His God* is
not so much about undeserved suffering, the man expresses an awareness of
the sinfulness of all people[98] and does not argue the justice of his own cause.
The sufferer in the Babylonian text *Ludlul bēl nēmeqi,* however, does argue
on his own behalf, certifying that he has been rigourous in fulfilling his
religious obligations[99] and seems perplexed by his inexplicable and sudden
change of fortune. *The Babylonian Theodicy* deals more explicitly with the
problems of unjust suffering. The problem is stated by the sufferer:

Those who do not seek the god go the way of prosperity,
While those who pray to the goddess become destitute and impoverished.
In my youth I tried to find the will of my god;
With prostration and prayer I sought my goddess.
But I was pulling a yoke in a useless corvée.
My god decreed poverty instead of wealth (for me).
A cripple does better than I, a dullard keeps ahead of me.
The rogue has been promoted, but I have been brought low.[100]

The traditionalist friend defends the concept of retribution as well as the
justice of the gods by reference to their incomprehensibility.[101] Here is a clear
parallel to the theodicy in Israel. The deity is regarded as responsible for
justice and retribution but man experiences the scourge of unjust suffering.

The second feature of the book of Proverbs discussed in relation to the
transcendence of the Lord was his role as creator. In the wisdom literature we
find occasional references to the creation of man. A Sumerian proverb states:

A perverse child—his mother should never (have) give(n) birth to him,
his (personal) god should never (have) fashion(ed) him.[102]

---

[95] Gordon (1959:307), Fensham (1962:130–131), Jacobsen (1976:134).

[96] Gordon (1959:84, proverb 1.86 and 1.87).

[97] See The *Babylonian Book of Proverbs,* § H, I, M in Langdon (1923:90–91), *Counsels of Wisdom* 57–65, 127–130. Shamash was the sun-god and not one of the prominent deities in the Babylonian pantheon, but the *Shamash Hymn* praises her as the giver of light who cares for every creature, reveals secrets, and observes everything. Lines. 37–38 reminds of Proverbs 15:11: "Samaš, your glare reaches down to the abyss So that the monsters of the deep behold your light" (Lambert 1960:128–129).

[98] *Man and his God* 102–103, *ANET* (1969:590).

[99] *Ludlul* II 23–32, *ANET* (1969:597).

[100] *The Babylonian Theodicy* 70–77, *ANET* (1969:602).

[101] *The Babylonian Theodicy* 58, 256–257, *ANET* (1969:602, 604).

[102] Gordon (1959:124, proverb 1.157).

The suffering young man in *Man and his God* pleads:

> My god, you who are my father who begot me, [*lift up*] my face,
> *like* an innocent cow, in *pity* ... the groan,
> How long will you neglect me, leave me unprotected?
> Like an ox, ...,
> (How long) will you leave me unguided?[103]

While the creation of the world is attributed to the great gods the creation of man is evidently associated with the personal god.[104] There is no explicit reference to the creation of the world in the wisdom texts, but *Ludlul bēl nēmeqi*, which opens by praising of Marduk as lord of wisdom, describes him as the supreme god who rules over day and night and over all other gods.[105] We conclude that the creation motif is not a prominent feature in the description of the gods in Mesopotamian wisdom texts. When it occurs it is as man creation attributed to the personal god.

The third feature in the depiction of the Lord in the book of Proverbs which indicates his transcendent nature, is the absence of direct address by God to man and the consequent, intermediary function of wisdom. An interesting parallel to this is the role of the Mesopotamian personal god. In *Ludlul bēl nēmeqi* it appears that Marduk, as the supreme god, was regarded as ultimately responsible for the suffering of the main character. This is made clear by the introduction as well as the conclusion of the story. In spite of this, the sufferer directs his prayer to his personal god and goddess[106] and it is mainly about his/her absence and silence that he complains.[107] An identification between the personal god/goddess and Marduk is never clearly made[108] and it is probable that the personal god here as elsewhere is called upon as an intermediary between the individual and the great gods, in this case Marduk.[109] Such a function is implied by the following proverb from Sumer:

> The destruction is from his own (personal) god;
> He knows no saviour.[110]

If the destruction comes from the personal god, the person has no one to intercede for him, and no other means of redress.[111]

---

[103] *Man and his God* 96–100, *ANET* (1969:590).

[104] Jacobsen (1976:158) notes that a common way of referring to one's personal god was as "the god who 'created' or 'engendered' me" or "the divine mother, who gave birth to me."

[105] *Ludlul* I 1–12, IV 27–48, *ANET* (1969:596, 600).

[106] *Ludlul* II 4–5, *ANET* (1969:597).

[107] *Ludlul* I 43–46, II 112–113, *ANET* (1969:596, 598). At times the sufferer speaks in a general way making it difficult to specify which god he is referring to, see II 36–38.

[108] Suggested by Albertz (1988:34).

[109] Gordon (1959:307) finds that the function of the personal god was "to act as intercessor on that man's behalf in the assembly of the gods." Lambert (1960:7): "Though the personal god was necessarily a small god, he was able to take his client's case to the greater gods, and to see that it received attention."

[110] Gordon (1959:45, proverb 1.7).

There is no example in the wisdom texts of a personal god appearing as an intermediary between man and the great gods. The conclusion of *Ludlul bēl nēmeqi* tells about three dreams in which "a remarkable young man," "a remarkable priest," and "a remarkable young woman" and an exorcist called Urnindinlugga appear to the sufferer.[112] The exorcist Urnindinlugga, though not a deity, definitely has an intermediary function and delivers a message from Marduk which bodes both recovery and future prosperity for the sufferer.

The priestly appearances in *Ludlul bēl nēmeqi* and the role of the personal god in Mesopotamian religion bridge the chasm between the supreme gods and man. The supreme gods seem remote and inaccessible to man and several wisdom texts assert the inability of man to understand the ways of the gods.[113] This pessimistic note seems to characterize Mesopotamian wisdom.

When we turn to Mesopotamian religion in general, the first thing of note is the diverse and complicated pantheon. Concerning the nature of these deities in general, Jacobsen questions whether "transcendent" is an appropriate attribute:

> ...one cannot but note a tendency to experience the Numinous as immanent in some specific feature of the confrontation, rather than as all transcendent. The ancient Mesopotamian, it would seem, saw numinous power as a revelation of indwelling spirit, as power at the center of something that caused it to be and thrive and flourish.[114]

In our chapter on creation theology the observation was made that the gods are viewed as dependent upon men in Mesopotamia.[115] This dependence is mutual: man is dependent on the help and protection of the gods[116] while the gods created men to help them in their toilsome labour and to supply them with offerings.[117] Still, in Mesopotamia there was a clear differentiation between the world of men and the world of the gods.[118] The essential distinction between the two worlds is found in the fact that the gods are immortal while

---

[111] Cf. the problem of Job who has no one that can help him against God.

[112] *Ludlul* III 9–53, *ANET* (1969:598–599). In the "Juste Souffrant" text translated by Nougayrol (1952:239–250) the friend of the sufferer appears to intercede before the deity.

[113] E.g., BM 38486 reverse 7–8: "The will of a god cannot be understood, the way of a god cannot be known. Anything of a god [is difficult] to find out" (Lambert [1960:265–266]). Cf. *Ludlul* II 36–38.

[114] Jacobsen (1976:5–6).

[115] Ch. 2, p. 70.

[116] Jacobsen (1976:158) points out that the Mesopotamian in the second millenium B C believed that the personal god dwelt in his body: "If 'his god removed himself from his body,'... the body was open for evil demons of disease to take over and 'possess' the man."

[117] This is to be compared with the Egyptian gods about whom Hornung (1973:211) says: "Die Götter bedürfen keiner materiellen Gaben, aber sie bedürfen der Antwort des Menschen auf ihre Existenz, sie wollen sich im Herzen des Menschen ereignen, erst dadurch erhält ihr Schöpfungswerk seinen bleibenden Sinn."

[118] Lambert (1960:3–4) notes: "According to the Sumerians and Babylonians two classes of persons inhabited the universe: the human race and the gods. Pre-eminence belonged to the gods, though they were not all equal. At the lower end of the divine scale came a host of minor deities and demons, while a trinity of great gods, Anu, Enlil, and Ea, stood at their head."

man dies without assurances of an afterlife.[119] Especially in relation to the great gods man was viewed as completely separated and subordinated. The highest authority in the Mesopotamian universe was the assembly of the gods where An/Anu presided and Enlil played a dominant role.[120] Between this body and mankind there was a wide chasm which could not be spanned. Thus man could not know anything about what was decided unless he was informed by one of the gods[121]. There is but one example where this distance between the gods and man was traversed and a man became a god, i.e. Utnapishtim.[122] This clearly was extraordinary, for not even the heroic Gilgamesh was able to acquire the eternal life.of the gods

The capriciousness, at least seemingly, of the Mesopotamia gods as they are depicted must be noted. Appeals could be made to them, especially to Utu/Shamash, the sun god and upholder of justice and equity, but in general man seems to have been consigned to their arbitrariness. An illustration of this: In the story of Atrahasis, the gods, who had created mankind, suddenly decided to decimate their number by a plague and ultimately to extinguish them simply because mankind had become too plentiful and made too much noise thus disturbing the gods.[123] In *Ludlul bēl nēmeqi* the sufferer laments that it is impossible to know what pleases the god and that a person's fortune may be suddenly and unexpectedly reversed.[124] The only alternative that remains for the sufferer is to appeal to the god in the hope that he will be merciful and rescue him. On this point there seems to be a certain difference in the book of Job where the problems of theodicy are approached from the perspective of a firm belief in God as just and righteous and where Job vehemently vindicates his innocence before God.

We conclude that the wisdom literature of Mesopotamia basically seems to share the view of the divine as is found in Mesopotamian religion in general. A great disparity exists between the world of the gods and the realm of men, especially in relation to the great gods. This disparity is to some extent ameliorated by the personal god who, even though also belonging to the world of the gods, stands closer to man and may function as his mediator before the great gods.

---

[119] Lambert (1960:11–12).

[120] Jacobsen (1976:86–91).

[121] This is what happens when the gods decide to cause a flood to extinguish mankind. Ea reveals this to Utnapishtim and gives him instructions concerning the ship and what to bring aboard the ship and in this way Utnapishtim and other living beings are saved (see Jacobsen [1976:206]).

[122] Gilgamesh epic, XI 189–195, *ANET* (1969:95).

[123] See Jacobsen (1976:118–120).

[124] *Ludlul* II 33–38, *ANET* (1969:597).

5. Conclusions concerning God's transcendence

a. Old Testament wisdom traditions

The understanding of God as responsible for justice and retribution is strongly emphasized in the wisdom literature of the Old Testament. The view of him as the only creator seems to be a basic assumption of the sages as well. The absence of direct communication between God and man characterizes the books of Proverbs and Ecclesiastes, while the book of Job presents a breakthrough in the usual impasse through the appearance of the Lord at the end of the book. The peculiar role of wisdom as God's representative is only attested in the book of Proverbs where it serves the function of bridging the chasm between God and man. In the book of Job the same effect is created by the theophany.

Our conclusion is that the view of God as transcendent is strongly emphasized not only in the book of Proverbs but in the wisdom traditions of the Old Testament as a whole. Each of these three features within the wisdom traditions indicate that God was conceived of as above man and not subject to terrestrial limitations. As the supreme God who transcends this world he is able to see and know each person and maintain justice among men. As the sole creator and upholder of the universe he transcends creation in the same way as the artisan stands above his own work. As the transcendent God he is ultimately beyond man's reach, but is free to communicate with man in different ways—through wisdom, theophanies, or messengers.

b. Other traditions of the Old Testament.

The understanding of God as transcendent permeates the Old Testament as a whole. We noticed that the view of the Lord as responsible for justice and retribution was strong especially in the prophetic and deuteronomistic traditions. The distinctiveness of the wisdom traditions lies in its pronounced focus on the individual.

The belief in God as the sole creator of all things is common to several Old Testament traditions. Points of contact with Genesis 1 and Isaiah 40–55 have already been noted and reference could also be made to the so-called creation psalms.[125] The connection between the creation of man and ethics in Proverbs 10–29 seems to be without a counterpart in the Old Testament.

The absence of direct address and the peculiar role of wisdom as the representative of the Lord before man can be compared to the role of Moses, the prophets and especially the angel of the Lord in other Old Testament traditions. Communication through intermediaries between the transcendent God and man is thus documented in several different forms in the Old Testament.

---

[125] Ps 8; 19A; 104; 139; (148), according to Westermann (1980:97). Westermann also lists some passages in Amos with the motif "praise of the creator": 4:13; 5:8–9; 9:5–6.

Thus it may be concluded that the wisdom traditions share with the rest of the Old Testament the view that God is transcendent. The parallels to the prophetic and deuteronomistic traditions suggest an interesting closeness in the concept of God between these traditions and the wisdom traditions.

c. Egypt

In Egyptian wisdom the view that the god is responsible for justice and retribution is present, but it is emphasized less than in Israelite wisdom. The almost complete absence of the problems of theodicy in Egyptian religious thought has been noted above. Wealth and success are referred to as gifts of the god in the instructions and it is also occasionally stated that the god punishes people for evil deeds against other men. It seems possible to say that in comparison to Old Testament wisdom traditions there is less of a juridical pattern to the description of the deity and his activity, and we also made the observation that the god and his way of acting in the texts involves a certain degree of arbitrariness.

The Instruction of Merikare as well as the late *Papyrus Insinger* include creation hymns, though with different purposes than the hymn in Proverbs 8, and in *The Instruction of Amenemope* there is, interestingly enough, a connection between the creation of man and ethics similar to that found in Proverbs 10–29, which is not paralleled elsewhere in the Old Testament.

The instructions do not contain any direct address from a deity to man; they are consistently from father to son or from teacher to student. The gap between the deity and man is nowhere bridged by any intermediary. Even though other similarities between *ma'at* and personified wisdom can be detected, *ma'at* never plays this role. It is the father/teacher who is in the position of authority in the instructions and his teaching is based upon experience, tradition, and theological considerations.

Even though it has been argued that Egyptian gods are not transcendent in the true sense of the word because they share their realm with man, the description of the deity in the instructions indicates the god's transcendence by depicting him as both beyond man and unrestricted by the limitations of this world.[126] Our conclusion is that though there are differences of detail in the depiction of God in Egyptian and Israelite wisdom, there is a shared view of God as simultaneously transcendent and engaged in the world of man.

d. Mesopotamia

The texts dealing with the problem of innocent suffering indicate that in Mesopotamia as well a belief in the retribution concept and in the gods as responsible for justice and retribution existed, though this view received less

---

126 See Morenz (1964) who argues that there is a development in the Egyptian concept of the deity from immanence, when the deity was incorporated in the king, to transcendence, especially in the age of personal piety, when the deity directly related to every being.

emphasis than in Israel. Mesopotamian descriptions of the gods are also marked by a higher degree of capriciousness. In this connection it is interesting to note that only Shamash/Utu is called righteous and just.

The creation motif is not prominent in the wisdom texts but, when it does occur, it deals with the creation of man and not with the creation of the "Ur-Mensch." This is the same practice which one encounters in Proverbs 10–29 where the "creation" referred to is that of the individual mentioned in the context.

Concerning the matter of an intermediary between god and man, there is an interesting Mesopotamian parallel. The great gods were for the most part regarded as transcendent and beyond man's reach in Mesopotamia, while the personal god was closer to man and seems to have had the function of representing his adherents before the great gods. This is as far as the parallel goes, however, the wisdom texts yield no example of a personal god representing any of the great gods as a spokesman, like personified wisdom in the book of Proverbs.

Jacobsen argues for the immanence of the gods of Mesopotamia since they were connected to the phenomena of nature. This may be true, especially of the earliest times, but the great gods which Jacobsen discusses seem to have possessed a set of characteristics that appear to be mutually exclusive. Thus while these gods clearly were regarded as immanent, they could also be simultaneously seen as residents of a world beyond man's reach, as immortal with potentialities far surpassing man's. At least one of them, Shamash/Utu is responsible for justice and retribution and they are all to a certain degree involved in the world of man. Creation is usually attributed to Enlil or Enki/Ea, but could be attributed to almost any of the great gods as, e.g., to Marduk in *Enūma elish*. Little is stated in the texts concerning the character of the personal god. It seems that this class of divinity, though divine and thus immortal, is restricted in power and the scope of his authority to act autonomously.

The differences between the understandings of God manifested in Israelite and Mesopotamian wisdom are quite large. The most noteworthy parallel is between Mesopotamian texts related to the problems of theodicy and the book of Job, certain psalms of lament and so called wisdom psalms. The differentiation between the great gods and the personal god should also be noted, even if it cannot serve as a clear-cut parallel to the role of wisdom as God's representative in the book of Proverbs.

B. The sovereign God

The aim of the preceding section of this chapter was to demonstrate the transcendent nature of the Lord in the book of Proverbs by focusing on some features that indicate that the sages regarded the Lord as transcendent. These features were then compared to similar characteristics found in other parts of the Old Testament and in non-Israelite wisdom. This present section will in a similar way focus on features that emphasize the sovereignty of the Lord. It seems to be a basic belief of the sages that the Lord as supreme God is without competition in his rule of the world and without limitations in the establishment of his will and purposes.

1. Definition of sovereignty

The term "sovereignty" is chosen to signify God's "otherness," i.e. his supremacy in relation to everything else in the universe and to signify his freedom to enact his will,[127] which means that no one, man or any other being, is able to thwart his purposes. The book of Proverbs seems to reflect a view of the Lord as one who in incomprehensible ways carries out his will, frequently without man's cooperation and, if necessary, even despite man's actions. This sovereignty is not limited to any particular realm and means that the Lord in his sovereignty carries out his purposes in the world of men, in a world where chance seems to rule and where people do not always act in accordance to his will.

2. The Lord as sovereign in the book of Proverbs

The sovereignty of the Lord in the book of Proverbs primarily appears when it is stated that he directs and rules all things, when his ways are declared to be incomprehensible to man, and in the assertion that God directs all things to suit his will and his purpose irrespective of or even contrary to man's actions. We will in the following deal more closely with each of these three areas.

a. The Lord as supreme ruler
The conviction that the Lord as supreme ruler acts sovereignly is the basis for exhortations like 16:3:

16:3. Commit thy work to Yahweh,
Then will thy plans succeed.[128]

---

[127] See Rendtorff (1977:344–353) for an insightful discussion of God's freedom vs. the concept of order in wisdom and historical traditions. Also Hermisson (1985:129–152), Mettinger (1988:142–148).

[128] Toy's translation (1977:319). Literally "roll on the Lord your deeds," cf. Ps 22:9, 37:5.

The decisive factor which brings about success according to this text is the pious commitment of one's plans and intended actions to the Lord. This is not necessarily in conflict with the advice given elsewhere to act wisely and diligently, but there is certainly a distinct emphasis here. Here the dominant anthropocentric approach is pushed into the background and is supplemented by a theocentric.

While 16:3 states that success is the consequence of commitment, 16:7 asserts that the Lord "automatically" gives success when someone's way of life pleases him:

> 16:7. When a man's ways please Yahweh,
> He makes even his enemies to be at peace with him.[129]

The second clause describes the complete harmony which the righteous man experiences.[130] The Lord acts in inscrutable ways and brings about results that man himself would not be able to accomplish.

A contrast to 16:7 is found in 22:14 which tells about the fate of the person whose ways are displeasing to the Lord:

> 22:14. The mouth of the adulteress is a deep pit,
> He with whom Yahweh is angry will fall thereinto.[131]

The relationship between cause and consequence is not specified, and no information is provided concerning the reason that the Lord's anger is roused. The saying constitutes a warning against falling into the wiles of a seductive woman, a recurring theme in the book, and the assertion of the importance of being in harmony with the Lord. But the saying also indicates the inscrutable character of the Lord's actions. The person who is trapped by the adulteress hardly knows that the ultimate reason for his bad fortune is the Lord's displeasure with him. In his sovereignty, the Lord directs everything in such a way that it resounds with his purposes and his execution of justice. It is not possible for man to distinguish between what he himself has caused and what is the result of the Lord's activity. We get the impression that the common, present-day dichotomy between "natural" and "supernatural" causes, were of

---

[129] Toy's translation (1977:319). Our comments to 16:3 apply here too. There is no necessary conflict between what man himself is able to bring about and what the Lord accomplishes. Toy correctly notes (1977:322): "...the happy condition of the righteous is brought about directly by divine action; but human causes, such as the kindliness and helpfulness of the good man, are probably not meant to be excluded."

[130] Cf. 19:23 which simply states the positive results of יראת יהוה.

[131] Toy's translation (1977:419). "Adulteress" is actually the "strange woman," זרה (here pl.), who is of dubious character appearing in Proverbs 1–9 a number of times (2:16; 5:3, 20; 6:24; 7:5). The warning against the strange woman may have been a common theme in wisdom traditions. Cf. the warning in The *Instruction of Any:* "Beware of a woman who is a stranger, one not known in her town; Don't stare at her when she goes by, Do not know her carnally. A deep water whose course is unknown, Such is a woman away from her husband" (Lichtheim [1976:137]).

only vague and minor interest to the contemporaries of the sages.[132] Their
conviction was that God rules this world in a sovereign way and that his action
is ultimately inscrutable to man.

Of importance in this respect is 21:1 which states that the Lord works
within the hearts of kings:

> 21:1. Like watercourses is a king's heart in the hands of Yahweh—
> Whither he will he turns it.[133]

The reference is to kings in general and the statement that the Lord steers their
thinking. The primary reference here is not to dreams, prophetic speech, or
other "supernatural" ways through which God can reveal his will to the king,
but rather to the unknown way God influences the king to think and act
according to his purposes. The king in the ancient Near East was an autocrat
and supreme ruler who was regarded as more or less divine, but this saying
looks to a higher authority who works out his will through the king.[134] The
saying is to be understood as a truism which emphasizes the power of the
Lord. None of the qualifications one might expect is inserted—e.g., the
importance of the king's religious attitude and obedience; furthermore, the
general character of the saying raises the following question: Does the
statement include all kings and countries?, etc. The main point is the assertion
that the Lord in incomprehensible ways directs also the minds of kings and
carries out his will through them. Other matters are ignored, at least in the
present context.

The book of Proverbs does not describe the Lord in royal terms, but it is
still relevant to say that he is depicted as supreme ruler, since he in a sovereign
way rules over all men and establishes his will in the world.

b. The incomprehensibility of the Lord's activity

Several passages implying the incomprehensibility of the Lord's activity have
already been commented upon. The view of God as sovereign in
accomplishing his will receives further impetus through the assertion that his
ways are inscrutable to man. Since man cannot understand his ways, he is
called upon to trust and commit himself to this sovereign ruler.

Proverbs 25:2 can be interpreted as either asserting the inevitable
inscrutability of the Lord's activity, or as stating that he consciously acts to
hide things from man. We believe the former understanding to be more

---

[132] 19:3 indicates that the sages were aware of the distinction between man's own activity as the cause
for trouble and God's involvement, but it is in accord with our statement that the two were seen as
closely related and even inextricably intertwined.

[133] Toy's translation (1977:398). Toy notes that the picture is that of a land like Egypt or Babylonia
watered by canals, whose flow can be regulated to water and fertilize every part.

[134] See our comments to 16:10, 12 in ch. 3, p. 123.

appropriate, that the concealment of matters was instead seen as a consequence of the empirical character of the sovereign Lord's activity:

> 25:2. It is the glory of God to conceal,
> It is the glory of kings to search out.[135]

This sentence is interesting for several reasons. First, the tension between God and the king which indicates a stark differentiation between the two. The king is not seen as equal to God, though he does occupy a special position among men in being able to understand the deeper mysteries of the cosmos. But God is elevated to a position high above even the most prominent men. Second, this sentence is one of the very few instances in the book of Proverbs where אלהים is used for God instead of יהוה.[136] Definite conclusions are difficult to draw on the basis of this, but it seems probable that the comparison originally was general and not specifically referring to the Lord of Israel. If one were to adopt this line of interpretation, אלהים in the first line in the plural, like מלכים in the second line would be translated: "It is the glory of gods to conceal a matter, but it is the glory of kings...." In such a case the sentence would state that incomprehensibility was not only characteristic of the God of Israel, but of gods in general. In its present setting the sentence asserts the incomprehensibility of the Lord. Whatever alternatives there may be concerning the original understanding of the sentence and the term אלהים, in the context of the book of Proverbs the sentence's primary reference is to the Lord. The use of the term "glory," כבד, indicates that inscrutability exalts the Lord as supreme and sovereign God[137] in the same way as the ability to find out the secrets of the world confers glory on a king.[138]

The contrast between the Lord's sovereign control of all things and man's inability to have insight into his life situation is formulated in 20:24:

> 20:24. A man's steps are ordered by Yahweh;
> How, then, can man understand his way?[139]

---

[135] Toy's translation (1977:458). "Conceal" and "search out" are both followed by דבר in the MT, designating "anything and everything" (Toy 1977:459). The repetition of דבר may indicate that what is concealed by God is not identical to what is sought out by kings.

[136] See ch. 1, pp. 35–36.

[137] Cf. the designation of the Lord in Isa 45:15, אל מסתתר, and the assertion in Deut 29:28 that what is hidden belongs to the Lord, הנסתרת ליהוה, while what is revealed belongs to us and our sons, והנגלת לנו ולבנינו . Cf. also Job 11:7, 26:14.

[138] Cf. the queen of Sheba's astonishment and her subsequent praise of king Solomon because of his ability to answer all her questions.

[139] Toy's translation (1977:392). Toy notes (1977:393): "This Division of the book is thus at one with the first Division in the recognition of absolute divine sovereignty, and no attempt is made to reconcile this belief with the belief (held with equal distinctness) in human freedom." This is the tension between what we have termed the anthropocentric and the theocentric approaches of the book. 20:24a is also found in Ps 37:23, one of the psalms often included as a wisdom psalm. In the psalm there is no contrast between the Lord's involvement and man's inability to understand; instead the continuation expresses confidence in the Lord's help and protection. Cf. RS 25.130:11'–12', 24'–27', Nougayrol (1968:293–295).

The formulation of the sentence implies that precisely because a man's steps are from the Lord,[140] they are incomprehensible. Left to his own devices he would perhaps be able to exert some control over the situation, but when the Lord inscrutably directs his deeds and their consequences, he does not have full insight into his life situation. There are two possible consequences of this: a fatalistic despair or commitment to the Lord and confidence in his help and guidance.

c. The independence of the Lord in relation to man's actions

In the book of Proverbs there are a number of passages which relate to God's sovereignty in their assertion that the Lord is able to accomplish his will independently of man's cooperation or corresponding action. Gese, who regards Israelite wisdom as closely related to Egyptian wisdom in its being based upon the concept of world order, identifies a number of sentences as "israelitische Sondergut," since they teach that the Lord is not bound to a concept of world order, but is free to act "gegen" or "unabhängig" of the plans and actions of man, i.e. the Lord is free to bring blessings or punishment upon man even if these do not correspond exactly to the person's deeds.[141] The Lord's freedom to act entails his sovereignty—he is not bound by any laws confining his activity to mere response to human actions.

The fact that the sovereign Lord is not limited to acting in response to man's action, but is free to carry out actions which are even contrary to the plans of man is illustrated by 16:9:

16:9. Man devises his way,
But Yahweh directs his steps.[142]

A literal translation makes it clear that the contrast is between man's heart as the seat of thought, חשב (pi), and the Lord's activity which directs, כון, his steps. A close parallel is found in 16:1 where "the plans of man's heart" are contrasted with "the answer of the tongue" which is stated to be "from the Lord." Above all these sentences assert the sovereignty of the Lord who directs everything to serve his purposes. As we have noted before, sentences are not normally qualified in detail and nothing indicates whether or not the focus is on general rules or particular cases into which the Lord "breaks in" to overturn the normal correspondence between act—in this case devising and planning—and consequence. Conditional statements have no place within the

---

[140] The literal translation of the first line is: "From the Lord are a man's steps." The insertion of "are ordered" is an attempt to bring out the sense of the indefinite formulation which probably is meant to indicate the involvement of the Lord in everything that a person does.

[141] Gese (1958:47) Passages mentioned by Gese are 10:22; 16:1, 9, 33; 20:24; 21:1, 30, 31; 25:2.

[142] Toy's translation (1977:320). 16:9 is very similar in thought to 16:1 which also contrasts man's plans to the actual result which the Lord brings about. There is no indication of how God is able to direct man's step and tongue, nor is it stated whether or not this maxim applies only to certain circumstances or is to be regarded a general rule.

wisdom traditions where the focus is on discovering the general truths about life.

Preuss, who shares and further develops the view that Israelite wisdom is more or less identical to Egyptian wisdom in being built upon the basis of world order, does not share Gese's view "...dass durch das Wissen um Jahwe diese Lehre vom Tun-Ergehen-Zusammenhang in Israel 'durchbrochen' worden sei, da einige Texten die Unabhängigkeit Jahwes von dieser Ordnung bezeugen würden."[143] He detects this "Durchbrechung" in the books of Ecclesiastes and Job, but not in the older parts of the book of Proverbs.

We believe that 16:1 and 9 should be interpreted as antithetical sentences which bring out the tension between man's activity and God's. Preuss interprets the "Sondergut" passages differently. He suggests that these sentences do not have to be understood as antithetical and mentions 16:33 as an example of this: "Wenn man z. B. im Gewandbausch das Los schüttelt, dann kommt eben von JHWH der Entscheid (16:33), dabei geht es doch um keinen Gegensatz!"[144] But Preuss' main view of the "Sondergut" sentences is that they express the incapacity of man to grasp the world order:

> Folglich hat H. Gese gemeint, dass schon sehr früh in Israel die Lehre vom Tun-Ergehen-Zusammenhang durch das Wissen um JHWH durchbrochen worden sei. Dem aber ist zu widersprechen, denn diese Texte handeln nicht von einer Durchbrechung des Tun-Ergehen-Zusammenhangs durch JHWH, sondern davon, dass dieser Zusammenhang und damit der ihm zugrundeliegende Plan der Weltordnung dem Menschen nicht einsichtig ist (21,30; vgl. 14,12; 16,33; 20,9; 21,1). Der rechte Weise bleibt auch in seiner Erkenntnis demütig (21,30). Gottes Ehre ist es auch, etwas zu verbergen (25,2).[145]

It is certainly the case that one element in the interpretation of sentences like 16:1 and 16:9 is the acknowledgement of man's inability to understand God's plan. But the sentences also have a particular perspective on the Lord's involvement in human affairs, how he accomplishes his purposes even if man's activity pulls in the opposite direction. The Lord is the sovereign God who actively takes part in and directs all the events in the world of man. In sentences like these there is a tension between the anthropocentric and theocentric approach of the book, a tension between what man accomplishes and what the Lord brings about. This is demonstrated by 21:30–31:

> 21:30. There is no wisdom nor understanding
> nor counsel against Yahweh.
> 31. The horse is prepared for the day of battle,
> But to Yahweh belongs the victory.[146]

---

[143] Preuss (1972:125). See also Skladny (1962:73–75), Schmid (1966:147–148).

[144] Preuss (1987:53).

[145] Preuss (1987:53).

[146] Toy's translation (1977:412). Toy comments: "Victory in battle, the couplet says, is decided by God, in spite of human arrangements."

These sentences could be interpreted as asserting that human effort is of no avail, a view which would contradict the rest of the book, which in its anthropocentric approach endows man with great potentialities. We suggest an interpretation along similar lines to those followed earlier for 16:1 and 9. According to this interpretation, human activity—in this case the use of wisdom or prepare for battle—is neither down-played nor given a primary or even decisive role in the outcome because the Lord is in control and will not allow his purposes to be thwarted by human schemes and ambitions.

We agree with Preuss that 16:33 does not represent an antithesis between man's action and God's. But there is an implied antithesis between the arbitrariness of the action and God's control of the situation to bring about his will, his משפט.

16:33. The lot is cast into the lap,
But the whole decision of it is from Yahweh.[147]

The point here is that the seeming arbitrariness of the situation is in fact under the control of the Lord, who in his sovereign and inscrutable way makes the lot fall in a certain way. The combination of גורל[148] and משפט[149] may indicate that this sentence has to do with those occasions on which lots were cast in order to reach a conclusion on matters of God's will and law.

There are various alternatives concerning the translation of 10:22, a sentence which has to do with the tension between the anthropocentric and theocentric approach. The main crux to resolve here is whether to translate עצב of the second line as "toil" or "sorrow." Toy prefers the latter alternative and translates:

10:22. The blessing of Yahweh, it makes rich,
And he adds no sorrow with it.[150]

Toy's translation implies an antithesis between the wealth of good men and that of bad men. When wealth is the result of the Lord's blessing it is free from negative after-effects, while the negative potential of ill gotten gain constantly lurks in the background. The understanding of עצב as sorrow of heart or mind, Toy finds attested in 15:13 and Gen 3:16.

---

[147] Toy's translation (1977:333). Toy notes (1977:334): "The determination of the divine will by casting lots was probably universal in the ancient world; the deity was supposed to direct the throw;.... In OT. important public and private affairs are so determined...; the priestly decision by Urim and Thummin was probably by lot." Cf. Prov 18:18 which indicates that the use of the lot was a means of solving personal disputes.

[148] The employment of the lot was used in OT times on many occasions: to apportion the land among the tribes, to identify the guilty party, for the two goats at the Day of Atonement, to choose Saul as the first king, etc. See Mendelsohn (1962:163–164..

[149] McKane (1985:499) restricts the use of משפט to legal matters in 16:10 where it is used in parallel to the קסם of the king. This may be an excessively restricted understanding of the term which is employed also in contexts which are not strictly legal, see, e.g., Prov 12:5 and BDB (1980:1048–1049).

[150] Toy (1977:212). The subject of the second clause can also be indefinite, e.g., with McKane (1985:226): "and there is no increase of vexation with it."

There are two problems with this translation. First, עצב occurs in 5:10, 14:23, 15:1, Psalms 127:2 and Genesis 3:16, denoting "hard work, toil"; in 15:1 it stands in antithesis to "soft" and means something like "harsh/harshness." The exceptions are 10:10 and 15:13 that have a related noun, עצבה, in the text, which apparently means "sorrow, pain."[151] The second problem is the implied antithesis to ill-gotten gain. It is true that wealth is not thought of as good in and of itself by the sages.[152] However, there is no other example in the book of Proverbs where wealth is described as causing psychological turmoil. There are statements to the effect that wealth is not profitable,[153] that it does not last,[154] or that honest poverty is to be preferred,[155] but these are not true parallels to this rendering of 10:22.

This means that the alternative translation of the second line: "and toil adds not to it" should probably be preferred. It is a somewhat remarkable statement, but in the context of the sentences just studied it is not totally out of place. It contrasts sharply with a number of other sayings in the book which ascribe great potentialities to man, e.g., 14:23 which goes so far as to state that in all labour, using the same term עצב, there is profit. On the other hand, the tendency toward a radicalized depiction of the tension between the anthropocentric and theocentric world view has already been observed. The important point here is to enhance the role of the Lord's blessing for success in life and it should be noted that the "adding" in the second line refers to the blessing of the Lord and not directly to riches. Blessing comes from the sovereign Lord and only he can give or take, increase or decrease it. The sentence deals with the sovereignty of the Lord as the one granting blessings and the consequences of that sovereignty rather than with man's capacity to influence his own life situation.

In several sentences we find a tension between the Lord's activity and man's corresponding to the tension in the book between a theocentric and an anthropocentric interpretation of phenomena. The sages believed in the Lord as the supreme ruler who in inscrutable ways was involved in the world of man but whose activity could never be fully understood. The consequences of this attitude of the sages is described by Crenshaw in the following way:

> Ultimately the wise man or woman had to concede the poverty of intellect, for "man proposes but God disposes" (Pr. 16:9; 19:21; 21:30–31). The ever present incalculable ingredient to every experience promoted an openness to various possibilities and a recognition of one's limits.[156]

---

[151] Cf. Job 9:28, Ps 16:4; 147:3.
[152] Toy (1977:213) mentions 13:11; 15:6; 16:19; 21:6; 28:6.
[153] 10:2.
[154] 13:11; 15:6 , 21:6.
[155] 28:6.
[156] Crenshaw (1976 A:24).

This "openness" may explain how it is was possible for the anthropocentric and theocentric approaches as well as outright contradictions[157] to exist side by side in the book. Israelite wisdom was an open system at least until a tendency toward dogmatization developed in the later wisdom books.

Von Rad comments upon these passages in his book on wisdom:

> The ancients became aware of this limitation in that utterly incalculable and therefore mysterious factor which seemed to intrude between the preparation of a project and its realization. Here, so the teachers thought, one can experience the hand of God. Of course, such sentences do not purport to be sound doctrines about the theological distinction between human and divine activity (man in planning, God in action). They are simply examples from life by means of which one can demonstrate clearly the intervention of the divine mystery.[158]

Von Rad emphasizes the sages' optimistic quest for understanding and their simultaneous awareness that any success in that quest will be limited by their lack of ability to understand the sovereign way in which God accomplishes his purposes.[159]

3. Comparison between the book of Proverbs and other Old Testament traditions

The view of the Lord as sovereign God is not peculiar to the book of Proverbs. In the following an attempt will be made to compare our observations from the book of Proverbs to other wisdom books as well as to other traditions of the Old Testament.

a. The wisdom traditions
The understanding of God as sovereign in action is also well attested in the books of Job and Ecclesiastes. Neither Job nor his friends doubt that God has the power to do whatever he desires.[160] At the same time the argument in the dialogue is built upon the common belief that God does not act arbitrarily, but rewards righteousness and punishes evil. But it is belief in precisely this doctrine which is the source of Job's confusion. Since he cannot see any reason for the "punishment" he has suffered, his view that God is righteous is shaken to the point that he accuses God of being unfair, of destroying the guiltless and the guilty without regard to their moral character.[161] To Job the issue is whether or not God is in fact righteous, while to his friends God's righteousness is beyond dispute. The whole discussion never departs from the assumption of God's sovereignty even though the question of whether or not God's activity is limited by ethical considerations is brought into the picture.

---

[157] See 26:4–5.
[158] Von Rad (1981:100). Similarly, Skladny (1962:75).
[159] Von Rad (1981:97–101).
[160] See Job 5:12–14, 9:4–10, 11:10, etc.
[161] Job 9:22.

Würthwein maintains that Job reacts against the traditional view of God as the righteous retributor and instead finds that he "acts irresistibly, in absolute sovereignty" without being limited by either external powers or internal ethical principles.[162] This may be an accurate description of Job's view of God in his darkest moments, but it should be noted that at times Job also expresses confidence in God's justice. But Würthwein is right when he observes that the sovereignty of God is emphasized throughout the book, though we cannot follow him in applying such a simplistic model of God's action to such a complex piece of literature as the book of Job. His view is that in the book of Proverbs God is depicted as a retributor who is calculable and bound to a determinable law in all his dealings, while the concept of God in the book of Job is a reaction against this view in its stress on the total arbitrariness of God in the experience of Job.[163] The history of the struggle between a rigid traditionalism built upon a view of reality in which everything can be calculated, and the view in which God is sovereign and the world is ultimately impenetrable and mysterious, is more complicated than the creation of simplistic dichotomies between the book of Proverbs and the books of Job and Ecclesiastes will allow.

Even though the arguments of Job's friends are built upon the conviction that some transgression is the root cause of Job's situation, they also include in their arguments the notion that God is inscrutable and that the secrets of life are known only to him.[164] In effect, these assertions of God's inscrutability are intended as a rebuke to Job whose demand for an exhaustive explanation for his suffering is seen as unreasonable, dangerous and impious by the friends.

The book of Ecclesiastes exhibits a profound belief in God's sovereignty through the repeated declaration that his designs for the world are irrevocable, inscrutable to man, and the controlling factor in man's life situation.[165] In addition references to God's activity in the present also depict him as acting sovereignly to accomplish his will and establish justice.[166] The theme and theological implications of Ecclesiastes 7:27 are similar to Proverbs 22:14.[167] The relationship between God's activity and man's is the topic addressed in

---

[162] Würthwein (1976:129).

[163] Würthwein (1976:122–123, 129–130).

[164] 4:16–19; 15:14–16; 25:2–6 discuss the contrast between fallible man and supreme God, but also point out the unknown character of the transcendent God. See also 11:7; 15:7–8; 26:7–14 (must be attributed to Bildad, see Habel [1985:366]). God's transcendence, righteousness, and inscrutability are seen by Elihu as closely interwoven: 33:12–13; 34:10–15; 35:2–7; 36:22–26; 37:14–18, 22–23.

[165] Eccl 1:13–15; 3:10–15; 7:13–14; 8:16–17; 9:1–3.

[166] Eccl 2:24–26; 3:17–18; 5:1–6, 17–19; 8:11–13, 15; 9:7; 11:5, 9. Parallel to these assertions of God's justice are observations that justice is not always accomplished, 6:1–2; 8:10, 14; 9:2. The tension between these two groups of passages are kept within the book and there is no indication that the belief in God's sovereignty is affected. It is rather as in the book of Job the question of God's righteousness or, less pointedly, the justice of life that is the issue.

[167] See our comments to Proverbs 22:14 above, p.170.

7:14, with the fundamental difference that here it is abundantly clear that man is unable to change anything that God already has done, while in Proverbs God tends to be portrayed more as intervening when human action contradicts his purposes rather than as strictly determining the course of events.

Gese discusses the incomprehensibility of divine action and man's limitation in the book of Ecclesiastes and concludes that despite everything Qoheleth holds fast to a monistic view of the world. He also notes Qoheleth's emphasis on the "fear of the Lord."[168] Both the monistic view of the world and the emphasis on the fear of the Lord can be traced back to early wisdom. In Ecclesiastes God is sovereign and has designed the world in such a way that man can neither fully appreciate nor change it.[169] Man's proper attitude, therefore, is to fear God.[170]

Psalm 127 is often referred to as one of the wisdom psalms[171] and the psalm is of interest in the present context. In the psalm man's toil is set in contrast to the Lord's blessing. The text even goes as far as to state that building, guarding and working are of no avail, שוא, if the Lord does not take part in the project. This radical way of expressing the need for the Lord's cooperation in a project is especially reminiscent of Proverbs 21:31 and 10:22.

b. Other Old Testament traditions

It is probably correct to say that a belief in God's sovereignty more or less characterizes the Old Testament as a whole and that the belief in the Lord as supreme ruler constitutes a basic, shared assumption of the biblical authors. This belief is shaken at times when personal or national disaster give indications to the contrary, but in the end it survived even these vicissitudes. The biblical authors seem to have acknowledged the fact that God's will was somehow hindered by the corruption of man and man's tendency to work against God's ordinances and directions.[172] This tension between God's will and man's disobedience pervades the historic and the prophetic books of the Old Testament. The interpretation of history manifest in the writings of the prophets and history writers is that the cause of national disasters lies not in God's incapacity but in man's disobedience. This is illustrated already in the primeval history by the transgression of Adam and Eve and the corruption of man before the flood. It is a recurrent motif in the deuteronomistic as well as in the prophetic traditions.

The Psalter and especially the hymns in the Old Testament provide a number of confessions of the sovereignty of God in sustaining and redeeming

---

[168] Gese (1983:150–151).

[169] Eccl 3:11; 8:17; 11:5.

[170] Eccl 3:14. Cf. Zimmerli (1964:156–158).

[171] E.g., Fichtner (1933:9), Crenshaw (1976 A:15).

[172] The fact that the sin of the people restricts the Lord's sovereignty is illustrated by Hos 11:8–9 where it appears that God's feelings conflict with his zeal for justice. The people have to bear the consequences of their actions, at least as long as they refuse to repent.

his people.[173] The incomprehensibility of the Lord's activity is also implied in these descriptions of God's majesty and glory.[174]

It is difficult to find parallels to the passages in the book of Proverbs that deal with the particular relationship between the Lord's and man's activity and results.[175] Von Rad advocates the view that the Succession Narrative represents an understanding of God as acting secretly through the "normal" circumstances of life and he also discusses the relevant passages from the book of Proverbs which corroborate this view.[176] The Succession Narrative as well as the Joseph story also show signs of a wisdom perspective, von Rad asserts. However, it should be noted that while these text certainly can be used as illustrations of wisdom teachings and the way the Lord leads everything to serve his purposes in spite of man's interference, the texts themselves have few explicit statements concerning the relationship between God's activity and man's[177] that can serve as parallels to the passages in the book of Proverbs.

4. Comparison between the book of Proverbs and non-Israelite wisdom

The decisive factor that made Gese term some sentences "Sondergut" was that he regarded them to be uniquely Israelite, without counterpart in Egyptian instructions. In the following an attempt will be made to relate our observations concerning the sovereignty of God in the book of Proverbs to the wisdom literature of Egypt and Mesopotamia.

a. Egypt
Hornung lists the attributes of the generic "god" of the instructions in order to demonstrate that the designation can refer to almost any deity:

> Aber die Lehren sagen nicht mehr, als dass der *nr* die verschiedensten Wohltaten spendet, dass er ins Weltgeschehen eingreift und seine "Befehle" Wirklichkeit werden lässt, dass er richtet, belohnt und straft, dass ohne oder gegen ihn nichts gelingt—alles Eigenschaften und Aktionsarten, die auch konkreten Gottesgestalten zugeschrieben werden.[178]

Hornung's characterization indicates that the god of the instructions was characterized as sovereign in his actions. The descriptions of the deity in the instructions do not indicate any limitation such as the restriction of the god to acting only within the normal circumstances of life or to acting in strict accordance to *ma'at*. The statement that without or against the deity nothing will succeed, is reminiscent of Proverbs 10:22, 21:31 and Psalms 127:1–2.

---

[173] See esp. Ps 33; 65; 89:6–19; 113; 135; 136; 145.

[174] See, e.g., Ps 65:9, 89:9–12, 113:5–9, 145:3–6.

[175] Since these passages point out the limitation of wisdom, it could be argued that there is a parallel in the critique of wisdom in the prophetic books, see Collins (1980:10–11).

[176] Von Rad (1981:97–101).

[177] See, however, Gen 45:5–8.

[178] Hornung (1973:191).

Hornung shares the view of other Egyptologists that there is a development in Egyptian religion towards more emphasis on the free will of the god[179]:

> Wie der König, so beugen sich auch die Verfasser der Lehren im Laufe der ägyptischen Geschichte immer tiefer unter Willen, Handeln und Einsicht der Gottheit; im "Zeitalter der persönlichen Frömmigkeit", dem auch Amenemope (um 1200 v. Chr) angehört, gibt sich der Mensch ganz in die Hand Gottes und erhofft kaum noch Heil von menschlichen Wirken.[180]

This development, which precedes Old Testament times, indicates that the belief in the sovereignty of the god is especially strong in those instructions which happen to be the most relevant comparative material for Old Testament wisdom.

Chapter 20 in *The Instruction of Amenemope* is about justice and non-partiality in the courts of law and states that: "*Ma'at* is a great gift of god, He gives it to whom he wishes,"[181] which stresses the sovereignty of the god in his office as overseer of justice and order. *Ma'at* is not an automatic retributive force, but completely controlled by the god.

The view of God as supreme ruler is well attested in the instructions from earliest times. It is stated repeatedly in *The Instruction of Ptahhotep* that the good things in life: wealth, advancement, a good son and eating, are from the god. As stated by Hornung above, *Amenemope* puts strong emphasis on humility before the god since his will is the determining factor in life.

Gese discusses a passage from *Ptahhotep* which provides an explanation for the differing fates of men:[182]

> He who hears is beloved of god,
> He whom god hates does not hear.
> The heart makes of its owner a hearer or non-hearer,
> Man's heart is his life-prosperity-health![183]

This passage must be understood by reference to the concept of determinism in Egypt which is here used to explain the cause of a physical handicap. It should be noted, however, that this passage at the same time stresses the responsibility of the individual for his own destiny—it is his heart which makes the difference! Thus the two contrasting views function in a complementary way, appearing side by side![184]

The determinism of the Egyptian view of reality can also be observed in the 25th chapter of *Amenemope* cited above.[185] It should be noted that the

---

[179] See our comments on *ma'at* in ch. 3, pp. 95–96.

[180] Hornung (1973:191).

[181] *Amenemope* xxi 5–6, Lichtheim (1976:158).

[182] Gese (1958:47).

[183] Lichtheim (1975:74). Lichtheim comments (1975:80, n. 68): "Once again the note of determinism is sounded; and it is quickly countered by the assertion that it is a man's own heart that determines his behaviour."

[184] Cf. above concerning the same phenomenon in Israelite wisdom.

[185] P. 156.

determination of the course of an individual's life here is completely in the hands of the god and is not regarded as some kind of impersonal force.

The incomprehensibility of the god and his actions is also attested in Egypt, at least from the Middle Kingdom onward. Crenshaw notes that a new tone can be detected in *The Instruction of Merikare:* "life's shadow-side lurks nearby. God hides from humans, who sin unwittingly if not consciously. Although a judgment is set, one's fate cannot be altered through magical acts which aim at controlling the gods."[186] This understanding of the god in the instructions appears explicitly in the following passage from *Merikare:*

> While generation succeeds generation,
> God who knows characters is hidden;
> One can not oppose the lord of the hand,
> He reaches all that the eyes can see.
> One should revere the god on his path,
> Made of costly stone, fashioned of bronze.[187]

The passage emphasizes the inscrutability of the god, his omnipotence as well as his omniscience. According to Lichtheim the last two lines probably refer to the cult statues of the gods carried in procession during festivals.[188] There was apparently no tension in Egyptian religion between the hiddenness and unboundedness of the deity and identifying him with a statue. Hornung refers to the images of the gods in Egypt as a "metalanguage," as hieroglyphs, expressing "Wesen und Funktion der gemeinten Gottheit," and continues:

> Aber all diese Tiere, Pflanzen und Dinge, die mit der Erscheinung der Götter verbunden werden, sagen nichts über die wahre, eigentliche Gestalt einer Gottheit aus. Diese ist nach den Texten "verborgen" und "geheimnisvoll", nach den Sargtexten darf nur der wissende Tote die wahre Gottesgestalt schauen. Kein denkender Ägypter wird sich vorgestellt haben, Amun sei in seiner wahren Gestalt ein Mensch mit Widderkopf.[189]

Amenemope advises caution in retributive action against other men by referring to the inscrutability of the god and his plans:

> Do not say: "Find me a strong superior,
> For a man in your town has injured me";
> Do not say: "Find me a protector,
> For one who hates me has injured me."
> Indeed you do not know the plans of god,
> And should not weep for tomorrow;...[190]

It seems possible to conclude that the deity in Egyptian instructions was regarded as inscrutable both in his nature and in the way he acts in the world.

---

[186] Crenshaw (1982:218).
[187] Lichtheim (1975:105–106). Lichtheim (1975:109, n. 25) explains that the expression "lord of the hand" refers to the sun-god in his role as creator.
[188] Lichtheim (1975:109, n. 26).
[189] Hornung (1973:113).
[190] *Amenemope* xxii 1–6, Lichtheim (1976:159).

The texts imply an awareness of the incomprehensibility associated with the deity and his relations to the world of men.

Concerning the peculiar relationship between man's action and God's in the book of Proverbs, a number of passages in the Egyptian material are particularly interesting. *The Instruction of Ptahhotep* expresses the conviction that it is the god who provides a person with wealth and success in a variety of ways. Maxim no. six lists a number of intentions of man which are instead turned against him and concludes with the words:

> People's schemes do not prevail,
> God's command is what prevails;
> Live then in the midst of peace,
> What they give comes by itself.[191]

Lichtheim finds the maxim to be "...interesting as a working of the theme of divine retribution through the reversal of fortune."[192] The last two lines are an assurance that the gods will provide the wise man with whatever he needs, indicating that he does not need to resort to scheming to get it. The difference between this text and Proverbs 16:1 and 9 is that the plans listed are more or less negative in character while the devising and planning of Proverbs 16:1 and 9 appear to be presented neutrally. The same theme occurs again in *Ptahhotep:*

> It is the god who gives advancement,
> He who uses elbows is not helped.[193]

Another maxim in *Ptahhotep* deals with how a poor man should relate to someone who has been able to move from the ranks of the poor to those of the prosperous. Such an individual is to be respected by the poor since his new status has been granted to him by the gods. At the same time this text indicates the man's own active part in the course of events:

> Respect him for what has accrued to him,
> For wealth does not come by itself.
> It is their law for him whom they love,
> His gain, he gathered it himself;
> It is the god who makes him worthy
> And protects him while he sleeps.[194]

The Instruction of Amenemope provides particularly interesting material in comparison to the "Sondergut" passages. Gese himself discusses a well-known passage ending the eighteenth chapter of *Amenemope:*

> Keep firm your heart, steady your heart,
> Do not steer with your tongue;

---

[191] *Ptahhotep* maxim 6, Lichtheim (1975:65).
[192] Lichtheim (1975:77, n. 13).
[193] *Ptahhotep* maxim 13, Lichtheim (1975:67).
[194] *Ptahhotep* maxim 10, Lichtheim (1975:66).

If a man's tongue is the boat's rudder,
The Lord of All is yet its pilot.[195]

Gese interprets this as an admonition to honesty where "tongue" in "steer with your tongue" stands in contrast to "heart." According to this interpretation, the message is that one should not attempt to hide what is in his heart by speaking falsehoods, for God will not allow such dishonesty to succeed. The important point in Gese's interpretation is that God always leads a person according to what is in his heart. He argues that this is compatible with the fundamental ideas of act-consequence relationship.[196]

Gese finds the Egyptian passage to be "ganz und gar nicht zu vergleichen mit dem äusserlich so ähnlichen Spruch Prov 16,1" since only the Proverbs passage represents a true overturning of the act-consequence relationship.[197] Gese's interpretation of the *Amenemope* passage appears somewhat strained and too much forced into the mold of his general theory on the act-consequence relationship.[198] The point of both sayings, even if they are not entirely identical thematically, seems to be that God is involved in and directs the workings of man's mind without his knowledge.[199] This interpretation is supported by the context of the eighteenth chapter of *Amenemope* which strongly emphasizes the qualitative distance between the perfect god and fallible man. One saying in the beginning of the chapter is quite similar to Proverbs 16:1:

The words men say are one thing,
The deeds of the god are another.[200]

The context indicates that these lines should be interpreted in the sense that the deeds of the god are reliable while the words of man cannot be trusted. But "the words men say" and "the deeds of the god" are hardly unconnected, and it seems probable that here, as in, e.g., Proverbs 16:1, the contrast is between what men do and God's sovereign way of arranging it all so that the end result coincides with this purposes. The difference is that the Proverbs passage has a less negative view of human activity than this chapter of Amenemope.

A belief in the sovereignty of the god finds strong support in *The Instruction of Ptahhotep* and *The Instruction of Amenemope*. This support comes in the form of several passages that manifest a relationship between man's action and God's similar to the "Sondergut" passages in the book of

---

[195] *Amenemope* xx 3–6, Lichtheim (1976:158).

[196] Gese (1958:46–47).

[197] Gese (1958:47).

[198] The point of the passage appears to be that God is the pilot of the tongue. The passage does not actually differentiate between what is in a person's heart and his words.

[199] Hornung (1973:191) points out that the last verse of this *Amenemope* passage emphasizes the partnership of man and the deity. They are in the same boat—"die Nusschale des Seins auf dem Ozean des Nicht-seins."

[200] *Amenemope* xix 16–17, Lichtheim (1976:157).

Proverbs.[201] This corroborates our observation that *Amenemope* represents a new approach in the religious thinking in Egypt—an approach where God's free will is the decisive factor while *ma'at* is less prominent and subordinated to this sovereign will of the god.

In his interesting article on the concept of *ma'at,* Volten maintains that the maxim "Der Mensch denkt, aber Gott lenkt" represents a "fundamentalen ägyptischen Gedanken,"[202] which he finds attested already in maxim 6 of *The Instruction of Ptahhotep* quoted above. Volten states: "Der allmächtige und allwissende Gott hat alles aus Ewigkeit vorausbestimmt."[203] We have already noted the prominence of this deterministic view of life in Egyptian wisdom.[204] Among the passages referred to by Volten are the words of *Ptahhotep* on the disobedient son:

> His guilt was fated in the womb;
> He whom they guide can not go wrong,
> Whom they make boatless can not cross.[205]

Volten makes a valid point in his emphasis on the deterministic side of the world view of the Egyptian sages, something which must have been important in every epoch of Egyptian history. Even when the emphasis fell on God's sovereign will rather than on *ma'at,* this personal will does not have to be seen in stark contrast to a more calculating predeterminacy. According to Volten, God's will, ma'at, and man's fate were identical in Egyptian belief.[206]

b. Mesopotamia.

The relationship between the gods and man in Mesopotamia is described by Lambert as follows:

> ...in the ancient Mesopotamian view every aspect of human society was decreed by the gods. Nothing was left to be chosen by the human race as suitable and convenient for it at a particular stage of development and in a particular geographical location. The gods had decreed it all.[207]

The wisdom texts share the view that the great gods are supreme rulers. As has been noted already there are several texts that deal with the problems of theodicy. Lambert compares Babylonian with Sumerian thought and notes that when the gods were no longer simple personifications of parts or aspects of nature, intellectual problems arose: "The big problem in Babylonian thought

---

[201] The same thought appears in *Onkhsheshonqy* viii 6; xxvi 14, see Lichtheim (1983:73, 91). A similar line of thought can be observed in *Any* viii 9–10, Lichtheim (1976:142).

[202] Volten (1963:76).

[203] Volten (1963:81).

[204] For a thorough treatment of the subject, see Morenz (1960 A).

[205] Maxim 12, Lichtheim (1975:67). "They" in the last two lines refers to the gods.

[206] Volten (1963:98).

[207] Lambert (1972:67).

was that of justice. If the great gods in council controlled the universe, and if they ruled it in justice, why ...?"[208]

In Mesopotamia where there is no indication of a belief in an after-life[209] and consequently no possibility of postponing the execution of justice to a world beyond the present, the texts often refer to the inscrutability of the gods as provisional explanation to the theodicy. This comes out especially clearly in the so called *Babylonian Theodicy* where the friend seeks to defend the gods and the conventional belief that the gods are just in the face of the sufferer's accusations:

> Your are as stable as the earth, but the plan of the gods is remote....
> The mind of the god, like the centre of the heavens, is remote;
> Knowledge of it is very difficult; people cannot know it....
> Though it is possible to find out what the will of the god is,
>   people do not know how to do it[210]

The same view can be observed in *Ludlul bēl nēmeqi* as well as in a bilingual proverb:

> Who can know the will of the gods in heaven?
> Who can understand the plans of the underworld gods?
> Where have humans learned the way of a god?[211]
>
> It is you, O Marduk, who divines among the gods.
> No god can understand his plan.[212]
>
> The will of a god cannot be understood,
> the way of a god cannot be known.
> Anything of a god [is difficult] to find out[213]

The view that the gods are inscrutable appears to have been prominent in Mesopotamia and indicates the existence of a wide chasm between the world of men and of the gods. The great gods act in sovereignty and it is not possible for man to gain insight into their secrets. The sufferer in *Ludlul bēl nēmeqi* complains that man cannot even know what is pleasing to the god.[214] The sufferer may pray to his god and goddess, consult the clergy who by exorcism, magic and incantations may relieve him or elucidate his case,[215] but when this is of no avail, only lamenting and pleading to the gods for mercy remain as in the Sumerian *A Man and His God* and *Ludlul bēl nēmeqi* or perhaps one might

---

[208] Lambert (1960:10).

[209] Lambert (1960:11).

[210] *Babylonian Theodicy* 58, 256–257, 264, *ANET* (1969:602, 604).

[211] *Ludlul* II 36–38, *ANET* (1969:597).

[212] *Ludlul* I 31–32, Wiseman (1980:105–106).

[213] BM 38486 reverse 7–8, Lambert (1960:265–266).

[214] *Ludlul* II 33–35, *ANET* (1969:597).

[215] See *Ludlul bēl nēmeqi* II 4–9.

resort to revolt and accusing the gods of injustice as in the *Babylonian Theodicy*.[216]

The Mesopotamian wisdom texts provide no direct parallels to Gese's "Sondergut" passages. The basic assumption seems to be that good acts towards the deity or one's fellow man will be repaid with the deity's favour and well-being, and evil acts with punishment. The theodicy passages stress the incomprehensibility of the gods and the submission of man before them.

5. Conclusions concerning God's sovereignty

a. Old Testament wisdom traditions

The assertion of God's omnipotence and lordship over the world permeates the Old Testament wisdom traditions and leads to the pious exhortation to fear God and submit every plan to him. Job cannot accept the interpretation of his friends concerning his situation, refuses to humbly accept his change of fortune and thus accuses God of injustice. But in the end Job also confesses his allegiance to God and accepts God's supremacy. While Qoheleth questions whether or not justice is really established in the world, he never deviates from viewing God as the supreme ruler and the "fear of God" as man's appropriate attitude toward him. In the book of Proverbs especially, a theocentric world view is found side by side with an anthropocentric approach.

The incomprehensibility of God's action is expressed in a variety of ways in the wisdom traditions. God is depicted as actively involved in the affairs of men, but his ways can never be fully known to man. This is asserted especially in the books of Proverbs and Ecclesiastes. Job's friends use this notion in their arguments, but in the dialogue Job refuses to accept God's incomprehensibility as an explanation for his predicament.

Most intriguing in the book of Proverbs are the "Sondergut" passages which emphasize the freedom of the Lord to do what he chooses regardless of human schemes and actions. Since so much of the teaching in the wisdom tradition is built upon the view that God's action toward individuals is calculated to repay good with good and evil with destruction, and that man has enormous potential, these sentences are certainly noteworthy because of their insistence that it is impossible to place conditions upon God's action. These sentences are without close parallels in the books of Job and Ecclesiastes. One of the so-called wisdom psalms, Psalm 127, exhibits similarities to Proverbs 21:31 and 10:22 in stressing the worthlessness of human effort which is contrary to the will of the Lord.

We find that the sovereignty of God in carrying out his purposes is strongly maintained by the Old Testament wisdom traditions without significant qualifications. God is depicted in as subtly yet significantly engaged in all

---

[216]*Babylonian Theodicy* 70–75, 133–141, 251, *ANET* (1969:601–604).

human affairs, steering them and harmonizing their outcome to his own will and purpose.

b. *Other Old Testament traditions*

The main distinctive view of God's sovereignty in the historic and prophetic books of the Old Testament, is that according to these traditions man's corruptness hinders God's plans and the accomplishment of his will. God is regarded as actively engaged, working out his purposes in a variety of ways, but the accomplishment of his will is severely hampered by man's fallibility.

The incomprehensibility of the Lord's activity is indicated in several of the hymns in the book of Psalms and is in harmony with the general view of God in the Old Testament.

Even if we hesitate to classify the Succession Narrative or the Joseph story as wisdom texts, there is some value in von Rad's view that the "Sondergut" passages stand close to the texts deriving from the era of the "Solomonic enlightenment" which highlight the Lord's subtle way of bringing about his will in the world of man. Nevertheless, although these texts provide a number of pertinent illustrations of the teachings of the sages, it is difficult to find specific passages that assert the Lord's sovereignty in the outworking of his purposes independently of or contrary to man's actions.

c. *Egypt*

The god of the instructions is active in the world as a ruler who carries out his will in a sovereign way. In the instructions from the New Kingdom there is a strong emphasis on the unbounded free will of the god. From the times of the Old Kingdom and onwards it is stated that especially the good things of life come from the god. This providence of the gods is not, as e.g. in the book of Proverbs, directly related to ethical behaviour. It is simply stated, often without any explanation, that some receive that which is good while others experience hardship and deprivation.

A feature which is more characteristic of the Egyptian as opposed to the Israelite world view, is the concept of divine determinism where everything takes place in accordance with the god's decree at the beginning of time. This belief implies that what happens is irrevocable—such a view must have been of only minor importance during the so called "period of personal piety," i.e. at the close of the New Kingdom, but it appears in every period and most of all in the late Demotic instructions.

The notion of the incomprehensibility of the gods and their activity is attested in Egyptian instructions from *The Instruction of Merikare* and onwards and seems to have constituted an essential aspect of the Egyptian understanding of the gods.

When it comes to the "Sondergut" passages, the Egyptian material provides several examples of a similar view. The sovereignty of the god to accomplish his will and the limitations of man to fulfil his purposes are attested already as early as in *The Instruction of Ptahhotep*. Especially in the eighteenth chapter of *The Instruction of Amenemope* we see a view of the god's activity which closely resembles Proverbs 16:1.

d. Mesopotamia

The great gods of Mesopotamia, who were also seen as supreme rulers of the universe, are characterized by sovereignty in relation to man. It is a recurrent motif in the wisdom texts that the gods are inscrutable. It is even asserted that man cannot know what is right and wrong in the eyes of the gods. The sovereignty of the gods appears strongly, but in the case of certain texts it is also possible to say that the gods and their actions appear as arbitrary and capricious.

No parallels to the "Sondergut" sentences are found. In Mesopotamian religious thought, the focus on the power and sovereignty of the great gods appears to have steered attention away from the interrelationship between divine and human actions.

C. Conclusions

Our study has demonstrated that the concept of God in the book of Proverbs is characterized by transcendence and sovereignty. The texts certainly argue for a profound differentiation between God and man both in terms of nature and potentiality. In several areas, e.g., non-cultic and non-mythological depiction, a certain remoteness and transcendence, the depiction of the Lord is consistent with the characteristics of supreme beings in religion in general. Our survey has shown that such similarities are true also for the god of the Egyptian instructions as well as the great gods of Mesopotamia as they appear in the wisdom texts. It has also become evident that even if the Egyptian and Mesopotamian texts share the same basic view of the deity as transcendent and sovereign, there are also significant divergences in detail.

Concerning divine traits indicating transcendence, we noted that the belief that the Lord is responsible for justice and retribution was fundamental to Israelite wisdom and built upon the firm conviction that the Lord is omniscient, omnipotent, and righteous. Even if this belief is to some degree also present in Egyptian and Mesopotamian wisdom, it does not appear to have been of equal importance nor was there the same firm conviction that the gods were righteous. The Mesopotamian texts dealing with innocent suffering assume both the fairness of the god and the correspondence between act-character and consequences. A number of different reasons might be suggested for the absence of the problems of theodicy in Egyptian texts. It may indicate that the gods were not regarded as responsible in the same way for injustices but were viewed as also struggling against evil. It may also find its explanation in the absence of law codes and justice as a "right" of the individual in Egypt. The steadfast belief in the righteousness of the Lord and his maintenance of justice in the world has strong parallels especially in the prophetic and deuteronomistic traditions of the Old Testament, which, even if they are less individualistic in approach, are quite similar to the book of Proverbs in this respect.

The belief in the Lord as sole creator also implies his transcendence and is a view shared by the wisdom literature and the Old Testament as a whole. In Mesopotamian wisdom, however, the role of divine creator is of no significance, while in Egypt the peculiar connection between the creation of man and ethics along the lines of that found in Proverbs 10–29 is attested. This is an interesting connection since at this particular point the similarity of the Egyptian material to Proverbs is more direct than any connections to the other traditions of the Old Testament.

When it comes to the absence of direct address and the peculiar role of wisdom as God's representative, we noted certain similarities to the other traditions of the Old Testament, especially the function of the angel of the Lord as God's representative. The appearance of an intermediary between

God and man reinforces the notion of the transcendence of God while at the same time indicating his involvement in the affairs of men. In the book of Job the theophany ends God's conspicuous silence, in the Mesopotamian *Ludlul bēl nēmeqi* Marduk answers by sending different messengers to the sufferer in dreams. With the exception of these cases; we find the absence of direct address to be characteristic of the wisdom literature. No parallels to the role and function of wisdom in Proverbs 1–9 were found elsewhere. *Ma'at* in Egypt never had this function, nor is there any evidence in Mesopotamian wisdom literature that the personal god played this role. The messengers of Marduk mentioned above is the closest parallel to be found.

The Lord is depicted as sovereign in the book of Proverbs in connection with three different themes. First, notions of sovereignty lie behind the depiction of the Lord as the supreme ruler who leads and helps those who submit to him and live a life pleasing to him. The books of Job and Ecclesiastes likewise stress God's omnipotence and sovereign rule over the earth. In other traditions of the Old Testament there is a noteworthy emphasis on the limitation imposed upon God's sovereignty by man's disobedience. The god of the Egyptian instructions and especially the great gods of Mesopotamia are also characterized as supreme rulers who govern all things in the world including men's lives.

Second, the incomprehensibility of God also entails his sovereignty. This feature is well attested in the wisdom traditions of the Old Testament as well as in Egypt and Mesopotamia. While the notion of incomprehensibility is present in other Old Testament traditions as well, it seems to be particularly concentrated in the wisdom texts, something which can probably be explained by their "philosophical" character.

Third, the sovereignty of the Lord is implied in the "Sondergut" passages in the book of Proverbs with their focus on God's freedom to bring all things into harmony with his purposes. No close parallels to this were found in the Old Testament, nor in the Mesopotamian material, but, interestingly enough, *The Instruction of Amenemope* which exhibits other similarities to the book of Proverbs contains such parallels.

The conclusion that can be drawn from the study of the Lord as supreme God in the book of Proverbs, is that the concept of God in the book of Proverbs finds its closest parallel context in the Old Testament, first and foremost, of course, in the other wisdom literature. This comparison shows that the book of Proverbs also has certain affinities on this point with the prophetic and deuteronomistic traditions of the Old Testament. A relationship between Israelite and Mesopotamian wisdom appears primarily in texts that relate to the problems of theodicy, a problem which is not so prominent in the book of Proverbs, as it is in the book of Job and to some extent also in the book of Ecclesiastes. In the Egyptian instructions we observed some remarkable parallels to the book of Proverbs—the connection between the creation of man and ethics, as well as the subtle and sovereign way God acts to bring about his purposes in men's lives independently of their own actions. The mysterious side of God and his action is common to the wisdom literature of Israel, Egypt, and Mesopotamia, and it is possible that this characteristic in the understanding of God may be considered a characteristic of wisdom literature *per se*.

Chapter five

The Lord as personal God in the book of Proverbs

Introduction

In a previous chapter we noted that the Lord in the book of Proverbs appears as the supreme god who transcends human limitations and is sovereign in accomplishing his purposes without any qualification. In this chapter we will see that there are a number of other complementary features in the depiction of the Lord in the book of Proverbs. Not only does the Lord appear as the supreme god, the sages also depict him as a personal god.

The term "personal god" is employed by Jacobsen in his description of Mesopotamian religion to describe the particular god of a person which serves as that person's "own" god and to whom he stands in a close relationship and from whom he expects personal success and well-being in his worldly affairs.[1] The intimacy of this relationship stands in contrast to the relationship between the great gods and the individual where supplication was only made in extra-ordinary situations and even then only through intermediaries.[2] Normally the relationship between the god and man is described as that of master and slave, while the relationship to one's personal god is associated with the intimate imagery of parent and child.[3] Jacobsen terms the latter religious attitude "personal religion" and argues that it originated in Mesopotamia in the beginning of the second Millenium[4] and from there eventually spread out all over the Ancient Near East.[5] He defines this "personal religion" in these words:

> We use it to designate a particular, easily recognized, religious attitude in which the religious individual sees himself as standing in close relationship to the divine, expecting help and guidance in his personal life and personal affairs, expecting divine anger and punishment if he sins, but also profoundly trusting to divine compassion, forgiveness and love for

---

[1] Jacobsen (1946:203–204; 1976:145–164).

[2] Jacobsen (1946:203).

[3] Jacobsen (1976:158).

[4] Cf. Klein (1982:295–297) who on the whole agrees with Jacobsen, but maintains that there is evidence of personal religion in Mesopotamia already in the Sumerian era, though the more refined and developed attitude of personal religion does not appear until the beginning of the second millenium.

[5] Jacobsen (1976:152). Cf. Römheld (1989:135–150).

him if he sincerely repents. In sum: the individual matters to God, God cares about him personally and deeply.[6]

Vorländer points out that the term "personal god" is not employed to signify a anthropomorphic description of a god, but rather the personal relationship between a god and man:

> Unter dem Begriff "persönlicher Gott" ist im folgenden die Funktion einer Gottheit zu verstehen, zu einem Individuum und dessen Familie in einer dauernden, engen Beziehung als sein spezieller Gott zu stehen. "Persönlich" wird hier also nicht im Sonne von "personhaft" verwendet, sondern meint die persönliche Zugehörigkeit eines Menschen zu einer bestimmten Gottheit.[7]

Vorländer and Albertz maintain that personal religion should be regarded as a a distinct facet of religion that co-existed with official religion. Both Vorländer and Albertz have applied this model of religion to the interpretation of the Old Testament.[8] Especially in the case of the patriarchal narratives, personal names and psalms of individual lament they argue that it is possible to demonstrate the existence of a religious attitude and relationship to God that deviates from that of official religion.

The similarities between the description of personal religion above and the religious attitude that frequently appears in the book of Proverbs is the reason why we have chosen the term "personal god" in this chapter.[9] The following analyses of the text material will seek to demonstrate that the relationship between God and man is often described in such a way in the book of Proverbs that it indicates a close personal relationship between the Lord and the individual. One important characteristic of the personal religion found in the Old Testament is the absence of references to Israel's salvation history. This feature constitutes another link between the book of Proverbs and the other wisdom literature of the Old Testament.

In his book Vorländer summarizes the concept of personal god in the Ancient Orient, by stating that any of the great gods as well as minor deities could serve as a personal god.[10] In so doing, Vorländer highlights his opposition to the prevailing view that only the minor deities in the pantheon could function as personal gods.[11] Furthermore, his approach also allows him to maintain that, e.g., the Lord in Israel could be related to as a personal god.

---

[6] Jacobsen (1976:147).

[7] Vorländer (1975:3). Vorländer notes that in the study of religions the term "Schutzgott" has often been used with the same meaning.

[8] Vorländer (1975), Albertz (1978).

[9] Albertz (1978:92) indicates that further support for his views may be found in other text corpora of the Old Testament, e.g. the books of Samuel, Kings and Proverbs.

[10] Vorländer (1975:165). The same applies also for Egypt, see Brunner (1982:953).

[11] E.g., Jacobsen (1946:203). In a later book Jacobsen notes (1976:152) that attitudes from "personal religion" in later times could be directed toward almost any god while in the earliest examples it were limited to one's "personal" god or goddess only. This of course makes it difficult to differentiate between a personal god and other deities.

Vorländer summarizes the function of the personal god towards the individual in the Ancient Orient:

> 1. Als Garant für sein Wohlergehen schenkt er dem Menschen Gesundheit, Erfolg, Harmonie mit der Umwelt und die Gunst der Vorgesetzten....
> 2. Der persönliche Gott schützt den ihm anvertrauten Menschen gegen alle sein Leben bedrohenden Feinde. Dies können sowohl politische und militärische Feinde als auch (insbesondere in Mesopotamien) Zauberer und Dämonen sein.
> 3. Der persönliche Gott vertritt den Menschen als Mittler und Fürsprecher bei den anderen Göttern....[12]

Developments in Egypt characterized by a shift in emphasis from *ma'at* in early times to the god's free will in the Late Kingdom has already been noted. In the early 1900's Breasted designated the latter period "the age of personal piety" because of its different religious emphasis.[13] In the new situation where the benevolence of the god was crucial for the successful completion of a project, there was an evident desire to influence the god in every possible way in order to succeed. These developments thus ushered in an era marked by religious attitudes that remind one very much of the phenomena in Mesopotamian personal religion described by Jacobsen.[14] In a similar way the individual in Egypt of this period stood in a special relationship to a particular deity from whom he expected help and refuge.[15] The texts reflect a relationship to the gods which is intimate and personal.[16] Morenz emphasizes that there does not seem to be any tension between the official cult and personal piety in Egyptian religion,[17] though the latter is different in not being restricted to certain localities and to the assistance of cult personnel. The inclusive nature of Egyptian religion appears to have permitted official and personal religion to be complementary without conflict.[18] Brunner notes that the influences of personal piety are especially noticeable in the instructions from the end of the eighteenth dynasty, such as *The Instruction of Amenemope*.[19] Towards the end of the New Kingdom personal piety had become superficial (Brunner uses the word "verflacht")[20] and in the late

---

[12] Vorländer (1975:166).

[13] Breasted (1912:344–370).

[14] Morenz (1984:131) defines "frömmigkeit" as: "die persönliche Beziehung des einzelnen zu Gott ausserhalb des Gottesdienstes. Anders ausgedrückt: Frömmigkeit ist Innesein und Nutzung der neuen, allgemeinen Verfügbarkeit Gottes für jeden, der ihn bittend anruft." Brunner (1983:103) finds it characterized by the fact "dass der einzelne Mensch unmittelbaren Zugang zu seinem Gott sucht und findet."

[15] Brunner (1982:953–954; 1983:104).

[16] See Brunner (1983:104), Morenz (1984:98–99,155).

[17] Morenz (1960 B:115–116; 1984:131, 138). Also Sadek (1987:294).

[18] Morenz (1960 B:110–112) points out that Amun functioned as the king of the gods, the god of the kings, as well as lord and refuge for the average man, thereby serving as example of the merging of official state cult and the piety of the average man.

[19] Brunner (1963:116–117). Cf. Otto (1971:9–22).

[20] Brunner (1963:112).

Demotic *Papyrus Insinger* it had become systematized to such an extent that it had completely transformed the thought world of ancient wisdom.[21]

Jacobsen concludes his observations on personal religion by applying them to the Old Testament:

> As far as we can see, it is only Israel that decisively extended the attitude of personal religion from the personal to the national realm. The relationship of Yahweh to Israel—his anger, his compassion, his forgiveness, and his renewed anger and punishment of the sinful people—is in all essentials the same as that of the relation between god and individual in the attitude of personal religion.[22]

Personal religion applies both to the individual and to the nation in Israel. Our interest here is with the former. There are Old Testament texts which indicate that the Lord relates to the Israelites as a personal god on an individual level. Among these Old Testament texts are a number of sayings in the book of Proverbs where the Lord is repeatedly depicted as a deity who relates personally to individuals, protecting and guiding them in their private lives and bringing about the success and well-being of those who follow the way of wisdom and righteousness.

The Lord, e.g., sees to it that the needs of the righteous are fulfilled, while on the other hand the evil desires of the wicked remain unfulfilled:

> 10:3. Yahweh suffers not the righteous to hunger,
> But he disappoints the desire of the wicked.[23]

The Lord not only keeps starvation away, but guides and helps when it comes to personal matters:

> 18:22. If one finds a wife, it is a piece of good fortune,
> A favour bestowed on him by Yahweh.[24]

The Lord listens to the prayer of the righteous, indicating that the relationship is one of an individual to his personal god. This intimacy is to be contrasted with remoteness of the Lord for the wicked:

> 15:29. Yahweh is far from the wicked,
> But he hears the prayer of the righteous.[25]

The Lord also appears as the personal god who protects and avenges for the person who confides in him:

> 20:22. Say not: "I will take revenge for wrong";
> Trust to Yahweh and he will save thee.[26]

---

[21] Brunner (1963:114–115, 117).

[22] Jacobsen (1976:164). Note esp. Isa 40–55, see Mettinger (1988:158–174).

[23] Toy's translation (1977:199).

[24] Toy's translation (1977:365). Cf. 19:14, contrast in 22:14.

[25] Toy's translation (1977:316). Toy (1977:316) explains "far from" as "inaccessible to, deaf to the appeal of."

[26] Toy's translation (1977:392).

A . God and the weak

We have noted that the book of Proverbs depicts the Lord as intimately involved in the world of man. This is made especially clear by a number of sayings expressing the Lord's concern over certain social issues, which constitutes the focus of our interest in this section. In these sayings the Lord is portrayed as a god who is closely related to individuals and desires a society characterized by justice and honesty where certain groups are not mistreated by others.

1. The Lord's concern for the weak and defenceless in the book of Proverbs

A number of sayings are significant in their depiction of the Lord as especially associated with the "weak" and defenceless. Groups that are vulnerable to mistreatment are thus given protection by religious-ethical teaching. In this view, the Lord is the personal god who protects and defends the rights of the "weak."

a. The weak and defenceless as social groups and their counterparts

The main group of people in socially difficult situations, for whom it is stated that the Lord has a special concern, are the poor.[27] Several of the creation of man passages, which we discussed in chapter two, refer to the poor man[28] and express the close relationship between the Lord and these people. This is made abundantly clear when it is said that to mistreat the poor man is to insult, חרף,[29] the Lord himself.

Two other groups who found themselves in a difficult position in Israelite society are the widow[30] and the orphan.[31] As in the case of the poor, it is explicitly stated that the widow and the orphan are helped and protected by the Lord.[32].

Proverbs 24:11–12 has been discussed above.[33] The passage seems to refer to a person who has been subject to some kind of miscarriage of justice and is, despite his innocence, about to be executed. This person represents the inno-

---

[27] This does not mean that poverty is always treated with sympathy. In other sayings it is, e.g., connected with laziness, 10:4; 19:15; 20:13, greediness, 11:24, ignorance, 13:18, and extravagances, 21:17; 23:21. Gowan (1987:348) correctly maintains that in this kind of sayings: "The proverbs were not explaining why people are poor but why a person should work."

[28] רש (17:5; 22:2; 29:13), דל (14:31), אביון (14:31). See the discussion of the terms in ch. 2, p. 59, nn. 67, 68, 71. Also Bammel (1968:888–889), Donald (1964:27–41), Kvalbein (1981:17–20).

[29] 14:31; 17:5. See ch. 2, p. 59.

[30] Hoffner (1974:287–291). Toy (1977:314) concerning 15:25: "*Widow* here stands for any poor, helpless person, the natural prey of the powerful and unscrupulous,..."

[31] See Ringgren (1982:1075–1079).

[32] 15:25; 23:10–11. For the special needs of these groups, see Fensham (1962:139).

[33] Ch. 3, pp. 108–109; ch. 4, p. 147.

cent who are in serious trouble without anyone to turn to for help. Again, the expression of the Lord's concern is noteworthy.

The poor man is twice referred to as God's creation on a par with other categories of people: the rich man (22:2) and the oppressor (29:13). In both sentences the main point is the assertion of the personal rights and value of the poor man. It seems reasonable to believe, in the light of other statements in the book, that the implication here is that the rich and the oppressor should be aware of the fact that they are accountable to God for their way of life.[34]

The widow in 15:25 is contrasted to the proud, גאים. The proud, as in 16:19, appears to be a powerful and unscrupulous person who in such a case would take advantage of the defencelessness of a widow.

b. The involvement of the Lord on behalf of the weak and defenceless
The antithetical structure of the sentence in 15:25 depicts the Lord as actively engaged in two different but complementary directions: negatively, against the proud man and positively, for the benefit of the widow:

> 15:25. Yahweh uproots the house of the proud,
> But establishes the border of the widow.[35]

It is not easy to provide details on precisely how the two parts of this sentence relate to one another—i.e., whether they simply illustrate the way the Lord acts towards different social groups, or indicate that the proud actually threaten the weak, which are here represented by the widow. The latter seems the more probable. While the Lord will violently "tear down," נסח (qal), the house of the proud man, he will "establish," נצב (hi), the boundary of the widow. Toy comments:

> The word *border* alludes to the Israelitish law which endeavored to maintain intact the landed property of every family by forbidding its alienation (Dt.19:14);....[36]

It must have been difficult for a woman on her own to maintain, guard and defend family property. The texts hint that the widow's already inferior position in society was plagued by the constant danger of being exploited by neighbours who would simply move their boundary markers.[37] The sentence emphasizes the active role of the Lord in defending the weak and maintaining the ancient boundaries of family property. It indicates the Lord's concern for both the weak and the defenceless as well as for the conservation of the land allotments of former generations. The sentence depicts the Lord as the

---

[34] See the interpretation given in ch. 2, pp. 65–67.

[35] Toy's translation (1977:314).

[36] Toy (1977:314).

[37] Baab (1962:842): "Many references to the widow indicate that hers was an unfortunate state and that she was frequently subjected to harsh treatment." Reference to the encroachment on the land of the weak and poor by the rich and powerful is supplied by Toy (1977:427): Deut 27:17; 1 Kings 21:19; Job 24:2; Isa 5:8; Hos 5:10.

personal god who defends the rights of an individual against threats, in this case unscrupulous men.[38]

The Lord's concern for the poor man is expressed in 19:17:

19:17. He who has pity on the poor lends to Yahweh,
And he will repay him his deed.[39]

What it means to "have pity on, show mercy, be kind to," חנן, the poor man is explained in the second clause where the general word for "deed," גמול, is used, presumably referring to any deed that would have benefitted the poor man. To act in this way towards the poor man is seen as giving a "loan," מלוה, to the Lord who will "repay," שלם (pi), it. The first clause expresses the closeness of the Lord to the poor with the remarkable assertion that compassion towards the poor is like lending to the Lord—a formulation which implies that the Lord thus would be regarded as in some sense indebted to a human creditor.[40] Although one should be careful not to carry the metaphor too far, the clause certainly emphasizes the intimate relationship between the poor man and his personal god, the Lord. The second clause of the sentence with the verb שלם (pi)[41] and גמול[42] give distinct formulation to the belief that one will be recompensed in accordance with one's way of life.

In chapter three we commented upon the position and special significance of 22:22–23 and 23:10–11.[43]

22:22. Rob not the poor because he is poor,
And oppress not the lowly in the gate.
23. For Yahweh will plead their cause,
And rob their robbers of life.[44]

23:10. Remove not the landmark of 'the widow,'
Into the field of the orphan enter not;
11. For their redeemer is mighty,
He will plead their cause against thee.[45]

Again we are faced with a situation in which the Lord promises to act as vindicator on behalf of the vulnerable groups in society. The language used here is legal with a clear retributional force: the Lord himself will "take up their case," יריב ריבם, and "rob the robbers" not merely of their possessions,

---

[38] In 16:19 "proud" appears in antithetical parallelism to "lowly spirit." Toy comments (1977:328): "The terms *lowly* and *proud* are here ethical, = the unassuming or inoffensive, and the overbearing or oppressive: they have, perhaps, also a religious import, = those who submit themselves to God, and those who disobey and disregard him."

[39] Toy's translation (1977:375).

[40] For the metaphor, see McKane (1985:534–535), Plöger (1984:224).

[41] See our discussion of the verb in ch. 3, p. 104, n. 78; p. 108, n.99; pp. 121–122, 138–139.

[42] Cf. the use of נמול with שוב (hi Qere) in 12:14

[43] See ch. 3, pp. 106–107.

[44] Toy's translation (1977:425).

[45] Toy's translation (1977:431). See ch. 3 , p. 107, n. 89 concerning the emendation to "widow" instead of MT "ancient landmark."

but of their lives. There is a heightened significance in the reference to the
Lord as the "redeemer," נאל, of the widow and the orphan. This is a legal
term that presupposes blood ties between the redeemer and the redeemed.[46]
When it is said that the Lord acts as the redeemer of the widow and the orphan
to defend their rights, it points to a family relationship in which the Lord
places on his own shoulders a social responsibility which no one else will
accept. 23:10–11 and 15:25 constitute examples of the belief in divine concern
for the preservation of family property and ancient tribal borders.[47]

The main focus in 24:11–12 is not primarily on the man about to be executed, but on the Lord's concern for justice.[48] and on the responsibility of the
person who is aware of the unjust way in which the case was handled.[49]

> 24:11. Deliver those who are taken to death,
> Save those who are tottering to slaughter.
> 12. If thou say: "'I' did not know this,"
> He who weighs hearts, does he not perceive?
> He who observes thy soul, does he not know?
> And will he not requite every man according to his deed?[50]

It is difficult to specify exactly which circumstances the saying is applicable to,
but it seems probable that it would have applied in cases where inadequate or
corrupt legal procedures have caused the condemnation of innocent people.[51]
The interesting feature of this text for the purposes of the present investigation
is the fact that the Lord makes even the seemingly uninvolved spectator
responsible for the fate of the victim. The Lord appears as closely attached to
and actively involved in the case of the condemned person, while, interestingly
enough, he at the same time is portrayed as being dependent upon men to act
on the person's behalf.[52]

c. The Lord's concern for social justice

There are some sayings in the book of Proverbs that indicate the concern of
the Lord for a more general concept of social justice which is not directly

---

[46] Stamm (1940:27–46), Stuhlmueller (1970:104), Ringgren (1977:350–355).

[47] This concern for the preservation of the land allotment of the fathers is especially found and
motivated in property laws like Lev 25:23ff where also the function of the נאל is specified. See
Stuhlmueller (1970:102–103).

[48] Cf. 17:15.

[49] See n. 33 for references to our discussion of the passage in ch. 3.

[50] Toy's translation (1977:445–446). Toy notes that the verb translated "save" literally is "hold back,"
but finds that the parallelism requires the former alternative. If we understand אם not to carry the
function of an emphatic but as the negative particle of an oath (as, e.g., McKane [1985:400]), the
translation of Gemser (1963:88), "nicht entzieh dich ihnen," seems possible.

[51] Ringgren (1980:66) finds that the saying applies either to the situation where a person has been
condemned on the basis of false or insufficient evidence or else that it refers to the oppressed person in
general. The former interpretation seems to be shared by McKane (1985:401–402) who regards "the
religious character of the arguments by which the imperatives are reinforced" as strengthening the
assumption that the saying applies to the rescue of innocent victims.

[52] Cf. our observations concerning the Lord's sovereignty and independence of men in ch. 4.

related to the oppression of particular social groups. Of course, these sayings still assume that the Lord is deeply involved in the affairs of men and that he reacts with severity against those who mistreat or cheat fellow-men and thereby disrupt the social order.

In chapters 10:1–22:16 we find several sentences that deal with the same motif—the use of accurate or false measures:

11:1. A false balance is an abomination to Yahweh,
But a just weight is well-pleasing to him.[53]

16:11. The balance and true scales are Yahweh's concern,
All the weights in the bag are his affair.[54]

20:10. Divers weights, divers measures,
Abomination to Yahweh are they both.[55]

20:23. Divers weights are an abomination to Yahweh,
And a false balance is not good.[56]

In every case except 16:11 the use of false measures is condemned by referring to it as an "abomination to the Lord," תועבת יהוה.[57] The expression implies the Lord's revulsion toward a variety of fraud in the marketplace which, of course, strikes the poor and the weak hardest of all. In 11:1b the contrast is the "full weight," אבן שלמה, which is told to be "pleasing," רצון, to the Lord. This pair of expressions, תועבה and רצון, occurs elsewhere in the book of Proverbs as an indication of the Lord's strong reactions to different kinds of behaviour.[58]

There are four sentences in the book of Proverbs that deal with this specific motif and it is worthy of note that they all occur in the same collection. As we will see this motif is common both to the Old Testament in general and to non-Israelite wisdom. The use of false weights and scales seems to have been a

---

[53] Toy's translation (1977:220)

[54] McKane's translation (1985:235). McKane (1985:500) seems to be correct in relating משפט to the preceding מאזני and regarding it as contrast to מאזני מרמה in 11:1. Toy (1977:324–325) finds it a problem that משפט is singular and that it can relate to only one of the preceding nouns. He considers omitting פלס but finds the sentence more satisfactory if משפט is omitted. Toy also reads "the king" instead of MT "the Lord" because of the context where vv 10–15 all deal with the functions of kings. He explains the emendation (1977:324) by saying that "the word *king* may have been interpreted by some scribe as meaning the divine king, Yahweh." It is true that the immediate context favours the reading "king," but the parallels in the larger context make it probable that "the Lord" is to be retained.

[55] Toy's translation (1977:385).

[56] Toy's translation (1977:392).

[57] תועבה is used of ritual as well as ethical abominations and occurs in the OT often to denote practices and behaviours of the worst kind, e.g. idolatry, child sacrifice, etc. (BDB [1980:1072–1073], Gerstenberger [1976:1053–1054]).

[58] Cf. 11:20; 12:22; 15:8. Other combinations with תועבה can be found in 3:32; 6:16–19; 15:9, 26. See Fichtner (1933:79–81) for a discussion of the expressions in Israelite and non-Israelite wisdom; more generally for the term, see Humbert (1960:235–236). Cf.Weinfeld (1972:267–269, 296). McKane (1985:439) suggests that the phrase תועבת יהוה may represent "a modification of an expression which is derived from international wisdom."

common problem to the ancient Near East. Unfortunately the descriptions of the problem are framed in such general terms that it is not possible to arrive at any certain conclusions concerning date and setting of sentences containing this motif.

Of prime interest to us is the way this socio-economic issue is seen to be related to God. After all, one might ask, why is it that a very common problem of the market place is specifically discussed from a religious point of view? Even if we cannot ascertain to what degree the background of these sayings was a specific concern for certain groups in society, it is still remarkable that the Lord is portrayed as so intimately related to the issue. However, the use of this line of religious reasoning against economic injustice is hardly surprising in the light of the general tenor of the book. The notion that the Lord is intimately involved in the world and the life of the individual permeates Proverbs and prompts these theologically based condemnations of unjust economic practices.

Another passage which could be mentioned is 6:16–19:

6:16. There are six things that Yahweh hates,
Yea, seven are an abomination to him:
17. Haughty eyes, a lying tongue,
And hands that shed innocent blood,
18. A mind that devises wicked schemes,
Feet that make haste to do harm,
19. A false witness who utters lies,
And he who sows discord among brethren.[59]

This saying illustrates the strong connection between religious issues and socio-ethical questions in the teaching of the sages. The different kinds of behaviour that are listed as hateful and abominable to the Lord are all behaviours that are destructive to society and to inter-personal relationships. Toy comments: "The things enumerated belong all together; they portray the character of the man who schemes to despoil and ruin his fellows,"[60] and McKane classifies the verses under the heading "Anti-social Behaviour."[61] Behaviour of this kind strikes the hardest against weaker social groups, though the saying is not restricted to the mistreatment of certain groups but has a general focus. The theocentric line of reasoning should be noted—behaviour of this kind is not condemned so much because of its effects on other people, but because it is abhorrent to the Lord who as a personal god watches over people and is concerned about justice and fair treatment of the individual.

---

[59] Toy's translation (1977:127).
[60] Toy (1977:127).
[61] McKane (1985:326).

2. Comparison between the book of Proverbs and other Old Testament traditions.

a. The wisdom traditions

God's concern for the weak and unprotected, primarily the poor, widows and orphans, is also attested in the book of Job. Job's friends imply from the start that Job must have committed some sin which caused his misfortune. In the end Eliphaz levels a direct accusation at Job:

> 22:6. For you take your brother's pledge without cause
> And so strip the naked of their garments.
> 7. You give no water to the weary
> And you hold back bread from the hungry.
> 8. The land belongs to the one with a strong arm!
> The privileged person inhabits it!
> 9. Widows you sent away empty,
> And you broke the arms of orphans.[62]

It is interesting to note that the sins Eliphaz mentions are all various forms of the mistreatment of the weak and defenceless in society. It seems to be a shared conviction of the friends and Job[63] that this kind of behaviour against fellow-men in difficult circumstances is a gross sin for which God is expected to punish a person severely.[64] But until the end, Job, in his "oath of purity" maintains his innocence and the inadequacy of his "punishment":

> 31:13. Have I dismissed the case of my manservant
> Or my maidservant, when they made a complaint against me?
> 14. What then would I do when El rises in court?
> When he examines me, how will I answer?
> 15. Did not he who made me in the belly make them,
> The One fashion us both in the womb?
> 16. Have I denied the poor their needs?
> Or let the eyes of the widow fail,
> 17. By eating my morsel alone
> While the orphan ate none of it?
> 18. Why, from his youth he grew up with me as with a father
> And from his mother's womb I guided him.
> 19. Have I watched any perish from lack of clothes
> Or the poor from lack of garment?
> 20. Did their loins not bless me
> As they warmed themselves by the fleece of my sheep?
> 21. If I raised my hand against the orphan
> Because I saw my support in the gate.

---

[62] Habel's translation (1985:331).

[63] See esp. Job 24:2–12.

[64] Hempel (1936:250) regards the accusations as built upon the concept of talion. Since Job has become poor, he must have oppressed the poor. This seems less probable in light of our observations from Proverbs that do not indicate a retribution pattern with offence and punishment strictly corresponding to each other (see Koch [1955:4]). Neither does the book of Job supply evidence for belief in the kind of retribution that differentiates the penalty according to the crime, a system that presupposes some kind of legal code.

22. May the blade fall from my shoulder
And my arm be broken from its socket.
23. For I dread a calamity from El
And I cannot face his majesty.[65]

Job's declaration of innocence also covers other areas of life such as adultery, idolatry and hypocrisy, but both the accusations against Job and this oath make it clear that the concern for the poor, the needy and the defenceless, was a posture which the sages considered to be crucial from a theological point of view.[66]

The book of Ecclesiastes deals sparingly with ethical matters and there is hardly anything in the book which relates to the issue before us. Qoheleth makes some observations concerning wickedness "in the place of justice,"[67] oppression of the powerful against the weak[68] and oppression of the poor.[69] Qoheleth's observations leads him at times to express trust in ultimate justice but more often to hopelessness. The examples indicate that these social issues were of importance to the sages in the days when the book was written.

The psalms usually included among the wisdom psalms do not deal with this issue,[70] though the motif of the oppression of the poor man and God's concern for him is attested in a number of psalms of other genres.[71]

The motif of accurate and false measures is not attested in other Old Testament wisdom books, but it occurs in Sirach 42:4 where the reference is to honesty in trade. God's interest in social issues permeates the speeches of Job's friends, who often refer to the anti-social behaviour of the wicked man.

b. Other traditions of the Old Testament

The divine concern for the poor, the widow, the orphan, and other groups in society that live under difficult circumstances are attested in various traditions of the Old Testament. The law codes express a special concern that justice not be perverted to discriminate against the poor man,[72] stating that God himself will bring justice to the orphan and the widow,[73] and commanding that provision be made for these groups.[74] The prophets express God's concern and

---

[65] Habel's translation (1985:423–424). For comments, see also Fohrer (1974:1–22).

[66] Fohrer (1974:13).

[67] Eccl 3:16.

[68] Eccl 4:1.

[69] Eccl 5:7.

[70] This absence probably says more about the criteria for defining wisdom psalms than about the concept of God in a certain kind of poetry.

[71] See, e.g., Ps 35:10; 68:5–7; 72:12–14; 82:1–4; 109:16, 22. Especially in the Psalms the term "poor" often designates not only a social group, but even more a particular religious affiliation—i.e. those who are pious, faithful to God and his covenant in contrast to the wicked (see Wolf [1962:844], Kvalbein [1981:61]).

[72] E.g., Ex 23:6 (cf. v 3; Lev 19:15), Deut 24:17; 27:19. For a survey of this motif in the Pentateuch, see Kvalbein (1981:28–33, 40–41).

[73] Ex 22:22–24; Deut 10:17–18.

[74] Lev 19:10; Deut 14:28–29; 15:7–11; 26:12–13. Peculiar to Deut is the Levite.

care for these social groups and condemn people who oppress and mistreat them.[75] The psalms refer to the poor man, often in contrast to the wicked person,[76] which indicates that the term is not only a socio-economic designation but also has religious connotations which at times are even dominant.[77] The Lord appears in the psalms as the helper, protector and refuge of the pious/poor man, the widow, the orphan and other people in need.[78] One notable difference in comparison to other Old Testament traditions is that in the wisdom texts the sojourner does not appear.[79]

The motif of accurate and false measures can also be found elsewhere in the Old Testament—in the Holiness Code[80] and in Deuteronomic law,[81] where we also note the presence of the term "abomination to the Lord," תועבת יהוה,[82] to indicate the Lord's negative reaction against the use of false measures. There is also some example of the motif in prophetic teaching.[83]

The wider issue of the Lord's concern for social justice in the Old Testament cannot be dealt with here. Suffice it to say that a considerable part of the legislative material and the prophetic teaching in the Old Testament is related to God's concern for the individual. The fact that the law codes in Israel are put in the mouth of the Lord indicates that he was seen as personally involved on behalf of individuals.[84] Especially noteworthy in this connection are Psalms 15 and 24:3–6, which are entrance liturgies spelling out requirements for entrance into the temple. It is remarkable that none of the requirements mentioned are cultic in nature, but all purely relational.

3. Comparison between the book of Proverbs and non-Israelite wisdom.

Our observations from the book of Proverbs concerning the Lord as personal god, especially of the weak and defenceless, will at this point be compared with the non-Israelite wisdom material.[85]

---

[75] E.g., Isa 1:23; Ez 22:7; Amos 2:6; 4:1; Mic 2:1–2; Mal 3:5. For an overview, see Kvalbein (1981:34–35, 41), Epzstein (1986:90–103). Pleins (1987:61–78) compares the views of poverty in wisdom and in the prophets and argues that they stand in stark contrast to each other. His observations are noteworthy, though he tends to exaggerate the differences, which to a large degree could as well be explained by different genre rather than by different perspectives.

[76] Ps 9:19; 10:2, 9–18; 12:6; 35:10; 37:14; 40:18; 41:2, etc.

[77] See Kvalbein (1981:43–60).

[78] See, e.g., Ps 9:13, 19; 10:14, 17–18; 12:6; 14:6; 35:10; 68:5–7; 69:34; 76:10; 109:31; 113:7; 140:13; 146:5–10.

[79] See, however, Job 31:32, where ארח indicates hospitality to wayfarers.

[80] Lev 19:36.

[81] Deut 25:13–16.

[82] Cf. Prov 11:1; 20:10, 23.

[83] Ez 45:10–12.

[84] See Gamper (1966:203).

[85] See Fensham (1962:129–139), Malchow (1982:120–124), Epzstein (1986). Malchow (1982:120) points out that texts like *Keret* and *Aqhat* demonstrate the existence of a similar phenomenon of a social concern in Ugarit as well by making it clear that Canaanite kings were expected to protect the

a. Egypt

Brunner notes that in the Old Kingdom riches were regarded as a gift from the gods while little was said about poverty, even though in all times it was regarded as a religious duty of kings and other people to help the poor.[86] The reason given for assisting the poor is frequently a statement to the effect that the wealthy himself may suddenly become poor and find himself in need charity. Both richness and poverty are from the gods. The breakdown of the social system of the Old Kingdom brought about a change in mentality[87] and at the time of the New Kingdom views concerning wealth and poverty had changed considerably. In the age of personal piety, the poor man was lifted up as an example of humility. The poor are mentioned so frequently and described in such positive terms in the texts from the period of the 19–20th dynasties, especially in prayers and hymns, that the religion of this age has been called "the religion of the poor."[88]

The Instruction of Ptahhotep emphasizes that it is the god who makes a person successful and rewards him with riches.[89] It also urges mercy and circumspection towards the poor.[90] The instruction also includes general statements on proper conduct in society.

The instructions of *Merikare, Amenemhet* and *The Eloquent Peasant* all contain references to a ruler's responsibility for the welfare of the poor, the widow and the orphan.[91] But again it is in *Amenemope* that the closest correspondences to the Israelite material are found. The second chapter admonishes its hearers not to mistreat certain groups, warning that the lot of those who oppress will be destruction:

> Beware of robbing a wretch,
> Of attacking a cripple;....
> He who does evil, the shore rejects him,
> Its floodwater carries him away.[92]

---

unprotected. See also Ringgren (1982:1075, 1077) and Hoffner (1974:289) for references to the orphan and the widow in Ugaritic texts.

[86] Brunner (1961:322, 343; see also 1961/2:538–540, 543).

[87] Brunner (1961:323) mentions the text *All Men Created Equal in Opportunity* as an example of the new mentality. This text explicitly states that the creator-god made the winds that every man should be able to breathe thereof and "the great inundation that the poor man might have rights therein like the great man" (*ANET* [1969:7–8]). Malchow (1982:120) finds social justice to be a dominant theme in Egyptian literature, esp. during the First Intermediate and the Middle Kingdom period as evidenced by texts like *The Eloquent Peasant, Merikare, Amenhet, Ipuwer.*

[88] Brunner (1961:330).

[89] Maxims 10, 22, 30, Lichtheim (1975:66, 69, 71).

[90] Maxim 4 , Lichtheim (1975:64).

[91] Lichtheim (1975:100, 136, 172).

[92] *Amenemope* iv 4–5, 12–13, Lichtheim (1976:150).

The sixth chapter deals with the motif of respect for property lines and explicitly commands that the reader not encroach upon the boundaries of the widow,[93] since such behaviour leads to destruction:

Do not move the markers on the borders of fields,
Nor shift the position of the measuring-cord.
Do not be greedy for a cubit of land,
Nor encroach on the boundaries of a widow....
Beware of destroying the borders of fields,
Lest a terror carry you away;
One pleases god with the might of the lord
When one discerns the borders of fields.[94]

The eleventh chapter admonishes against greed for the property and bread of the poor since they will never bring any satisfaction:

Do not covet a poor man's goods,
Nor hunger for his bread;
A poor man's goods are a block in the throat,
It makes the gullet vomit.[95]

The thirteenth chapter provides an example of concern for the poor and counsels mercy concerning the negotiation of his debts:

If you find a large debt against a poor man,
Make it into three parts,
Forgive two, let one stand.[96]

The sixteenth chapter deals with the motif of accurate and false measures and admonishes against cheating, since the god Thoth who invented the measures watches over their accurate use:

Do not move the scales nor alter the weights,
Nor diminish the fractions of the measure;
Do not desire a measure of the fields,
Nor neglect those of the treasury.
The Ape sits by the balance,
His heart is in the plummet;
Where is a god as great as Thoth,
Who invented these things and made them?
Do not make for yourself deficient weights,
They are rich in grief through the might of god.[97]

---

[93] *Amenemope* vii 15. The widow occurs also in the twenty-eighth chapter where it is commanded that the widow not be prevented from gleaning in the fields (Lichtheim [1976:161, see n.29]).

[94] *Amenemope* vii 12–15, viii 9–12, Lichtheim (1976:151–152).

[95] *Amenemope* xiv 5–8, Lichtheim (1976:154–155).

[96] *Amenemope* xvi 5–7, Lichtheim (1976:155). Cf. the twenty-eighth chapter: "God prefers him who honours the poor To him who worships the wealthy" (xxvi 13–14, Lichtheim [1976:161]).

[97] *Amenemope* xvii 18–xviii 5, Lichtheim (1976:156–157). See also ch. 17 against falsifying the bushel with the motivation: "The bushel is the eye of Re" (xviii 23, Lichtheim [1976:157]).

The twenty-fifth chapter forbids the mistreatment of the blind man, the dwarf, the lame or the insane based on the idea that the god was the "builder" of man who designs different men in different ways.[98]

The correspondences between *The Instruction of Amenemope* and the passages from the book of Proverbs on social issues are numerous and thematically related. Several of the admonitions in *Amenemope* contain theological argumentation which demonstrates that in Egypt as well there was a conviction that such issues were seen as important to the deity. The Egyptian texts do not express the close personal involvement of the deity as clearly as does the book of Proverbs and this constitutes one difference between these traditions.

The Demotic instructions refer occasionally to social issues and the concern of the god for the socially weak. *Papyrus Insinger* includes the motif of accurate and false measures, but as a metaphor for human character:

> The great god Thoth has set a balance in order to make right measure on earth by it.
> He placed the heart hidden in the flesh for the right measure of its owner.
> If a learned man is not balanced his learning does not avail.
> A fool who does not know balance is not far from trouble.[99]

Papyrus Insinger maintains the ancient belief that it is the god who gives either riches or poverty and that man can do little to change the situation:

> There is one who lives on little so as to save, yet he becomes poor.
> There is one who does not know, yet the fate gives (him) wealth.
> It is not the wise man who saves who finds a surplus.
> Nor is it the one who spends who becomes poor.
> The god gives a wealth of supplies without an income.
> He also gives poverty in the purse without spending.[100]

In *Papyrus Insinger* the view that the god has deep personal interests in helping the poor is expressed in a similar way to what we have seen in the book of Proverbs:

> The heart of the god is content when the poor man is sated before him.
> If property accrues to you give a portion to the god; that is the portion of the poor....
> The god lets one acquire wealth in return for doing good.
> He who gives food to the poor, the god takes him to himself in boundless mercy.
> The heart of the god is pleased by the giving of food (more than) the heart of the
>   recipient.[101]

Regarding God's concern for social issues, especially the concern for the weak, we find that there are many similarities between the book of Proverbs

---

[98] *Amenemope* xxiv 9–18, Lichtheim (1976:160).

[99] *Papyrus Insinger* iv 17–20, Lichtheim (1980:188–189). Here the motif of accurate measurements is employed in relation to the belief that a person's heart is weighed on the scales after his death and that the result determines his destiny. This is alluded to in *Papyrus Insinger* v 7–8: "The god lays the heart on the scales opposite the weight. He knows the impious and the pious man by his heart" (Lichtheim [1980:189]).

[100] *Papyrus Insinger* vii 13–18, Lichtheim (1980:191).

[101] *Papyrus Insinger* xvi 3–4, 11–14, Lichtheim (1980:197–198).

and Egyptian instructions, especially those from the New Kingdom period and later. These instructions contain examples of theological argumentation, but it is not until the late Demotic text, Papyrus Insinger, that we find a view of the deity's close personal involvement in the affairs of men similar to what we have noted in the case of the book of Proverbs. To be noted is the correspondence to Israelite wisdom in the lack of references to the sojourner's rights.

b. Mesopotamia

We turn now to Mesopotamian wisdom to look for parallels to the depiction of the Lord in the book of Proverbs as involved in social life for the sake of the individual, especially the depiction of him as a personal god for the weak and defenceless.[102] The Sumerian and Babylonian proverbial material[103] yield little that relates to our issue. In the Babylonian *Counsels of Wisdom,* one section refers to the displeasure of the personal god and Shamash, the omnivisionary sun god of justice,[104] when the "downtrodden" are insulted:

> Do not insult the downtrodden and [..]
> Do not sneer at them autocratically.
> With this a man's god is angry,
> It is not pleasing to Šamaš, who will repay him with evil.
> Give good to eat, beer to drink,
> Grant what is asked, provide for and honour.
> In this a man's god takes pleasure,
> It is pleasing to Šamaš, who will repay him with favour.
> Do charitable deeds, render service all your days.[105]

Ethical injunctions are "a well-known feature of some Sumerian hymns."[106] *The Šamaš Hymn,* included in Lambert's *Babylonian Wisdom Literature,* stresses the attention and help which Shamash gives to the individual, especially those who are particularly needy. One section states that Shamash helps refugees and fugitives, captives and the sick, and that he punishes the person who covets his neighbour's wife, the villain and the judge who takes bribes.[107] Alongside of this occurs the motif of false and accurate measures, recounting the reactions of Shamash as well as of the people:

---

[102] Lambert (1960:18) argues that the attention given to the widow and orphan in Sumerian texts shows the antiquity of the theme "kindness to those in need," a theme which is based upon the authority of Shamash, the god of justice. See Donald (1964:27–41) concerning the poor in Akkadian wisdom literature.

[103] Gordon (1959), Lambert (1960:222–282).

[104] Concerning the role of Shamash, see our comments in ch. 4, pp. 161–162, 168. See also Fensham (1962:130–132).

[105] *Counsels of Wisdom* 57–65, Lambert (1960:100–103).

[106] Lambert (1960:118) from the introduction to *A Bilingual Hymn to Ninurta* which on the obverse of the tablet enumerates incorrect behaviours like adultery, slander, oppression of the poor and weak and on the reverse addresses the god as he enters his shrine.

[107] *The Shamash Hymn* 71–100, Lambert (1960:130–133). Lines 132–145 (Lambert [1960:134–135]) are about different groups of people that call to Shamash and line 146 makes it clear that they are all heard by Shamash.

The merchant who [practices] trickery as he holds the balances,
Who uses two sets of weight, thus lowering the ....,
He is disappointed in the matter of profit and loses [his capital.]
The honest merchant who holds the balances [and gives] good weight—
Everything is presented to him in good measure [...]
The merchant who practices trickery as he hold the corn measure,
Who weighs out loans (or corn) by the minimum standard, but requires a large quantity in
    repayment,
The curse of the people will overtake him before his time,
If he demanded repayment before the agreed date, there will be guilt upon him.
His heir will not assume control of his property,
Nor will his brothers take over his estate.
The honest merchant who weighs out loans (or corn) by the maximum standard, thus
    multiplying kindness,
It is pleasing to Šamaš, and he will prolong his life.[108]

Fensham notes that references to Shamash's protection of the poor are frequent in Babylonian wisdom literature, but the widow and the orphan are
never explicitly mentioned[109] nor do we find any references to the sojourner.

In the reflective essays from Mesopotamia not much is found that relates to
God and the weak. It is worth noting that when the sufferers in *Ludlul bēl
nēmeqi, A Dialogue about Human Misery* and *The Babylonian Theodicy*
bemoan their misery and injustice, they insist on their innocence almost exclusively in terms of cultic rather than social categories.[110] This fact underscores
our previous observation that there is no tension between wisdom and cult in
Mesopotamia and that they were more naturally related to one another than in
Israel. Social issues were of importance in Mesopotamian wisdom as well, but
they seem to have been given less emphasis as matters of primary importance
to the deity.[111] Social concern in general is demonstrated when the sufferer in
The Babylonian Theodicy refers to the disorder he experiences around him:

People extol the word of a strong man who has learned to kill
But bring down the powerless who has done no wrong.
They confirm (the position of) the wicked for whom what should be an abomination is
    considered right
Yet drive off the honest man who heeds the will of his god.
They fill the [storehouse] of the oppressor with gold,
But empty the larder of the beggar of its provisions.
They support the powerful, whose...is guilt,
But destroy the weak, and trample the powerless.[112]

---

[108] *The Shamash Hymn* 107–119, Lambert (1960:132–133).
[109] Fensham (1962:131). The widow and the orphan occur elsewhere, esp. in the law codes, see
Ringgren (1982:1076), Hoffner (1974:288) for references.
[110] Cf., e.g., Job 31.
[111] Cf. van der Toorn (1985:13–20, 41–44) who argues that the ethical codes of Israel and
Mesopotamia were basically the same and that in both religions the ethical code was based on the
emotional interest of the deity.
[112] *Babylonian Theodicy* 267–274, ANET (1969:604).

4. Conclusions concerning God and the weak

a. The wisdom traditions

The social concern of God is well attested in the books of Proverbs and Job and demonstrates that Israelite sages viewed the Lord as having a close relationship to the individual. The emphasis on this aspect of the concept of God is in harmony with the stress upon the act-consequence relationship in the wisdom literature. The common basis of these two aspects must be found in the highly individualistic viewpoint which permeates this literature. The fact that the Lord appears as the defender of the rights of those groups which have no other recourse for the vindication of their rights, is noteworthy and indicates that the sages regarded the Lord as a personal god who related intimately to the individual, regardless of social status, and that his presence with the person meant protection and help when every other means of procuring them failed. The use of the term redeemer, גאל, to refer to the Lord in 23:11 strengthens this characterization considerably. The sentences that deal with the motif of accurate and false measures may also have some thematic relationship to this description of the Lord, since the cheating of the merchants had its most disastrous effects on the weakest in society. The theological reasoning in support of honesty and justice as well as the condemnation of other forms of anti-social behaviour demonstrate that the sages regarded their God as concerned about every area of life in which the individual was affected.

b. Other traditions of the Old Testament

When we turn to other Old Testament traditions, we find an essentially harmonious description of the Lord as concerned about social justice and about the welfare of the individual. God's concern for the poor, the widow and the orphan, and the oppressed seems to be a theme shared by the main traditions of the Old Testament which indicates the presence of a wide-spread belief that the Lord acted in a special way as a personal god for these groups of people. The motif of accurate and false measures and honesty in trading constitutes a link between wisdom and law traditions.

c. Egypt

We have previously made the observation that a concern for social issues is present in the wisdom literature of Egypt. The theological argumentation found in instructions from the New Kingdom era and the late period indicate that the gods in Egypt were viewed as concerned about mercy and justice towards the weak and defenceless. The motif of accurate and false measures also appears in a late text, where it is used as a metaphor for the human character. Compared with the book of Proverbs, these instructions, with the exception of one relatively late text, have a tendency to avoid formulations that express close personal attachment of the god to the individual. The close relationship between the deity and man appears however in non-wisdom texts, especially texts from "the age of personal piety."

d. Mesopotamia

Evidence for the personal involvement of the gods in social issues in Mesopotamia wisdom texts is hard to come by. The best examples are related to the sun god Utu/Shamash, who, as the god of justice, was evidently regarded as concerned about justice, compassion, and proper social behaviour. Shamash is described as a kind of personal god when he appears as the protector of the weak and defenceless on the one hand, and as the judge of trespassers on the other. We have also noted the more important role played by cultic themes in Mesopotamian wisdom and that they, in the declarations of innocence in the reflective essays, play the role that social matters do in the book of Job.

B. God and the righteous man

In the book of Proverbs the Lord is depicted as close to the person who is righteous, fears the Lord, trusts him and is obedient to the wisdom teachings. The sayings that are most noteworthy in this respect will now be studied in order to determine what characterizes the concept of God in this material and what relationship it has both to the rest of the Old Testament and to non-Israelite wisdom.

1. The Lord as personal god of the righteous man in the book of Proverbs

a. The righteous man and his counterpart

There are a number of different expressions used to designate the person who stands in a special relationship to the Lord in the book of Proverbs. For the sake of convenience we have chosen to use the term "righteous" as an umbrella term for such persons in general. "Righteous" is used to predicate man several times in God-sayings[113] and occurs around 60 times in the sentences[114] as a designation of the person who lives an upright life and who will consequently experience success.

It is stated that the righteous man speaks wisely,[115] knows how to administer his property,[116] is considerate,[117] etc, and therefore will endure and escape evil. The term "righteous" designates a man who knows how to avoid evil and live correctly. In this sense, the term is synonymous with "wise." But the meaning of "righteous" is not limited to designating correct behaviour. McKane is right when he argues that terms like צדיק and רשע in the book of Proverbs are evidence of Yahwistic piety.[118] Even in contexts which are not explicitly theological, the term צדיק has religious connotations. The righteous man lives correctly because he is obedient both to God and to the teachings of the sages. This characterization also applies to the other main designation for the person who is close to the Lord—the man who "fears the Lord."

The "fear of the Lord" and wisdom are connected in Proverbs 1:7 and 9:10 where the fear of the Lord bears the function of promoting wisdom.[119] The

---

[113] 3:33; 10:3; 15:29; 18:10. Related expressions are present in 15:9 which tells that the Lord loves the person who pursues righteousness, מרדף צדקה, and in 21:3 which in general states that to do right and justice, עשה צדקה ומשפט, is of primary importance to the Lord.

[114] Almost all the occurrences are in the sentence genre, especially in the section of antithetical sentences, i.e. Prov 10–15.

[115] 10:11, 20–21, 31–32; 13:5; 15:28.

[116] 10:16; 15:6.

[117] 12:10.

[118] McKane (1985:15). We do not agree, though, with McKane that this presence of Yahwism in Proverbs is a later reinterpretation of an original, almost secular wisdom.

[119] Becker (1965:213). Cf. parallels in Job 28:28; Ps 111:10; Prov 15:33.

expression occurs a number of times in the book of Proverbs[120] designating the correct attitude of the wise man towards God and life.[121] This expression is attested in the different sections of the book and is lacking only in chapters 25–29, where the paucity of theological references makes it difficult to attribute any special significance to its absence, beyond the general comments we have already made on the theological character of that section.[122]

Becker points out in his detailed study *Gottesfurcht im Altes Testament* that "fear of the Lord" in the book of Proverbs "ist ausnahmslos sittlicher Prägung, und zwar ohne nomistischen Einschlag;" and also: "Der sittliche Begriff ist vor allem typischer Begriff der Weisheitsliteratur."[123] Von Rad argues that this expression in the wisdom literature must be understood in a broad sense designating, as in the Elohistic narratives, "obedience to the divine will" or "commitment to, knowledge about Yahweh."[124] Our view is that the expression is used about a person who lives in a relation of obedience and trust towards the deity, but it does also, in the same way as "righteous," designate a certain life-style of socio-ethical qualities.

Other terms used to designate the person close to the Lord in the book of Proverbs are "upright," ישר, "those who walk in integrity," הלכי תם, "pious," חסיד,[125] עניים/ענוים[126] and "those who trust in the Lord," בוטח על-יהוה.[127] Parallel to our conclusions concerning "righteous" and "fear of the Lord," it should be noted that the meaning of these terms can be summarized by saying that they denote a person who lives both according to the wisdom teachings and in a close relationship to God.

The terminology for the opposite character, i.e. the person from whom God holds himself separate, is also varied. The main term used in this connection is "wicked," רשע, often the antithesis of "righteous."[128] Other terms and expressions are "man of violence," איש חמס,[129] "iniquitous person," נלוז,[130]

---

[120] 1:7, 29; 2:5; 8:13; 9:10; 10:27; 14:26, 27; 15:16, 33; 16:6; 19:23; 22:4; 23:17; in verbal form 3:7; 14:2; 24:21; 31:30.

[121] Fichtner (1933:52).

[122] 28:14 is about the man who "fears always." The object of the verb may be God and in that case the verse is to be included in the sayings on the "fear of God." The strange thing in that case is that it is not spelled out. The object can also be, e.g., "sin" (Toy [1977:501]) or the participle may just denote in a general way the opposite attitude to the arrogance of the person who "hardens his heart."

[123] Becker (1965:210, 261). Similarly Plath (1963:55, 62–63). Plath (1963:68–72, 125) finds few parallels in non-Israelite wisdom to "fear of God(s)" in this ethical-normative sense and draws the conclusion that the sages in this case were influenced by the prophets.

[124] Von Rad (1981:66).

[125] 2:7–8.

[126] 3:34. Ketib עניים, literally "poor," is possible in the narrow as well as the wider context, even though Qere ענוים, "humble, meek," in this saying better contrasts scoffers, לצים.

[127] 28:25, בוטח ביהוה in 29:25.

[128] E.g. 3:33; 10:3, 16, 24, 25; 11:5, 8, 31; 12:12; 14:19, 32; 15:6, 29; 17:15; 18:5; 24:15; 25:26; 28:1; 29:2, 7, 27.

[129] 3:31.

[130] 3:32.

"scoffers," לצים,[131] "workers of iniquity," פעלי און[132]—terms which, in the same way as the positive terminology, refer both to the character and behaviour of the person and his relationship to God.

b. *The Lord as protector of the righteous man*

In the book of Proverbs there are a number of sayings that illustrate the view that the Lord acted as the personal god and protector of the righteous man.[133] The first passage comes from chapter two which is a unified instruction.[134] This instruction is addressed to "my son," i.e. to anyone willing to adhere to the teachings. The introduction admonishes the reader to be attentive to the teachings and search for wisdom with all his heart. Verse 5, which continues in the second person singular form, relates this knowledge and wisdom to piety, יראת יהוה, and constitutes a bridge to the following three verses which are construed in the third person singular. These verses provide the explanation that it is the Lord who gives wisdom, and that he helps, guides and protects the person who lives a life according to his will:[135]

> 2: 5. Then shalt thou understand the fear of Yahweh,
> And find the knowledge of God;
> 6. For Yahweh gives wisdom,
> Out of his mouth come knowledge and discernment;
> 7. He lays up deliverance for the upright,
> Is a shield to those who walk in integrity;
> 8. He guards the paths of probity,
> And protects the way of the pious.[136]

The designations for those under the Lord's protection correspond to the ideals of wisdom: the upright, ישרים, those who walk in integrity, הלכי תם, those who keep to the paths of probity, נצר ארחות משפט and the pious, חסיד.[137] These

---

[131] 3:34.

[132] 10:29.

[133] Cf.above, p. 195, Vorländer's characterization of the personal god.

[134] McKane (1985:278) hesitates in designating chapter 2 as instruction because of the absence of imperatives and use instead of conditional clauses. Also because "there is a lack of concrete, authoritative instruction on specific matters in this passage." McKane's strict criteria leads him to conclude (1985:278–279) that the chapter "exemplifies a process of formal development of the Instruction" without the authoritative element.

[135] It is common to understand 2:5–8 as an editorial insertion, which is possible since these verses stand out from the context and can be excluded without damage to the total structure. Another possibility is that verses 6–8 were already included in the original composition as a quotation (in that case the exact original is unknown to us) or quotation-like statement with verse 5 as an introduction. The change in verb-form could be regarded as intentional to mark the verses out and highlight them in the context. See Plöger (1984:24–26) for a view of vv 1–11 as a coherent structure.

[136] Toy's translation (1977:34–35). Note the presence of Elohim, see ch.1, pp. 35–36. דעת אלהים is parallel to יראת יהוה and probably retained for sake of rhetorical variation.

[137] The basic meaning of ישר is "straight, right," and in the wisdom literature it is often used in the plural denoting people of upright character, see 2:21; 3:32; 11:3, 6, 11, etc; Job 4:7; 17:8; Ps 49:15. תם means "completeness, integrity," and is used also in 10:9; 13:6; 19:1; 20:7; 28:6, indicating the character of the righteous man. ארחות משפט denotes the paths that are legally right as well as pleasing to God. חסיד means "kind, pious." This is the only occurrence in Proverbs of the term which is commonly used in the psalms to designate the person who obeys and trusts in God.

designations paint a portrait of a person who is dedicated to honesty and devotion in his moral and religious life. The Lord is described as deliverer,[138] shield,[139] guardian[140] and protector.[141] All the four terms give the assurance that he who lives close to God and according to the recommendations of wisdom will live in safety and security.

The instruction in 3:21–35 opens in the traditional manner with an exhortation to adhere to the teachings and is embroidered with an assurance of the positive results that will follow:

> 3:21b. My son, keep [with thee] wisdom and discretion,
> 21a. Let them not depart from thy sight;
> 22. They will be life to thy being,
> Adornment to thy neck.
> 23. Then wilt thou go thy way securely;
> Thy foot will not stumble;
> 24. When thou 'sittest down' thou wilt not be afraid,
> Thou wilt lie down, and thy sleep will be sweet.
> 25. Thou wilt not fear the calamity that befalls the 'foolish,'
> Nor the storm that strikes the wicked;
> 26. For Yahweh will be thy protector,
> And will keep thy feet from snares.[142]

The main theme of this assurance to the obedient person is the safety he will experience at all times, even when calamity and storm befall others. Verse 26 concludes the introductory section of the instruction by giving a rationale for trusting the Lord who acts as the "protector," כסל, literally "confidence," of those devoted to him. Several of the expressions in the passage allude to the symbolism depicting life as a path which occurs quite frequently in this first collection of the book of Proverbs.

The antithetical sentence in 10:29 describes the contrasting views of the Lord in the eyes of the righteous and the wicked:

---

[138] תושיה, here probably with the meaning "deliverance," occurs only twice in the OT (Isa 28:29; Mic 6:9) apart from the books of Job (5:12; 6:13; 11:6; 12:16; 26:3; 30:22) and Proverbs (3:21; 8:14; 18:1). We agree with Toy (1977:36): "It appears to signify the act or power of establishment or arrangement, and so fertility in expedients, wisdom, and, as result, achievement, help, deliverance. The last sense is the one here naturally suggested by the parallel *shield*." McKane (1985:282) regards the term as belonging to the vocabulary of old wisdom with the meaning "power, capacity, competence," but here without its practical meaning by being conditional on rectitude and piety.

[139] The term emphasizes the protective aspect of the Lord's presence.

[140] The formulation of this clause is somewhat unusual since the object of the Lord's guarding is not explicitly stated. Toy translates "He guards the paths of probity" but it can hardly be anything but the people who keep to these paths that are the object of the Lord's activity.

[141] שמר, as נצר in the preceding parallel clause, expresses the Lord's observation and protection of the righteous man.

[142] Toy's translation (1977:73). Toy transposes the clauses of v 21 to solve the problem of the missing subject in the first clause.

10:29. Yahweh is a stronghold to the 'man of integrity,'
But destruction to the workers of iniquity.[143]

"The man of integrity," חם דרך, or, more literally, "he who is perfect in his way," signifies someone who is devoted to blameless conduct before God and men, while the contrasting term, "the workers of iniquity," describes those whose lives are characterized by qualities like falsehood, wickedness and idolatry. The main message of this sentence is that the members of each group see the Lord in very different ways—to the first group he is a stronghold,[144] a place of refuge and protection especially in times of hardship and danger, but to the second group he is destruction.[145] It is difficult to pinpoint the exact significance of these designations, especially the latter. The meaning must be related to the character-consequence relationship of which the Lord was considered the guarantor and at times even the direct agent of retribution. The Lord is destruction to the evil-doers since he symbolizes and supervises their inevitable doom. The other side of the same coin is that he rewards the righteous by watching over and protecting him.

The individualism of wisdom was not a strictly defined view as the content of 14:26 indicates. As in Mesopotamian religion, the protection of the personal god in the book of Proverbs also includes that individual's family:

14:26. He who fears Yahweh has strong ground of confidence,
And his children will have a refuge.[146]

The parallels make it clear that the confidence, מבטח, of the God-fearing man as well as the refuge, מחסה, of his children is none other than the Lord himself. The following sentence, 14:27, continues on the same theme:

14:27. The fear of Yahweh is a fountain of life,
Whereby one avoids the snares of death.[147]

The second clause of this sentence is interesting since it puts more emphasis on man's own role in escaping misfortune.[148] By living a pious life man avoids

---

[143] Toy's translation (1977:216). Toy notes (1977:217) that the first line according to the MT reads: "a stronghold to perfection is the way of Yahweh" and argues that the parallelism requires that we read with LXX "perfect" instead of "perfection," and that, as elsewhere in the OT, we understand the Lord to be the stronghold. The second clause is identical to 21:15b where "workers of iniquity" stand in contrast to the righteous.

[144] מעוז, only here in Proverbs.

[145] מחחה, used also in v 14 in reference to the thoughtless speech of the fool which constantly constitutes an impending threat to himself and others.

[146] Toy's translation (1977:297). Toy argues that the MT text must be changed from ביראת יהוה to ליֹרא יהוה in order to see an allusion to the God-fearing person, which is needed to correspond to the masculine suffix in בניו in the second clause. McKane's suggestion (1985:232) seems possible: "The fear of Yahweh is a (man's) stronghold,....."

[147] Toy's translation (1977:297). Toy connects the two clauses by inserting "whereby one...." The MT has only the infinitive with preposition, לסור, in the second clause.

[148] 13:14 is identical to 14:27 except that, instead of "the fear of Yahweh," it has "the law/instruction of the wise man," תורת חכם.

the snares of death, i.e. the destruction that threatens the life of the wicked. The more common way of expressing the safety of the righteous—that the Lord is his stronghold or rescuer—is here exchanged for a more anthropocentric approach to the issue.[149]

The description of the Lord as a safe place to which the righteous can run for cover is vivid in 18:10:

> 18:10. The name of Yahweh is a strong fortress,
> To which the righteous runs and is safe.[150]

The sense of the last verb, שׂגב (ni), is literally that the person is raised to a position of safety, which lends a dramatic element to the description. The expression "the name of Yahweh" instead of just Yahweh as in 10:29 is peculiar to this sentence. This Name-theology, well-known from Deuteronomistic circles, is not found elsewhere in the book of Proverbs and may be a sign of Deuteronomistic influence. We suggest that the reason for its inclusion here might be the strongly anthropomorphic connotations conveyed by the formulation of the sentence. This may have motivated the insertion of an indirect reference to the Lord in order to minimize the emphasis on this aspect.[151]

The pious man in 19:23 is promised long life and presented with a blank check against all kinds of evil:

> 19:23. The fear of Yahweh leads to life,
> 'Who hopes in him' will be unvisited by harm.[152]

The verb with the meaning "exalt" used in 18:10 occurs also in 29:25:

> 29:25. The fear of man brings a snare,
> But he who trusts in Yahweh is safe.[153]

The antithesis in 29:25 between "fear of man," חרדת אדם, and "trusting in the Lord," בוטח ביהוה, is worth noticing. Trusting in the Lord is an expression of the proper attitude of the pious and is close in meaning to "the fear of the Lord," יראת יהוה—an expression which might have been expected due to the parallelism of the sentence since the lexical meanings of חרדה and יראה are essentially synonymous. On the other hand, the use of an expression like "trusting in the Lord" emphasizes the difference in attitude which one should have before man and before the Lord. The fear in relation to man that is

---

[149] A similar view appears in, e.g., 1:10–19 and 2:16–19 where the person is instructed to keep away from men of violence and the foreign woman since they lead others to destruction.

[150] Toy's translation (1977:360). Strong fortress, מגדל־עז, parallel to strong confidence, מבטח־עז, in 14:26.

[151] The possibility of this suggestion is strengthened by the lack of anthropomorphisms in wisdom literature, probably explained not only by genre and setting, but by a conscious effort to avoid them for theological reasons.

[152] Toy's translation (1977:379). Toy reads ושבר עליו instead of the somewhat awkward "he dwells satisfied," ושבע ילין, in the second clause.

[153] Toy's translation (1977:515). The rare expression "fear of man," חרדת אדם, occurs only here in Proverbs.

referred to here is not synonymous to the fear referred to in the expression "fear of the Lord." The relationship of the righteous man to the Lord is not at all reminiscent of the fright and terror a person might experience before certain men. "Fear of the Lord" on the contrary is used in reference to the person who is close to the Lord and puts his trust in him as his personal god and is rewarded with protection and safety.

Agur's queries, which imply the incomprehensibility of God, are followed by a pious affirmation of trust in God:

> 30:5. Every word of God is pure;
> He is a shield to those who trust in him.[154]

Whether "every God's word," כל־אמרת אלוה, in the first clause refers to written revelation[155] or an expression of more general character can be debated. The prohibition against additions in verse six favours the former alternative. In any case, close identity between God himself and his words is expressed since in the second clause God appears as subject—as a shield to those who seek refuge in him.[156] The wording of this verse is also found in Psalms 18:31 and 2 Samuel 22:31 and it is usually assumed that a quotation from the psalm has been inserted here as a kind of response to Agur's words. In that case it is highly interesting that the divine name Eloah is used here while it is Yahweh in the other two passages, especially since this is the only time Eloah occurs in the book.[157] The probable explanation of the change is the fact that Agur appears not as an Israelite and because of this a more general God-designation is employed.[158]

c. The Lord as the one granting success and well-being to the righteous man
A number of sayings in the book of Proverbs place an emphasis on the way in which the Lord rewards those who put their trust in him. As Jacobsen has pointed out, this is probably the most fundamental aspect of the relationship between a man and his personal god.

The instruction in Proverbs 1–9 which, in its content, is the most theological is 3:1–12, especially verses 5–10. This instruction consists of a number of exhortations, several of them specifically advocating piety. Of special

---

[154] Toy's translation (1977:522). The literal meaning of חסה (qal) is "to flee, seek refuge in" which is a preferable translation, though the imagery of the clause becomes somewhat inconsistent.

[155] So Toy (1977:523) and similarly McKane (1985:648). If this interpretation is correct, the following verse with its prohibition against additions (cf. Deut 4:2) easily makes sense. Such a reference to a written codex is not attested elsewhere in Proverbs (תורה in 1:8; 6:20, 23; 13:14; 28:4, 7, 9; 29:18 does not seem to refer to any written codex, but to the instruction of parents or wise men) and would indicate a late date for this addition to the book.

[156] Cf. 2:7.

[157] The name Eloah occurs frequently in the book of Job, elsewhere rarely in the OT.

[158] This argument presumes that the following verses should not be ascribed to Agur since Yahweh occurs in v 9.

interest to us are the supportive arguments given, which consist of firm assurances of the positive results that obedience and piety will bring.

> 3:5. Trust to Yahweh with all thy heart,
> And lean not on thine own understanding;
> 6. In all thy ways acknowledge him,
> And he will smooth thy paths.
> 7. Be not wise in thine own eyes—
> Fear Yahweh, and turn away from sin—
> 8. Then will there be health to thy 'body'
> And refreshment to thy bones.
> 9. Honor Yahweh with thy wealth,
> With the best of all thy revenue—
> 10. Then will thy barns be filled with 'corn'
> And thy vats will overflow with must.[159]

The person who trusts in the Lord is assured that the Lord will smooth his paths, i.e. that God will remove hindrances and hardships along his life journey. Health and bodily vigour are assured for the person who fears Yahweh, and the person who generously shares his wealth with others will prosper.[160] Relating to different areas of life these three supportive arguments do indeed deal with the success and well-being of a person. They represent an individualistic approach to piety in which the well-being of a person is contingent exclusively upon the relationship between that individual and the Lord as his personal god.

The instruction in 3:21–35[161] ends with a theological statement concerning the Lord's attitude towards different groups of people:

> 3:33. The curse of Yahweh is on the house of the wicked,
> But the habitation of the righteous he blesses.
> 34. Scoffers he scoffs at,
> But to the pious he shows favour.[162]

The antithesis in verse 33 is between the curse and the blessing of the dwellings of the wicked and the righteous respectively, while the antithesis in verse 34 is built upon the notion that the Lord's reaction to a persons actions is reciprocal; to the good he does good while to the evil he brings destruction. The Lord's blessing of the habitation of the righteous probably has a broad application beyond the individual to the household, signifying prosperity[163] as well as protection, honour, and well-being. The expression that the Lord shows "favour" to the pious indicates the positive appearance of the person in

---

[159] Toy's translation (1977:56).

[160] It seems probable in the context of the book that "honouring, כבד (pi), the Lord" here does not refer to cultic obligations, but rather to more general prescriptions to help and respect fellow-man, esp. the poor and needy, attested elsewhere in the book.

[161] Concerning the structure of the chapter, see ch. 2, pp. 48–49.

[162] Toy's translation (1977:79–80). See our comments in ch. 3, pp. 98–99.

[163] See our comments to 10:22, ch. 4, pp. 175–176.

the eyes of the Lord[164] with the further implication that the Lord as his personal god will protect him and assist him in his endeavours.

The Lord watches over the righteous and does not allow him to suffer want:

10:3. Yahweh suffers not the righteous to hunger,
But he disappoints the desire of the wicked.[165]

The sentence forcefully expresses the Lord's rejection of the aspirations of the wicked, while he as personal god cares for the needs of the person close to him.

In a context in which the concept of life beyond the grave is not present, long life was an important indication of divine blessing. The sages regarded longevity as the consequence of a life of piety and obedience:

10:27. The fear of Yahweh prolongs life,
But the life of the wicked will be shortened.[166]

Despite our comments on 14:27 above,[167] there can be no doubt that the long life of the God-fearing person and the short life of the wicked man were primarily seen as dependent on the view of the Lord as guarantor of justice in his world.

The teachings of the sages included also exhortations which urged the readers to entrust all things to the Lord:

16:3. Commit thy work to Yahweh,
Then will thy plans succeed.[168]

The imperative form is not the norm in this section and it is possible that the use of the form here is to be explained by the fact that the sentence can be seen as concluding a small corpus consisting of verses 1–3, which all deal with the plans and ways of man and their relation to the Lord.[169] The advice of the first clause to entrust one's activity to the Lord[170] is followed by the assurance of its success in the second clause.[171] The subject of the first clause is works, deeds, מעשה (pl), denoting the actual undertaking, while the subject of the second clause is the plans and thoughts, מחשבת (pl), of the person's mind. The tension may be intentional indicating that while a man might commit each project to the Lord, the Lord has the entire situation under control and will work out everything with the best interests of that individual in mind. The

---

164 Cf. v 4.
165 Toy's translation (1977:199). The literal sense of הדף is stronger: "thrust away, reject."
166 Toy's translation (1977:216).
167 P. 217–218.
168 Toy's translation (1977:319).
169 The fact that 16:1–3 are missing from the LXX may further indicate that these verses constitute a separate minor corpus.
170 Literally: "Roll on Yahweh thy deeds."
171 The literal meaning of כון (ni) is "to be established, stand firm."

exhortation clearly establishes the relationship between the piety and devotion of the righteous man and the success bestowed upon him by his God.

The relationship between trust and a positive end is also evident in 16:20:

16:20. He who gives heed to the word will prosper,
And the man that trusts in Yahweh, happy is he![172]

The expression משכיל על־דבר in the first clause is a combination of a wisdom term, here translated "he who gives heed," and "word," the latter of which is very common and is also used to designate the messages of the prophets.[173] It seems probable, though, that דבר in this context refers to the teachings of the scribes. However, the use of דבר here and תורה elsewhere to refer to the teachings of the sages, implies that the different traditions: prophetic, legal, and wisdom, were not totally distinct.

The expression translated "prosper" here means literally "find good," probably to be understood as a general designation for "being successful" in all areas of life. The parallel in the second clause is a beatitude formula[174] which occurs elsewhere in the book of Proverbs[175] and is also frequently found in the Psalms.[176]

Obedience to the teachings of the sages and trust in the Lord are complementary to each other. He whose life is characterized by such obedience and trust is assured of success and happiness in all areas of life. Even if it is not explicitly spelled out in this sentence, the context of other similar sayings and the theological message of the book indicates that the sages believed that these positive results were granted to the individual by the Lord himself.

The assertion that the person who puts his trust in the Lord will prosper is spelled out in 28:25:

28:25. A greedy man stirs up strife,
But he who trusts in Yahweh will prosper.[177]

The antithesis between "greedy" and "trust in Yahweh" appears strange at first sight. The expression translated "greedy" means literally "large/wide of appetite," רחב נפש, and a more appropriate translation might be "self-indulgent," signifying a person whose appetite for wealth, pleasure, etc., is insatiable. The second line would then constitute a description of a person who has a more balanced attitude toward the positive things in life and who derived his primary satisfaction from piety and obedience to the will of the Lord.

---

[172] Toy's translation (1977:328). The first word of the sentence is משכיל which is a term common in wisdom with the meaning "act wisely," here in reference to "word, thing," דבר.

[173] See Jer 18:18.

[174] Here with a 3 sg masc suffix.

[175] Also in 3:13; 8:32; 14:21; 28:14; 29:18.

[176] Ps 1:1; 65:5; 84:5; 89:16; 119:1; 128:2; 137:8; 144:15; 146:5.

[177] Toy's translation (1977:505).

It is stated that he who trusts in the Lord will "prosper." The word used in this connection is דשן (pu), literally "be made fat."[178] It also has a broader meaning signifying something like the contentment a person experiences when all is well, under control and in order. The antithetically parallel "stirs up strife" alludes to the unpleasantness of the disorder which surrounds the self-indulgent man.

In 28:25 it is made clear that the pious person will experience prosperity. The person himself and his behaviour no doubt affects the situation, but the context of other sayings, as well as the main theological trends in the book, strongly suggest that for the sages the active involvement of the Lord as the personal god of the pious person was decisive.

d. Friendship, love, and discipline

The instruction in 3:1–12 concludes with two verses that should be regarded as a separate paragraph and a moderated view of the bold assurances of divine protection for the pious man previously expressed:

> 3:11. Reject not, my son, the instruction of Yahweh,
> And spurn not his reproof,
> 12. For whom 'he' loves he reproves,
> And he afflicts 'him' in whom he delights.[179]

In this context these verses indicate that the sages were aware that the theodicy posed a number of important problems for their individualistic approach to retribution. We must assume that from the very beginning the unqualified promises of protection, safety and freedom from all evil were not viewed as unproblematic. These verses introduce the motif of chastisement as an explanation for the difficulties that even the righteous inevitably experience. The terms used: "instruction," מוסר, "reproof," תוכחת, and "reprove," יכח (hi), occur elsewhere in the book,[180] often describing the educational activity of the teacher or parent who in exercising these prerogatives serves as prototype for God.

Toy's translation cited above does not accurately represent the text's emphasis on the father-son relationship in the last clause.[181] According to the Masoretic vocalization, verse 12 ought to be translated:

---

[178] Also used in 11:25; 13:4; 15:30.

[179] Toy's translation (1977:64). Toy (1977:65) reads "afflict," יכאב (hi) with LXX in the second clause of v 12 instead of "as a father," כאב, and exchanges "son" by "him" for sake of parallelism.

[180] מוסר seems to be a typical wisdom term and, except in chs. 25–31, is found through the book: 1:2, 3, 7, 8; 3:11; 4:1, 13; 5:12, 23; 6:23; 7:22; 8:10, 33; 10:17; 12:1; 13:1, 18, 24; 15:5, 10, 32, 33; 16:22; 19:20, 27; 22:15; 23:12, 13, 23; 24:32. תוכחת (v 11) occurs almost exclusively in Proverbs, often in parallelism to מוסר: 1:23, 25, 30; 3:11; 5:12; 6:23; 10:17; 12:1; 13:18; 15:5, 10, 31, 32; 27:5; 29:1, 15. יכח (hi): 3:12; 9:7–8; 15:12; 19:25; 24:25; 25:12; 28:23; 30:6.

[181] Toy's reason for altering the vocalization (1977:65) is that it makes the correspondence to Job 5:17–18 even closer and also that the conception of the Lord as father occurs only here in Proverbs.

3:12. for Yahweh disciplines the one whom he loves,
like a father with the son in whom he takes pleasure.[182]

This reading of the text renders the close relation between an individual and his god more forcefully, in a way reminiscent of Jacobsen's characterization of the relationship not as the common master—slave relationship, but rather in terms of the intimacy between father and son. The tenderness of this relationship is also brought into relief through the use of the word "love"—a term rarely employed in this book or elsewhere in the Old Testament as a description of the Lord's feelings towards man.

The close relationship between the Lord and the righteous man is especially evident in the second line of 3:32:

3:32. For a bad man is an abomination to Yahweh,
But between him and the upright there is friendship.[183]

In this verse, the upright is part of the Lord's council or inner circle of close friends, סוד,[184] which corresponds well to the translation "friendship" The relationship between the Lord and the upright person is thus here described in terms that points in the direction of a close, personal bond between God and man.

Finally, let us examine two sentences which contrast the abhorrence of the Lord for the life of the wicked and his sacrifices with the Lord's love toward the righteous man and his pleasure in the prayer of the upright:

15:8. The sacrifice of the wicked is an abomination to Yahweh,
But the prayer of the upright is acceptable to him.
9. Abomination to Yahweh is the life of wicked,
But him who practices righteousness he loves.[185]

This is one of the few sayings in the book of Proverbs that refer to the cult and sacrifices. It is the wicked man's sacrifice that is rejected, not sacrifices as such. It is difficult to ascertain if there is also a tension between prayer and sacrifice, the former signifying the type of piety preferred by the sages. The main antithesis, however, is between the wicked and the upright or righteous.[186]

Again it is stated that the Lord "loves" the man whose life is characterized by righteousness. The words express affection as well as a close bond between the Lord and the individual. Verse eight uses the term "pleasure," רצון, to

---

[182] McKane's translation (1985:214).

[183] Toy's translation (1977:79).

[184] Toy (1977:80–81) translates סוד as friendship with the meaning "private, intimate converse and friendly relation." Cf. Job 29:4–5; Ps 25:14; 55:14–15. An aspect of the term סוד, not dominating here, is its meaning of secrecy and secret counsel for planning, cf. 11:13; 20:19; 25:9. On סוד, see Sæbø (1976:144–148).

[185] Toy's translation (1977:305–306).

[186] The description in the last clause, lit. "the one who pursues righteousness," denotes an active search for the way of life characterized by righteousness.

denote the Lord's appreciation of a person and his way of life. As we have already noted, this is a term occurring frequently in antithetical parallelism to "abomination."

2. Comparison between the book of Proverbs and other Old Testament traditions

Our treatment of passages relating to the Lord as personal God in the book of Proverbs demonstrates that the close relationship between the Lord and righteous man depicted in the book of Proverbs can be described as a relationship between a person and his personal god. We will now proceed to make some comparisons between our observations on the book of Proverbs and the other Old Testament traditions.

a. The wisdom traditions

The depiction of God as protector of the righteous man is attested also in other wisdom books of the Old Testament. In the book of Job it occurs in the speeches of Job as well as of his friends. This is the way Job has believed in and experienced his God throughout his life,[187] and he still clings to this belief even though the reality of the situation no longer corresponds to his theology.[188] God, who had in the past been his protection and safety, now appears to be his brutal enemy.[189] Job's friends, who concentrate for the most part on the disaster and lack of safety of the wicked man, also state, in what we may presume was the conventional manner, that God's presence in the life of the righteous man is the only sure source of protection from harm.[190]

The book of Ecclesiastes supplies no support for this view of God as the special protector of the righteous. On the contrary, when Qoheleth sets his mind to investigate the matter, he arrives at the conclusion that there is no difference—the righteous and the wicked share the same fate.[191]

Among so-called wisdom psalms several express the conviction that the Lord protects the righteous person.[192] In particular, Psalm 37 deals with this issue and asserts confidence in 1) God's punishment of all wickedness, 2) his protection of the pious man and 3) the ultimate victory of the person who trusts in the Lord even if he temporarily experiences difficulties. The psalmist asserts that this point of view is in essential harmony with his life-long experience:

---

[187] See Job 29:2–25.
[188] See Job 31:1–4.
[189] See esp. Job 9:12, 16–17; 10:3–22; 16:12–14; 19:8–11; 30:21.
[190] See Job 5:19–27; 11:18–20.
[191] See Eccl 9:1–3. There are passages, though, that express more confidence in justice, 3:17; 8:12–13 (cf. v 14).
[192] Ps 34; 37; 49; 91; 112.

37:25. I have been young, and now am old;
Yet I have not seen the righteous forsaken
or his children begging bread....
28. For the Lord loves justice;
He will not forsake his saints.
The righteous shall be preserved for ever,
but the children of the wicked shall be cut off.
29. The righteous shall possess the land,
and dwell upon it for ever....
39. The salvation of the righteous is from the Lord;
He is their refuge in the time of trouble.
40. The Lord helps hem and delivers them,
He delivers them from the wicked, and saves them,
Because they take refuge in him. (RSV)

The depiction of the Lord as the one who grants success and well-being is closely connected to the view in which he functions as protector and both aspects appear similarly in other wisdom books. Job not only remembers the protection of God, he also looks back to the days when everything went his way, when he was held in high esteem by everyone and was successful in all his endeavours:

Job 29:2. Oh, if only I were as in months gone by,
As in the days when Eloah watched over me.
3. When his lamp shone over my head
And I walked by its light in the dark;
4. When I was in the days of my prime,
When the friendship of Eloah graced my tent;
5. When Shaddai was still at my side
And my boys were all around me;
6. When my feet were bathed in cream
And the rock poured out streams of oil for me.
7. When I passed through the city gate
to take my seat in the square,
8. Boys saw me and hid,
Elders rose and stood.
9. Nobles refrained from arguing
And clapped their hands on their mouths[193]

This text also expresses the "friendship" to signify the warmth of the bygone relationship Job which had experienced with his god. The Masoretic text of verse 4 used the same word, סוד, as in Proverbs 3:32 to designate this close fellowship between God and man.[194]

Job's friends assert that success and well-being as well as safety and protection are the consequences of a right relationship with God. This is especially well illustrated in the words of Eliphaz who enumerates God's blessings to the

---

[193] Habel's translation (1985:402).
[194] See our comments above to Proverbs 3:32, p. 224.

righteous man: deliverance from all evil, harmony and peace, prosperity, large family, health and long life:

Job 5:19. In six calamities he will deliver you;
In seven no evil will befall you.
20. In famine he will redeem you from death;
In war from the power of the sword.
21. From the roving tongue you will be hidden,
Nor will you fear the demon when he comes.
22. At plunder and famine you will laugh;
The beast of the earth you will not fear.
23. For you will have a pact with the stones of the field
And the beast of the field will be at peace with you.
24. You will know your tent is at peace;
When you visit your fold, nothing will be missing.
25. You will know your progeny is great;
Your offspring will be as the grass of earth.
26. You will reach the grave full of vigour,
Like a sheaf of grain in season.
27. Yes, we have searched all this! It is true!
Hear it! Know it for yourself![195]

The book of Ecclesiastes states time and again that the good things a person receives should be regarded as from the hand of God and appreciated as such.[196] These passages may be referred to as portraying a close relationship between God and man where God as the personal god blesses the individual. But the emphasis of the book is so much upon man's inability to understand God and his ways that we are forced to surmise that these passages do not so much indicate the close fellowship between God and man as they give a theological-philosophical basis and legitimation for the enjoyment of the simple pleasures that life offers to everyone.

Several of the so-called wisdom psalms proclaim the success and well-being of the righteous man and affirm that the Lord helps those who trust in him.[197] About the man who shuns evil in favour of delighting in the law of the Lord, Psalm 1 says:

Ps 1:3. He is like a tree planted by streams of water,
that yields its fruit in its season, and its leaf does not wither.
In all that he does, he prospers. (RSV)

The depiction of the righteous man as a close friend and ally of the Lord has been noted in connection with a previous discussion of Job 29. The formulation asserting that God "loves" the righteous does not occur elsewhere in the wisdom traditions. The chastisement motif is attested in the book of Job,

---

[195] Habel's translation (1985:114–115).
[196] Eccl 2:24–25; 3:12–13, 22; 5:17–19; 8:15; 9:7–9; (11:9).
[197] Ps 1:3; 37:3–6, 17–19; 128:1–6.

especially in the speeches of Eliphaz and Elihu,[198] as well as in a few psalms which have been classified as wisdom psalms.[199]

b. Other traditions of the Old Testament

The close fellowship between God and righteous man in which God acts in the manner of a personal god, giving protection, success and well-being to the righteous man, is not unique to the wisdom literature of the Old Testament. In the introduction to this chapter, we referred to the research of Vorländer and Albertz who both maintain that the characterization of God in the patriarchal narratives as well as in the individual psalms of lament must in large measure be understood from a perspective which regards him as the personal god of the individual. The theophoric personal names, which, remarkably, contain no references to Israel's salvation history, predominantly have meanings indicating God's "Mit-Sein" with the individual.[200] This fact argues that the personal relationship between God and man should not be characterized as a phenomenon exclusive to one single period in Israel's history, since it is to be found in every period as a phenomenon complementary to the more aloof relational style of official religion . Vorländer also notes this kind of relationship between the Lord and David and David's dynasty.[201]

To the prophets God is mainly the national God even though their messages often direct a challenge toward individuals, admonishing them to obey the message from God and experience his deliverance and help. The prophets themselves may serve as examples of individuals who are portrayed as experiencing this intimate, personal relationship between their God and themselves.

The concept of the Lord as the personal god of the individual appears to be attested throughout the whole Old Testament. There also appears to be an interrelationship in Israel between this concept of God and the description of him as the god of the nation, where personal and official religion were never completely separate and exerted significant influences on one another through the course of Israelite history.[202]

3. Comparison between the book of Proverbs and non-Israelite wisdom.

The broader contours of the concepts of a personal god in the surrounding cultures of Egypt and Mesopotamia have already been described. It now remains to survey the wisdom literature of these two cultures in order to compare their concepts of the personal god with that of the book of Proverbs.

---

[198] Eliphaz, Job 5:17–18; Elihu, Job 33:19–24; 34:23–37; 36:7–15.
[199] Ps 32:3–5; 39:9–12; 73:13–17.
[200] Albertz (1978:49–77).
[201] Vorländer (1975:231–244).
[202] See Vorländer (1975:293–301), Jacobsen (1976:164), Albertz (1978:165–198).

a. Egypt

Among other features, Hornung notes in his summary of the function of the god in Egyptian Instructions[203] that "ohne oder gegen ihn nichts gelingt"—a formulation that indicates that the *ntr* in the instructions was referred to as the individual's personal god, close to man and able to give him success in his efforts.

The consistent practice of referring to the deity by the generic term *ntr* in the instructions, indicates that no specific deity was in focus.[204] The instructions, designed to be read and followed by individuals, made this allowance for the freedom of each individual to apply what was stated concerning the deity to his own personal god.[205]

It is not difficult to find evidence in the instructions for the belief that the god stands in a personal relationship to the person who adheres to and lives according to the teachings of the sages. In early times this was deeply interconnected with the concept of *ma'at,* a connection which was intended to encourage one to live a life according to the dictates of the all-embracing order. In later times this emphasis shifted toward what has been called "personal piety." A man who merited the favour of his god was characterized by both highly ethical behaviour and respect for the gods. For a man of this kind, the instructions assert that the god will make his work prosper and give him the best of life in all its fulness. Statements about the protective aspect are less common.

In the early *Instruction of Ptahhotep* the personal involvement of the god is noted repeatedly in the context of assertions that everything a person owns is allowed by the grace of the god, and that it is the god who is completely responsible for the advancement of a person:

> If you plow and there's growth in the field,
> And god lets it prosper in your hand,....[206]

> If you are a man of worth
> And produce a son by the grace of god,....[207]

> It is the god who gives advancement,
> He who uses elbows is not helped.[208]

> Sustain your friends with what you have,
> You have it by the grace of god;....[209]

---

[203] Hornung (1973:191)

[204] See comments and references in ch. 1, pp. 44–45.

[205] Hornung (1973:38–49, esp. 46–47).

[206] *Ptahhotep*, maxim 9, Lichtheim (1975:66).

[207] *Ptahhotep*, maxim 12, Lichtheim (1975:66).

[208] *Ptahhotep*, maxim 13, Lichtheim (1975:67).

[209] *Ptahhotep*, maxim 22, Lichtheim (1975:69).

If you are great after having been humble,...
Do not put trust in your wealth,
Which came to you as gift of god;....[210]

Lo, the good son, the gift of god,....[211]

The Instruction of Amenemope includes a reference to prayer and its results
that demonstrates the close relationship between the sun god and the individual
and asserts that the god supplies all the needs of the pious man including safety:

You shall pray to the Aten when he rises,
Saying: "Grant me well-being and health";
He will give you your needs for this life,
And you will be safe from fear.[212]

The late Demotic instructions, and especially *Papyrus Insinger,* supply quite a
bit of material containing the notion that protection, wealth and well-being,
spring out of a personal fellowship with the god.   The teachings in
Onkhsheshonqy run along similar lines

S[erve your] god, that he may guard you.[213]

Do not say "I have this wealth, I will not serve god nor will I serve man."
Wealth comes to an end; serving the god is what creates (it).[214]

All god fortune is from the hand of the god.[215]

If [a woman is at peace] with her husband it is the influences of the god.[216]

Papyrus Insinger places considerable emphasis upon the fact that everything in
human life comes through the active involvement of the god who determines
people's lives. This is brought out especially by the use of the same refrain,
with minor variations, to close each of the twenty-five chapters of the book:

The fate and fortune that come, it is the god who sends them.[217]

Papyrus Insinger ascribes protection as well as prosperity to the god:

It is the god who gives wealth; it is a wise man who guards [it].[218]

---

[210] *Ptahhotep,* maxim 30, Lichtheim (1975:71).

[211] *Ptahhotep,* epilogue, Lichtheim (1975:76).

[212] *Amenemope* x 12–15, Lichtheim (1976:153). See also the expression "safe in the hand of the god"
in xiv 1.

[213] *Onkhsheshonqy* vi 1, Lichtheim (1983:71).

[214] *Onkhsheshonqy* xviii 16–17, Lichtheim (1983:83).

[215] *Onkhsheshonqy* xx 6, Lichtheim (1983:85).

[216] *Onkhsheshonqy* xxv 5, Lichtheim (1983:89).

[217] *Papyrus Insinger* ii 20, v 11, etc, Lichtheim (1980:187, 189, etc.).

[218] *Papyrus Insinger* v 15, Lichtheim (1980:189).

The god gives a wealth of supplies without an income.[219]

[It is the god who] gives protection to the wise man because of (his) service.[220]

There is no true protection except the work of the god.[221]

The god blesses trust with protection.[222]

The god gives wealth to the wise man because of (his) generosity.[223]

The seventeenth chapter of *Papyrus Insinger* is of special interest since it demonstrates that there was an awareness among the Egyptian sages of the fact that the wise and pious man may also experience hardships. This problem is dealt with by asserting that the god is able to turn evil into good for the pious man if he only has patience to persevere:

> It is the god who gives patience to the wise man in misfortune....
> Do not be heartsore during an imprisonment; the work of the god is great.
> The man of god is in prison [for his very gain].[224]

We find that from the earliest times the sages of Egypt taught that success and well-being were brought to man by the god. Though certain developments created changes in world view and the concept of the divine, the presence of this belief can be detected in the instructions of every era. In earlier times, this belief was connected to *ma'at,* in the late New Kingdom it was associated with "personal piety" and in the late period it became companion to a variety of deistic fatalism. Nevertheless, the formulation of the belief remains essentially the same: the *nṯr,* the god of the individual, is responsible for a man's fortune in life.

b. Mesopotamia

Perhaps the best evidence that the references to a deity in Mesopotamian wisdom usually refer to a personal god, is the very frequent use of the possessive pronoun connected to the term for god. It is also noteworthy that reference to deities as couples, e.g. my god and my goddess, is relatively frequent.

Vorländer describes the relationship between man's well-being and the personal god in the Mesopotamian wisdom literature in the following way:

> Die Weisheitstexte ermahnen den Menschen, Erfolg und Wohlergehen allein von seinem persönlichen Gott zu erwarten. Nicht auf Reichtum oder sein Alter soll der Mensch bauen, sondern auf seinen persönlichen Gott....

---

[219] *Papyrus Insinger* vii 17, Lichtheim (1980:191).

[220] *Papyrus Insinger* x 1, Lichtheim (1980:193).

[221] *Papyrus Insinger* xi 13, Lichtheim (1980:194).

[222] *Papyrus Insinger* xii 2, Lichtheim (1980:194).

[223] *Papyrus Insinger* xv 10, Lichtheim (1980:197).

[224] *Papyrus Insinger* xix 9; xx 4–5, Lichtheim (1980:200–201).

Voraussetzung für die Gegenwart des persönlichen Gottes und damit für ein glückliches und erfolgreiches Leben ist die regelmässige Darbringung von Gebeten und Opfern. Auf diesen Zusammenhang von Opfer und Wohlergehen weisen die Weisheitslehrer immer wieder mahnend hin.[225]

Even if the cultus is more pronounced in Mesopotamian than in Israelite wisdom, there are also texts that make it clear that a right relationship with the deity had an ethical basis as well.

In the bilingual so-called *Assyrian Collection* there are proverbs that demonstrate that "having a god" and "having success" are synonymous expressions.[226]   In addition it is asserted that it is the presence and help of the personal god that is the most important factor in determining a person's fate:

> When you exert yourself, your god is yours.
> When you do not exert yourself, your god is not yours.[227]

> It is not wealth that is your support. It is (your) god.
> Be you small or great, it is (your) god who is your support.[228]

> ....may he not stand in the presence of (his) god and king; his gods will forsake him, his lordship will be driven out, and his god will not be his.[229]

The arguments of the sufferer in the Sumerian *Man and his God* are built upon the conviction that his personal god has for some reason deserted him, leaving him vulnerable to the sickness and suffering which then afflicted him. The text expresses the necessity of having a god to look after one's sustenance and protection, and formulates the close relationship between the personal god and man in the following way:

> Let his lament soothe the heart of his god,
> (For) a man without a god would not obtain food....

> My god, you who are my father who begot me, [*lift up*] my face,
> *like* an innocent cow, in *pity*...the groan,
> How long will you neglect me, leave me unprotected?[230]

The sufferer in *Ludlul bēl nēmeqi* also experiences the abandonment of the personal god/goddess, leaving him deserted and without protection:

> My god has forsaken me and *disappeared,*
> My goddess has cut me off and stayed removed from me.

---

[225] Vorländer (1975:75).

[226] Jacobsen (1976:155): "The personal god was, *ab ovo,* intimately connected and concerned with one individual's fortunes. So much so that one might almost say that the god was a personification of the power for personal success in that individual."

[227] ii 23–26, Lambert (1960:227,230).

[228] ii 42–45, Lambert (1960:227–228, 232).

[229] ii 9–12, Lambert (1960:228, 232).

[230] *Man and his God* 8–9, 96–98, ANET (1969:589–590).

The benevolent spirit who was (always) beside [me] has departed,
My protective spirit has flown away and seeks someone else.[231]

The personal god is even referred to as "his protective god"[232] in this text, underlining the protective nature of his presence with the person. In the end the sufferer is assured that Marduk has heard his prayers, he is restored to health and prosperity and again experiences close fellowship with his personal deity.[233]

The sufferer's friend in the *Babylonian Theodicy* represents what may be assumed to have constituted the traditional view—that the humble man could expect protection and success from his personal god:

He who looks to his god has a protective spirit,
The humble man who fears his goddess accumulates wealth.[234]

Unless you seek the will of the god, what success can you have?
He that bears his god's yoke never lacks food, even though it be sparse.
Seek the favorable breath of the god,
What you have lost in a year you will make up in a moment.[235]

The sufferer is troubled that the rules do not appear to be consistent, that his service to the god and his righteous life have not led to prosperity and success and he expresses the suspicion that his unfortunate situation was from the very beginning decreed by his god:

Those who do not seek the god go the way of prosperity,
While those who pray to the goddess become destitute and impoverished.
In my youth I tried to find the will of my god;
With prostration and prayer I sought my goddess.
But I was pulling a yoke in useless corvee.
My god decreed poverty instead of wealth (for me).[236]

It is in the religion and wisdom literature of Mesopotamia that the concept of personal god is the most clearly defined. The Mesopotamian wisdom literature demonstrates the basic function of the personal god as the one who brings success and well-being to man and as the protector against all kinds of evil. However, it is important to note that this belief is both asserted and debated within this corpus of literature.

---

[231] *Ludlul* I,43–46, *ANET* (1969:596).

[232] *Ludlul* I,97, *ANET* (1969:597).

[233] See Tablet IV, *ANET* (1969:600).

[234] *Babylonian Theodicy* 21–22, *ANET* (1969:602).

[235] *Babylonian Theodicy* 239–242, *ANET* (1969:603).

[236] *Babylonian Theodicy* 70–75, *ANET* (1969:602).

4. Conclusions concerning God and the righteous man

a. Wisdom traditions

The close fellowship between the Lord and righteous man as it is found in the book of Proverbs also appears in the book of Job and several of the so-called wisdom psalms. The man with whom God is especially present in the manner of a personal god is a man whose life is characterized by piety as well as high ethical standards. The texts assure the reader that such a man will experience the protection of the Lord as well as success and the good life. In the book of Job there is tension between the confident assertions of the friends and Job's confusion concerning his predicament. The book of Proverbs repeatedly proclaims that the righteous man and his family can live in peace and safety because of the protection of the Lord. The contrasting position is one of instability and the impending catastrophe, portrayed by the image of the wicked man running headlong, often unknowingly, into destruction. The assertion that the righteous are kept safe by the protection of God is also a strong motif in the wisdom psalms, e.g. Psalm 37.

The book of Ecclesiastes differs from the other wisdom books in this respect. Although the book contains exhortations to piety and trust, its main theme is the incomprehensibility of God and his activity in the world, which tends to deemphasize the portrayal of God as a personal god while emphasizing his status as the god of transcendence and mystery. In his observation of the way things actually work out in the world, Qoheleth maintains a point of view which is the opposite of traditional wisdom, namely that the wicked and the righteous share the same fate.

b. Other traditions of the Old Testament

Vorländer and Albertz have demonstrated that the concept of a personal god in the different traditions of the Old Testament represents one particular aspect of religion which is usually co-existent with official religion. In Israel this personal religion is characterized by an absence of references to Israel's salvation history and a lack of expressed interest in the official cult. Personal religion is instead characterized by an emphasis on God's presence with the individual, his protection and his help in achieving success in life. Vorländer and Albertz demonstrate that this picture of personal religion applies to Mesopotamia as well as to Israel and note that, in this respect, there are more similarities between the two cultures than at the level of official religion.

The studies of Vorländer and Albertz mainly deal with the patriarchal narratives, the history of the Davidic dynasty, the psalms of individual lament and theophoric personal names. Our study indicates that the wisdom literature ought to be included among the traditions that yield positive evidence relating to personal religion. It seems likely that closer study would lead to a similar conclusion in the case of the historic and prophetic traditions.

c. Egypt

In the Egyptian instructions there is a close connection between adhering to wisdom teachings and God's granting of prosperity and success to the person. This is clearly the case in the Old Kingdom text *The Instruction of Ptahhotep*. *The Instruction of Amenemope* also contains some evidence which points in this direction and this view is strongly asserted in the late Demotic instructions *Onkhsheshonqy* and *Papyrus Insinger*. The god's protective function is much more prominent in the later instructions. *The Instruction of Amenemope,* which is the prime example of an instruction from the "age of personal piety," contains several sayings which are formulated in a way that indicates close fellowship with the god,[237] but the number of sayings is not exceptionally large. We conclude from this that the motifs of protection and success granted by the god to the obedient played a role in the wisdom teachings of every age, with some variation in emphasis and meaning.

d. Mesopotamia

The study of Mesopotamian religion has indicated to us the importance of the concept of a personal god. When we examine the wisdom texts we find the argument for the presence of this concept supported by references to the protection as well as the success which the personal god awards to the individual. When sickness, suffering and hardship strike a person, it is taken as a sign that his personal god has deserted him and that person then goes through a period of soul-searching in order to find out how he may have offended the god. By the confession of sins and pleas of mercy[238] the person tries to influence his god and regain his presence. Several of the so-called reflective essays from Mesopotamia deal with the problems that arise when a person feels deserted by his god because he has been stricken by bad fortune but cannot come up with any reason for it. As in the book of Job, the sufferer complains of injustice and arbitrariness in the god's behaviour.

---

[237] See above, also *Amenemope* ix 5–6, xxii 7.

[238] Interestingly, the concept of God's mercy seems to play a minor role in Israelite wisdom (Prov 28:13, Job 7:21; 11:6), but appears more in apocryphal works (Fichtner [1933:126])

C. Conclusions

It has been the aim of this chapter to demonstrate that the concept of God in the book of Proverbs is characterized to a large degree by closeness to man and the personal involvement of God in the affairs of the individual. Terms used in the study of the other religions of the ancient Orient, "personal religion" and "personal god," have been employed to signify the depiction of the deity in this manner.

The book of Proverbs contains a considerable number of sayings that depict the Lord as a "personal god." This portrayal of the Lord as personal god is particularly pertinent to individuals in difficult circumstances like the poor man, the widow and the orphan. In addition to this connection with the weak and defenceless, the Lord is also depicted as the personal god of an individual whose life is characterized by wisdom, honesty, piety, humility, etc., whom we have been referring to in this chapter as the righteous man. We also noted that the Lord is portrayed as having profound concern for the situation of the weak and defenceless, to the point that he is even declared their "redeemer," גאל.[239] In relation to the righteous man the most prominent feature of the Lord is his appearance as protector and refuge against all the evil that will befall the wicked. Several sayings indicate the blessing the Lord gives to the righteous man, that he as personal god makes the righteous prosperous and successful in his work.

Within the book there are certain divergences. For example, there are hardly any references to the concern of the Lord for the weak in chapters 1–9 while the motif of accurate and false measures is confined to 10:1–22:16. However, we find it difficult to arrive at any definite conclusions on the basis of these thematic divergences since they may be due to genre or the differing background of the sections of the book. Other themes, like the close fellowship between the righteous man and the Lord, are attested throughout the book. This last observation is probably best explained by the fact that close fellowship between the Lord and individuals is a basic ingredient of Old Testament faith, and not the least in the wisdom literature with its sharp contrasts between different groups of people.

The comparison of our observations on the book of Proverbs with other wisdom texts of the Old Testament showed a close correspondence between the books of Proverbs and Job while Ecclesiastes was largely silent on these issues. The so-called wisdom psalms show parallels especially in the assertion of God's protection and granting success to the righteous man. It seems possible to conclude that the depiction of the Lord as close to man in the manner of a personal god is a shared feature of the different wisdom traditions of the Old Testament. The book of Ecclesiastes differs in its radical, philosophical-

---

[239] Prov 23:10–11.

theological and empiricist position, which put its author in a position where he was unable to agree with the optimistic assertions of traditional wisdom.

The comparison of our observations on the book of Proverbs and other Old Testament traditions as well as non-Israelite wisdom, did first of all demonstrate that this kind of literature in the Ancient Near East had much in common. In the wisdom literature of Egypt and Mesopotamia it is possible to find correspondences to the Lord's concern for the weak[240] as well as to the description of the close fellowship between the Lord and righteous man in the book of Proverbs. The fact that these features in the characterization of God also occur in the various Old Testament traditions indicates that the situation cannot be simplistically described as Israelite sages merely copying the wisdom teachings and adopting the thought patterns of the surrounding cultures.[241] Differences in emphasis, approach and argumentation indicate that the interrelationship is more complicated and that the similarities to a large extent can be explained as due to the common values and traditions of neighbouring cultures. Even close correspondences, e.g. the motif of accurate and false measures, do not necessarily lead to the conclusion of direct dependence as the presence of this motif in the other Old Testament traditions clearly illustrates. The weightiest argument for asserting that Israelite wisdom was in some way dependent upon non-Israelite wisdom, seems to be provided by the lack of references to the sojourner in both Israelite and non-Israelite wisdom, for this is precisely where Israelite wisdom deviates from the other Old Testament traditions.

The Mesopotamian wisdom literature provides us with the closest parallels to the book of Proverbs when it comes to expressions of the protection and blessing associated with divine presence with the individual. Nevertheless, the fact that there is less emphasis on the ethical presuppositions on the part of man in Mesopotamian wisdom is an important distinguishing characteristic. There is some limited evidence in the Mesopotamian wisdom literature pointing toward the concern of the deity for the weak in society.

Egyptian wisdom literature, especially the instructions from the New Kingdom and later, runs parallel to the book of Proverbs in its emphasis on the concern of the deity for the weak. In the Egyptian instructions of every period a strong emphasis on the teaching that the god grants success to the individual in all his deeds is detectable. This corresponds to the Mesopotamian approach

---

[240] Fensham (1962:137) concludes that there are "remarkable similarities and analogies between the conception of protection of the weak in Mesopotamian, Egyptian, and Israelite literature," including the basic conception that the protection of the weak is the will of the god.

[241] Malchow (1982:120–124) argues against the view that the sages adopted their concept of social justice from the prophets and maintains that instead it came from the Near Eastern culture in general. We agree with Malchow that the sages should not be viewed as dependent upon the prophets and that they, especially on this subject, made a substantial contribution to the OT thought. However, this concern for social justice, which is common to the ANE, appears in different OT traditions like the law collections, the prophetic writings and the wisdom books. It is by no means possible to ascertain the extent to which the sages were directly dependent upon non-Israelite sources.

where "having a god" was even used as a synonym for "having luck, being successful." This feature is also present in the book of Proverbs and other wisdom texts, though it is not greatly emphasized and is always closely related to piety and ethics.

Our general conclusion is that the concept of God in the book of Proverbs exhibits the most fundamental relationship to the wisdom traditions and other traditions of the Old Testament. Correspondences to the wisdom traditions of Egypt and Mesopotamia are frequent and significant. However, in light of the differences noted above, these parallels do not necessarily lead to the conclusion that non-Israelite wisdom traditions had direct literary influences upon the book of Proverbs. The correspondences are mostly of such nature that they are best explained as due to a common cultural context with a variety of inter-relationships between countries and people.

Summary and final conclusions

Our study of the book of Proverbs has shown that the concept of God within this book and within the wisdom traditions in Israel is founded upon a variety of concepts. The themes of the Lord as the creator of the world and the creator of man appear separately in the book, each with a particular emphasis—creation of the world in order to promote and enhance wisdom, and creation of man to supply a basis for social ethics, especially concern for the poor. The notion that the Lord is the sole creator is beyond doubt. It is never questioned, but uniformly presupposed, and is, therefore, freely employed by the sages to support their precepts. With this as a theological background there is a certain relevance in referring to the "creation theology" of the wisdom traditions. God is the sole creator of the world and of man—this had implications for the cosmology as well as the anthropology of wisdom. It is surprising that this belief in the Lord as creator is not applied more extensively and more systematically to different areas of teaching, but in the book of Proverbs remained confined to the promotion of wisdom and social ethics. This indicates that though "creation theology" constitutes an essential aspect of the theology of the sages, it cannot be regarded as the only aspect of their theology, not even as the most important.

Closely related to "creation theology" is the notion of order within wisdom thinking. Our investigation of relevant passages in the book of Proverbs showed that the sages built their teachings upon an understanding of the world as "ordered," i.e. a world that was not chaotic, but could be trusted and where things generally happened in a way that could be predicted and planned for. Prominent in their teachings was the idea that there was justice in the world and that the wicked must face the dire consequences of their life-style in the same way as the righteous could enjoy the benefits of his. This order does not appear, however, to be something impersonal and automatic, but is built upon the belief that the Lord is deeply involved in his creation, maintaining justice and "order" in the world.

Our study of the text material in the book of Proverbs led to the conclusion that the sages believed that the connection between a person's life-style and his fate was determined by a number of factors—e.g., the Lord's execution of justice and the "natural" consequences of certain actions and behaviours, such as laziness, the reaction of other people, etc. On the whole, the sages showed little interest in the specifying the exact consequences of certain actions or behaviour. Their main interest was to make use of the act/character-consequence relationship as the philosophical basis for their teachings, primarily in the field of ethics. This specific function of the character-consequence relationship must be regarded as the main reason for the impersonal, passive and general formulations that abound in the book. A further reason for this indefiniteness was that it left a number of possible alternatives open for the realization of the predicted consequences.

Our investigation of the concepts of retribution and order as they appear in the texts, indicate that the sages viewed God as involved in the world and responsible for the maintenance of justice. The majority of sayings in the book contain no reference to God or any over-arching principle but are restricted predominantly to the expression of ethical views and the moral implications of certain kinds of behaviour. Though the interpretation of certain sayings may indicate that the sages regarded evil, and probably also good, as to some degree independent forces which could be "contagious," we have not found this concept to be dominant and therefore have not adopted the view that the idea of consequences being built into actions was the basis of the sages' affirmations of the act/character-consequence relationship. We have argued that the non-specified descriptions of actions as well as consequences in the book of Proverbs point in another direction. The examination of these non-specified descriptions led us to suggest that the expression "character-consequence relationship" would be more appropriate than the customary "act-consequence relationship". Further study of the text material led to the conclusion that the sages believed that the consequences of a person's life could be realized in different ways, while at the same time they regarded God as the guarantor that justice would be ultimately upheld.

Several features in the description of God in the book of Proverbs indicate that the sages regarded the Lord as a transcendent being and sovereign lord actively involved in the world. The fact that he is able to establish justice for each individual, that he is in no way portrayed as belonging to creation but rather is the creator of all things and that wisdom functions as his intermediary, indicate his transcendence in relation to the world. The depiction of him as supreme ruler, as inscrutable, and as able to accomplish his will and purposes in spite of human resistance, reveals his sovereignty. All these features together embody the fundamental differentiation between the Lord and everything in creation, including man, and thus we have argued that in the view of the sages the designation "supreme God" is quite appropriate. The description of the Lord as simultaneously transcendent over and engaged in the world of man, corresponds to the contours of the phenomenon of a "supreme being" or "Hochgott," in other religions. Our comparative study of other traditions of the Old Testament and non-Israelite wisdom, demonstrates that the depiction of the Lord in the book of Proverbs shares a number of features related to the portrayal of divine beings in these traditions. This correspondence owes its explanation, to a large degree, to the shared, conventional depiction of the deity as the supreme being. The general way the deity was referred to in Egyptian, Mesopotamian and Israelite wisdom explains some of the similarities in the characterization of the deity as well as making room for the specific differences which did in fact exist between the theologies of the different religions. The reasons for this generality in referring to the deity were not the same in each of the traditions; in Egypt and Mesopotamia the non-specific reference had the function of leaving the saying open to application in a number of different situations and in the name of a number of different deities in the pantheon. In Israel, on the other hand, we may assume that the main reason for the same practice was a certain internationalism built upon the view that God is the supreme ruler of the world. This feature—which to some extent is visible in all three Israelite wisdom books in the lack of references to Israel's salvation history—is most readily apparent in the book of Ecclesiastes where designations of God are kept as general as possible.

Another perspective, which is complementary to the view of the Lord as supreme God in the book of Proverbs, is the depiction of him as intimately related to the world and the individual. We have identified and analysed a number of sayings that emphasize this aspect of the theology of the sages under the heading "The Lord as personal God." This particular line of theological thinking appears especially in sayings expressing the Lord's concern for the weak and mistreated in society and in the depiction of the intimate relationship between the righteous man and the Lord. Comparisons with other wisdom books and the various Old Testament traditions show that the Lord is depicted as the personal god of the individual in a similar way in the rest of the Old Testament as well.

The depictions of the personal god and goddess frequently referred to in Mesopotamian wisdom texts and the kind of deity referred to by the generic term *nṯr* in Egyptian instructions are in many ways similar to the portrayal of the Lord as a personal god in the book of Proverbs. God's concern for the weak and victimized is emphasized in the main Old Testament traditions and Egyptian wisdom, but less pronounced in Mesopotamian wisdom as well as in Proverbs 1–9. Mesopotamian wisdom literature has a high frequency of references to the protective presence of the personal god which finds parallels in a number of sayings in the book of Proverbs. However, the book of Proverbs is distinctive for its pronounced emphasis on the ethical prerequisites for the protective presence of the deity and for its uniformly strong commendations of ethical behaviour as an essential ingredient in a life characterized by wisdom. Egyptian wisdom books exhibit the closest similarities with the book of Proverbs in their expression of the deity's concern for the weak and mistreated. A slight difference between the two can, however, be detected. Compared to the book of Proverbs, even the Egyptian wisdom books from the age of personal piety appear to be more reluctant to express an intimate relationship between the deity and human beings.

The first part of this book is about creation and order. Crenshaw has rightly argued for a thematic connection between creation faith and the justice of God.[1] Since the world and man was created by the Lord, the universe is comprehensible and at least part of its mysteries can be fathomed. Chaos never gains the upper hand since the Lord who created all things is involved in the world and upholds creation. The implications of this relate not only to one's view of the cosmos, but also of society. The very fact that the teachings of the sages preserved in the book of Proverbs express the belief that God is the transcendent and sovereign Lord who is also personally involved in the situation of individuals, provided the necessary basis for belief in justice and correspondence between life-style and consequences. Our study has led to the conclusion that this belief in justice and the character-consequence relationship did not serve a primarily *theological* purpose in the book of Proverbs, but rather was employed to provide a *philosophical* basis for the ethical teachings of the sages. The repeated and bold assertions of justice for each individual in the sayings of the book of Proverbs must inevitably have provoked doubts and theological problems. There are indications in the book that the sages were aware of the incredible complexity of the questions concerning individual justice and theodicy. Nevertheless, the ethical-didactic focus which characterizes the sayings did not permit discussions of these problematic issues but rather concentrated on the concrete application of ethical principles to human behaviour.

The second part of the present work treats the depiction of the Lord as supreme God and personal God. It needs to be noted that the monotheistic, Israelite setting of the book of Proverbs led to the fusion of diverse perspectives on the understanding of the deity. Van der Toorn argues that there is no substantial difference between the ethical codes of Mesopotamia and Israel and that both cultures were characterized by belief in the divine enforcement of the ethical code. But he notes the difference in the fact that "in Old Testament religion the personal god and the divine Patron of justice are one;...."[2] Within the monotheistic perspective of the Old Testament, the god of justice and the personal god *could not be separated,* in the religions of the surrounding cultures we find examples where these concepts of the deity were combined, but such a combination was not necessary. In Egypt and Mesopotamia the best examples of the combination of the traits of supreme being and personal god in one deity appear to be the sun god, i.e. Utu/Shamash and Re-Amun. Like Yahweh in the book of Proverbs, these gods are

---

[1] See Crenshaw (1976:33–34).
[2] Van der Toorn (1985:44).

the deities of choice in wisdom texts, were connected to the execution of justice and were portrayed as both supreme and personal deities. It must be emphasized that there is no inherent conflict between the concept of a personal god and the concept of a supreme being just as there is no necessary conflict between official and personal religion. It is rather the case, at least in a monotheistic setting, that the view of the deity as the personal god is inseparable from the concept of God as a supreme being. Only a supreme god is able to know, protect and give justice to each individual.[3] Sperling expresses these facets of the concept of God in Hebrew religion in the following way: "Paradoxically, Yahweh is at once the most transcendent god of the ancient Near East and the most human."[4]

The goal of our investigation has been to trace the concept of God in the book of Proverbs in order to gain a better general grasp of the theology of Israelite wisdom. In the book of Proverbs—a book which by no means delineates a systematic theology—a number of important features of the theological understanding of the sages of ancient Israel can be detected. It will never be possible for us to provide a comprehensive reconstruction of the mental concept of God held by the Israelite sages. It is our hope that this study has contributed to the recognition of some of these features in the theological thinking of the Old Testament wisdom literature. It is our conviction that the theological thinking of these sages is of vital importance to our understanding of the entire Old Testament. We conclude with a quote from Buss concerning the relationship between the teachings of the Bible and those of other religions, an issue that is crucial in the evaluation of Old Testament wisdom:

> Individuality is not opposed to comparability. It may be noted that this observation applies also to the field of religion; the meaningful individuality of biblical faith is enhanced, not denied, through a wide range of contacts.[5]

---

[3] Morenz (1964:30). Cf. Assmann (1977:773; 1983:273–274).
[4] Sperling (1987:7).
[5] Buss (1974:54).

Abbreviations. Technical Remarks

I have used the abbreviations listed in *Journal of Biblical Literature* 107, 1988, 579–596. These abbreviations are essentially the same as those found in *Elenchus Bibliographicus Biblicus* and in Eissfeldt's *The Old Testament: An Introduction*. In addition to the abbreviations listed in *JBL* I have also used the following:

ANE   Ancient Near East.
FS   Festschrift
LÄ   *Lexikon der Ägyptologie*. Hsgb. W. Helck & W. Westendorf. Wiesbaden: Harrasowitz. 1975–.
RdE   *Revue d'Egyptologie*.
RLA   *Reallexikon der Assyriologie und vorderasiatischen Archäologie*. Leipzig, Berlin, New York, 1932–.
SAIW   *Studies in Ancient Israelite Wisdom*. Ed. J. L. Crenshaw. Library of Biblical Studies. New York: KTAV, 1976.
THAT   *Theologisches Handwörterbuch zum Alten Testament*. 2 vols. Hsgb. Ernst Jenni–Claus Westermann. München: Kaiser/Zürich: Theologischer Verlag, 1971/76.
TUMSR   Trinity University Monograph Series in Religion.
TynBul   *Tyndale Bulletin*

References to biblical passages follow the numbering of the Hebrew text.
Texts cited from the secondary literature and quotations in general have been reproduced as faithfully as possible here. This means that parentheses, etc., except footnote references, are included as they appear in the original work.

Bibliography

Albertz, R., 1974. *Weltschöpfung und Menschenschöpfung.* Calwer Theologische Monographien 3. Stuttgart: Calwer.

—, 1978. *Persönliche Frömmigkeit und Offizielle Religion: Religionsinterner Pluralismus in Israel und Babylon.* Calwer Theologische Monographien 9. Stuttgart: Calwer.

—, 1988. "Ludlul bel nemeqi—eine Lehrdichtung zur Ausbreitung und Vertiefung der persönlichen Mardukfrömmigkeit." AOAT 220 (=FS K. Deller). Kevelaer: Butzon & Bercker/Neukirchen-Vluyn: Neukirchener.

Alster, B., 1974. *The Instruction of Suruppak: A Sumerian Proverb Collection.* Mesopotamia: Copenhagen Studies in Assyriology 2. Copenhagen: Akademisk forlag.

—, 1975. *Studies in Sumerian Proverbs.* Mesopotamia: Copenhagen Studies in Assyriology 3. Copenhagen: Akademisk forlag.

—, 1978. "Sumerian Proverb Collection Seven." *RA* 72, 97–112.

Alt, A., 1976. "Solomonic Wisdom." *SAIW,* 102–112. Orig. in German: *TLZ* 76 (1951) 139–144.

Anderson, B. W., 1962. "God, OT View of." *IDB* 2, 417–430.

—, 1984. "Introduction: Mythopoeic and Theological Dimensions of Biblical Creation Faith." *Creation in the Old Testament.* Issues in Religion and Theology 6. Ed. B. W. Anderson. Philadelphia: Fortress/London: SPCK, 1–24.

Assmann, J., 1975. *Ägyptische Hymnen und Gebete.* Die Bibliothek der Alten Welt. Zürich und München: Artemis.

—, 1977. "Gott." *LÄ* 2, 756–786.

—, 1979. "Weisheit, Loyalismus und Frömmigkeit." *Studien zu altägyptischen Lebenslehren.* OBO 28. eds. Erik Hornung und Othmar Keel. Freiburg: Universitätsverlag/Göttingen: Vandenhoeck & Ruprecht, 11–72.

—, 1983. *Re und Amun: Die Krise des polytheistischen Weltbilds im Ägypten der 18.–20. Dynastie.* OBO 51. Freiburg: Universitätsverlag/Göttingen: Vandenhoeck & Ruprecht.

—, 1984. "Schöpfung." *LÄ* 5, 677–690.

Aulén, G., 1967. *Dramat och symbolerna: En bok om gudsbildens problematik.* 3rd ed. Stockholm: Diakonistyrelsen.

Baab, O. J., 1962. "Widow." *IDB* 4, 842–843.

Bammel, E., 1968. "πτωχός, B.The Poor in the Old Testament." *TDNT* 6, 888–894. German original in *TWAT* 6 (1959) 888–894.

Barns, J., 1956. *Five Ramesseum Papyri.* Oxford: University Press.

—, 1968. "A New Wisdom Text from a Writing-Board in Oxford." *JEA* 54, 71–76.

Becker, J., 1965. *Gottesfurcht im Alten Testament.* AnBib 25. Rom: Päpstlichen Bibelinstitut.

Beyerlin, W. (ed.), 1975. *Religionsgeschichtliche Textbuch zum Alten Testament.* GAT. Göttingen: Vandenhoeck & Ruprecht.

Blenkinsopp, J., 1983. *Wisdom and Law in the Old Testament: The Ordering of Life in Israel and Early Judaism.* Oxford Bible Series. Oxford: Oxford University.

Blumenberg, H., 1962. "Transzendenz und Immanenz." *RGG* 6, 989–997.

Bolle, S. D., 1982. *Wisdom in Akkadian Literature: Expression, Instruction, Dialogue.* Los Angeles: University of California.

Bonnet, H., 1952. "Maat." *Reallexikon der ägyptische Religionsgeschichte.* Berlin: de Gruyter, 430–434.

Brandon, S. G. F., 1963. *Creation Legends of the Ancient Near East.* London: Hodder and Stoughton.

Breasted, J. H., 1912. *Development of Religion and Thought in Ancient Egypt.* London: Hodder & Stoughton.

Brekelmans, C., 1979. "Wisdom Influence in Deuteronomy." *La Sagesse de l'Ancien Testament.* Ed. M. Gilbert. Gembloux: Leuven University Press, 28–38.

Brunner, H., 1958. "Gerechtigkeit als Fundament des Thrones." *VT* 8, 426–428.

—, 1961. "Die religiöse Wertung der Armut im Alten Ägypten." *Sæculum* 12, 319–344.

—, 1961/2. "Magische, kultische und ethische Elemente ägyptischer Religiosität." *Antaios* 3, 534–543.

—, 1963. "Der freie Wille Gottes in der ägyptischen Weisheit." *Les Sagesses du Proche-Orient ancien.* C.E.S.S. Université de Strasbourg. Paris: Presses Universitaires, 103–120.

—, 1980. "Lehren." *LÄ* 3, 964–968.

—, 1982. "Persönliche Frömmigkeit." *LÄ* 4, 951–963.

—, 1983. *Grundzüge der altägyptischen Religion.* Grundzüge 50. Darmstadt: Wissenschaftliche Buchgesellschaft.

Bryce, G. E., 1979. *A Legacy of Wisdom: The Egyptian Contribution to the Wisdom of Israel.* London: Associated University Press.

Buccellati, G., 1981. "Wisdom and Not: The Case of Mesopotamia." *JAOS* 101, 35–47.

Buss, M. J., 1974. "The Study of Forms." *Old Testament Form Criticism.* TUMSR 2. Ed. John H. Hayes. San Antonio: Trinity University, 1–56.

Caminos, R. A., 1954. *Late-Egyptian Miscellanies.* Brown Egyptological Studies 1. London: Oxford University.

Collins, J. J., 1980. "Proverbial Wisdom and the Yahwist Vision." *Semeia* 17, 1–17.

Cox, D., 1973. "The Desire for Oblivion in Job 3." *SBFLA* 23, 37–49.

Crenshaw, J. L., 1969. "Method in Determining Wisdom Influence upon 'Historical' Literature." *JBL* 88, 129–142. Reprinted in *SAIW,* 481–494.

—, 1974 A. "The Eternal Gospel (Eccl. 3.11)." *Essays in Old Testament Ethics. J. P. Hyatt in Memorian.* Eds. J. L. Crenshaw and J. T. Willis. New York: KTAV, 23–55.

—, 1974 B. "Wisdom." *Old Testament Form Criticism.* TUMSR 2. Ed. John H. Hayes. San Antonio: Trinity University, 225–264.

—, 1976 A. "Prolegomenon." *SAIW,* 1–60.

—, 1976 B. "Wisdom in the Old Testament." *IDBSup,* 952–956.

—, 1980. "The Birth of Skepticism in Ancient Israel." *The Divine Helmsman: Studies on God's Control of Human Events. Presented to Lou H. Silbermann.* New York: KTAV, 1–19.

—, 1982. *Old Testament Wisdom: An Introduction.* London: SCM. Orig.: Atlanta: John Knox, 1981.

—, 1985. "Education in Ancient Israel." *JBL* 104, 601–615.

Delekat, L., 1971. "Yáho-Yahwáe und die alttestamentlichen Gottesnamenkorrekturen." *Tradition und Glaube: Das frühe Christentum in seiner Umwelt* (FS K. G. Kuhn). Ed. Gert Jeremias. Göttingen: Vandenhoeck & Ruprecht, 23–75.

Dijk, J. J. A. van, 1953. *La Sagesse suméro-accadienne: Recherches sur les genres littéraires des textes sapientiaux.* Commentationes Orientales 1. Leiden: Brill.

Doll, P., 1985. *Menschenschöpfung und Weltschöpfung in der alttestamentlichen Weisheit.* SBS 117. Stuttgart: Katholisches Bibelwerk.

Donald, T., 1964. "The Semantic Field of Rich and Poor in the Wisdom Literature of Hebrew and Accadian." *OrAnt* 3, 27–41.

Eichrodt, W., 1962. "In the Beginning: A Contribution to the Interpretation of the First Word of the Bible." *Israel's Prophetic Heritage: Essays in Honor of James Muilenburg.* Eds. B. W. Anderson and W. Harrelson. New York: Harper & Row, 1–11. Reprinted in *Creation in the Old Testament.* Issues in Religion and Theology 6. Philadelphia: Fortress/London: SPCK, 1984, 65–73.

Eissfeldt, Otto, 1965. *The Old Testament. An Introduction.* Oxford: Blackwell. Transl. from 3rd German edition.

Emerton, J. A., 1979. "Wisdom." *Tradition and Interpretation.* Ed. G. W. Anderson. Oxford: Clarendon, 214–237.

Epzstein, L., 1986. *Social Justice in the Ancient Near East and the People of the Bible.* London: SCM. French orig.: Paris: Les Editions du Cerf, 1983.

Fabry, H.-J., 1978. "דל." *TDOT* 3 (1978) 208–230. German orig. *TWAT* 2 (1977) 221–244.

Fahlgren, K. Hj., 1972. "Die Gegensätze von *ṣᵉdaqā* im Alten Testament." *Um das Prinzip der Vergeltung in Religion und Recht des alten Testaments.* Wege der Forschung 125. Ed. K. Koch. Darmstadt: Wissenschaftliche Buchgesellschaft, 87–129. Orig. 1932.

Fensham, F. C., 1962. "Widow, Orphan, and the Poor in Ancient Near Eastern Legal and Wisdom Literature." *JNES* 21, 129–139.

Fichtner, J., 1933. *Die altorientalische Weisheit in ihrer israelitisch-jüdischen Ausprägung: Eine Studie zur Nationalisierung der Weisheit in Israel.* BZAW 62. Giessen: Töpelmann.

—, 1951. "Zum Problem Glaube und Geschichte in der israelitisch-jüdischen Weisheitsliteratur." *TLZ* 76, 145–150.

—, 1976. "Isaiah among the Wise." *SAIW*, 429–438. Orig. in German in *TLZ* 74 (1949) and *Gottes Weisheit*. Stuttgart:Calwer, 1965, 18–26.

Fishbane, M., 1971. "Jeremiah 4:23–26 and Job 3:3–13: A Recovered Use of the Creation Pattern." *VT* 21, 151–167.

Fisher, L. R., 1965. "Creation at Ugarit and in the Old Testament." *VT* 15, 313–324.

Fohrer, G., 1964. "σοφια." *TWNT* 7, 476–496. English transl. in *TDNT* 7 (1971) 476–496.

—, 1969. "Die Weisheit im Alten Testament." *Studien zur alttestamentlichen Theologie und Geschichte* (1949–66). BZAW 115. Berlin: Töpelmann, 242–274.

—, 1974. "The Righteous Man in Job 31." *Essays in Old Testament Ethics. J. Philip Hyatt, In Memorian.* Eds. J. L. Crenshaw and John T. Willis. New York: KTAV, 1–22.

Fontaine, C. R., 1982. *Traditional Sayings in the Old Testament: A Contextual Study.* Bible and Literature 5. Sheffield: Almond Press.

Fox, M. V., 1968. "Aspects of the Religion of the Book of Proverbs." *HUCA* 39, 55–69.

—, 1980. "Two Decades of Research in Egyptian Wisdom Literature." *Zeitschrift für Ägyptologische Studien* 107, 120–135.

Frankfort, H., 1961. *Ancient Egyptian Religion: An Interpretation.* New York: Harper & Brothers. Orig. published by Columbia University Press, New York, 1948.

Franklyn, P., 1983. "The Sayings of Agur in Proverbs 30: Piety or Skepticism?" *ZAW* 95, 238–252.

Gammie, J. G., 1970. "The Theology of Retribution in the Book of Deuteronomy." *CBQ* 32, 1–12.

Gamper, A., 1966. *Gott als Richter in Mesopotamien und im Alten Testament.* Innsbruck: Universitätsverlag Wagner.

Gaster, T. H., 1962. "Cosmogony." *IDB* 1, 702–709.

Geels, A., 1983. "Gudspresentation och gudsbild." *Årsbok 1983 för föreningen lärare i religionskunskap,* 83–90.

Gemser, B., 1960. "The Instructions of 'Onchsheshonqy and Biblical Wisdom Literature." VTSup 7, 102–128. Reprinted in *SAIW*,.134–160.

—, 1963. *Sprüche Salomos.* 2. Auflage. Handbuch zum Alten Testament 16. Tübingen: Mohr.

Gerleman, G., 1956. *Studies in the Septuagint: III. Proverbs.* Lunds Universitets Årsskrift. N. F. Avd. 1. Bd. 52. Nr 3. Lund: Gleerup.

Gerstenberger, E., 1965. *Wesen und Herkunft des "apodiktischen Rechts."* WMANT 20. Neukirchen-Vluyn: Neukirchener.

—, 1969. "Zur alttestamentlichen Weisheit" *VF* 14, 28–44.

—, 1976, "תעב *tʿb* pi. verabscheuen." *THAT,* vol 2. Eds. Jenni-Westermann. München: Kaiser/Zürich: Theologischer, 1051–1055.

Gese, H., 1958. *Lehre und Wirklichkeit in der alten Weisheit: Studien zu den Sprüchen Salomos und zu dem Buche Hiob.* Tübingen: Mohr.

—, 1963. "Die Krisis der Weisheit bei Koheleth." *Les Sagesses du Proche-Orient ancien.* C.E.S.S. Université de Strasbourg. Paris: Presses Universitaires, 139–151.

Gladson, J. A., 1978. *Retributive Paradoxes in Proverbs 10–29*. Unpubl. diss., Vanderbilt University. Available from University Microfilms International, Ann Arbor, Michigan, no. 7909275.

Goldingay, J., 1979. "The 'Salvation History' Perspective and the 'Wisdom' Perspective within the Context of Biblical Theology." *EvQ* 51, 194–207.

Golka, F. W., 1983. "Die israelitische Weisheitsschule oder 'des Kaisers neue Kleider'." *VT* 33, 257–270.

—, 1986. "Die Königs- und Hofsprüche und der Ursprung der israelitischen Weisheit." *VT* 36, 13–36.

Gordon, C. H., 1965 *The Ancient Near East* . 3rd rev. ed.. New York: Norton.

Gordon, E. I., 1959. *Sumerian Proverbs: Glimpses of Everyday Life in Ancient Mesopotamia*. Museum Monographs. Philadelphia: University Museum of the University of Pennsylvania.

—, 1960. "A New Look at the Wisdom of Sumer and Akkad." *BO* 17, 122–152.

Gowan, Donald E., 1987. "Wealth and Poverty in the Old Testament: The Case of the Widow, the Orphan, and the Sojourner." *Int* 41, 341–353.

Grønbæk, J. H., 1985. "Baal's Battle with Yam—A Canaanite Creation Fight." *JSOT* 33, 27–44.

Grumach, I., 1972. *Untersuchungen zur Lebenslehre des Amenemope*. Münchner Ägyptologische Studien 23. München/Berlin: Deutscher Kunstverlag.

Gunkel, H., 1984. "The Influence of Babylonian Mythology upon the Biblical Creation Story." *Creation in the Old Testament*. Issues in Religion and Theology 6. Ed. B.W. Anderson. Philadelphia: Fortress/London: SPCK, 25–52. Orig. publ. in *Schöpfung und Chaos in Urzeit und Endzeit* (1895) 3–120.

Habel, N. C., 1972. "Yahweh, Maker of Heaven and Earth." *JBL* 91, 321–337.

—, 1985. *The Book of Job*. OTL. Philadelphia: Westminster.

Halbe, J., 1979. "'Altorientalisches Weltordnungsdenken' und alttestamentliche Theologie: Zur Kritik eines Ideologems am Beispiel des israelitischen Rechts." *ZTK* 76, 381–418.

Helck, W., 1980. "Maat." *LÄ* 3, 1110–1119.

Hempel, J., 1936. *Gott und Mensch im Alten Testament: Studie zur Geschichte der Frömmigkeit*.. 2., Auflage. BWANT 38. Stuttgart: Kohlhammer.

Hermisson, H.-J., 1968. *Studien zur israelitischen Spruchweisheit*. WMANT 28. Neukirchen-Vluyn: Neukirchener.

—, 1978. "Observations on the Creation Theology in Wisdom." *Israelite Wisdom: Theological and Literary Essays in Honor of Samuel Terrien*. Eds. John G. Gammie et al. New York: Scholars Press for Union Theological Seminary, 43–57.

—, 1985. "Gottes Freiheit—Spielraum des Menschen." *ZTK* 82, 129–152).

Herrmann, S., 1961. "Die Naturlehre der Schöpfungsgeschichtes: Erwägungen zur Vorgeschichte von Genesis 1." *TLZ* 86, 413–424.

Hildebrandt, T., 1988. "Proverbial Pairs: Compositional Units in Proverbs 10–29." *JBL* 107, 207–224.

Hoffner, H. A., 1974. "אלמנה." *TDOT* 1, 287–291. German orig. in *TWAT* 1 (1973) 308–313.

Hornung, E., 1973. *Der Eine und die Vielen: Ägyptisches Gottesvorstellungen*. 2nd ed. Darmstadt: Wissenschaftliche Buchgesellschaft. Orig. 1971.

Humbert, P., 1953. "L'emploi du verbe *pā'al* et de ses dérivés substantifs en hébreu biblique." *ZAW* 65, 35–44.

—, 1960. "Le substantif *to'ēbā* et le verbe *t'b* dans l'Ancien Testament." *ZAW* 72, 217–237.

Humphreys, W. L., 1978. "The Motif of the Wise Courtier in the Book of Proverbs." *Israelite Wisdom: Theological and Literary Essays in Honor of Samuel Terrien*. Eds. John G. Gammie et al. New York: Scholars Press for Union Theological Seminary, 177–190.

Hutter, M., 1987. "Das Werden des Monotheismus im alten Israel." *Anfänge der Theologie: Xapisteion Johannes B. Bauer*. Eds.N. Brox et al. Graz: Styria, 25–39.

Jacobsen, T., 1946. "Mesopotamia." *The Intellectual Adventure of Man: An Essay on Speculative Thought in the Ancient Near East.* Henri Frankfort et al.. Chicago & London: University of Chicago Press, 123–219.

—, 1976. *The Treasures of Darkness: A History of Mesopotamian Religion.* New Haven/London: Yale University.

—, 1987. "The Graven Image." *Ancient Israelite Religion: Essays in Honor of Frank Moore Cross.* Eds. P.D. Miller et al. Philadelphia: Fortress, 15–32.

Jenks, A. W., 1985. "Theological Presuppositions of Israel's Wisdom Literature." *Horizons in Biblical Theology* 7, 43–75.

Jónsson, G. A., 1988. *The Image of God: Genesis 1:26–28 in a Century of Old Testament Research.* ConBib OT Series 26. Stockholm: Almqvist & Wiksell.

Kaiser, O., 1959. *Die mythische Bedeutung des Meeres in Ägypten, Ugarit, und Israel.* BZAW 78. Berlin: Töpelmann.

Kaiser, W. C. Jr, 1978. "Wisdom Theology and the Centre of Old Testament Theology." *EvQ* 50, 132–146.

Kapelrud, A. S., 1979. "Die Theologie der Schöpfung im Alten Testament." *ZAW* 91, 159–170.

—, 1981. "The Relationship between El and Baal in the Ras Shamra Texts." *The Bible World: Essays in Honor of Cyrus H. Gordon.* Ed. G. Rendsburg et al. New York: KTAV, 79–85.

Kayatz, C., 1966. *Studien zu Proverbien 1–9: Eine form- und motivgeschichtliche Untersuchung unter Einbeziehung ägyptischen Vergleichsmaterials.* WMANT 22. Neukirchen-Vluyn: Neukirchener.

Keel, O., 1974. *Die Weisheit spielt vor Gott: Ein ikonographischer Beitrag zur Deutung des m^esaḥāqät in Sprüche 8,30f.* Freiburg: Universitätsverlag/Göttingen: Vandenhoeck & Ruprecht.

—, 1978. *Jahwes Entgegnung an Ijob: Eine Deutung von Ijob 38–41 vor dem Hintergrund der zeitgenössischen Bildkunst.* Göttingen: Vandenhoeck & Ruprecht.

—, 1979. "Eine Diskussion um die Bedeutung polarer Begriffspaare in den Lebenslehren." *Studien zu altägyptischen Lebenslehren.* OBO 28. Eds. Erik Hornung und Othmar Keel. Freiburg: Universitätsverlag/Göttingen: Vandenhoeck & Ruprecht, 225–234.

Keller, C.-A., 1977. "Zum sogenannten Vergeltungsglauben im Proverbienbuch." *Beiträge zur alttestamentlichen Theologie. FS Walter Zimmerli.* Ed. H. Donner. Göttingen: Vandenhoeck & Ruprecht, 223–238.

Khanjian, J., 1973. *Wisdom in Ugarit and in the Ancient Near East with Particular Emphasis on Old Testament Literature.* Unpubl. diss., Claremont Graduate School. Available from University Microfilms, Ann Arbor, Michigan, no. 74–14,883.

—, 1975. "Wisdom." *Ras Shamra Parallels.* Eds. Loren R. Fisher et al. *AnOr* 50, 373–400.

Kitchen, K A., 1969. "Studies in Egyptian Wisdom Literature I." *OrAnt* 8, 189–202.

—, 1970. "Studies in Egyptian Wisdom Literature II." *OrAnt* 9, 203–210.

—, 1977. "Proverbs and Wisdom Books of the Ancient Near East: The Factual History of a Literary Form." *TynBul* 28, 69–114.

—, 1979. "The Basic Literary Forms and Formulations of Ancient Instructional Writings in Egypt and Western Asia." *Studien zu altägyptischen Lebenslehren.* OBO 28. Eds. Erik Hornung und Othmar Keel. Freiburg: Universitätsverlag/Göttingen: Vandenhoeck & Ruprecht, 236–282.

Klassen, W., 1962–3. "Coals of Fire: Sign of Repentance or Revenge?" *NTS* 9, 337–350.

Klein, J., 1982, "'Personal God' and Individual Prayer in Sumerian Religion." *AfO* Beiheft 19, 295–306.

Koch, K., 1955. "Gibt es ein Vergeltungsdogma im Alten Testament." *ZTK*, 52, 1–42. Also in K. Koch (ed.), *Um das Prinzip der Vergeltung in Religion und Recht des alten Testaments.* Wege der Forschung 125. Darmstadt: Wissenschaftliche Buchgesellschaft, 1972.

Kovacs, B. W., 1974. "Is There a Class-ethics in Proverbs." *Essays in Old Testament Ethics.* Eds J. L. Crenshaw and John T. Willis. New York: KTAV, 171–187.

Kramer, S. N., 1955. "'Man and his God': A Sumerian variation on the 'Job' Motif." VTSup 3 (=FS H. H. Rowley), 170–182.

Krause, M., 1980. "חכם. 3. Egyptian," *TDOT* 4, 368–370. Orig. *TWAT* 2 (1977) 925–927.

Kubina, V., 1979. *Die Gottesreden im Buche Hiob: Ein Beitrag zur Diskussion um die Einheit von Hiob 38,1–42,6.* Freiburger theologische Studien 115. Freiburg/Basel/Wien: Herder.

Kvalbein, H., 1981. *Jesus og de fattige: Jesu syn på de fattige og hans bruk av ord for "fattig."* Oslo: Luther.

Lambert, W. G., 1960. *Babylonian Wisdom Literature.* Oxford: Clarendon.

—, 1972. "Destiny and Divine Intervention in Babylon and Israel." *OTS* 17, 65–72.

Landes, G. M., 1974. "Creation Traditions in Proverbs 8:22–31 and Genesis 1." *Old Testament Studies in Honor of Jacob M. Myers.* Gettysburg Theological Studies 4. Eds. H. N. Bream et al. Philadelphia: Temple University, 279–293.

Lang, B., 1972. *Die weisheitliche Lehrrede: Eine Untersuchung von Sprüche 1–7.* SBS 54. Stuttgart: Katholische Bibelwerk.

—, 1986. *Wisdom and the Book of Proverbs: An Israelite Goddess Redefined.* New York: Pilgrim Press.

Langdon, S., 1923. *Babylonian Wisdom.* London: Luzac and Co/Paris: Geuthner.

Lemaire, A., 1981. *Les écoles et la formation de la Bible dans l'ancien Israel.* OBO 39. Göttingen: Vandenhoeck & Ruprecht/Fribourg: Editions Universitaires.

—, 1984. "Sagesse et écoles." *VT* 34, 270–281.

Lichtheim, M., 1975. *Ancient Egyptian Literature: vol I: The Old and Middle Kingdoms.* Berkeley/Los Angeles/London: University of California. (paperback edition [Orig. 1973]).

—, 1976. *Ancient Egyptian Literature: vol II: The New Kingdom.* Berkeley/Los Angeles/London: University of California.

—, 1980. *Ancient Egyptian Literature: vol III: The Late Period.* Berkeley/Los Angeles/London: University of California.

—, 1983. *Late Egyptian Wisdom Literature in the International Context: A Study of Demotic Instructions.* OBO 52. Freiburg: Universitätsverlag/Göttingen: Vandenhoeck & Ruprecht.

Lindblom, J., 1955. "Wisdom in the Old Testament Prophets." VTSup 3 (=FS H. H. Rowley), 192–204.

Lindenberger, J. M., 1983. *The Aramaic Proverbs of Ahiqar.* John Hopkins Near Eastern Studies. Baltimore/London: John Hopkins University Press.

—, 1985. "Ahiqar. A New Translation and Introduction." *The Old Testament Pseudepigrapha,* vol. 2. Ed. James M. Charlesworth. London: Darton, Longman & Todd, 479–507.

Lindström, F., 1983. *God and the Origin of Evil. A Contextual Analysis of Alleged Monistic Evidence in the Old Testament.* ConB OT Series 21. Lund: Gleerup.

Luyten, J., 1979. "Psalm 73 and Wisdom." *La Sagesse de l'Ancien Testament.* Ed. M. Gilbert. Gembloux: Leuven University, 59–81.

Lyons, E. L., 1987. "A Note on Proverbs 31:10–31." JSOT suppl. series 58 (=FS R. E. Murphy), 237–245.

McCarthy, D., 1984. "'Creation' Motifs in Ancient Hebrew Poetry." *Creation in the Old Testament.* Issues in Religion and Theology 6. Ed. B. W. Anderson. Philadelphia: Fortress/London: SPCK, 74–89. Revised reprint from *CBQ* 29 (1967) 393–406.

McCreesh, T. P., 1985. "Wisdom as Wife: Proverbs 31:10–31." *RB* 92, 25–46.

McKane, W., 1965. *Prophets and Wise Men.* SBT 44. London: SCM.

—, 1985. *Proverbs: A New Approach.* 4th impr. OTL. London: SCM (first publ. 1970).

Malchow, B. V., 1982. "Social Justice in the Wisdom Literature." *BTB* 12, 120–124.

Mendelsohn, I., 1962. "Lots. 1. In the OT." *IDB* 3, 163–164.

Mettinger, T. N. D., 1971. Solomonic State Officials: A Study of the Civil Government Officials of the Israelite Monarchy. ConB OT Series 5. Lund: Gleerup.

—, 1982. *The Dethronement of Sabaoth: Studies in the Shem and Kabod Theologies.* ConB OT Series 18. Lund: Gleerup.

—, 1988. *In Search of God: The Meaning and Message of the Everlasting Names.* Philadelphia: Fortress.

—, 1989. "The Study of the Gottesbild—Problems and Suggestions." *SEÅ* 54, 135–145.

Miller, P. D., 1980. "El, the Creator of the Earth." *BASOR* 239, 43–46.

—, 1982. *Sin and Judgment in the Prophets: A Stylistic and Theological Analysis.* SBLMS 27. Chico: Scholars Press.

Mogensen, B., 1975. "Profeterne, kulten og visdommen." *Hilsen til Noack.* København: Gad, 168–180.

Moor, J. C. de, 1980. "El, the Creator." *The Bible World: Essays in Honor of Cyrus H. Gordon.* New York: KTAV, 171–187.

—, 1983. *Uw God is mijn God: Over de oorsprong van het geloof in de ene God.* Serie Kamper Cahiers 51. Kampen: J. H. Kok.

—, 1986. "The Crisis of Polytheism in Late Bronze Ugarit." *OTS* 24, 1–20.

Morenz, S., 1953. "Feurige Kohlen auf dem Haupt." *TLZ* 78, 187–192.

—, 1960 A. *Untersuchungen zur Rolle des Schicksals in der ägyptischen Religion.* Abhandlungen der sächsischen Akademie der Wissenschaften zu Leipzig, Philologisch-historische Klasse 52/1. Berlin: Akademie-Verlag.

—, 1960 B. *Ägyptische Religion.* Die Religionen der Menschheit 8. Stuttgart: Kohlhammer.

—, 1963. "Ägyptologische Beiträge zur Erforschung der Weisheitsliteratur Israels." *Les Sagesses du Proche-Orient ancien.* C.E.S.S. Université de Strasbourg. Paris: Presses Universitaires, 63–71.

—, 1964. *Die Heraufkunft des transzendenten Gottes in Ägypten.* Sitzungsberichte der Sächsischen Akademie der Wissenschaften zu Leipzig, Philologisch-historische Klasse 109. Berlin: Akademie-Verlag.

—, 1984. *Gott und Mensch im alten Ägypten.* 2., erweiterte Auflage. Zürich und München: Artemis.

Morgan, D. F., 1979. "Wisdom and the Prophets." *Studia Biblica 1978 I.* JSOTsup 11. Ed. Elisabeth A. Livingstone. Sheffield, JSOT, 209–244.

Mowinckel, S., 1928. "Hypostasen," *RGG* (2nd ed.) 2, 2065–2068.

—, 1955. "Psalms and Wisdom." VTSup 3 (=FS H. H. Rowley), 205–224.

Müller, H.-P., 1968. "Wie sprach Qohälät von Gott?" *VT* 18, 507–521.

—, 1978 A. *Das Hiobproblem: Seine Stellung und Entstehung im alten Orient und im Alten Testament.* Erträge der Forschung 84. Darmstadt: Wissenschaftliche Buchgesellschaft.

—, 1978 B. "Neige der althebräischen 'Weisheit': Zum Denken Qohäläts," *ZAW* 90, 238–264.

—, 1980. "חכם." *TDOT* 4, 364–368, 370–385. German orig. *TWAT* 2 (1977) 920–925, 927–944.

Murphy, R. E., 1962. "A Consideration of the Classification 'Wisdom Psalms'," VTSup 9, 156–167. Reprinted in *SAIW*, 456–467.

—, 1966. "The Kerygma of the Book of Proverbs." *Int* 20, 3–14.

—, 1969. "The Interpretation of Old Testament Wisdom Literature." *Int* 23, 289–301.

—, 1975. "Wisdom and Yahwism. *No Famine in the Land.* (FS J. L. McKenzie). Ed. J. W. Flanagan et al. Claremont: Scholars Press, 117–126.

—, 1981 A. *Wisdom Literature. Job, Proverbs, Ruth, Canticles, Ecclesiastes, and Esther.* The Forms of the Old Testament Literature 13. Grand Rapids: Eerdmans.

—, 1981 B. "Hebrew Wisdom," *JAOS* 101, 21–34.

—, 1981 C. "The Faces of Wisdom in the Book of Proverbs." AOAT 212 (=FS H. Cazelles). Kevelaer: Butzon & Bercker/Neukirchen-Vluyn: Neukirchener, 337–345.

—, 1987. "Religious Dimensions of Israelite Wisdom." *Ancient Israelite Religion: Essays in Honor of Frank Moore Cross.* Eds. P. D. Miller et al. Philadelphia: Fortress, 449–458.

Nel, P. J., 1981. "The Genres of Biblical Wisdom Literature." *JNSL* 9, 129–142.

—, 1982. *The Structure and Ethos of the Wisdom Admonitions in Proverbs.* BZAW 158. Berlin/New York: de Gruyter.

Nielsen, E., 1976–77. "Homo faber—sapientia dei." *SEÅ* 41–42, 157–165.

Noth, M., 1955. "Die Bewährung von Salomos 'göttlicher Weisheit'." VTSup 3 (=FS H. H. Rowley), 225–237.

Nougayrol, J., 1952. "Une version ancienne du 'Juste Souffrant'." *RB* 59, 239–250.

—, 1968. "Textes Suméro-Accadiens des archives et bibliotheques privées d'Ugarit." *Ugaritica V.* Mission de Ras Shamra 16. Paris: Imprimerie Nationale..., 1–446.

Ogden, G. S., 1977. "The 'Better'-Proverb (Tôb-Spruch), Rhetorical Criticism, and Qoheleth." *JBL* 96, 489–505.

Olivier, J. P. J., 1975. "Schools and Wisdom Literature." *JNSL* 4, 49–60.

Olsson, T., 1983. "Gudsbild, talsituation och litterär genre." *Årsbok 1983 för föreningen lärare i religionskunskap,* 91–109.

—, 1985 A. "Gudsbildens dimensioner." *Lundaforskare föreläser 17.* Lund: Gleerup. 27–35.

—, 1985 B. "Gudsbildens gestaltning: litterära kategorier och religiös tro." *Svensk Religionshistorisk Årsskrift,* 42–63.

Otto, E., 1971. "Gott als Retter in Ägypten." *Tradition und Glaube* (FS K. G. Kuhn). Eds. G. Jeremias et al. Göttingen: Vandenhoeck & Ruprecht, 9–22.

—, 1977. "Die 'synthetische Lebensauffassung' in der frühköniglichen Novellistik Israels." *ZTK* 74, 371–400.

Pax, E., 1960. "Studien zum Vergeltungsproblem der Psalmen." *SBFLA* 11, 56–112.

Pedersen, J., 1959. *Israel. Its Life and Culture I–IV.* Copenhagen: Branner og Korch/London: Oxford University Press. First publ. in 1926.

Perdue, L. G., 1977. *Wisdom and Cult: A Critical Analysis of the Views of Cult in the Wisdom Literature...* SBLDS 30. Missoula, Montana: Scholars Press.

—, 1983. "The Testament of David and Egyptian Royal Instructions." *Scripture in Context II: More Essays on the Comparative Method.* Eds. William W. Hallo et al. Winona Lake: Eisenbrauns, 79–96.

Pettazoni, R., 1956. *The All-Knowing God: Researches into early Religion and Culture.* London: Methuen.

Pettinato, G., 1971. *Das altorientalische Menschenbild und die sumerischen und akkadischen Schöpfungsmythen.* Abhandlungen der Heidelberger Akademie der Wissenschaften: Philosophisch-historische Klasse 1971/1. Heidelberg: Carl Winter Universitätsverlag.

Pfeifer, G., 1967. *Ursprung und Wesen der Hypostasenvorstellungen im Judentum.* Berlin: Evangelische Verlagsanstalt.

Plath, S., 1963. *Furcht Gottes: Der Begriff* ירא *im Alten Testament.* Arbeiten zur Theologie, R. 2: 2. Stuttgart: Calwer.

Pleins, J. D., 1987. "Poverty in the Social World of the Wise." *JSOT* 37, 61–78.

Plöger, O., 1984. *Sprüche Salomos (Proverbia).* BKAT 17. Neukirchen-Vluyn: Neukirchener.

Pope, M. H., 1955. *El in the Ugaritic Texts.* VTSup 2. Leiden: Brill.

Posener, G., 1950. "Section Finale d'une Sagesse Inconnue." *RdE* 7, 71–84.

—, 1955. "L'Exorde de l'Instruction éducative d'Amennakhte." *RdE* 10, 61–72.

—, 1976. *L'enseignement loyaliste: Sagesse égyptienne du Moyen Empire.* Hautes Études Orientales 5. Geneve: Librairie Droz.ok

—, 1979. "L'enseignement d'un homme a son fils." *Studien zu altägyptischen Lebenslehren.* OBO 28. Eds. Erik Hornung und Othmar Keel. Freiburg: Universitätsverlag/Göttingen: Vandenhoeck & Ruprecht, 307–316.

Postel, H. J., 1976. *The Form and Function of the Motive Clause in Proverbs 10–29.* Unpublished diss., Univ. of Iowa. Available from University Microfilms, Ann Arbor, Michigan, no. 77–3762.

Preuss, H. D., 1970. "Erwägungen zum theologischen Ort alttestamentlicher Weisheitsliteratur." *EvT* 30, 393–417.

—, 1972. "Das Gottesbild der älteren Weisheit Israels." VTSup 23 (=*Studies in the Religion of Ancient Israel*.), 117–145.

—, 1977. "Jahwes Antwort an Hiob und die sogenannte Hiobsliteratur des alten Vorderen Orients." *Beiträge zur alttestamentlichen Theologie* (FS W. Zimmerli). Eds. H. Donner et al. Göttingen: Vandenhoeck & Ruprecht, 323–343.

—, 1987. *Einführung in die alttestamentliche Weisheitsliteratur.* Kohlhammer Urban-Taschenbücher 383. Stuttgart: Kohlhammer.

Priest, J. F., 1963. "Where is Wisdom to be Placed?" *JBR* 31, 275–282. Reprinted in *SAIW*, 281–288.

Rad, G. von, 1962, *Old Testament Theology vol I: The Theology of Israel's Historical Traditions.* New York: Harper & Row. German original, Munich: Kaiser, 1957.

—, 1981. *Wisdom in Israel,* reprint. London: SCM. First publ. in GB 1972. German orig. *Weisheit in Israel,* Neukirchen: Neukirchener, 1970.

—, 1984. "The Theological Problem of the Old Testament Doctrine of Creation." *Creation in the Old Testament.* Issues in Religion and Theology 6. Philadelphia: Fortress/London: SPCK, 53–64. Orig. Engl. transl. in *The Problem of the Hexateuch and Other Essays.* New York: McGraw-Hill/Edinburgh: Oliver & Boyd, 1966, 131–143.

Rainey, A. F., 1969. "The Scribe at Ugarit: His Position and Influence." *Proceedings of the Israel Academy of Sciences and Humanities* 3, 126–147.

Rankin, O. S., 1964. *Israel's Wisdom Literature: Its Bearing on Theology and the History of Religion,* reprint. Edinburgh: T & T Clark.

Rendtorff, R., 1977. "Geschichtliches und Weisheitliches Denken im Alten Testament." *Beiträge zur alttestamentlichen Theologie* (FS W. Zimmerli). Eds. H. Donner et al. Göttingen: Vandenhoeck & Ruprecht, 344–353.

Reventlow, H. G., 1960. "Sein Blut komme über sein Haupt." *VT* 10, 311–327.

Richter, W., 1966 A. *Recht und Ethos: Versuch einer Ortung des weisheitlichen Mahnspruches.* SANT 15. München: Kösel-Verlag.

—, 1966 B. "Urgeschichte und Hoftheologie." *BZ* NF 10, 96–105.

Ringgren, H., 1947. *Word and Wisdom: Studies in the Hypostatization of Divine Qualities and Functions in the Ancient Near East.* Lund: Håkan Ohlsson.

—, 1977. "נאל." *TDOT* 2 (rev. ed.), 350–355. German orig. TWAT 1 (1973:884–890).

—, 1980. *Sprüche/Prediger.* 3., Auflage. ATD 16/1. Göttingen: Vandenhoeck & Ruprecht.

—, 1982. "יחם." *TWAT* 3, 1075–1079.

Roberts, J. J. M., 1976. "Myth *versus* History." *CBQ* 38, 1–13.

Rodhe, S. E., 1957. "Transcendens-Immanens." *Nordisk Teologisk Uppslagsbok,* vol 3. Lund: Gleerups/Köpenhamn: Ejnar Munksgaard, 935–938.

Römheld, D., 1989. *Wege der Weisheit: Die Lehren Amenemopes und Proverbien 22,17–24,22.* BZAW 184. Berlin/New York: de Gruyter.

Ruffle, J., 1977. "The Teaching of Amenemope and its Connection with the Book of Proverbs." *TynBul* 28, 29–68.

Rylaarsdam, J. C., 1946. *Revelation in Jewish Wisdom Literature.* Chicago: University of Chicago.

Sadek, A. I., 1987. *Popular Religion in Egypt during the New Kingdom.* Hildesheimer ägyptologische Beiträge 27. Hildesheim: Gerstenberger.

Sæbø, M., 1971. "חכם ḥkm weise sein." *THAT,* vol 1, 557–567.

—, 1972. "Den gammeltestamentlige visdomslitteratur." *TTKi* 43, 35–54.

—, 1976. "סוד sōd Geheimnis." *THAT,* vol 2, 144–148.

—, 1976–77. "Hvem var Israels teologer?: Om struktureringen av 'den gammeltestamentlige teologi'." *SEÅ* 41–42, 189–205.

—, 1979. "Creator et Redemptor: Om skapelsens teologiske plass og funksjon i Det gamle testamente." *Ordene og Ordet: Gammeltestamentlige Studier.* Oslo: Universitetsforlaget, 138–165. Orig. in *Deus Creator* (FS I. P. Seierstad). Oslo: Universitetsforlaget, 1971, 1–28.

Saggs, H. W. F., 1978. *The Encounter with the Divine in Mesopotamia and Israel.* Jordan Lectures 1976. London: Athlone Press.

Scharbert, J., 1972. Šlm im Alten Testament." *Um das Prinzip der Vergeltung in Religion und Recht des alten Testaments.* Wege der Forschung 125. Ed. K. Koch. Darmstadt: Wissenschaftliche Buchgesellschaft, 300–324.

Schmid, H. H., 1966. *Wesen und Geschichte der Weisheit: Eine Untersuchung zur altorientalischen Weisheitsliteratur.* BZAW 101. Berlin: Töpelmann.

—, 1968. *Gerechtigkeit als Weltordnung: Hintergrund und Geschichte des alttestamentlichen Gerechtigkeitsbegriffes.* BHT 40. Tübingen:Mohr.

—, 1973. "Schöpfung, Gerechtigkeit und Heil: 'Schöpfungstheologie' als Gesamthorizont biblischer Theologie." *ZTK* 70, 1–19. Transl. in *Creation in the Old Testament.* Issues in Religion and Theology 6. Ed. Bernhard W. Anderson. Philadelphia: Fortress/London: SPCK, 1984, 102–117.

—, 1974. *Altorientalische Welt in der alttestamentliche Theologie.* Zürich: Theologischer Verlag.

Schmidt, W. H., 1964. *Die Schöpfungsgeschichte der Priesterschrift.* WMANT 17. Neukirchen-Vluyn: Neukirchener.

—, 1982. "A Theologian of the Solomonic Era? A Plea for the Yahwist." *Studies in the Period of David and Solomon...* Ed. Tomoo Ishida. Winona Lake: Eisenbrauns, 55–73.

Scobie, C. H. H., 1984. "The Place of Wisdom in Biblical Theology." *BTB* 14, 43–48.

Scott, R. B. Y., 1955. "Solomon and the Beginnings of Wisdom in Israel." *VTSup* 3 (=FS H. H. Rowley), 262–279. Reprinted in *SAIW,* 84–101.

—, 1960. "Wisdom in Creation: The *'Āmôn* of Proverbs 8:30." *VT* 10, 213–223.

—, 1961. "Folk Proverbs of the Ancient Near East." *Transactions of the Royal Society of Canada* 15, 47–56. Reprinted in *SAIW,* 417–426.

—, 1970. "The Study of the Wisdom Literature." *Int* 24, 20–45.

—, 1982. *Proverbs-Ecclesiastes,* 2nd ed. AB 18. New York: Doubleday. Orig. publ. 1965.

Shupak, N., 1987. "The 'Sitz im Leben' of the Book of Proverbs in the Light of a Comparison of Biblical and Egyptian Wisdom." *RB* 94, 98–119.

Simpson, W. K.(ed.), 1973. *The Literature of Ancient Egypt: An Anthology of Stories, Instructions, and Poetry.* New Haven and London: Yale University.

Skehan, P., 1971 A. "A Single Editor for the Whole Book of Proverbs" (revised). *Studies in Israelite Poetry and Wisdom.* CBQMS 1. Washington: The Catholic Biblical Association of America, 15–26. Orig. in *CBQ* 10 (1948) 115–130.

—, 1971 B. "Wisdom's House" (revised). *Studies in Israelite Poetry and Wisdom.* CBQMS 1. Washington: The Catholic Biblical Association of America, 27–45. Orig. in *CBQ* 29 (1967) 162–180.

Skladny, Udo, 1962. *Die ältesten Spruchsammlungen in Israel.* Göttingen: Vandenhoeck & Ruprecht.

Soden, W. von, 1957. "Zu einigen altbabylonischen Dichtungen." *Or* 26, 315–319.

—, 1965. "Das Fragen nach der Gerechtigkeit Gottes im Alten Orient." *MDOG* 96, 41–59.

Sommerfeld, W., 1989. "Marduk." *RLA* 7, lfg. 5–6, 360–370.

Sperling, S. D., 1987. "God in the Hebrew Scriptures." *The Encyclopedia of Religion* 6, 1–8.

Stamm, J. J., 1940. *Erlösen und Vergeben im Alten Testament.* Bern: Francke.

Stecher, R., 1953. "Die persönliche Weisheit in den Proverbien Kap 8." *ZKT* 75, 411–451.

Stuhlmueller, C., 1970. *Creative Redemption in Deutero-Isaiah.* AnBib 43. Rome: Biblical Institute.

Sullivan, L. E., 1987. "Supreme Beings." *The Encyclopedia of Religion* 14, 166–181.

Taylor, A., 1931. *The Proverb.* Cambridge, Mass: Harvard University.

Terrien, S., 1962. "Amos and Wisdom." *Israel's Prophetic Heritage* (FS J. Muilenburg). Eds. B. W. Anderson and W. Harrelson. New York: Harper & Row, 108–115. Reprinted in *SAIW,* 448–455.

—, 1981. "The Play of Wisdom: Turning Point in Biblical Theology." *Horizons in Biblical Theology* 3, 125–153.

Toombs, L. E., 1955. "Old Testament Theology and the Wisdom Literature." *JBR* 23, 193–196.

Toorn, K. van der, 1985. *Sin and Sanction in Israel and Mesopotamia: A Comparative Study.* Studia Semitica Neerlandica 22. Assen: Van Gorcum.

Towner, W. S., 1976. "Retribution." *IDBSup*, 742–744.

Toy, C. H., 1977. *A Critical and Exegetical Commentary on the Book of Proverbs* (reprinted). ICC. Edinburgh: T & T Clark. Orig. publ. 1899.

Vawter, B., 1980. "Proverbs 8:22: Wisdom and Creation." *JBL* 99, 205–216.

Volten, A., 1963. "Der Begriff der Maat in den ägyptischen Weisheitstexten." *Les Sagesses du Proche-Orient ancien.* C.E.S.S. Université de Strasbourg. Paris: Presses Universitaires, 73–101.

Vorländer, H., 1975. *Mein Gott: Die Vorstellungen vom persönlichen Gott im Alten Orient und im Alten Testament.* AOAT 23. Kevelær: Butzon & Bercker/Neukirchen-Vluyn: Neukirchener.

Waltke, B. K., 1979. "The Book of Proverbs and Ancient Wisdom Literature." *BSac* 136, 221–238.

Weinfeld, M., 1972. *Deuteronomy and the Deuteronomic School.* Oxford: Clarendon.

Westermann, C., 1967. "Das Reden von Schöpfer und Schöpfung im Alten Testament." *Das ferne und nahe Wort* (FS L. Rost). BZAW 105. Stuttgart: Kohlhammer, 238–244.

—, 1971. "Weisheit im Sprichwort." *Schalom: Studien zu Glaube und Geschichte Israels* (FS A. Jepsen). Ed. Karl-Heinz Bernhardt. Stuttgart: Calwer, 73–85.

—, 1974 A. *Creation.* London: SPCK/Philadelphia: Fortress. German orig.:*Schöpfung.* Stuttgart-Berlin: Kreuz, 1971.

—, 1974 B. *Genesis: I. Teilband. Genesis 1–11.* BKAT I/1. Neukirchen-Vluyn: Neukirchener.

—, 1980. *The Psalms: Structure, Content & Message.* Minneapolis: Augsburg.

—, 1981 *The Structure of the Book of Job: A Form-critical Analysis.* Philadelphia: Fortress. German orig., 1977.

White, J. B., 1987. "The Sages' Strategy to Preserve Šalôm." JSOT Suppl ser. 58 (FS R. E. Murphy), 299–311.

Whybray, R. N., 1965 A. *Wisdom in Proverbs: The Concept of Wisdom in Proverbs 1–9.* SBT 45. London: SCM.

—, 1965 B. "Proverbs 8:22–31 and its Supposed Prototypes." *VT* 15, 504–514. Reprinted in *SAIW*, 390–400.

—, 1974. *The Intellectual Tradition in the OT.* BZAW 135. Berlin/New York: de Gruyter.

—, 1979. "Yahweh-sayings and their Contexts in Proverbs 10:1–22:16." *La Sagesse de l'ancien Testament.* Ed. M. Gilbert. Paris-Gembloux: Leuven University Press, 153–165.

—, 1982. "Wisdom Literature in the Reigns of David and Solomon." *Studies in the Period of David and Solomon and Other Essays.* Ed. Tomoo Ishida. Tokyo: Yamakawa-Shuppansha, 13–26.

—, 1989. "The Social World of the Wisdom Writers." *The World of Ancient Israel.* Ed. R. E. Clements. Cambridge: Cambridge University, 227–250.

Widengren, G., 1938. *Hochgottglaube im alten Iran.* Uppsala Universitets Årsskrift 1938:6. Uppsala: Lundequistska/Leipzig: Harrasowitz.

—, 1969. *Religionsphänomenologie.* Berlin: de Gruyter.

Wildberger, H., 1963. "Jesajas Verständnis der Geschichte." VTSup 9, 83–117.

Williams, J. G., 1980. "The Power of Form: A Study of Biblical Proverbs." *Semeia* 17, 35–58.

—, 1987. "Proverbs and Ecclesiastes." *The Literary Guide to the Bible.* Eds. Robert Alter and Frank Kermode. London: Collins, 261–282.

Williams, R. J., 1956. "Theodicy in the Ancient Near East," *CJT* 2, 14–26.

—, 1975. "A People Come Out of Egypt." VTSup 28, 231–252.

—, 1981. "The Sages of Ancient Egypt in the Light of Recent Scholarship." *JAOS* 101, 1–19.

Wilson, F. M., 1987. "Sacred and Profane? The Yahwistic Redaction of Proverbs Reconsidered." JSOTSup 58 (=FS R. E. Murphy), 313–334.

Wiseman, D. J., 1977. "Israel's Literary Neighbours in the 13th Century B. C." *JNSL* 5, 77–91.

—, 1980. "A New Text of the Babylonian Poem of the Righteous Sufferer." *Anatolian Studies* 30, 104–107.

Wolf, C. U., 1962. "Poor." *IDB* 3, 843–844.

Wolff, H. W., 1964. *Amos' geistige Heimat.* WMANT 18. Neukirchen-Vluyn: Neukirchener.

Wolters, A., 1988. "Proverbs 31:10–31 as Heroic Hymn: A Form-Critical Analysis." *VT* 38, 446–457.

Wright, A. G., 1968. "The Riddle of the Sphinx: The Structure of the Book of Qoheleth." *CBQ* 30, 313–334. Reprinted in *SAIW,* 245–266.

Würthwein, E., 1967. "μισθός. 2. The Old Testament Belief in Recompense." *TDNT* 4, 706–712. German orig. in *TWNT* 4 (1942) 710–718.

—, 1976. "Egyptian Wisdom and the Old Testament." *SAIW,* 113–133. German original in Würthwein, E., *Wort und Existenz: Studien zum Alten Testament,* Göttingen: Vandenhoeck & Ruprecht, 1970, 197–216.

Zerafa, P. P., 1978. *The Wisdom of God in the Book of Job.* Studia Universitatis S. Thomae in Urbe 8. Roma: Herder.

Zimmerli, W., 1964. "The Place and Limit of Wisdom in the Framework of Old Testament Theology." *SJT* 17, 146–158. Orig. in *Gottes Offenbarung. Gesammelte Aufsätze zum Alten Testament.* TBü 19. Munich: Kaiser, 1963.

—, 1974. "Erwägungen zur Gestalt einer alttestamentlichen Theologie." *Studien zur alttestamentlichen Theologie und Prophetie: Gesammelte Aufsätze II.* TBü 51. Munich: Kaiser, 27–54.

—, 1933. "Zur Struktur der alttestamentlichen Weisheit." *ZAW* 51, 177–204. Engl. transl. in *SAIW,* 175–207.

Selective index of Bible passages

Included in this index are mainly references to biblical passages in the main text. Of the large number of references found in the footnotes, only the relatively small number considered to be especially noteworthy appear in the index.

CONIECTANEA BIBLICA

OLD TESTAMENT SERIES

Editors: Tryggve N. D. Mettinger, Lund, and Magnus Y. Ottosson, Uppsala.

1. *Albrektson, Bertil,* History and the Gods. 1967.
2. Johnson, Bo, Die armenische Bibelübersetzung als hexaplarischer Zeuge im 1. Samuelbuch. 1968.
3. Ottosson, Magnus, Gilead. Tradition and History. 1969.
4. Erlandsson, Seth, The Burden of Babylon. A Study of Isaiah 13:2–14:23. 1970.
5. *Mettinger, Tryggve N.D.,* Solomonic State Officials. A Study of the Civil Government Officials of the Israelite Monarchy. 1971.
6. Hidal, Sten, Interpretatio syriaca. Die Kommentare des heiligen Ephräm des Syrers zu Genesis und Exodus mit besonderer Berücksichtigung ihrer auslegungsgeschichtlichen Stellung. 1974.
7. Tengström, Sven, Die Hexateucherzählung. Eine literargeschichtliche Studie. 1976.
8. Mettinger, Tryggve N.D. King and Messiah. The Civil and Sacral Legitimation of the Israelite Kings. 1976.
9. Norin, Stig, Er spaltete das Meer. Die Auszugsüberlieferung in Psalmen und Kult des Alten Israel. 1977.
10. Hyvärinen, Kyösti, Die Übersetzung von Aquila. 1977
11. Kronholm, Tryggve, Motifs from Genesis 1–11 in the Genuine Hymns of Ephrem the Syrian. 1978.
12. Ljung, Inger. Tradition und Interpretation. A Study of the Use and Application of Formulaic Language in the so-called Ebed YHWH-psalms. 1978.
13. Johnson, Bo, Hebräisches Perfekt und Imperfekt mit vorangehenden w^e. 1979.
14. Steingrimsson, Sigurdur Ö, Vom Zeichen zur Geschichte. Eine literar- und formkritische Untersuchung von Ex 6,28–11,10. 1979.
15. Kalugila, Leonidas, The Wise King. Studies in Royal Wisdom as Divine Revelation in the Old Testament and Its Environment. 1980.
16. André, Gunnel, Determining the Destiny. PQD in the Old Testament. 1980.
17. Tengström, Sven, Die Toledotformel und die literarische Struktur der priesterlichen Erweiterungsschicht im Pentateuch. 1982.
18. Mettinger, Tryggve N.D., The Dethronement of Sabaoth. Studies in the Shem and Kabod Theologies. 1982.
19. Strömberg Krantz, Eva, Des Schiffes Weg mitten im Meer. Beiträge zur Erforschung der nautischen Terminologie des Alten Testaments. 1982.
20. *Porter, Paul A.,* Metaphors and Monsters. A literary-critical study of Daniel 7 and 8. 1983.
21. Lindström, Fredrik, God and the Origin of Evil. A Contextual Analysis of Alleged Monistic Evidence in the Old Testament. 1983.
22. Wiklander, Bertil, Prophecy as Literature. A Text-linguistic and Rhetorical Approach to Isaiah 2–4. 1984.
23. Haglund, Erik, Historical Motifs in the Psalms. 1984.
24. Norin, Stig, Sein Name allein ist hoch. Das Jhw-haltige Suffix althebräischer Personennamen untersucht mit besonderer berücksichtigung der alttestamentlichen Redaktionsgeschichte. 1986.
25. Axelsson, Lars Eric, The Lord Rose up from Seir. Studies in the History and Traditions of the Negev and Southern Judah. 1987.
26. Jónsson, Gunnlaugur A, The Image of God. Genesis 1:26–28 in a Century of Old Testament Research. 1988.
27. Aurelius, Erik, Der Fürbitter Israels. Eine Studie zum Mosebild im Alten Testament. 1988.
28. Kartveit, Magnar, Motive und Schichten der Landtheologie in I Chronik 1–9. 1989.
29. Boström, Lennart, The God of the Sages. The Portrayal of God in the Book of Proverbs. 1990.

* Out of print.

DATE DUE